BUTLER'S LIVES OF THE SAINTS

THE LIVES OF THE SAINTS

SAINTS

Originally Compiled by the

REV. ALBAN BUTLER

Now Edited, Revised, and Copiously Supplemented by

HERBERT THURSTON, S.J.

AND

NORAH LEESON

VOL. V
MAY

LONDON

BURNS OATES & WASHBOURNE LTD

PUBLISHERS TO THE HOLY SEE

NIHIL OBSTAT:

INNOCENTIUS APAP, S.Th.M., O.P.
Censor deputatus.

IMPRIMATUR:

✠ JOSEPH BUTT,
Vic. Gen.

WESTMONASTERII,
die 21a Martii, 1936.

MADE AND PRINTED IN GREAT BRITAIN
FOR
BURNS OATES & WASHBOURNE LTD
1936

PREFACE

IN this present volume, as in those which have preceded, I have to thank Miss Norah Leeson for doing most of the spade-work. Even where she has followed more or less closely the narrative provided by Alban Butler, she has generally found it necessary to rewrite the text in her own words, partly because the style of the original can hardly be accommodated to the prose of our own day, partly because much compression was everywhere necessary to keep the bulk of this instalment of the work from exceeding due limits. In place of the 137 entries in Butler's May volume (several of these being concerned with the writings, etc., of Saints whose biography is separately printed), the present book deals with 258 independent lives of holy people, a considerable proportion of whom have been raised to the altars of the Church by beatification or a *confirmatio cultus* since Butler compiled his lists. With regard to all these new additions, there can be no question as to the propriety of prefixing an asterisk to their names in the table of contents. I must plead guilty, however, to having introduced the same indication of novelty in a certain number of other cases in which the text of the original has been notably departed from. Such festivals as those of SS. Philip and James, the Invention of the Holy Cross, the Apparition of St Michael, St Mamertus, St Paschal Baylon, St Gregory VII, St Philip Neri, etc., were necessarily dealt with, sometimes at great length, in Alban Butler's work, but, for one reason or another, it seemed desirable to depart from his treatment, and though I fear that the good old-fashioned Garden-of-the-Soul Catholic may feel that some of the eighteenth-century unction has been sacrificed, still it seemed necessary to make some effort to avoid too obvious a patchwork. Did not Our Lord say : " No man putteth a piece from a new garment upon an old garment ; otherwise he both rendeth the new, and the piece taken from the new agreeth not with the old " ?

It may also be noted that in deference to the existing text of the Roman Martyrology, or sometimes in view of the usage prevailing in churches when a feast is principally celebrated, the date under which certain Saints are treated does not always agree with that indicated in Butler. For example, Butler speaks of " St Nicholas," Bishop of Linköping, on May 9 ; but here, in deference to what has (perhaps erroneously) been supposed to be the Swedish usage, a short account of him has been given on July 24. Similarly, Butler provides a notice of Blessed John of Avila under March 8, but his biography is inserted here on May 10, the day on which his feast is kept in Spain and by the Society of Jesus. Similar changes of date, though confined within the range of a few days, may be noted in the case of St Pachomius, St Isidore Agricola, St Ivo of Chartres, St Felix of Cantalice, and St Mary Magdalen de'Pazzi.

It is hoped that the present year will see the publication of both the June and the October volumes of this revised edition of a work which, in spite of drawbacks, Alban Butler's sound scholarship has made famous throughout the Catholic world.

HERBERT THURSTON.

February 14, 1936.

CONTENTS OF VOLUME V

(The entries marked with an asterisk are either additions to Butler's text, or represent biographies which, in their substance as well as in their form, have been entirely rewritten for the present work.)

CONTENTS OF VOLUME V

CONTENTS OF VOLUME V

xi

CONTENTS OF VOLUME V

CONTENTS OF VOLUME V

xiii

CONTENTS OF VOLUME V

xiv

CONTENTS OF VOLUME V

CONTENTS OF VOLUME V

THE LIVES OF THE SAINTS

MAY 1

SS. PHILIP AND JAMES, APOSTLES

FIRST CENTURY

ST PHILIP THE APOSTLE came from Bethsaida in Galilee, and seems to have belonged to a little group of earnest men who had already fallen under the influence of St John the Baptist. In the synoptic gospels there is no mention of Philip except in the list of apostles which occurs in each. But St John's gospel introduces his name several times, recording in particular that the call of Philip came the day after that given to St Peter and St Andrew. Jesus, we are told, "found Philip" and said to him, "Follow Me." More than a century and a half later Clement of Alexandria avers that St Philip was the young man who, when our Lord said to him, "Follow Me," begged leave to go home first and bury his father, which occasioned the reply, "Let the dead bury their dead; but go thou and preach the kingdom of God" (Luke ix 6o). It seems probable that this identification was based on no firmer ground than the use of the phrase "Follow Me" in both cases. The position of the incident of the rebuke ("Let the dead," etc.) in the narrative of St Luke, and also in that of St Matthew, clearly suggests that it occurred some time after the beginning of the public life, when our Lord was already attended by His little company of apostles. On the other hand, St Philip was certainly called before the marriage feast at Cana, though, as our Saviour Himself declared, His hour had not yet come, *i.e.* He had not yet embarked on the public activities of His great mission.

From the account given by the evangelist, we should naturally infer that Philip responded without hesitation to the call he had received. Though his knowledge was imperfect, so much so that he describes Jesus as "the son of Joseph of Nazareth," he goes at once to find his friend Nathanael (in all probability to be identified with the apostle Bartholomew) and tells him, "We have found him of whom Moses, in the law and the prophets did write," being plainly satisfied that this was in truth the Messias. At the same time Philip gives proof of a sober discretion in his missionary zeal. He does not attempt to force his discovery upon unwilling ears. When Nathanael objects, " Can anything good come from Nazareth ? " his answer is not indignant declamation, but an appeal for personal inquiry— " Come and see." In the description of the feeding of the five thousand Philip figures again. " When Jesus," we are told, " had lifted up His eyes and seen that a very great multitude cometh to Him, He said to Philip, ' Whence shall we buy bread that these may eat ? ' And this He said to try him ; for He Himself knew what He would do." Once more we get an impression of the sober literalness of St Philip's mental outlook when he replies : " Two hundred pennyworth of bread is not sufficient for them that every one may take a little." It is in accord with the same amiable type of character which hesitates before responsibilities that, when certain Gentiles among the crowds who thronged to Jerusalem for the pasch came to Philip saying, " Sir, we would see Jesus," we find him reluctant to deal with the request without taking counsel. " Philip cometh and telleth Andrew. Again Andrew and Philip told Jesus." Finally another glimpse is afforded us of the same apostle's earnestness and devotion conjoined with defective spiritual insight, when on the evening before the Passion our Lord announced, " No man cometh to the Father but by Me. If you had known Me, you would without doubt have known My Father also : and from henceforth you shall know Him, and you have seen Him." Philip saith to Him : " Lord, show us the Father, and it is enough for us." Jesus saith to him : " Have I been so long a time with you ; and have you not known Me ? Philip, he that seeth Me seeth the Father also. How sayest thou: Show us the Father ? " (John xiv 6–9).

Apart from the fact that St Philip is named with the other apostles who spent ten days in the upper room awaiting the coming of the Holy Ghost at Pentecost, this is all we know about him with any degree of certainty.

On the other hand, Eusebius, the church historian, and some other early writers, have preserved a few details which tradition connected with the later life of Philip. The most reliable of these is the belief that he preached the gospel in Phrygia, and died at Hierapolis, where he was also buried. Sir W. M. Ramsay found among the tombs of that city a fragmentary inscription which refers to a church there dedicated to St Philip. We know also that Polycrates, Bishop of Ephesus, writing to Pope Victor towards the close of the second century, refers to two daughters of St Philip the Apostle, who had lived in virginity until old age at Hierapolis, and mentions also another daughter who was buried in his own city of Ephesus. Papias, who was himself Bishop of Hierapolis, seems to have known personally the daughters of St Philip and to have learnt from them of a wonderful miracle attributed to him, no less than the raising of a dead man to life. Heracleon, the Gnostic, about the year 180, maintained that the apostles Philip, Matthew and Thomas died a natural death, but Clement of Alexandria contradicted this, and the opinion commonly accepted at a later date was that Philip was crucified head downwards under Domitian. One fact which introduces much uncertainty into these obscure fragments of evidence is the confusion which undoubtedly arose between Philip the Apostle and Philip the Deacon, sometimes also called the Evangelist, who figures so prominently in chapter viii of the Acts of the Apostles. Both, in particular, are alleged to have had daughters who enjoyed exceptional consideration in the early Church. It is stated that the remains of St Philip the Apostle were eventually brought to Rome, and that they have been preserved there in the Basilica of the Apostles since the time of Pope Pelagius (A.D. 561). A late apocryphal document in Greek, dating from the close of the fourth century at earliest, purports to recount the missionary activities of St. Philip in Greece, as well as in the land of the Parthians and elsewhere, but it echoes the received tradition so far as regards his death and burial at Hierapolis.

The apostle St James—the Less, or the younger (Jacobus minor)—here associated with St Philip, is most commonly held to be the same individual who is variously designated " James, the son of Alpheus " (*e.g.* Matt. x 3, and Acts i 13), and " James, the brother of the Lord " (Matt. xiii 55 ; Gal. i 19). He may also possibly be identical with James son of Mary and brother of Joseph (Mark xv 40). This, however, is not the place to discuss the rather intricate problem of the " brethren of our Lord " and the questions connected with it. It may be assumed then, as Alban Butler infers, that the apostle James who became Bishop of Jerusalem (Acts xv and xxi 18) was the son of Alpheus and " brother " (*i.e.* first cousin) of Jesus Christ. Although no prominence is given to this James in the gospel narrative, we learn from St Paul that he was favoured with a special apparition of our Lord before the Ascension. Further, when the same St Paul, three years after his conversion, went up to Jerusalem and was still regarded with some suspicion by the apostles who remained there, James, with St Peter, seems to have bid him a cordial welcome. Later we learn that Peter after his escape from prison sent a special intimation to James, apparently as to one whose pre-eminence was

3

recognised among the Christians of the holy city. At what is called the Council of Jerusalem, where it was decided that the Gentiles who accepted Christian teaching need not be circumcised, it was St James, as we learn from chapter xv of the Acts of the Apostles, who, after listening to St Peter's advice, voiced the conclusion of the assembly in the words, " it hath seemed good to the Holy Ghost and to us." He was, in fact, the Bishop of Jerusalem, as Clement of Alexandria and Eusebius expressly state. Even Josephus, the Jewish historian, bears testimony to the repute in which James was held, and declares, so Eusebius asserts, that the terrible calamities which fell upon the people of that city were a retribution for their treatment of one " who was the most just of men." The story of his martyrdom, as told by Hegesippus in the latter part of the second century, has been preserved by Eusebius, and runs as follows :

" Together with the apostles, James, our Lord's brother, succeeded to the government of the Church. He received the name of ' the Just ' from all men from the time of our Lord even to our own ; for there were many called James. Now he was holy from his mother's womb, drank no wine nor strong drink nor ate anything in which was life. No razor came upon his head ; he anointed himself not with oil, and used no bath. To him alone it was permitted to enter the holy place ; for he wore nothing woollen, but linen garments [*i.e.* the priestly robes]. And alone he entered into the sanctuary and was found on his knees asking forgiveness on behalf of the people, so that his knees became hard like a camel's, for he was continually bending the knee in worship to God and asking forgiveness for the people. In fact, on account of his exceeding great justice he was called ' the Just ' and ' Oblias,' that is to say, bulwark of the people."

We learn further from Hegesippus that :

" As many as came to believe did so through James. When, therefore, many also of the rulers were believers, there was an uproar among the Jews and Scribes and Pharisees, for they said : ' There is danger that the whole people should expect Jesus as the Christ.' Coming together, therefore, they said to James : ' We beseech thee, restrain the people, for it is gone astray unto Jesus, imagining that he is the Christ. We beseech thee to persuade all who come for the day of the Pasch concerning Jesus, for in thee do we all put our trust. For we bear thee witness, as do all the people, that thou art just and that thou acceptest not the person of any. Persuade, therefore, the multitude that they go not astray concerning Jesus. For, of a truth, the people, and we all, put our trust in thee. Stand, therefore, upon

4

the pinnacle of the temple, that from thy lofty station thou mayest be evident, and thy words may easily be heard by all the people. For on account of the Pasch all the tribes, with the Gentiles also, have come together.' Therefore the aforesaid Scribes and Pharisees set James upon the pinnacle of the temple, and cried aloud to him saying : ' O Just One, in whom we ought all to put our trust ; inasmuch as the people is gone astray after Jesus who was crucified, tell us what is the door of Jesus ' (*cf.* John x 1-9). And he replied with a loud voice : ' Why ask ye me concerning the Son of Man, since He sitteth in Heaven on the right hand of the Mighty Power, and shall come on the clouds of Heaven ? ' And when many were fully persuaded and gave glory at the testimony of James and said : ' Hosanna to the son of David,' then once more the same Scribes and Pharisees said among themselves : ' We do ill in affording such a testimony to Jesus. Let us rather go up and cast him down, that being affrighted they may not believe him.' And they cried aloud saying : ' Ho, ho, even the Just One has gone astray ! ' And they fulfilled the scripture that is written in Isaias : ' Let us take away the just one, for he is troublesome to us. Therefore they shall eat the fruit of their doings.' Going up therefore they cast the Just One down. And they said to each other : ' Let us stone James the Just.' And they began to stone him, for the fall did not kill him. But turning he kneeled down and said : ' I beseech Thee, O Lord God, Father forgive them, for they know not what they do.' And while they thus were stoning him, one of the priests of the sons of Rechab, the son of Rachabim, who had witness borne to them by Jeremias the prophet, cried aloud, saying : ' Cease ye ; what do ye ? The Just One is praying on your behalf.' And one of them a fuller, took the club with which he beat out the clothes, and brought it down on the Just One's head. Thus he was martyred. And they buried him at the spot beside the temple, and his monument still remains beside the temple."

The story is told somewhat differently by Josephus, who says nothing about the Apostle's having been thrown down from the pinnacle of the temple. He informs us, however, that he was stoned to death, and assigns this to the year 62. In relation to the festivals kept by the Church liturgically under the designation of " St Peter's Chair," it is interesting to note that Eusebius speaks of the " throne " (or chair) of St James as still preserved and venerated by the Christians of Jerusalem. It was this St James who was the author of the Epistle in the New Testament which bears his name and which, by its in-sistence on the merit of good works, was highly obnoxious to those who preached the doctrine of justification by faith alone. Luther rejected it from his canon, calling it contemptuously an " epistle of straw."

Philip said, " Lord, show us the Father," and Jesus answered, " Have I been so long a time with you, and have you not known me ? " St Philip's ardent desire to see the Father was not in itself a subject of rebuke. What our Lord reproved, but still in gentle terms, was the failure to recognise the illumination, the privileges, the opportunities, already within the grasp of those who lived in His company. Full understanding only came to the apostles when it was too late, when they had lost what should abundantly have sufficed for their contentment. There was, it is true, a more perfect vision of God than that which they enjoyed in the daily spectacle of their Master's human form. But such bliss was reserved for the time when, after many tribulations and after the fiery ordeal of martyrdom itself, they should be released from the trammels of existence in the flesh. Meanwhile it behoved them to put to profit what they already possessed. In ages to come countless multitudes of holy souls would envy them a single hour of the companionship they took so much as a matter of course. As it was, their eyes were often heavy when they watched. They heard His words but forgot them, or failed to understand. Though the spirit, no doubt, was willing, the flesh was weak. The outpouring of grace was continuous, but, as they came to see afterwards, these fountains of living water in large measure had run to waste.

We are inclined perhaps to think the apostles very favoured, to blame them for wanting more assurance. But meanwhile are we making the most of what we have ourselves ? We cannot look into the eyes of the Saviour, or hear the sound of His voice, but yet we, too, can surely see the Father. We can see Him reflected in the beautiful things around us, in the limitless depths of the sky, in the glory of the sunset, in the marvellous structure of all organic life, in the renewal of the seasons, in the lavish prodigality of Nature, in the courage and generosity of noble deeds. God is revealing Himself at every moment of the day, and yet we, immersed in our grievances or our disappointments, still ask to be shown the Father, as though His very existence were in doubt.

Outside the New Testament, and such not wholly reliable traditions as we find recorded in the pages of Eusebius, there is very little we can appeal to as sources for the history of either St Philip or St James. In the *Acta Sanctorum*, May, vol. i, the Bollandists have gathered up most of the allusions to be met with in the early ecclesiastical writers. The apocryphal Acts of St Philip, which probably date from the third or fourth century, have been edited by R. A. Lipsius in his *Apokryphen Apostelgeschichten und Apostel-*

legenden, vol. ii, part 2, pp. 1–90. See also E. Hennecke, *Neutestamentliche Apokryphen* (2nd edn., 1924) ; and the *Handbuch* brought out by the same editor. The life of the two apostles with whom we are here concerned is discussed in nearly all scriptural encyclopædias, such, for example, as the *Dictionnaire de la Bible* with its supplements, and with regard to the treatment of these saints in art consult Künstle, *Ikonographie der christlichen Kunst* and R. P. Bedford, *St James the Less*, 1911. The authorship of the canonical Epistle of St James, which is commonly attributed by Catholic scholars to the saint commemorated on this day, has been the subject of much heated discussion. The matter does not concern us here, and the text of the epistle itself throws little light upon the history or character of the writer who penned it. As the martyrdom of St James the Less is commonly assigned to the year A.D. 62 or 63, the Epistle, on the assumption that he is the author, must be of early date.

Mgr Duchesne has suggested that the association of St James with St Philip on May 1, which is common both to the Gelasian and the Gregorian sacramentaries, may be traced to the dedication of the church " of the Apostles " at Rôme by Pope John III, *c.* A.D. 563. This church though later spoken of vaguely as the church " of the Apostles " was originally dedicated to the Apostles SS. Philip and James in particular, the inscription long preserved there said :

> Quisquis lector adest Jacobi pariterque Philippi
> Cernat apostolicum lumen inesse locis.

But there are indications in certain MSS. of the Hieronymianum and in other documents such as the Félire of Œngus that Philip's name on May 1 once stood alone, and that James is a later addition.

ST ANDEOLUS, Mart.

A.D. 208

According to a legend, which rests on no reliable foundation, St Irenæus after his death appeared to the Bishop of Smyrna, asking him to send missionaries to Gaul. Amongst others Andeolus, who was a subdeacon, responded to the call. He is said to have been actively employed, and most successful, as a preacher on the left bank of the Rhône until, in the year 208, he was arrested and put to death by Septimius Severus near Viviers. It is stated that the Emperor himself ordered the martyr's head to be cleft crosswise with a wooden sword. His relics are said to be preserved in the town called after him, Bourg-Saint-Andéol, a few miles south of Viviers.

The apocryphal Acta are printed in the *Acta Sanctorum*, May, vol. i. Their unhistorical character is sufficiently proved by the fact that St Polycarp is named as the bishop of Smyrna who sent Andeolus to Gaul, though Polycarp suffered martyrdom nearly half a century before the death of St Irenæus. The legend, however, must have been current at the beginning of the ninth century. See Quentin, *Les Martyrologes Historiques*, pp. 253–254.

ST GRATA OF BERGAMO, WIDOW

(?) A.D. 305

Much confusion and uncertainty surrounds the story of St Grata. A local tradition declares that she built three churches and a hospital, and there is evidence that what were believed to be her relics were translated in 1027 to a church dedicated in her honour. Legend affirms that she married a German nobleman, converted him, and went with him to Germany, but after his death returned to Bergamo. There she spent her great possessions in works of charity, and herself nursed the sick poor. She is said to have shown hospitality to St Alexander, the principal patron of Bergamo, a soldier of the Theban legion, who was martyred for the faith. Grata buried his body with her own hands and built a church over his tomb.

The Bollandists have printed two fabulous medieval accounts of St Grata in the *Acta Sanctorum*, September, vol. ii, under September 4. It is not even certain whether she lived in the fourth century or in the eighth, and it is possible that there were two holy widows of this name whose legends have been confused.

ST AMATOR, BP.

A.D. 418

For details of the life of St Amator we have to rely upon a biography written 160 years after his death by an African priest called Stephen at the bidding of St Aunarius, a later Bishop of Auxerre. The contents of the narrative prove it to have been for the most part an audacious fiction. Amator, we read, was the only son of distinguished citizens of Auxerre, who affianced him to a young heiress named Martha, although he had expressed a strong disinclination for the married state. On the wedding day the guests assembled, the bride appeared in gorgeous apparel, and the aged Bishop Valerianus came to perform the ceremony. Accidentally or providentially Valerianus, instead of reading the nuptial blessing, recited the form which was used in the ordination of deacons—a mistake which was noticed only by the bride and bridegroom. When the service was over the young couple agreed to live a life of virginity, and Martha within a short time retired into a convent. Amator, after having laboured for some years as a priest, was unanimously elected Bishop of Auxerre. In the course of a long episcopate he converted the remaining pagans of the district, performed many miracles, and built two churches, that of St Stephen in Auxerre and an oratory on Mount Atre to contain the reputed relics of St Cirycus and St Julitta which he had brought back from Antioch. The governor of Auxerre during St Amator's later years was Germanus, a high-spirited young patrician, wholly devoted to the pleasures of hunting. That all men might admire his prowess he continued, although he was a Christian, to observe the pagan custom of hanging the heads of the animals he killed on a tall pear-tree in the middle of the city—an offering to Woden. This practice caused great scandal, and St Amator, after having repeatedly but vainly remonstrated with Germanus, had the tree cut down during the governor's absence. Greatly incensed, the young man on his return threatened to kill the Bishop, who thought it advisable to retire for a time from the city. He was now well advanced in years, and had been for some time desirous of handing on his office to another. While he was staying at Autun with the provincial prefect, Julius, it was suddenly borne in upon him—by revelation or by intuition—that the worthy successor he was seeking was none other than Germanus himself. Having obtained the sanction of his host, under whom the governor of Auxerre served, Amator returned to Auxerre where, at his summons, the people—Germanus included—came to him in the cathedral. All arms having been laid down outside at the bishop's request, the doors were shut, and the prelate, with the help of some of his clergy, seized Germanus, stripped him of his secular garb, gave him the tonsure, and pronounced him bishop-designate of Auxerre.

St Amator's work was now done. He had laboured for many years, and had secured as his successor one who was destined to become the greatest of all the Bishops of Auxerre. A few days later the aged saint asked to be conveyed once more into his cathedral, where he peacefully breathed his last.

The body of St Amator was laid in the church on Mount Atre, to which he had translated the relics of Blessed Martha, his betrothed, eight years earlier.

The Latin life written by Stephen is printed in the *Acta Sanctorum*, May, vol. i. Its extravagant details are, of course, quite fabulous, but there is no reason to doubt St Amator's historical existence. Mgr Duchesne in his *Fastes Épiscopaux* (vol. ii, pp. 427–446) speaks well of the episcopal lists of Auxerre. See also Baudrillart, *Dictionnaire d'Histoire et de Géographie ecclésiastique*, vol. ii, *c.* 981, and Father Delehaye's commentary on the *Hieronymianum* (p. 224) in which martyrology St Amator is commemorated.

ST BRIEUC, ABBOT

c. A.D. 510

Although some writers have striven to prove that St Brieuc was of Irish descent, it is now commonly admitted that he was born in Cardiganshire, probably about the year 420. A life of him, which purports to be written by a contemporary but which is certainly of much later date, describes his career in some detail. The saint, who in this Latin narrative is generally called Brioccius, but also Briomaglus,* is said to have been the son of noble parents named Cerpus and Eldruda. They were pagans, but good and charitable people. Before his birth an angel appeared, first to his mother and then to his father, in their sleep, demanding of them that the child should be sent to France to be brought up by St Germanus. This injunction was in due time complied with, and in the household of Germanus the boy Brioccius met and formed ties of friendship with both St Patrick and St Iltyd. Before he was ten years old he had learnt all the psalms by heart, and his charity to the poor was such that he gave away everything which belonged to him. We read of violent attacks of the demon under the form of a wolf, which he triumphantly overcame, and also of his success in exorcising possessed persons. When in due course he had been ordained priest, a vision in his sleep recalled him to his own country, and there he converted his parents to Christianity, seemingly as a consequence of the miracles of healing which he wrought. After a while he was bidden by an angel to return to Gaul, and accordingly he set sail with no less than 168 disciples whom he had already gathered about him. On the journey the ship's progress was suddenly arrested in the middle of the night. Great consternation prevailed, but they eventually discovered that they had struck an obstacle, which was really the devil, who, in the form of a huge monster, was lying right across their path. Yielding to the prayers and conjurations of the saint this primitive sea-serpent, though with a very bad grace, vanished into thin air. "*Evanescit ut fumus*," is the biographer's phrase.

Pursuing their journey, they landed at some unidentified place where the local chieftain, named Conan, was converted from paganism by Brieuc's miracles. This, however, was not their final destination, and they sailed on to a little estuary on the coast of Brittany near Tréguier, where they settled and built a monastery,

* Briomaglus seems to be the full form of the name ; Briocus the hypocoristic abbreviation so common among Celtic peoples.

of which St Brieuc became abbot. A flourishing and fervent community was formed which attracted many recruits, but before long news came of a grievous pestilence which was devastating his native Cardigan. His family implored him to visit them once again, and he, though very reluctantly, yielded to their entreaties, leaving his nephew, St Tugalus, to rule the abbey in his absence. On his arrival in Wales his parents were consoled, and the pestilence was arrested by his prayers, but he would not consent to abide with them long. He was gladly welcomed back in Brittany, but finding that everything prospered under the government of Tugalus, he determined to leave him in charge, and himself to found another monastery in a different part of the country. It is said that 84 volunteers accompanied him, who all travelled by sea, and, finding a suitable spot, with a good water supply, proceeded to encamp and make themselves at home. The ruler of the district, Rigualis, was at first infuriated by this invasion, but falling ill himself he was cured by St Brieuc. Having further discovered that he was a blood relation he became his warm friend and patron. Chronology is little heeded in these Celtic biographies. We are told, however, that Brieuc, after the foundation of the new abbey on the lands which the chieftain bestowed, assisted Rigualis on his death-bed, and himself, to the great sorrow of his brethren, passed away shortly after. He is said to have been then one hundred years old. All this is supposed to have happened on the site of the present cathedral and town of Saint-Brieuc, but in the middle of the ninth century the saint's remains, for fear of the Norman marauders, were translated partly to Angers and partly to Lehon. In 1210, at the prayer of the then Bishop of Saint-Brieuc, a portion of the relics was given back by the monks of Angers, and after happily surviving the outrages of the Revolution, they are preserved in the cathedral to this day. It is possible that St Brieuc was himself a missionary bishop, but the see which bears his name was not formed until many centuries later.

The complete text of the " Vita S Brioci " was printed for the first time in the *Analecta Bollandiana*, vol. ii (1883), pp. 161–190. In the same collection, vol. xxiii (1904), pp. 246–251, is an interesting fragment in verse of a life in which he is called " Briomaglus." From this we learn that when his remains were exhumed (*c.* 853[?]) he was found wearing a dalmatic, a fact which pointed to episcopal consecration. See also Duchesne, *Fastes Épiscopaux*, vol. ii, pp. 269 and 390 ; Baring-Gould and Fisher, *Lives of the British Saints*, vol. i, p. 288 ; Forbes, *Kalendars of Scottish Saints*, p. 291 ; du Bois de la Villerabel, *Vie de Saint Brieuc*; Gougaud, *Christianity in Celtic Lands*, p. 115. Most valuable of all, however, is the essay of Canon G. H. Doble, *St Brioc, a Celtic Saint*, 1929 (no. 17 in the series of Cornish Saints). At least one Cornish church is dedicated to St Brieuc.

ST SIGISMUND, KING

A.D. 523

The kingdom of Burgundy, at the beginning of the sixth century, comprised a great portion of south-eastern France and of south-western Switzerland. It was ruled by a prince of Vandal extraction named Gundobald, who had obtained the throne by murdering his brother, Chilperic, together with his wife and his two sons. Gundobald was an Arian, but a year before his death his son and successor, Sigismund, was converted to the Catholic faith by St Avitus, Bishop of Vienne. Though a devout man and a benefactor to the Church, Sigismund seems to have remained something of a barbarian —subject at times to uncontrollable fits of rage. On one occasion, when worked upon by the false accusations of his second wife, he ordered his son Sigeric to be strangled, because he had incensed his stepmother by upbraiding her for wearing his dead mother's clothes. No sooner had the cruel deed been perpetrated than Sigismund came to his senses and was overpowered with horror and remorse at his crime, a sin which he lamented for the rest of his life. Perhaps the greatest service Sigismund rendered to the Church was the rebuilding of the monastery of St Maurice at Agaunum in the present canton of Valais. He endowed it liberally and, in order that the " laus perennis," the unbroken chant, should be celebrated within its walls, he brought to it monks from Lérins, Gigny, Ile-Barbe, and Condat. It was during Sigismund's reign that the Burgundian bishops assembled at the Council of Epaon, where many wise measures were passed for the reform of ecclesiastical discipline. Shortly afterwards, on the feast of the martyrs of the Theban Legion, the church of Agaunum was dedicated, St Avitus preaching a sermon of which fragments are still preserved. Sigismund in his repentance had prayed that God would punish him in this life, and his prayer was granted. The three kings of France, sons of Clovis, thinking the moment propitious, declared war against him with the avowed intention of avenging their maternal grandfather, Chilperic, whom Sigismund's father had put to death, and of conquering the kingdom of Burgundy. Sigismund, after he had been defeated in battle, escaped in the direction of Agaunum, where he took the habit of a monk. For a time he lived as a hermit in the vicinity of St Maurice, but eventually he was captured and taken to Orleans. There he was put to death by King Clodomir, in spite of the remonstrances of St Avitus. His body was thrown into a well, from which it was recovered by pious hands, and his relics are now preserved at

Prague in Bohemia. St Sigismund is invoked in cases of fever and hernia.

There is a *Passio Sancti Sigismundi* which is a valuable historical document compiled by a monk of Agaunum. It is printed in the *Acta Sanctorum*, May, vol. i, but more critically edited by Bruno Krusch in *M. G. H. Scrip. rer. Meroving.*, vol. ii, pp. 333–340. We also learn something from Gregory of Tours, both in his *Historia Francorum*, bk. iii, and in his *De Gloria Martyrum*, ch. 74. A full bibliography is available in Dom H. Leclercq's article on Agaunum in the *Dictionnaire d'Archéologie et de Liturgie*, vol. i, cc. 850–871, and in Hefele–Leclercq, *Histoire des Conciles*, vol. ii, pp. 1017–1022 and pp. 1031–1042.

ST MARCULFUS, OR MARCOUL, HERMIT

c. A.D. 558

The name of St Marcoul was formerly celebrated throughout the length and breadth of France because for centuries it was usual for the king, after his coronation at Rheims, to proceed to Corbény to venerate the relics of St Marcoul, in whose honour a novena was observed by the sovereign in person or, vicariously, by his grandalmoner. It was through St Marcoul that the King was popularly believed to derive the gift of healing known as " touching for the King's evil," or scrofula. As recently as 1825, after the coronation of Charles X at Rheims, the relics were brought to the hospital of St Marcoul at Rheims, and the novena was kept. Afterwards the monarch laid his hands on a number of patients, making the sign of the cross and saying : " *Le roi te touche : Dieu te guérisse.*"

Marcoul was born at Bayeux of noble parents, who eagerly fostered the piety which he evinced from his earliest years. Even as a little child he would deprive himself of his meals in order to give them away to the poor, and was remarkable for the sweetness of his disposition, as well as for his love of prayer. At the age of thirty he was ordained priest by Possessor, Bishop of Coutances, who sent him forth to preach as a kind of diocesan missioner. Although successful in winning souls, Marcoul always longed for solitude and closer union with God, and would often retire to a lonely island, where he would spend his days as a hermit. After some time he obtained from King Childebert a grant of land at Nanteuil, on which he built some simple huts for a few disciples who also wished to live a retired life. From this small nucleus there soon grew up a great monastery. Many of the monks continued to live, like their founder, the eremitic life, and several of them, including St Helier, went to settle in the island of Jersey. We read that St Marcoul at one period stayed there with them, and by his intercession saved the inhabitants from a raid of marauding Saxons. So violent a storm arose when he prayed that the invaders were dashed to pieces on the rocks. King Childebert and Queen Ultrogotha had a great regard for the holy man : not only did they heap privileges upon Nanteuil for his sake, but they helped him to found religious houses elsewhere. St Marcoul died about the year 558, on May 1, and tradition says that his two most faithful disciples, St Domardus and St Cariulfus (St Criou), passed away on the same day. Famous for his miracles during his life and after his death, St Marcoul was regarded as a patron who cured skin diseases. As late as the year 1680 sufferers made pilgrimages to his shrine at Nanteuil and bathed in the springs connected with the church. The shrine was completely destroyed by the revolutionaries in 1793.

Mabillon and the Bollandists in the *Acta Sanctorum* (May, vol. i) have printed an ancient life of St Marculfus, which, however, as B. Baedorf has shown, can hardly be older than the early ninth century. A somewhat expanded recension is also included in the same collection. Consult further F. Duine, *Mémento des Sources hagiographiques de Bretagne*, p. 44. Popular accounts of St Marculfus have been published by Ch. Gautier, 1899, and H. Scholl, 1932.

ST ASAPH, Bishop

c. A.D. 600

After St Kentigern (Bishop of Glasgow in Scotland) had been driven from his diocese, he founded a great monastery on the banks of the river Elwy in North Wales. According to the somewhat un-reliable testimony of John of Tynemouth, the community consisted of 965 monks, of whom 300 being quite illiterate tilled the soil or tended the cattle, 300 did the work of the monastery, whilst the remaining 365, observing strict enclosure, chanted the divine office in successive shifts in such wise that the praises of God never ceased by day or night. Pre-eminent amongst the monks for his piety, his good looks, his learning, and his miracles was Asaph, the grandson of St Pabo, " the Bulwark of Pictland." As a lad he is reported to have received miraculous proof of the merit of obedience by carrying hot embers in his tunic at the bidding of his superior without suffering the least injury to his person or his habit. St Kentigern formed such a high opinion of his disciple's virtue and abilities that when he himself was recalled to Glasgow he left St Asaph in charge of the monastery, besides consecrating him bishop of the surrounding district. St

Asaph wrote sundry canons or ordinances for the administration of his diocese, and is credited with the composition of a life of St Kentigern as well as other works. He was an eloquent preacher, and his memory was so dear to the people that at a later date the name of his see was changed from Llanelwy to St Asaph. He is usually reckoned the first bishop of St Asaph, but there is no record of his successors in that office for several hundred years after his death. In the twelfth century we find Geoffrey of Monmouth appointed Bishop of St Asaph, in succession to a certain prelate called Gilbert.

The Bollandists, in their brief account of this saint, draw mainly from the legends in the Aberdeen breviary. See, however, A. P. Forbes, *Kalendars of Scottish Saints*, pp. 271–272 ; Baring-Gould and Fisher, *Lives of the British Saints*, vol. i, pp. 177 *seq.*

ST EVERMARUS, Mart.

c. A.D. 700

On May 1 in the village of Rousson, near Tongres, an annual procession takes place in honour of St Evermarus, who was slain there more than 1200 years ago, and whose relics are venerated in the church built over the spot where he fell. He was a native of Friesland, a nobleman whose piety induced him to make a number of pilgrimages. After his return from a visit to St James's shrine at Compostella in Spain, he was led to visit the tombs of more recent saints in Belgium and northern France. Having venerated the relics of St Fursey, St Ultan, St Foillan, St Remaclus, St Gertrude of Nivelles, and St Trudo, he started off with seven companions to seek the grave of St Servatius at Maestricht. Late one evening they reached the outskirts of the forest of Ruth, and, as they could not hope to find their way through it in the dark, they sought shelter in a house which stood on the edge of the wood upon the bank of the Meuse. It actually was the residence of a brigand chieftain called Hacco, who preyed upon travellers—despoiling those who passed through the forest and exacting a toll from the boats which sailed up and down the river. Because he was away from home, his wife, a good Christian, gave them hospitality but sent them forth early next morning, cautioning them to avoid Hacco. However, the brigand and his followers came upon them in the midst of the forest and killed them. Their bodies were accidentally discovered one day when Pepin of Heristal was hunting in the wood, and after they had been identified they were honourably buried by his orders. The relics of St

Evermarus were translated more than once before they were deposited in their present resting-place.

Two medieval accounts, one of them extremely verbose, are printed in the *Acta Sanctorum*, May, vol. i, but they possess little historical value. See also Balau, *Sources de l'histoire de Liége*, pp. 114–117.

ST THEODARDUS, ARCHBISHOP OF NARBONNE

A.D. 893

The birthplace of St Theodardus was Montauriol, a little town which formerly occupied a site covered by the present city of Montauban. About his family nothing is known except that his parents or forefathers were part founders of the Abbey of St Martin at Montauriol. He appears to have studied law at Toulouse, for we first hear of him as the advocate retained by the cathedral authorities in a curious suit brought against them by the Jews of Toulouse, who, not unnaturally, objected to a sort of religious pageant in the course of which a Jew was publicly struck on the face before the cathedral doors. This ceremony took place three times a year—at Christmas, on Good Friday, and on the Feast of the Assumption. Archbishop Sigebod, who came to Toulouse for the hearing of the case, was so greatly taken with the young lawyer that he took him back with him to Narbonne. Soon afterwards Theodardus received holy orders and became Sigebod's archdeacon, winning golden opinions for his charity and sanctity. The Montauban breviary describes him as " an eye to the blind, feet to the lame, a father of the poor, and the consoler of the afflicted." Amongst other reforms carried through by him was the resumption of the recital of the canonical hours at their correct times. Greatly beloved by all, he was unanimously chosen Archbishop of Narbonne at the death of Sigebod, who had nominated him as his successor. The perils which then beset travellers did not deter the newly-elected prelate from undertaking a visit to Rome, where he received the pallium from the Holy Father. As an archbishop he worked unremittingly to repair the ravages wrought by the Saracens and to revive the drooping faith of the people. He practically rebuilt his own cathedral, and in 886 he restored the bishopric of Ausona, now Vich, which had long fallen into abeyance. To buy back those who were taken captive by the Saracens in their frequent raids, and to feed the hungry during a three years' famine, he not only spent his whole income, but he also sold some of the sacred vessels and other treasures of his church. The strenuous life he led and his anxieties for his flock, after a few years seriously impaired his health ; he could not sleep and suffered from continual fever. It was thought that he might recover in his native air, and he accordingly returned to Montauriol. The monks of St Martin received him joyfully, but they soon realised that he had only come back to die. After making a general confession in the presence of all the brethren he received the last sacraments and passed peacefully away as if in sleep. Afterwards the Abbey was renamed St Audard in his honour, and he became the principal patron of Montauban.

The life of St Theodardus printed in the *Acta Sanctorum*, May, vol. i, dates only from the close of the eleventh century. See also *Gallia Christiana*, vol. vi, pp. 19–22, and Duchesne, *Fastes Épiscopaux*, vol. i, p. 306. A popular account of the saint has been written in French by J. A. Guyard, of which a second edition appeared in 1887.

ST ALDEBRANDUS, Bishop
EARLY IN THE THIRTEENTH CENTURY

A native of Sorrivolo, or Sorbetulo, in the Romagna, St Alde-brandus received his education in Ravenna, at the monastery of Santa Maria de Porto. Elected provost by the Augustinian canons of Rimini, he used to preach to the people in the open square before the church, at a period when the preaching office was usually con-fined to bishops. His strictures, however, roused the populace against him, and he was practically driven from the city. Afterwards he was made Bishop of Fossombrone, in which capacity he survived to the age of 100, respected and beloved by his people for his charity, austerity, and his many reputed miracles. He rebuilt on a much larger scale the cathedral church of Fossombrone, but did not see it completed. The belfry which is his symbol in art refers to the legend that when, after his death, the cathedral bells were carried off by the citizens of Fano during a raid on Fossombrone, no sound could be extracted from them until they had been replaced in the tower in which St Aldebrandus had caused them to be hung.

The Bollandists in their account of this saint had to content themselves with a summary of uncertain date extracted by Ughelli (*Italia Sacra*, vol. ii, cc. 915–917) from the archives of the See of Fossombrone. Eubel, *Hierarchia Catholica*, vol. i, p. 254, has called attention to serious chronological diffi-culties in this version of the story.

BLESSED AUGUSTE SCHÖFFLER AND J. L. BONNARD,
MARTYRS
A.D. 1851–1852

These two devoted young priests, both of them alumni of the Société des Missions Etrangères at Paris, patiently endured the same form of martyrdom in Annam (French Indo-China), each suffering decapitation on May 1, but with a year's interval between. Auguste Schöffler was a native of Lorraine, and belonged to the diocese of Nancy. He had come from his studies at Paris to Tonquin in 1848, and at once threw himself with great energy into the work of learning the native languages. He was soon able to hear confessions and deliver instructions, though three times within less than that number of years he had nearly died of fever. In 1851 owing to certain political disturbances a new persecution of the Christians broke out. Father Schöffler was arrested on March 1, and, although he was not tortured, he must have suffered terribly from the great wooden frame (*cangue*) round his neck, and the fetters which confined his limbs, not to speak of the vermin and of the company in the common prison into which he was thrown. His execution was attended with much parade, but the martyr's courage and bearing impressed even his enemies.

Father Jean Louis Bonnard was a member of a most pious French family, and had entered the *grand séminaire* at Lyons, but volunteering for the foreign missions finished his course in Paris. He reached Tonquin in 1850, at the crisis of the cholera epidemic then raging, but laboured strenuously among the plague-stricken while continuing his study of the language. The Vicar-Apostolic, under whose orders he served, wrote of him with the tenderest affection and admiration. A very beautiful letter of his is preserved in which, when under sentence of death, he took leave of his family in France. His head was struck off on May 1, 1852, and, as was usual in such cases, his remains, heavily weighted, were thrown into the river. In the case of the martyr last named the native Christians, by incredible exertions, succeeded in recovering the body, which is still preserved with veneration.

A full account of these martyrdoms will be found in the *Annals of the Propagation of the Faith* for 1852 and 1853. See also Canon J. R. Shortland, *The Persecutions of Annam*, pp. 275–282 ; and more fully, Abbé A. Launay, *Les Cinquante-deux Serviteurs de Dieu, etc.* (1893), pp. 127–180, with other more recent works of the same writer dealing with the French missions in Indo-China.

MAY 2

ST ATHANASIUS, Bp., Doctor of the Church

A.D. 373

S T ATHANASIUS, "the Champion of Orthodoxy," was probably
born about the year 297 at Alexandria. Of his family nothing is
known except that his parents were Christians, and that he had a
brother called Peter. All that has come down to us concerning his childhood is a tradition, preserved by Rufinus, to the effect that he first
attracted the notice of the Patriarch Alexander when he was playing at
church ceremonies on the beach with other little boys. Having watched
Athanasius baptising some of his companions in the sea, the prelate
summoned them, and, having satisfied himself by questioning them
that the baptisms were valid, he undertook to have them trained for
the priesthood. The truth of this story is more than questionable, if
only on the ground that at the time of Bishop Alexander's accession
Athanasius must have been at least fifteen or sixteen years old.
Whether or not he owed his training to the Patriarch, it is certain
that he received an excellent education, which embraced Greek
literature and philosophy, rhetoric, jurisprudence and Christian
doctrine. His familiarity with the text of Holy Scripture was quite
exceptional. We have it on his own authority that he learnt theology
from teachers who had been confessors during the terrible persecution under Maximian, which had raged in Alexandria when he was
almost an infant. It is interesting to note that from his early youth
Athanasius appears to have had close relations with the hermits of
the desert—more especially with the great St Anthony. "I was his
disciple," he wrote, "and like Eliseus I poured water on the hands of
that other Elias." The friendship he then formed with the holy men
was to prove of inestimable assistance to him in his later life. But
it is not until the year 318, when he was about 21, that Athanasius
makes his first actual appearance upon the stage of history. He
then received the diaconate, after having been a lector for six years,
and he was appointed secretary and amanuensis to Bishop Alexander.
It was probably at this period that he produced his first literary work,
a discourse against the Gentiles, the latter part of which deals with

19

the Incarnation. In it he also sets forth clearly the true doctrine of the Trinity.

Almost from the dawn of Christianity in Egypt two strong and often divergent forces made themselves felt in the Church: that of the hierarchy represented by the patriarch, and that of the intellectuals, who cared very little for ecclesiastical tradition. The latter stood for freedom of theological speculation, and were impatient of ecclesiastical control. Occasionally, if they went too far, the leaders of this section were obliged, like the great Origen, to leave the country ; but the party remained—ever ready to criticise the Bishop and to withstand him on the slightest provocation. When, for instance, after the close of Maximian's persecution, the Patriarch Peter sanctioned clemency in reconciling the lapsed, Meletius Bishop of Lycopolis found a ready following in the opposition when he not only denounced his metropolitan but proceeded to set up a rival hierarchy. So also during the pontificate of Alexander, a priest named Colluthus obtained similar support even when he claimed the power of ordaining priests and deacons. These schisms concerning administration were embarrassing enough to the rulers of the Church, but matters became much more serious when one of the fundamental doctrines of Christianity came to be assailed. It was probably about the year 323 that scandal began to be aroused in Alexandria by the priest of the church of Baucalis, Arius by name, who was publicly teaching that the Word of God is not eternal, that He was created in time by the Eternal Father, and that therefore He could only figuratively be described as the Son of God. The Bishop demanded a statement of these doctrines, which he laid first before the Alexandrian clergy and afterwards before a council of Egyptian bishops. With only two dissentients the assembly condemned the heresy, deposing Arius together with eleven priests and deacons of Alexandria who adhered to his tenets. The heresiarch retired to Cæsarea, where he continued to propagate his teaching, having enlisted the support of Eusebius of Nicomedia and other Syrian prelates. In Egypt he had won over the Meletians and many of the intellectuals, whilst his doctrines, embodied in hymns or songs set to popular tunes, were popularised in the market-place and were carried by sailors and traders in an incredibly short time all along the Mediterranean shores. That Athanasius, as the Bishop's archdeacon and secretary, already took a prominent part in the struggle, and that he even composed the encyclical letter announcing the condemnation of Arius, has been assumed with a great show of probability. All that is actually certain, however, is that he was present, as attendant upon his bishop, at the great Council of Nicæa in which the true doctrine of the Church was set forth, the sentence of excommunication against Arius confirmed, and the confession of faith known as the Nicene Creed promulgated and subscribed. It is unlikely that Athanasius actually participated in the discussions of this assembly of bishops in which he had not even a seat, but even if he did not exercise any influence upon the great council, it assuredly influenced him, and as a modern writer has well said, the rest of his life was at one and the same time a testimony to the divinity of the Saviour, and a heroic testimony to the profession of the Nicene Fathers.

Shortly after the close of the Council, Bishop Alexander died, and Athanasius, whom he had nominated as his successor, was chosen Patriarch of Alexandria, although he was not yet thirty years old. Almost immediately after his consecration he undertook a visitation of his enormous diocese, including the Thebaïd and other great monastic settlements, where he was warmly welcomed as being himself an ascetic. He also appointed a bishop for Abyssinia, a country in which the Christian faith had recently found a footing. Nevertheless almost from the first he was faced by dissensions and opposition. In spite of his strenuous efforts to bring about union, the Meletians continued their schism, and made common cause with the heretics, whilst Arianism, though temporarily crushed by the Council of Nicæa, soon reappeared with renewed vigour in Egypt as well as in Asia Minor, where it had powerful support. In 330 the Arian Bishop of Nicomedia, Eusebius, returned from exile and succeeded in persuading the Emperor Constantine, whose favourite residence was in his diocese, to write to Athanasius, bidding him readmit Arius into communion. The Patriarch replied that the Catholic Church could hold no communion with heretics who attacked the divinity of Christ. Eusebius then addressed an ingratiating letter to Athanasius, in which he sought to justify Arius; but neither his flattering words nor the threats he induced the Emperor to utter could shake the determination of the lion-hearted though weakly-looking young bishop whom Julian the Apostate, at a later date, was angrily to stigmatise as " that mannikin." The Bishop of Nicomedia's next move was to write to the Egyptian Meletians urging them to carry out a design they had formed of impeaching Athanasius. They responded by bringing against him charges of having exacted a tribute of linen for use in his church, of having sent gold to a certain Philomenus, suspected of treason against the Emperor, and of having authorised one of his deputies to destroy a chalice which was being used at the altar by a Meletian priest called Ischyras. In a trial before the Emperor, Athanasius cleared himself of all these accusations and returned in triumph to Alexandria, bearing with him a commendatory letter from Constantinople. His enemies, however, were not discouraged. He was now charged with having murdered a Meletian bishop of the name of Arsenius, and was cited to attend a council at Cæsarea. Aware that his supposed victim was alive and in hiding, the Patriarch ignored the summons. Nevertheless he found himself compelled by a definite command from the Emperor to appear before another council summoned at Tyre in 335—an assembly which, as it turned out, was packed by his opponents and presided over by an Arian who had usurped the see of Antioch. Various offences were preferred against him, of which the first was that of the broken chalice. Several of the charges he disposed of at once : in regard to others he demanded time in which to obtain evidence. Realising, however, that his condemnation had been decided beforehand, he abruptly left the assembly and embarked for Constantinople. Upon his arrival he accosted the Emperor in the street in the attitude of a suppliant, and obtained the favour of an interview. So completely did he seem to have vindicated himself that Constantine, in reply to an encyclical from the Council of Tyre announcing that Athanasius had been condemned and deposed, wrote to the signatories a severe letter summoning them to Constantinople for a re-trial of the case. Then, for some reason which has never been satisfactorily cleared up, the monarch suddenly changed his mind. Ecclesiastical writers naturally shrank from attaching blame to the first Christian Emperor, but it would appear that he took umbrage at the outspoken language of the Patriarch in a further interview. Before the first letter could reach its destination a second one was despatched which confirmed the sentences of the Council of Tyre and banished Athanasius to Treves in Belgian Gaul.

History records nothing about this first exile which lasted two years, except that the saint was hospitably received by the local bishop and that he kept in touch with his flock by letters.

In 337 the Emperor Constantine died, shortly after he had been baptised by Eusebius of Nicomedia, and his empire was divided between his three sons, Constantine II, Constantius, and Constans. The various exiled prelates were immediately recalled, and one of the first acts of Constantine II, who inherited Britain, Spain, and Gaul, was to restore Athanasius to his see. The Patriarch re-entered his diocesan city in seeming triumph, but his enemies were as relentless as ever, and Eusebius of Nicomedia had completely won over the Emperor Constantius, within whose jurisdiction Alexandria was situated. He was accused before the monarch of raising seditions, of promoting bloodshed, and of detaining for his own use corn which was destined for widows and the poor. His old adversary, Eusebius of Nicomedia, furthermore obtained from a council which met at Antioch a second sentence of deposition, and the ratification of the election of an Arian bishop of Alexandria. By this assembly a letter was written to Pope Julius inviting his intervention, and the condemnation of Athanasius. This was followed by an encyclical, drawn up by the orthodox Egyptian hierarchy and sent to the Pope and to the Catholic bishops, in which the case for Athanasius was duly set forth. The Roman Pontiff replied, accepting the suggestion of the Eusebians that a synod should be held to settle the question.

In the meantime a Cappadocian named Gregory had been installed Patriarch of Alexandria by the prefect Philagrius, Pagans and Arians having joined forces against the Catholics. In the face of the scenes of violence and sacrilege that ensued, Athanasius withdrew, and betook himself to Rome to await the hearing of his case. The synod was duly summoned, but as the Eusebians who had demanded it failed to appear, it was held without them. The result was the complete vindication of the saint—a declaration which was afterwards endorsed by the Council of Sardica. Nevertheless he was unable to return to Alexandria till after the death of the Cappadocian Gregory, and then only because the Emperor Constantius, on the eve of a war with Persia, thought it politic to propitiate his brother Constans by restoring Athanasius to his see. After an absence of eight years the Patriarch returned to Alexandria amidst scenes of unparalleled rejoicing, and for three or four years the wars and disturbances in which the rulers of the empire were involved left him in comparatively peaceful possession of his chair. But the murder of Constans removed the most powerful support of orthodoxy, and Constantius, once he felt himself securely master of the west and of the east, set himself deliberately to crush the man whom he had come to regard as a personal enemy. At Arles in 353 he obtained the condemnation of the saint from a council of time-serving prelates, and again in 355 at Milan where he declared himself to be the accuser of Athanasius. The few friendly bishops were exiled, including Pope Liberius, who was kept in isolation in Thrace until, broken in body and spirit, he was temporarily beguiled into acquiescence with the censure.

In Egypt Athanasius held on with the support of his clergy and people, but not for long. One night, when he was celebrating a vigil in the Church of St Theonas, a troop of soldiers under Duke Syrianus forced open the doors, killing some of the congregation and wounding others. As though by a miracle, Athanasius escaped —he never knew how—and disappeared into the desert, where the watchful care of the monks kept him safely hidden for six years. If, during that time, the world had few tidings of him, he was kept well informed of all that was going on, and his untiring activity, repressed in one direction, expressed itself in literary form. To this period are ascribed many of his chief writings—an Encyclical to the Bishops of Egypt and Libya, an Apology to Constantius, another Apology for his Flight, a History of the Arians, three letters to Serapion and a treatise on the Synods of Rimini and Seleucia.

The death of Constantius in 361 was followed soon afterwards by the murder, at the hands of the populace, of the Arian who had usurped the Alexandrian patriarchate. The new Emperor, Julian, had revoked the sentences of banishment enacted by his predecessor, and Athanasius returned to his own city. But it was only for a few months. The Apostate's plans for the paganising of the Christian world could make little way as long as the champion of the Catholic faith ruled in Egypt. Julian therefore banished him from Alexandria as " a disturber of the peace and an enemy of the gods," and Athanasius once more sought refuge in the desert, regardless of the imperial edict which forbade him to leave Egypt. He only very narrowly escaped capture. He was in a little boat on the Nile when his companions in great alarm called his attention to an imperial galley which was fast overhauling them. Athanasius, unperturbed, bade them turn the boat and row towards it. The pursuers shouted out, asking for information about the fugitive. " He is not far off," was the reply. " Row fast if you want to overtake him." The stratagem succeeded, and Athanasius again eluded his would-be captors. During this fourth exile he seems to have explored the Thebaïd from end to end. He was at Antinopolis when he was informed by two solitaries of the death of Julian, who had at that moment expired, slain by an arrow in Persia.

At once he returned to Alexandria, and some months later he proceeded to Antioch at the invitation of the Emperor Jovian, a soldier of Catholic sympathies, who had revoked his sentence of banishment and desired of him an exposition of the true doctrine of the Trinity. The monarch, after receiving him with honour, accepted the treatise he had written and refused to listen to the complaints of the Arians against the saint. Jovian's reign, however, was a short one ; and the Emperor Valens in May 365 issued an order banishing all the orthodox bishops who had been exiled by Constantius and restored by his successors. Again Athanasius was forced to withdraw. The ecclesiastical writer, Socrates, says that he concealed himself in the vault in which his father lay buried, but a more probable account states that he remained in a villa in one of the suburbs of Alexandria.   Four months later Valens revoked his edict—possibly fearing a rising among the Egyptians who had become devotedly attached to their much persecuted bishop.   With great demonstrations of joy the people escorted him back and the authorities restored to him the possession of the Church of St Dionysius.   Five times the great patriarch had been exiled : seventeen years he had spent in exile : but for the last seven years of his life he was left in the unchallenged occupation of his see.   It was probably at this time that he wrote the life of St Anthony.

St Athanasius died in Alexandria on May 2, 373, and his body was subsequently translated first to Constantinople and then to Venice.

The greatest man of his age and one of the greatest religious leaders of any age, the saintly Patriarch of Alexandria rendered services to the Church the value of which can scarcely be exaggerated, for he defended the faith against almost overwhelming odds and emerged triumphant.   Most aptly has he been described by Cardinal Newman as " a principal instrument after the Apostles by which the sacred truths of Christianity have been conveyed and secured to the world."

Although the writings of St Athanasius deal mainly with controversy, there is beneath this war of words a deep spiritual feeling which comes to the surface at every turn and reveals the high purpose of him who writes.   Take, for example, his reply to the objections which the Arians raised from the texts :   " Let this chalice pass from Me," or " Why hast Thou forsaken Me ? "

" Is it not extravagant, then," he asks, " to admire the courage of the servants of the Word, yet to say that that Word Himself was in terror, through whom they despised death ?   For that most enduring purpose and courage of the holy martyrs demonstrates that the Godhead was not in terror, but that the Saviour took away our terror.   For as He abolished death by death, and by human means all human evils, so by this so-called terror did He remove our terror, and brought about for us that never more should men fear death. His word and deed go together. . . . For human were the sounds : ' Let this chalice pass from Me,' and ' Why has Thou forsaken Me ? ' and divine the action whereby He, the same being, did cause the sun to fail and the dead to rise.   And so He said humanly : ' Now is My soul troubled ' ; and He said divinely : ' I have power to lay down My life and power to take it again.'   For to be troubled was proper to the flesh, but to have power to lay down His life and take it again when He would, was no property of man, but of the Word's power.   For man dies not at his own arbitrament, but by necessity of nature and against his will ; but the Lord being Himself immortal, not having a mortal flesh, had it at His own free will, as God, to become separate from the body and to take it again, when He would.

"Concerning this, too, speaks David in the psalm : ' Thou shalt not leave my soul in hell, neither shalt Thou suffer Thy Holy One to see corruption.' For it beseemed that the flesh, corruptible as it was, should no longer after its own nature remain mortal, but because of the Word which had put it on, should abide incorruptible. For as He, having come in our body, was conformed to our condition, so we, having received Him, partake of the immortality that is from Him.

"Idle, then, is the excuse for stumbling, and narrow are the notions concerning the Word, of those Ario-maniacs who are upset by its being written : ' He was troubled,' and ' He wept.' For they seem not even to have human feeling, if they are thus ignorant of man's nature and properties ; properties which do but make it the greater marvel, that He, the Word, though in a suffering flesh, neither prevented those who were conspiring against Him, nor took vengeance on those who were putting Him to death, though He was able, He who hindered some from dying, and raised others from the dead. And He let His own body suffer, for therefore did He come, as I said before, that in the flesh He might suffer, and thenceforth the flesh might be made impassible and immortal, and that, as we have many times said, contumely and the other troubles might fall upon Him, but come short of others after Him, being by Him annulled utterly, and that henceforth men might for ever abide incorruptible, as a temple of the Word."

The principal source of information for the life of St Athanasius is the collection of his own writings, but his activities were so interwoven with not only the religious, but the secular, history of his times, that the range of authorities to be consulted is very wide. For English readers Cardinal Newman, in his Anglican days, both in his special work on St Athanasius and in his tract on the " Causes of the Rise and Successes of Arianism," has rendered the whole complicated situation intelligible. There is also a brilliantly written chapter on St Athanasius in Dr. A. Fortescue's volume, *The Greek Fathers*. Two excellent little monographs have appeared in France, the one by F. Cavallera, and the other by G. Bardy in the series " Les Saints." Reference should also be made to four valuable papers by E. Schwartz in the *Nachrichten* of the Göttingen Akademie from 1904 to 1911. For a fuller bibliography see Bardenhewer in the latest edition of his *Patrologie*, or in his larger work, *Geschichte der altkirchlichen Literatur*.

SS. EXSUPERIUS AND ZOË, MM.

c. A.D. 135

Exsuperius (or rather Hesperus) and his wife Zoë were the slaves of a rich man named Catalus who lived in the reign of the Emperor Hadrian at Attalia, a town of Pamphylia in Asia Minor. They had been born Christians, and though negligent themselves, they brought up their two sons, Cyriacus and Theodulus in the true faith. Having been shamed out of their religious indifference by the example of their children, they refused to accept food offered to the gods, which their master sent them on the occasion of the birth of his son. Thereupon they were arrested and brought up for trial. All made a bold confession. After the two boys had been tortured in the presence of their parents, all four were roasted to death in a fiery furnace. The Emperor Justinian built a church in Constantinople dedicated to St Zoë—presumably to contain her remains—but some of the relics of all these martyrs appear to have been translated to Clermont, where they are still devoutly venerated.

Although these saints seem to be commemorated on May 2 in all the synaxaries (see in particular the *Synaxarium Constantinopolitanum*, ed. Delehaye, *cc.* 649–650), and a Greek *Passio* is printed in the *Acta Sanctorum*, May, vol. i, the account seems to be historically worthless. It is difficult to understand how the father's name, Hesperus, which appears in all the manuscripts, has been transformed into Exsuperius in the Roman Martyrology.

ST SATURNINUS AND COMPANIONS, MM.

c. A.D. 304

In the Roman Martyrology for this day we find the entry: " At Rome, of the holy martyrs Saturninus, Neopolus, Germanus and Celestine, who suffered many things, and at last were cast into prison and there found rest in the Lord." The greater part of this is incorrect and seems due to a confusion of names in the *Hieronymianum*, of which, unfortunately, we have hundreds of other examples. It is reasonably certain that at Alexandria a martyr named Saturninus was honoured on May 2, because the ancient Syriac calendar of the early fifth century preserves such a record. In the same document we have mention of " the presbyter Germanus," also at Alexandria, but three days earlier. Further, we may read in Eusebius a graphic description of the torments to which the Alexandrian martyrs were subjected, and the historian tells us that while some of them succumbed under torture, others were thrust back half-dead into their dungeons, where they perished in agony after a short interval. Of Neopolus and Celestine absolutely nothing is known.

Upon all the foregoing consult Père Delehaye's Commentary on the *Hieronymianum* in the *Acta Sanctorum*, November, vol. ii, part 2, p. 225. An extravagant suggestion that under Neopolus we should recognise a St Napoleon has been discussed by Père Delehaye in *Mélanges Henri Pirenne*, vol. i, pp. 81–88.

ST ULTAN, ABBOT

c. A.D. 675

St Ultan (or Ulain) and his more celebrated brothers, St Fursey and St Foillan, were Irish monks of high degree who crossed over to East Anglia, where they founded the abbey of Burgh Castle, near Yarmouth, on territory bestowed upon them by King Sigberct or Sigebert I. The monastery was destroyed in a raid by the soldiers of King Penda : the monks were dispersed : and St Fursey went to France, where he died. When St Foillan and St Ultan visited their brother's tomb at Péronne on their way back from a pilgrimage to Rome, they were warmly welcomed by St Gertrude of Nivelles, who offered them land at Fosses on which to build a monastery and a hospice for strangers. St Foillan became the first abbot of Fosses, while St Ultan, whom St Gertrude venerated greatly for his sanctity and supernatural gifts, was induced to remain for a time at Nivelles to teach the nuns to sing the divine office. By supernatural revelation St Ultan knew of the death of St Foillan, who was murdered by robbers in the forest of Soignies, and he foretold to St Gertrude, at her request, the day of her own death. He said that St Patrick was preparing to welcome her, and in point of fact she died on March 17. St Ultan became abbot of the two monasteries of Fosses and of Péronne, over which he ruled for the remainder of his life. He died at Péronne, but his relics were subsequently translated to Fosses.

What we know of St Ultan is mainly gleaned from the life of St Fursey and from that of St Gertrude of Nivelles. These texts have been edited by Bruno Krusch in the second and the fourth volume of the *Monumenta Germaniæ, Scriptores Rerum Merovingicarum*. See also Gougaud, *Christianity in Celtic Lands*, pp. 147–148, and *Gaelic Pioneers*, pp. 128–131 ; and *cf.* J. F. Kenney, *The Sources for the Early History of Ireland*, vol. i, pp. 502–505.

ST WALDEBERTUS, ABBOT OF LUXEUIL
c. A.D. 668

Amongst the numerous successors of Saint Columban in the monastery of Luxeuil the most famous during his life and the most revered after his death was undoubtedly St Waldebertus, the third abbot. This is partly due to the fact that his long rule coincided with the most glorious period of the abbey's history and partly to the numerous miracles attributed to the saint. Objects he had touched—notably his wooden drinking bowl—were long venerated for their healing properties, and in the tenth century Anso, a Luxeuil monk, wrote a book about the wonders the saint had wrought.

Waldebertus was a wealthy young Frankish nobleman, who had been a warrior until he decided to enter the religious life. In military attire he appeared at Luxeuil to ask admittance of the Abbot St Eustathius, and when he laid aside his weapons to receive the habit, they were suspended from the roof of the church, where they remained for centuries. Within a short time he proved so exemplary a monk that he obtained permission to lead the eremitic life in the cleft of a rock about three miles from the Abbey. After the death of St Eustathius and the refusal of St Gall to become his successor, the brethren chose St Waldebertus as their new superior. For forty years he ruled them wisely and well. Under his government the rule of St Columban was superseded by that of St Benedict, and he obtained for Luxeuil from Pope John IV the privilege already conceded to Lérins and Agaunum of being free from episcopal control. He had bestowed his own estates upon the abbey, which was also enriched during his lifetime by many liberal benefactions. Such assistance was indeed sorely needed, because Luxeuil itself could not contain or support all who sought to enter it. Parties of monks were continually being sent out from it to found fresh houses in other parts of France. Even over nunneries St Waldebertus was called to exercise control, and it was with his help and support that St Salaberga or Sadalberga founded her great convent at Lâon with its seven churches. The holy abbot died about the year 668 and was buried in the church of St Martin by his great friend St Migetius, Bishop of Besançon.

An account of the life and miracles of St Waldebertus or Walbert was written 300 years after his death by Adso, Abbot of Muntier-en-Der. This has been printed by Mabillon, and in the *Acta Sanctorum*, May, vol. i. See also J. B. Clerc, *Ermitage et Vie de S. Valbert* (4th edn., 1861); H. Baumont, *Étude historique sur Luxeuil*, 1896; A. Malnory, *Quid Luxovienses monachi, etc.*, 1894; J. Poinsotte, *Les Abbés de Luxeuil*, 1900.

ST WIBORADA, Virg. and Mart.

A.D. 925

Klingen, in the Swiss canton of Aargau, was the birthplace of St Wiborada, who is called in French Guiborat and in German Weib-rath. From her earliest years she evinced unusual piety, and when little more than a child, would sleep on the floor, undertake long fasts and daily walk barefoot a league and a half to the nearest church for Mass. Her parents, who belonged to the Swabian nobility, raised no opposition to her austerities and she led a retired life in the house of her father and mother, whom she nursed when they were ill and whose eyes she eventually closed. Her time was ordinarily divided between prayer and manual labour. After one of her brothers, Hatto by name, had decided to be a priest she not only made his clothes, but she also worked for the monastery of St Gall, where he prosecuted his studies. Many of the books in the abbey library were covered by her. Upon the death of her parents, Wiborada joined this brother who had been made provost of the Church of St Magnus. He taught her Latin so that she could join him in saying the offices and could answer when he said Mass. Their house became a kind of hospital to which Hatto would bring patients for Wiborada to tend. However, after the brother and sister had made a pilgrimage to Rome, Hatto resolved to take the habit at St Gall's—largely through Wiborada's influence. She, on the other hand, remained for some years longer in the world, though not of it. It may have been at this period—but more probably, as certain writers have argued, after she became a recluse—that she came into touch with St Ulric, who had been sent, as a delicate little lad of seven, to the monastic school of St Gall. We read that she prophesied his future elevation to the episcopate, and in after years he regarded her as his spiritual mother. According to some of the saint's biographers—but not the earliest—she suffered so severely from calumnies against her character that she underwent trial by ordeal at Constance to clear herself of the charges. Whether the story is true or false, she decided to withdraw into solitude that she might serve God without distraction. At first she took up her abode in an anchorhold which she built on a mountain not far from the Abbey of St Gall, but in 915 she was immured by Solomon, Bishop of Constance, in a cell beside the church of St Magnus. There she remained for the rest of her life, practising extraordinary mortifications. Many visitors came to see her, attracted by the fame of her miracles and prophecies. Other recluses also settled near her, but only one of them was admitted to

any sort of companionship. This was a woman of high degree
called Rachildis, a niece of St Notker Balbulus of St Gall. She was
brought to St Wiborada suffering from a disease which the doctors
had pronounced incurable. Having apparently been cured by the
ministrations of the recluse, she could never be induced to leave her
benefactress. But after the death of the latter the malady returned
with so many complications that she seemed a second Job, owing
to the multiplicity of her diseases and the patience with which she
bore them.

St Wiborada foretold her own death at the hands of the invading
Hungarians, adding that her friend Rachildis would be left unmolested. Her warnings enabled the clergy of St Magnus and the
monks of St Gall to escape in time, but she herself absolutely refused
to leave her cell. The barbarians burnt the church and, having made
an opening in the roof of the hermitage, entered the cell, as she
knelt in prayer. After they had stripped off her garments to the
hairshirt which she wore, they struck her on the head three times
with a hatchet and left her in a dying condition, the whole cell being
drenched with blood. Rachildis, however, remained unharmed,
and survived her friend for twenty-one years.

There is good evidence for most of the details given above. Hartmann, a
monk of St Gall, who first wrote a sketch of her life—it is printed by
Mabillon and in the *Acta Sanctorum*, May, vol. i—was almost a contemporary. A later life by Hepidannus is less reliable. But we have also other
references to St Wiborada, for example, in Gerhard's *Life of St Ulric of
Augsburg*, and in Ekkehard (iv) *Casus S. Galli*. This last is printed by
G. Meyer v. Knonau, *St Gallische Geschichtsquellen*, III. The statement made
in the July volume of this series (p. 38) that Wilborada's prophecy concerning
St Ulrich is " chronologically impossible," seems much too strong in the
face of A. Schröder's valuable article in the *Historisches Jahrbuch*, vol. xxii
(1901), pp. 276–284.

BLESSED CONRAD OF SELDENBÜREN, Conf.

A.D. 1126

The celebrated Benedictine Abbey of Engelberg, in Unter-
walden, owed its foundation to Blessed Conrad, a scion of the princely
family of Seldenbüren, whose main residence was near Zürich.
Upon the death of his parents Conrad resolved to devote part of
his patrimony to building a monastery, and tradition says that the
site was revealed to him by Our Lady in a vision. For some un-
recorded reason, delay must have occurred in the construction, for
although the work was begun in 1082, it was not completed until

1120. At that date the church was consecrated by Ulric, Bishop of Constance and St Adelhelmus was appointed abbot, bringing with him twelve monks from Einsiedeln, or—according to another authority—from the Abbey of St Blasien which one of Conrad's ancestors had built in the Black Forest. After devoting the rest of his fortune to establishing a convent for women, the founder went to Rome where he obtained recognition and privileges for his houses. He then retired from the world, receiving from St Adelhelmus the habit of a humble lay brother. From his peaceful retreat Conrad emerged at the bidding of his superior to meet a claim which had been made on some of the property he had bestowed upon the Abbey. At Zürich he went unsuspectingly to a meeting arranged by his opponents, who fell upon him and killed him. The body of Blessed Conrad was brought back to Engelberg where it remained incorrupt until the Abbey was burnt down in 1729.

There is no early life of Bd. Conrad, but a short account is furnished in the *Acta Sanctorum*, May, vol. i. See also two papers by A. Brackmann in the *Abhandlungen* of the Prussian Academy for 1928, and the sketch by B. Egger, *Konrad von Seldenbüren*, 1926.

BLESSED MAFALDA, Nun

A.D. 1252

In the year 1215, at the tender age of eleven, Princess Mafalda (*i.e.* Matilda), daughter of King Sancho I of Portugal, was married to her kinsman King Henry I of Castile, who was, like herself, a minor. The marriage was annulled the following year on the ground of the consanguinity of the parties, and Mafalda returned to her own country, where she took the veil in the Benedictine convent of Arouca. As religious observance had become greatly relaxed, she induced the community, with the approval of Pope Honorius III, to adopt the Cistercian rule. Her own life was one of extreme austerity. The whole of the large income bestowed upon her by her father was devoted to pious and charitable uses. She restored the cathedral of Oporto, founded a hostel for pilgrims, erected a bridge over the Talmeda and built an institution for the support of twelve widows at Arouca. When she felt that her last hour was approaching she directed, according to a common medieval practice, that she should be laid on ashes. Her last words were : " Lord, I hope in Thee." Her body after death shone with a wonderful radiance, and when it was exposed in 1617, in the presence of

Bishop Affonso Mexia of Lamego, it is said to have been as flexible and fresh as though the holy woman had only just died. Mafalda and two of her sisters are honoured with the title of Blessed, this being sanctioned by Pope Pius VI in 1793.

A notice of Bd. Mafalda, compiled mainly from late Cistercian sources, will be found in the appendix to the first volume for May in the *Acta Sanctorum*. An account of all three sisters, Sancha, Tereza, and Mafalda, is also contained in the *Portugal glorioso e illustrado, etc.*, by J. P. Bayão, 1727.

ST PEREGRINUS LAZIOSI, Conf.

A.D. 1345

The only son of well-to-do parents, St Peregrinus Laziosi was born in 1260 at Forli, in the Romagna. As a young man he took an active part in the politics of his native city, which belonged to the anti-papal party. On the occasion of a popular rising, St Philip Benizi, who had been sent by the Pope to act as a mediator, was severely mishandled by the popular leaders, and Peregrinus himself struck him on the face with his fist. The holy Servite's only reply was to offer the other cheek—an action which brought his assailant to immediate repentance. With tears he confessed his guilt and besought pardon. St Philip consoled his penitent, exhorting him at the same time to amend his life and to cultivate a childlike devotion to the Mother of God. From that time Peregrinus was a reformed character. Turning away from his worldly companions, he spent hours upon his knees in the Chapel of Our Lady in the Cathedral. One day the Blessed Virgin herself appeared to him in that place, and addressed him, saying : " Go to Siena : there you will find the devout men who call themselves my servants : attach yourself to them." Peregrinus instantly obeyed the order. Having received the Servite habit, he set about following with zeal the path of perfection. It became his guiding principle that one must never rest in the way of virtue, but must press on to the appointed goal. It is said that for thirty years he never sat down. As far as he could, he observed silence and solitude, for he regarded them as being of paramount assistance in the spiritual life. After he had spent some years in Siena, his superiors sent him to Forli to found a new house for the order. By this time he had been ordained and had proved himself to be an ideal priest—fervent in the celebration of the holy mysteries, eloquent in preaching, untiring in converting and reconciling sinners. A great affliction now befell him in the form of a loathsome cancer of the foot, which, besides being excruciatingly painful, made him an object of repulsion to his neighbours. He bore this trial without a murmur. At last the surgeons decided that the only thing to do was to cut off the foot. St Peregrinus spent the night before the operation in trustful prayer to God before his crucifix. He then sank into a light slumber from which he awoke completely cured—to the amazement of the doctors, who testified that they could no longer detect any trace of the disease. This miracle greatly enhanced the reputation which the holy man had already acquired by his exemplary life. He lived to the age of 80 and died in the odour of sanctity. He is the principal patron of Forli.

The Bollandists in the *Acta Sanctorum*, April, vol. iii, were able to print some portion of the documents presented in the cause of the canonisation of St Peregrinus. Since then many Italian accounts of the saint have been published, mostly devotional rather than historically critical ; for example, B. Albicini, *Vita e Morte del B. Pellegrino Laziosi*, 1648 ; F. A. Monsignani, *Notizie della Vita, Morte e Miracoli, etc.*, 1727, with a number of others. See also Giani, *Annales FF. Servorum B.V.M.*, vol. i, pp. 285 *seq.*

MAY 3

THE " INVENTION " OF THE HOLY CROSS

? A.D. 326

THE feast of the " Invention," that is to say the discovery of the Holy Cross, which is kept by the Church on May 3 with the rite of a double of the second class, would seem to take precedence of the September feast, the " Exaltation," which is only observed as a greater double. There is, however, a good deal of evidence which suggests that the September feast is the more primitive celebration, and that a certain confusion has arisen between the two incidents in the history of the Holy Cross which these festivals purport to commemorate. Strictly speaking, neither of them seems at first to have been directly connected with the discovery of the cross. The September feast took its rise from the solemn dedication in A.D. 335 of the churches which Constantine, at the instigation of his mother, St Helen, had caused to be built on the site of the Holy Sepulchre. We cannot be sure that the dedication was carried out precisely on September 14th. The month, however, was September,* and seeing that in the time of the pilgrim Ætheria, fifty years later, the annual commemoration of this inaugurating ceremony lasted for a week together, there is clearly no reason to be particular to a day or two. In any case, Ætheria herself tells us : " The dedication of these holy churches is therefore celebrated with the highest honour, and also because the Cross of our Lord was found on this same day. And it was so ordained that, when the holy churches above mentioned were consecrated, that should also be the day when the Cross of our Lord had been found, in order that the whole celebration should be made together, with all rejoicing, on the self-same day." From this it would follow that the discovery of the cross was honoured at Jerusalem in September, and the pilgrim Theodosius about A.D. 530, speaking expressly of the " *inventio crucis*," bears witness to the same fact.

But at present we commemorate in September an entirely different event, to wit, the recovery in 629 by the Emperor Heraclius

* See Hefele–Leclercq, *Histoire des Conciles*, vol. i, p. 666, n. 2.

35

of the relics of the cross which some years before had been carried off from Jerusalem by Chosroes II, King of Persia. The Roman martyrology and the lessons of the Breviary are explicit on the point, and a full account of the circumstances will be found in the September volume of this work, pp. 166–7. There is, however, reason to think that under the style "Exaltation of the Cross" we have reference to the physical act of the lifting ($ὕψωσις$) of the sacred relic when it was exhibited for the veneration of the people, and it is also probable that this designation was used in connection with the feast before the time of Heraclius.

As for the actual finding, with which we are here concerned, there is a distressing absence of early information. The Pilgrim of Bordeaux, in 333, says nothing of the cross. Eusebius, the Church historian, from whom, as a contemporary, we should have expected to learn much, makes no reference to the discovery, though he seems to know about the three separate places of worship within the Holy Sepulchre precincts. Thus, in stating that Constantine "adorned a shrine sacred to the salutary emblem," he may well be supposed to refer to that chapel, "Golgotha," in which, as Ætheria tells us, the relics of the cross were preserved. St Cyril, Bishop of Jerusalem, in his catechetical lectures which were delivered, about the year 346, on the very site where our Saviour was crucified, refers more than once to the wood of the cross. "It has been distributed," he declares, "fragment by fragment, from this spot and has already nearly filled the world." Furthermore, in his letter to Constantius, he expressly states that "the saving wood of the cross was found at Jerusalem in the time of Constantine." In all this there is no mention of St Helen, who died in 330. The first, perhaps, to ascribe the discovery to her active intervention is St Ambrose, in his sermon "De Obitu Theodosii," preached in 395; but about that date or a little later we find many others, St John Chrysostom, Rufinus, Paulinus of Nola, and Cassiodorus, together with the church historians Socrates, Sozomen and Theodoret—but notably not St Jerome, who lived on the spot—all repeating similar stories of the recovery of the cross in which St Helen plays a principal part. Unfortunately, the details of these accounts are by no means always in agreement. St Ambrose and St John Chrysostom inform us that in the excavations which were undertaken at the instance of St Helen, three crosses were discovered. They add that to the one in the middle the "title" was still attached, and that in this way our Saviour's cross was clearly identified. On the other hand, Rufinus, who is followed in this by Socrates, reports that in accordance with a special inspiration St Helen directed that excavations should be made in a certain place, that three crosses were found and an inscription, but there was no way of deciding to which of the three the inscription belonged. The Bishop of Jerusalem, Macarius, thereupon had a dying woman brought to the spot. She was made to touch the three crosses, and at the contact of the third she was healed, so that it was made plain to all that this was the cross of our Saviour. There are other divergences, at about the same date, regarding the miracle of healing by which the true Cross was identified, the finding and disposal of the nails, etc. On the whole, it seems probable that the statements made more than sixty years after the event by writers bent mainly on edification, were a good deal influenced by certain apocryphal documents which must already have been in circulation.

The most notable of these is the tractate *De inventione Crucis dominicæ* which is mentioned (*c.* 550) in the pseudo-Gelasian decree *De recipiendis et non recipiendis libris* as a writing to be regarded with mistrust. There can be no doubt that this little tractate was widely read. The compiler of the first redaction of the *Liber Pontificalis* (*c.* A.D. 532) must have had it in his hands, and he quotes from it in the account he gives of Pope Eusebius. It must also have been known to those who blunderingly revised the *Hieronymianum* at Auxerre early in the seventh century.* Neglecting the anachronisms in which the narrative abounds, the story in brief runs thus. The Emperor Constantine, in conflict with vast hordes of barbarians on the Danube, was in grave danger of defeat. There appeared to him, however, a vision of a brilliant cross in the sky, with the legend " In this sign thou shalt conquer." He was thereupon victorious, was instructed and baptised by Pope Eusebius in Rome, and out of gratitude despatched his mother, St Helen, to Jerusalem, to search for the relics of the holy cross. All the inhabitants professed ignorance of its whereabouts, but at last, by dint of threats she prevailed upon a learned Jew named Judas to reveal what he knew. They dug twenty fathoms deep and discovered three crosses. The identity of the true cross is determined by its raising a dead man to life. Judas is thereupon converted, and, as the bishop of Jerusalem happened just then to die, St Helen selects this new convert, who is henceforth called Cyriacus, or Quiriacus, to govern that see in his place. Pope Eusebius is summoned from

* It is curious to find Mgr Duchesne stating in his *Origines* (*Christian Worship*, p. 275, n. 2 ; and *cf.* the *Liber Pontificalis*, vol. i, p. 378, n. 29) that " in the Epternach MS. there is no mention of this festival of the cross." It occurs there on May 7, and also on the same day in St Willibrord's Calendar.

Rome to Jerusalem to consecrate him bishop, and shortly afterwards, through the miraculous appearance of a brilliant light, the hiding-place of the holy nails is also revealed. St Helen, having made generous donations to the holy places and the poor of Jerusalem, happened to die not long afterwards, charging all faithful Christians as her last behest to hold festival every year on the 3rd of May (*quinto nonas Maii*), the day on which the cross was found. Before the year 450, Sozomen (bk. ii, ch. i) seems to have been acquainted with this story of the Jew who revealed the hiding-place of the cross. He does not denounce it as a fabrication, but quietly passes it by as less probable.

Another apocryphal story which bears, though less directly, on the finding of the cross, is introduced, somewhat as a digression, into the document known as *the Doctrine of Addai*, of Syrian origin. What we are told here is that Protonike, the wife of the Emperor Claudius Cæsar, less than ten years after our Lord's Ascension, went to the Holy Land, compelled the Jews to reveal where the crosses were hidden, and distinguished that of our Saviour by a miracle wrought upon her own daughter. It is contended that this legend has suggested the story of St Helen and the discovery of the cross in the time of Constantine. Mgr Duchesne believed that the *Doctrine of Addai* was earlier in date than the *De inventione crucis dominicæ*, but there are strong arguments for the contrary opinion.*

In view of all this very unsatisfactory evidence, the most probable suggestion seems to be that the holy cross with the title was found during the excavations rendered necessary by the construction of Constantine's basilica on Mount Calvary. Such a discovery, which may well have involved some period of doubt and inquiry while the authenticity of the find was being discussed, is likely to have given rise to multifarious conjectures and rumours which before long took written shape in the *De inventione* tractate. It is probable that St Helen's share in the transaction actually amounted to no more than what we should gather from Ætheria's statement when she speaks of "the building which Constantine, under his mother's auspices (*sub præsentia matris suæ*) embellished with gold and mosaics and precious marbles." The credit of a victory is often given to a sovereign, though it is his generals and troops who have done all the fighting. What is certain in the whole matter is that from the middle of the fourth century reputed relics of the true cross spread through the world. This we know not only from St Cyril's reiterated

* See, for example, A. Stülcken in Hennecke's *Handbuch zu den Neutestamentlichen Apokryphen* (1904), p. 158.

statement, but also from dated inscriptions in Africa and elsewhere. Still more convincing is the evidence that before the end of the same century the stem of the cross and the title were both venerated in Jerusalem with intense devotion. Ætheria's account of the ceremony deserves to be quoted. She tells us how :

" A table covered with a linen cloth is placed before the Bishop ; the deacons stand round this table, and a silver-gilt casket is brought in which is the holy wood of the Cross. The casket is opened and the wood is taken out, and both the wood of the Cross and the Title are placed upon the table. Now, when it has been put upon the table, the Bishop, as he sits, holds the extremities of the sacred wood firmly in his hands, while the deacons who stand around guard it. It is guarded thus because the custom is that the people, both faithful and catechumens, come one by one, and bowing down at the table, kiss the sacred wood and pass on. And because, I know not when, some one is said to have bitten off and stolen a portion of the sacred wood, it is thus guarded by the deacons who stand around, lest any one approaching should venture to do so again. And as all the people pass by, one by one, all bowing themselves, they touch the Cross and the Title, first with their foreheads and then with their eyes ; then they kiss the Cross and pass through, but none lays his hand upon it to touch it."

This is the description of an eye-witness about the year 385 ; but only a dozen years or so later we have in the Life of St Porphyrius (see our February volume, pp. 360–361) another testimony to the veneration with which the relic was regarded by its custodians. And again, after nearly two centuries, the pilgrim, commonly, if incorrectly, known as Antoninus of Piacenza, tells us how : " In the basilica of Constantine, which adjoins the tomb and Golgotha, in the atrium of the church itself, is a chamber where the wood of the holy Cross is kept, which we adored (*adoravimus*) and kissed, for I also saw and held in my hand and kissed the title which was placed over the head of Jesus upon which is written, ' Jesus of Nazareth, King of the Jews.' " On the importance of the Title, still in part preserved, with its writing in three languages, as serving to guarantee the authenticity of the cross itself, see *The Month*, May 1930, pp. 426–429.

There is a considerable literature bearing upon the matters here discussed. For much of this the reader may conveniently be referred to the bibliographical references in Dom Leclercq's article on " Invention de la Croix " in the *Dictionnaire d'Archéologie*, etc., vol. iii, *cc.* 3131–3139. See also the *Acta Sanctorum*, May, vol. i ; Duchesne, *Liber Pontificalis*, vol. i, pp. cvii–cix and pp. 75, 167, 378 ; Kellner, *Heortology* (Eng. trans.), pp. 333–341 ; J. Straubinger, *Die Kreuzauffindungslegende* (1912) ; A. Halusa,

Das Kreuzesholz in Geschichte und Legende (1926) ; *The Month*, May 1930, pp. 420–429.

It is generally held that this feast of the " Invention of the Cross " on May 3 is not of Roman origin, since it is lacking in the Gregorian Sacramentary, but, so far as its prevalence in the West is concerned, must have arisen in Gaul. It occurs in the Félire of Oengus and in most MSS. of the *Hieronymianum*. In the Epternach MS., however, it is assigned, as noted above, to May 7. This seems to have reference to a feast celebrated in Jerusalem, and among the Armenians, in memory of the luminous cross in the heavens which appeared on May 7, A.D. 351, as St Cyril describes in his letter to the Emperor Constantius. As for the date, May 3, it is impossible not to believe that it is closely connected with the mention of that precise day in the apocryphal tract, *De inventione crucis dominicæ*. The earliest notice of a cross festival in the West seems to be the mention of a " *dies sanctæ crucis* " in a lectionary of Silos, *c.* 650.

SS. ALEXANDER, EVENTIUS AND THEODULUS, MM.

c. A.D. 113 (?)

In the official Roman Martyrology the second announcement for this day, May 3, runs as follows : " At Rome, on the Via Nomentana, the passion of the holy martyrs Alexander the Pope, Eventius and Theodulus, priests ; whereof Alexander, after suffering fetters, imprisonment, the rack and torture by hooks and the flame, was, under the Emperor Hadrian and the judge Aurelian, pierced with many sharp points in all his limbs, and slain, but Eventius and Theodulus, after long imprisonment, were tried by fire and at last beheaded." Although the whole of this notice has practically speaking been repeated in successive martyrologies for more than 1200 years, it unfortunately reposes upon a so-called " Passio " of the martyrs, which is a mere work of fiction and historically worthless. The Alexander mentioned is assumed to have been the Pope, but this is almost certainly an error. In the *Hieronymianum* the name Eventius stands first, and in a fragmentary inscription found in 1855 on the spot indicated as that of the burial in the Via Nomentana, another name must have come before Alexander's ; in neither is he styled *episcopus*. There were, no doubt, three martyrs interred on this spot, but we know nothing beyond their names. Of Pope Alexander I the *Liber Pontificalis* tells us very little. It attributes to him the insertion of the clause *Qui pridie quam pateretur* in the canon of the Mass, and also the pious custom of using holy water in private houses, but if it indicates the seventh milestone along the Via Nomentana as the place of his interment, it has borrowed this from some recension of the quite unreliable *Passio*.

The *Passio* itself is printed in the *Acta Sanctorum*, May, vol. i. But consult also Duchesne, *Liber Pontificalis*, vol. i, p. xci ; Quentin, *Les Martyrologes historiques*, p. 58 and *passim* ; Delehaye's commentary on the *Hieronymianum*, pp. 227–228 ; and Marucchi, *Il Cimitero e la Basilica di S. Alessandro alla Via Nomentana*, Rome, 1922.

SS. TIMOTHY AND MAURA, MM.

c. A.D. 286

The cruel edicts of Diocletian against the Christians were enforced with great severity in Upper Egypt by Arrian, the prefect of the Thebaïd. Amongst his victims were a young couple named Timothy and Maura, who were ardent students of the Holy Scriptures, Timothy being a lector of the Church at Penapeis, near Antinoë. They had only been married twenty days when Timothy was taken before the governor and was bidden to deliver up the sacred books that they might be publicly burned. Upon his refusal, red-hot iron instruments were thrust into his ears, his eyelids were cut off and other tortures were applied to him. As he remained steadfast, Maura was sent for that she might break down his resolution by her entreaties. Far from obeying the governor's orders, she declared herself willing to die with her husband. After her hair had been torn out, she and Timothy were nailed to a wall where they died, after lingering for nine days.

There was a considerable cultus of these martyrs in the East, though its introduction at Constantinople seems to have been relatively late. The Greek " Acts " have been printed in the *Acta Sanctorum*, May, vol. i (appendix), but see also the *Synaxarium Constantinopolitanum* (ed. Delehaye), *cc.* 649–652.

ST JUVENAL, BISHOP OF NARNI

c. A.D. 376

The chief patron of Narni and the titular of its cathedral is its first bishop, St Juvenal, whose oratory and original tomb are still venerated in the city. His history has been confused with that of other saintly prelates of the same name, and a connected biography, compiled by the Bollandists from fragmentary notices in print and manuscript, is quite obviously legendary in parts. According to this account, Juvenal, who was both a priest and a physician, came from the East to Narni, where he was hospitably entertained by a pious lady called Philadelphia. At the request of the Christian inhabitants,

Pope Damasus made Narni into a separate diocese and consecrated St Juvenal to be its bishop. One day, as he was passing a brazen bull in front of a heathen temple dedicated to Bacchus, a pagan priest struck him in the mouth with the hilt of his sword because the saint refused to sacrifice to the gods. The bishop held the weapon with his teeth, and the priest, in a violent effort to withdraw his blade, cut his own throat. This incident led to the immediate conversion of the heathen bystanders. In the fifth year of his pontificate, troops of Ligurians and Sarmatians who had captured Terni proceeded to invest Narni. St Juvenal climbed upon the city wall, where he chanted the 34th Psalm and prayed aloud for the town. Scarcely had the people responded Amen, when a great thunderstorm broke out, with torrents of rain, in which 3000 of the assailants perished. Thus was Narni saved. The saint ruled his diocese for seven years, dying in 376. St Gregory the Great speaks of him more than once and styles him martyr, but he seems to have made the mistake of identifying him with a namesake who suffered death for the faith at Benevento. In the ninth century, when the Margrave Adalbertus took Narni, the body of St Juvenal was removed to Lucca. Afterwards it was translated more than once, but it now rests again at Narni.

The Bollandists have collected much archæological material bearing on the cult of St Juvenal. See the *Acta Sanctorum*, May, vol. i ; and also Lanzoni, *Le Diocesi d'Italia*, vol. i, pp. 402 *seq.* ; the *Römische Quartalschrift*, 1905, pp. 42–49, and 1911, pp. 61–71. *Cf.* the *Neues Archiv.*, 1919, pp. 526–555.

ST CONLETHUS, OR CONLÆD, Bp. OF KILDARE

c. A.D. 519

History has preserved few reliable details concerning St Conlethus, the patron as well as the first bishop of Kildare. A priest, and like many of the early Irish ecclesiastics, a clever worker in metals, he was living the life of a solitary at Old Connell on the Liffey when he came into touch with St Brigid, who at once formed a very high opinion of him. Their intercourse ripened into friendship. A gloss on the Félire of Œngus calls St Conlæd " St Brigid's chief artificer " ; but, if she knew how to utilise his artistic talents in making sacred vessels, she knew still better how to employ his spiritual gifts, for she obtained his consecration as bishop over her people at Kildare. A leaf appended to the Martyrology of Donegal describes St Conlæd as " brazier of Brigid, first bishop of

Cilldara and archbishop also,"—meaning, perhaps, that he became metropolitan over the regionary bishops and abbots in that district of Ireland. Tradition ascribes to St Conlæd the fashioning of the crozier afterwards owned by St Finbar of Termon Barry and now preserved in the museum of the Royal Irish Academy. In the gloss upon the Félire of Œngus the curious statement is made that St Conlæd was devoured by wolves when he persisted in undertaking a journey to Rome against St Brigid's wishes. This seems to be an attempt to explain the name Conlæd, i.e. " half (*leth*) to wolves (*coin*)," and the gloss states further that his previous name was Roncenn.

There are no materials apparently for the life of St Conlæd except casual allusions in Cogitosus's account of St Brigid and other similar sources. See, however, Healy, *Ireland's Ancient Schools and Scholars*, pp. 112–118 ; Gougaud, *Christianity in Celtic Lands* ; and J. F. Kenney, *The Sources for the Early History of Ireland*, vol. i (1929).

ST PHILIP OF ZELL, HERMIT
EIGHTH CENTURY

During the reign of Charlemagne's father, King Pepin, there was living in the Rhenish palatinate, not far from the actual city of Worms, a hermit named Philip who had an extraordinary reputation for sanctity and miracles. An Englishman by birth, he had settled in the Nahegau after he had made a pilgrimage to Rome, where he was ordained priest. Amongst those who sought out the recluse was King Pepin himself, who, according to the legend, often visited him and conversed familiarly with him about holy things. The historian of St Philip, who wrote a century after his death, states that through his intercourse with the hermit, Pepin " began to fear as well as to love God and to place all his hope in Him." As is so often the case with solitaries, Philip exercised a great attraction over the wild creatures of the forest : birds perched on his shoulder and ate from his hands, whilst hares frisked about him and licked his feet. He was joined in his solitude by another priest, Horoscolfus by name, who served God with him in prayer and helped to cultivate the land which, under their care, proved very productive. One evening, thieves stole the two oxen which the hermits kept to aid them in their labours. All night long the miscreants wandered about the woods, unable to find their way out, and, in the morning, they discovered that they were back again in front of the hermitage. In dismay they threw themselves at St Philip's feet, begging for forgiveness. The holy man reassured them, entertained them as honoured guests and sped them on their way. Gradually disciples gathered round the two hermits and a church was built which was dedicated to St Michael. A story is told that Horoscolfus, on his return from a journey, found his master dead and lying in his coffin. With tears the disciple besought his master to give him the usual blessing which, for some reason, had been omitted when they had last parted. In reply the corpse sat up and said : " Go forth in peace, and may God prosper you abundantly in all things. Take care of this place as long as you live. Safe and sound you shall go forth : safe and sound shall you return." Then, having given the desired blessing, he sank back into death. Horoscolfus continued to reside in the hermitage until, at the age of 100, he passed away to rejoin his master. On the site of the cells was built a monastery, and then a collegiate church, in the midst of what became the flourishing parish of Zell. At a very much later date, the temporalities of the church were transferred to the Academy of Heidelberg, the precursor of the present University. The relics of St Philip are said to have been discovered in 973, and a great impetus was given to his cultus which, at one time, was very widespread.

The author of the life of St Philip, which is printed in the *Acta Sanctorum*, May, vol. i, is not known, but he was certainly not a contemporary, as has sometimes been stated. This text with other materials has been more critically edited by A. Hofmeister in the supplementary volume (*Scriptores*, vol. xxx, part 2, pp. 796–805) of Pertz, *Monumenta Germaniæ*. Some useful information also concerning St Philip and his cultus was printed in various numbers of *Der Katholik* of Mainz in 1887, 1896, 1898, and 1899.

BLESSED VENTURA SPELLUCCI, Abbot

Twelfth Century

The little Umbrian town of Spello, near Assisi, greatly venerates the memory of one of its citizens, Blessed Ventura Spellucci, whose relics are preserved in a church which bears his name. Born of a noble family and a man of piety, he was so greatly impressed by his intercourse with two members of the Order of Italian Crucifers, who were passing through Spello, that he accompanied them to Rome, whither they were bound in order to pray at the tombs of the apostles and to obtain further facilities for their work of establishing hospices for pilgrims. In the Holy City he received the habit of the order and when, on the death of some of his relations, he inherited their possessions, he built a hospice at Spello with a monastery, over which he ruled as abbot until his death.   The hospice church, built, as it was, in an exposed situation on the main road, was afterwards destroyed by soldiers during some political disturbances, but it was restored in 1625.   The following year the body of Blessed Ventura was elevated and then solemnly enshrined.

A short account of this Beato is furnished in the *Acta Sanctorum*, May, vol. i.   It is mainly derived from Jacobilli, *De Sanctis et Beatis Umbriæ*.

45

MAY 4

ST MONICA, Widow

A.D. 387

THE Church is doubly indebted to St Monica, the ideal of wifely forbearance and holy widowhood, whom we commemorate upon this day, for she not only gave bodily life to the great Doctor, St Augustine, but she was also God's principal instrument in bringing about his spiritual birth by grace. She was born in North Africa—probably at Tagaste, sixty miles from Carthage—of Christian parents, in the year 332. Her early training was entrusted to a faithful retainer who apparently had been nurse also to the head of the family and who treated her younger charges wisely, if somewhat strictly. Amongst the disciplinary regulations she inculcated was that of never drinking between meals. " It is water you want now," she would say, " but when you become mistresses of the cellar you will want wine—not water—and the habit will remain with you." But when Monica grew old enough to be charged with the duty of drawing wine for the household, she disregarded the excellent maxim, and from taking occasional secret sips in the cellar, she soon came to drinking whole cupfuls with relish. One day, however, a slave who had watched her and with whom she was having an altercation, called her a wine-bibber. The shaft struck home : Monica was overwhelmed with shame and never again gave way to the temptation. Indeed, from the day of her baptism, which took place soon afterwards, she seems to have lived a life exemplary in every particular.

As soon as she had reached a marriageable age, her parents gave her as a wife to a citizen of Tagaste, Patricius by name, a pagan not without generous qualities, but violent-tempered and dissolute. Monica had much to put up with from him, but she bore all with unfailing submission and with the patience of a strong, well-disciplined character. He, on his part, though inclined to criticise her piety and liberality to the poor, always regarded her with respect and never laid a hand upon her, even in his worst fits of rage. When other matrons came to complain of their husbands and to show the marks of blows they had received, she did not hesitate to tell them that they very often brought this treatment upon themselves by their tongues. In the long run, Monica's prayers and example resulted in winning over to Christianity not only her husband, but also her cantankerous mother-in-law, whose presence as a permanent inmate of the house had added considerably to the younger woman's difficulties. Patricius died a holy death in 371, the year after his baptism. Of their children, at least three survived, two sons and a daughter. Navigius, the younger boy, was gentle and piously disposed—he was to be his mother's support in after years—but it was in the elder son Augustine that the parents' ambitions centred, for he was brilliantly clever, and they were resolved to give him the best possible education. Nevertheless, his waywardness, his love of pleasure and his fits of idleness caused his mother great anxiety. He had been admitted a catechumen in early youth and once, when he was thought to be dying, arrangements were made for his baptism, but his sudden recovery caused the baptism to be deferred indefinitely. At the date of his father's death he was seventeen and a student in Carthage, devoting himself especially to rhetoric. Two years later Monica was cut to the heart at the news that Augustine was leading an immoral life and also—a thing which grieved her still more—that he had embraced the Manichæan heresy. For a time after his return to Tagaste she even went so far as to refuse to let him live in her house or eat at her table that she might not have to listen to his blasphemies. But she relented as the result of a consoling vision which was vouchsafed to her. She seemed to be standing on a wooden beam bemoaning her son's downfall when she was accosted by a radiant celestial being who questioned her as to the cause of her grief. He then bade her dry her eyes and added : "Your son is with you." Casting her eyes towards the spot he indicated, she beheld Augustine standing on the beam beside her. Afterwards, when she told the dream to Augustine he flippantly remarked that they might easily be together if Monica would give up her faith, but she promptly replied : "He did not say that I was with you : he said that you were with me." Her ready retort made a great impression upon her son, who in later days regarded it as an inspiration. This happened about the end of 377, almost nine years before Augustine's conversion. During all that time Monica never ceased her efforts on his behalf. She stormed heaven by her prayers and tears : she fasted : she watched : she importuned the clergy to argue with him, even though they assured her that it was useless in his actual state of mind. "The heart of the young man is at present too stubborn, but God's time will come," was the reply of a wise bishop who had formerly been a Manichæan himself. Then,

as she persisted, he said in words which have become famous :
" Go now, I beg of you : it is not possible that the son of so many
tears should perish." This reply and the assurance she had received
in the vision gave her the encouragement she was sorely needing,
for there was as yet in her elder son no indication of any change of
heart. Augustine was twenty-nine years old when he resolved to go
to Rome to teach rhetoric. Monica, though opposed to the plan
because she feared it would delay his conversion, was determined
to accompany him if he persisted in going, and followed him
to the port of embarkation. Augustine, on the other hand, had made
up his mind to go without her. He accordingly resorted to an
unworthy stratagem. He pretended he was only going to speed a
parting friend, and whilst Monica was spending the night in prayer
in the church of St Cyprian, he set sail alone. " I deceived her
with a lie," he wrote afterwards in his Confessions, " while she
was weeping and praying for me : and what did she ask of Thee, my
God, but that Thou wouldst not allow me to sail away. But Thou
didst graciously hear her main desire, namely, that I might be
enlisted in Thy service, and Thou didst refuse to grant what she
then asked in order to give what she always asked." Deeply grieved
as Monica was when she discovered how she had been tricked, she
was still resolved to follow him. So she set out, not long afterwards,
in a ship bound for Rome. During a severe squall which they
encountered in the Mediterranean she sustained the courage of the
sailors and other passengers by promising them a safe arrival at
their destination. Monica reached Rome only to find that the bird
had flown. Augustine had been taken ill in the Holy City, and upon
his recovery, had gone on to Milan. There he came under the influence of the great bishop St Ambrose. When Monica at last tracked
her son down, it was to learn from his own lips, to her unspeakable
joy, that he was no longer a Manichæan. Though he declared that he
was not yet a Catholic Christian, she replied with equanimity that
he would certainly be one before she died. To St Ambrose she turned
with heartfelt gratitude and found in him a true father in God.
She delighted in his discourses and hymns and deferred to him in
all things—abandoning at his wish practices which had become dear
to her. For instance, she had been in the habit of carrying wine,
bread and vegetables to the tombs of the martyrs in Africa and
had begun to do the same in Milan, when she was told that St
Ambrose had forbidden the practice as tending to intemperance and
as approximating too much to the heathen *parentalia*. She desisted
at once, though Augustine doubted whether she would have given
in so promptly to anyone else. At Tagaste she had always kept the

Saturday fast, which was customary there as well as in Rome. Perceiving that it was not observed in Milan, she induced Augustine to question St Ambrose as to what she herself ought to do. The reply she received has been incorporated into the Canon Law and runs as follows : " When I am here, I do not fast on Saturday, but I fast when I am in Rome : do the same, and always follow the custom and discipline of the church as it is observed in the particular locality in which you find yourself." St Ambrose, on his part, had the highest opinion of St Monica's sterling qualities and was never tired of singing her praises to her son. In Milan as in Tagaste, she was foremost among the devout women, both in her devotions and in her liberality to the poor. Morning and evening she was to be found in church and she never failed to assist at the Holy Sacrifice of the Mass. When the Arian Queen Mother, Justina, was persecuting St Ambrose, Monica was one of those who undertook long vigils on his behalf and who were prepared to die with him or for him. At last, in August 386, there came the long-desired moment when Augustine announced his complete acceptance of the Catholic faith. For some time previously Monica had been trying to arrange for him a suitable marriage, but he now declared that he would from henceforth live a celibate life. Then, when the schools rose for the season of the vintage, Augustine retired with his mother and some of his friends to the villa of one of the party named Verecundius at Cassiacum. There the time of preparation before Augustine's baptism was spent in pious and philosophical conversations, some of which are recorded in the " Confessions." In all these talks Monica took part, displaying remarkable penetration and judgement and showing herself to be exceptionally well versed in the Holy Scriptures. As they listened to her, we are told by her son, one and all forgot her sex. At Easter, 387, St Ambrose baptised St Augustine, together with several of his friends, and soon afterwards the party set out to return to Africa. They made their way to Ostia, there to await a ship, but Monica's life was drawing to an end, though no one but herself suspected it. In a conversation with Augustine shortly before her last illness she said : " Son, nothing in this world now affords me delight. I do not know what there is now left for me to do or why I am still here, all my hopes in this world being now fulfilled. All I wished to live for was that I might see you a Catholic and a child of heaven. God has granted me more than this in making you despise earthly felicity and consecrate yourself to His service." She had formerly often expressed a desire to be buried beside Patricius, and therefore one day, as she was expatiating on the happiness of death, she was asked if she would not be afraid to die and be buried in a place so far from home. " Nothing is far from God," she replied, " neither am I afraid that God will not find my body to raise it with the rest." Five days later she was seized with a fever, and on one occasion fainted, remaining insensible for several hours. Upon regaining consciousness she said to her sons, who were watching beside her : " Here you will bury your mother." Navigius expressed a hope that she would live to return home, but she said : " Lay this body anywhere : do not be concerned over that. The one thing that I ask of you both is that you should remember me at the altar of the Lord—wherever you may happen to be." As the disease developed she suffered acutely, until the ninth day, when she passed to her eternal reward. She was fifty-five years of age. Augustine, who closed her eyes, restrained his own tears and those of his son Adeodatus, deeming a display of grief out of place at the funeral of one who had died so holy a death. But afterwards, when he was alone and began to think of all her love and care for her children, he broke down altogether for a short time. He writes : " If any one thinks it a sin that I thus wept for my mother some small part of an hour—a mother who for many years had wept for me that I might live to Thee, O Lord—let him not deride me. But if his charity is great, let him weep also for my sins before Thee." In the Confessions, Augustine prays for her and implores the prayers of his readers for Monica and Patricius, but it is her prayers which have been invoked by successive generations of the faithful who venerate her as a special patroness of married women and as a pattern for all Christian mothers.

In the concluding chapter of his *Life of St Monica* Mgr Bougaud has occasion to touch upon the " Association des mères chrétiennes," founded in the middle of the last century by the Abbé Ratisbonne, under the patronage of St Monica. Its aim was to unite in a crusade of prayer those many Catholic mothers who, in these our days, so often have their hearts wrung by the godlessness, the indifference, or the depravity of their husbands and children. He ends his book with this eloquent passage :

" Complete thy work, O Monica, and from the height of that glory where thou claspest within thine arms that son upon whom thou didst bestow a second life, look down upon the multitude of Christian women who are now fulfilling the same noble and difficult mission which thou thyself didst accomplish : support them in those heavy trials through which God wills them to pass in order that they may insure the salvation of their sons. Sustain their courage, O happy mother, charm away their tears ; and in perusing thy life, teach them that the unhallowed fire which at times threatens to destroy their children's souls, is not so potent as the sacred flame which burns within a mother's heart.

"As for myself, who have so lovingly sought out the traces—alas! too faint—of thy footsteps here below, O incomparable St Monica, if my attempt prove unsuccessful, I shall not regret having essayed it. In revealing thy heart to me thou hast taught me to know my own. Thanks to thy teaching, I know now better than I did before, at what cost souls are to be ransomed, and that if a true mother must possess a priestly heart, the heart of a true priest must be a maternal one. Henceforth, bound by my office to reclaim so many Augustines, no longer will I kneel despairingly at the holy altar's foot. O mother, thou hast taught me how to set about my task. May I profit by thy lessons, and, inflamed by thy example, may I rise superior to my fears, and cheerfully submitting to the sacrifices required at my hands, may I dedicate myself, more entirely than I have ever done before, to the sublime art of saving souls from sin, and restoring them to truth, to virtue, and to God!"

We know practically nothing of St Monica apart from what can be gleaned from St Augustine's own writings and especially from bk. ix of the *Confessions*. A letter reviewing her life and describing her last moments, which purports to have been addressed by St Augustine to his sister, Perpetua, is certainly not authentic. The text of this will be found in the *Acta Sanctorum*, May, vol. i, and elsewhere. In the article "Monique" (*Dictionnaire d'Archéologie et de Liturgie*, vol. xi, cc. 2332–2356), Dom H. Leclercq has collected a good deal of information concerning Tagaste, now known as Souk Arrhas, and the newly discovered foundations of a basilica at Carthage. It is difficult, however, to see what connection this has with St Monica, beyond the fact that the name St Monica's has, in modern times, been given to a chapel in the neighbourhood. It must be confessed that little or no trace can be found of a cultus of St Monica before the translation of her remains from Ostia to Rome, which is alleged to have taken place in 1430, under the pontificate of Pope Martin V. Her body thus translated is believed to rest in the church of S. Agostino. Of the many Lives of St Monica which have been written in modern times that by Mgr Bougaud (Eng. trans., 3rd edn., 1896) may be specially recommended. There are others by F. A. M. Forbes (1915) and by E. Procter (1931), not to speak of those in French, German, and Italian.

ST CYRIACUS, or JUDAS QUIRIACUS, Bp.

A.D. 133 (?)

The principal patron of Ancona, St Judas Cyriacus, may possibly have been a local bishop who died or was killed during a pilgrimage he made to Jerusalem. On the other hand, he has been conjecturally identified with Judas, bishop of Jerusalem, who was slain during a riot in 133. The local tradition of Ancona, however, connects its patron with Judas Quiriacus, a legendary Jew who is supposed to have revealed to the Empress Helena the place in which the Holy Cross lay hidden, and after being baptised and made bishop of Jerusalem, to have suffered martyrdom under Julian the Apostate. A fantastic account of his dialogue with the Emperor Julian and of the torments endured by him and his mother Anna before death released them, is furnished in the so-called Acts of his martyrdom. Ancona is said to owe to the Empress Galla Placidia the relics of its patron, but the saint's head was brought over from Jerusalem by Henry, Count of Champagne, who built a church in the town of Provins to contain it.

The text of the *De Inventione Crucis dominicæ*, the second part of which is concerned with the martyrdom of Judas Cyriacus, has been printed both in Latin and in Greek in the *Acta Sanctorum*, May, vol. i. See also E. Pigoulewsky in the *Revue de l'Orient chrétien*, 1929, pp. 305–356. The legend of Judas Cyriacus has already been referred to above, p. 37.

ST PELAGIA, Virg. and Mart.

A.D. 304 (?)

The story of St Pelagia of Tarsus is one of those Greek romances which appear to have been originally fabricated to supply edifying fiction for the Christian public. She is described as the beautiful daughter of pagan parents who sought to betroth her to the son of the Emperor Diocletian. She did not wish to marry and obtained permission to go away on a visit to her former nurse. She seized the occasion to seek instruction from a holy bishop called Clino, who baptised her and gave her Holy Communion. When, on her return it transpired that she was a Christian, her fiancé committed suicide and her mother denounced her to the Emperor. So lovely was the maiden that Diocletian, instead of punishing her, would fain have married her, but she rejected his addresses and refused to abandon her faith. She was therefore roasted to death in a red-hot brazen bull. Her remains were cast forth, but lions guarded them until they were rescued by the bishop who buried them with honour on a mountain near the city.

There are many Pelagias, upon one of whom—Pelagia of Antioch—St John Chrysostom pronounced a panegyric. The stories of the others are almost entirely legendary, and are confused one with another. No data are preserved, in this case of Tarsus, upon which any reasonable presumption of a historic foundation can be based. The attempt, however, to reduce all these hagiographic fables to a recrudescence of the worship of

Aphrodite is quite unreasonable. The theories of H. Usener (in his *Legenden der heiligen Pelagia*, 1897) and other folk-lorists need to be controlled by such comments as Fr Delehaye has published in his *Légendes Hagiographiques* (3rd edn., 1927), pp. 186–195. There is, moreover, nothing suggestive of Aphrodite in these particular "Acts" printed in the *Acta Sanctorum*, May, vol. i, as the fabulous history of Pelagia of Tarsus.

ST FLORIAN, MART.   A.D. 304

The Saint Florian commemorated in the Roman martyrology on this day was an officer of the Roman army, who occupied a high administrative post in Noricum, now part of Austria, and who suffered death for the faith in the days of Diocletian. His legendary "acts" state that he gave himself up at Lorch to the soldiers of Aquilinus, the governor, when they were rounding up the Christians, and that after making a bold confession he was twice scourged, half-flayed alive and finally thrown into the river Enns with a stone round his neck. His body, recovered and buried by a pious woman, was eventually removed to the Augustinian Abbey of St Florian, near Linz. It is said to have been at a later date translated to Rome, and Pope Lucius III, in 1138, gave some of the saint's relics to King Casimir of Poland and to the Bishop of Cracow. Since that time St Florian has been regarded as the patron of Poland as well as of Linz and of Upper Austria. In these translations there may have been some confusion with other reputed saints of the same name, but there has been great popular devotion to St Florian in many parts of central Europe, and the tradition as to his martyrdom not far from the spot where the Enns flows into the Danube is ancient and reliable. Many miracles of healing are attributed to his intercession and he is invoked as a powerful protector in danger from fire or water.

In contrast to so many reputed Diocletian martyrs there is solid ground for the belief that Florian suffered at Lauriacum (Lorch). His "Acts" first printed in the *Acta Sanctorum*, May, vol. i, have been critically edited by Bruno Krusch in *Monumenta Germaniae, Scrip. rer. Meroving.*, vol. iii, pp. 68–71. They date from the end of the eighth century, but are admitted to have an historical foundation. There is also under May 4 a clear mention of his name and the manner of his martyrdom in the *Hieronymianum*. There has been much discussion of the case in the *Neues Archiv* and other learned German periodicals. For references see the *Lexikon für Theologie und Kirche*, vol. iv (1932), cc. 42–43. Consult further J. Zeiller, *Les Origines chrétiennes dans les Provinces Danubiennes*, 1919.

ST NEPOTIANUS, CONF.

A.D. 395

Among the writings of St Jerome is a touching letter of sympathy addressed to his friend St Heliodorus, Bishop of Altino, on the death of a favourite nephew. It is entitled *Epitaphium Nepotiani* and is actually a panegyric and an appreciation of the high principles which animated all his conduct. Even as a young officer in the Imperial bodyguard, Nepotianus had lived a spotless life, but he resigned a promising career in the army in order to live only for God. He gave away his possessions to the poor and was ordained by his uncle, although his humility made him hesitate to offer himself for the priesthood. After he had exercised his sacred ministry under St Heliodorus at Altino, he died, deeply mourned by all who had enjoyed his friendship. St Jerome had previously dedicated to him a treatise on the sacerdotal life.

It is difficult to trace any sort of cultus of this holy priest, but the Bollandists have printed a short notice of him in their second volume for May (under May 11).

ST VENERIUS, BP. OF MILAN

A.D. 409

The second Bishop of Milan after St Ambrose was St Venerius, who was one of his deacons and who succeeded St Simplicianus in 400. Very little is known about him, but his cultus received a great impetus when St Charles Borromeo elevated his relics in 1579 and translated them to the cathedral. The saint enjoyed the friendship of St Paulinus of Nola, of St Delphinus of Bordeaux and of St Chromatius of Aquileia, and was a warm sympathiser with St John Chrysostom in his sufferings. When the bishops of Africa, assembled at Carthage in 401, appealed for the support of Pope Anastasius, they also addressed a similar appeal to Bishop Venerius. The Christian poet Ennodius celebrated his praises and describes him as a man of singular eloquence.

All these testimonies are gathered up in the account furnished in the *Acta Sanctorum*, May, vol. i.

ST GODEHARD, or GOTHARD, Bp. of HILDESHEIM

A.D. 1038

The birthplace of St Godehard was the Bavarian village of Reichersdorf, where his father was an employee in the service of the Canons, who at that period occupied what had formerly been the Benedictine Abbey of Nieder-Altaich. The boy was educated by the Canons and showed so much promise that he attracted the notice of the Bishops of Passau and Regensburg and the favour of Archbishop Frederick of Salzburg. The last named not only took him to Rome, but also made him Provost of the Canons at the early age of nineteen. When, mainly through the efforts of the three prelates, the Benedictine rule was restored in Nieder-Altaich in 990, Godehard, by this time a priest, received the monastic habit together with several other canons. He rose to be prior and then abbot, the ceremony of his installation being honoured by the presence of St Henry, then Duke of Bavaria—afterwards Emperor—who always held him in the utmost esteem. A girdle worked for him by the Empress Cunegund was long venerated as a relic. The excellent order kept by Godehard at Nieder-Altaich prompted St Henry to send him to reform the monasteries of Tegernsee, in the diocese of Freising, Hersfeld, in Thuringia, and Kremsmünster in the diocese of Passau. This difficult task he accomplished satisfactorily whilst retaining the direction of Nieder-Altaich, which was ruled by a deputy during his long absences. In the course of twenty-five years he formed no less than nine abbots for various houses. Then came the call to a very different life. St Bernwald, Bishop of Hildesheim, died in 1022, and the Emperor Henry immediately decided to nominate Godehard to be his successor. In vain did the holy abbot, who happened to be at the court, plead his age and lack of suitable qualifications, he was obliged to comply with the wishes of the monarch, supported by the local clergy. Although he was sixty years of age he threw himself into the work of his diocese with the zest and energy of a young man. He built and restored churches : he did much to foster education, especially in the Cathedral school ; he established such strict order in his chapter that it resembled a monastery ; and, on a swampy piece of land which he reclaimed on the outskirts of Hildesheim, he built a hospice where the sick and poor were tenderly cared for. He had a great love for the really necessitous, but he looked with less favour on able-bodied, professional tramps ; he called them " peripatetics," and would not allow them to stay for more than two or three days in the hospice.

The holy bishop died in 1038 and was canonized in 1131. It is generally agreed that the celebrated Pass of St Gothard takes its name from a chapel built upon its summit by the dukes of Bavaria and dedicated to the great prelate of Hildesheim.

We have a full and trustworthy account of St Gothard written by his devoted disciple, Wolfher. There are, in fact, two lives by the same author, the one compiled before Gothard's death, the other revised and completed some thirty years later. Both are printed in Pertz, *Monumenta Germaniæ*, *Scriptores*, vol. xi, pp. 167–218. There are also some letters by and to him which have survived and which have been printed in the *Monumenta Germaniæ*, *Epistolæ Selectæ*, vol. iii, pp. 59–70 and 105–110. St Gothard figures prominently in the third volume of Hauck's *Kirchengeschichte Deutschlands*. There are also modern biographies by F. K. Sulzbeck (1863) and O. J. Blecher (1931). See further the *Acta Sanctorum*, May, vol. i, and E. Tomek, *Studien z. Reform d. deutsch. Klöster*, vol. i (1910), pp. 23 seq.

BLESSED CATHERINE OF PARC-AUX-DAMES, VIRG.

EARLY THIRTEENTH CENTURY

Blessed Catherine of Parc-aux-Dames was the daughter of Jewish parents, resident in the city of Louvain. Amongst the constant visitors to their house was the Duke of Brabant's chaplain, Master Raynerus, with whom his host used to have long discussions on religious subjects. From the time she was five years old, little Rachel—as she was then called—was an attentive listener to these talks and one day the priest, noticing her eager expression, said to her : " Rachel, should you like to become a Christian ? " " Yes —if you would tell me how ! " was the prompt reply. From that time Master Raynerus began to give her instruction in the faith as occasion offered. Rachel's parents, however, became uneasy at the change which was taking place in their child, and when she was in her seventh year, decided to send her away beyond the Rhine to remove her from Christian influences. Rachel was greatly distressed at the prospect, but one night she had a vision of Our Lady, clad in dazzling white, who gave her a staff and bade her escape. The girl arose at once, slipped out of the house and made her way to the priest, by whom she was taken to the Cistercian nuns in the Abbey of Parc-aux-Dames, a league and a half from Louvain. There she was baptised and clothed with the habit of the order, assuming the name of Catherine. Her parents appealed to the Bishop of Louvain, to the Duke of Brabant and even to Pope Honorius, that their daughter might be restored to them—at any rate till she was twelve years old. The Bishop and the Duke favoured the claim, but it was successfully opposed by Engelbert, Archbishop of Cologne, and William, Abbot of Clairvaux. Catherine accordingly remained at Parc-aux-Dames until her death, and became famous for her visions and miracles.

See the account in the *Acta Sanctorum*, May, vol. i, which is mainly compiled from such Cistercian sources as Cæsarius of Heisterbach and Henriquez. But the Dominican, Thomas de Chantimpré, also vouches for the truth of the story from his personal knowledge of Catherine.

BLESSED GREGORY OF VERUCCHIO, CONF. A.D. 1343

The father of the Blessed Gregory dei Celli of Verucchio died before his little son was four years old, and the child was brought up by a pious mother whose one object was to train him for God. When he was fifteen, they decided to dedicate themselves to St Augustine and St Monica : Gregory received the habit of the hermits of St Augustine, whilst his mother spent their fortune in founding as well as endowing a house for the order at Verucchio. For ten years Gregory lived in the monastery, leading an exemplary life and converting many sinners who had been led away into heresy. But after his mother's death, the brethren, instigated by jealousy at his success, or perhaps by resentment at his strictness, ungratefully drove him out of the house which had been built from the proceeds of his patrimony. Homeless and destitute, he made his way to the Franciscans of Monte Carnerio, near Reati, by whom he was so kindly received that, with several other hermits, he settled down permanently amongst them. He lived to extreme old age, dying, it is alleged, at the age of 118. It is averred that the mule which was bearing his coffin to the burial ground at Reati suddenly broke away and as though driven by an unseen force, carried its load back to Verucchio, where its arrival was announced by the spontaneous ringing of all the church bells. By local custom Blessed Gregory is invoked as a patron when rain is needed.

The account of this Beato printed in the *Acta Sanctorum*, May, vol. i, depends mainly upon a document, attested by a notary public of the Celli family, which was forwarded to the Bollandists by Father H. Torelli, the historiographer of the Hermits of St Augustine. It must be confessed that there are suspicious features about this notarial instrument, but there can be no doubt that the cultus of Bd. Gregory, alleged to have been signalised by many miraculous cures, was formally confirmed by Pope Clement XIV in 1769.

BLESSED MICHAEL GEDROYE, CONF.

A.D. 1485

The history of Blessed Michael Gedroye is the story of his infirmities and of his austerities. Born at Gedroye Castle, near Vilna, in Lithuania, the only son of noble parents, it soon became evident that he could never bear arms, being a dwarf and very delicate. Moreover, an accident at a very early age deprived him of the use of one of his feet. His father and mother therefore destined him for the Church, and his natural piety pointed in the same direction. His studies being frequently interrupted by ill-health and the lack of good teachers, the boy occupied himself in making sacred vessels for the church when he was not engaged in prayer. Weakly as he was, he had begun almost from childhood to practise mortification, speaking seldom, fasting strictly four days in the week and living as far as possible in retirement. He joined the Canons Regular of St Augustine in the Convent of Our Lady of Metro at Cracow, but was permitted at his own request to take up his abode in a solitary cell adjoining the church. There, in a space so restricted that he could scarcely lie down, he spent the rest of his life, only leaving his cell to go to church, and on very rare occasions to converse with holy men. He never ate meat, living on vegetables, or else on bread and salt. His austerities were extreme and were never relaxed during illness or in his old age. Moreover, he suffered much physical and mental torment from evil spirits. On the other hand, God gave him great consolations : once Our Lord spoke to him from the crucifix, and he was endowed with the gifts of prophecy and miracles.

An account of this Beato, based on materials which do not seem to be altogether reliable, is given in the *Acta Sanctorum*, May, vol. i. The Canons of " our Lady of Metro " were members of a penitential Order of which a brief description may be found in Hélyot, *Ordres religieux*, vol. ii (1849), pp. 562–567.

BB. CARTHUSIAN MARTYRS, WITH BLESSED RICHARD REYNOLDS AND JOHN HAILE, MM.

A.D. 1535–1540

To the Carthusian Order belongs the honour of having furnished the first martyr of the Tudor persecution in the person of

John Houghton, Prior of the London Charterhouse. After him, on the same day and at the same place, were martyred two other Carthusian Priors, as well as John Haile, Vicar of Isleworth, and a Bridgettine monk named Richard Reynolds.

John Houghton, who was a native of Essex and a graduate of Cambridge University, had been a secular priest for four years when he entered the London Charterhouse. There he spent twenty years of religious life, being conspicuous even amongst his austere brethren for his mortification, his patience and his humility. Maurice Chauncy, a fellow monk, has left us an edifying record of his heroic virtues, together with an interesting description of his person and bearing. He was short of stature, we read, graceful, venerable of countenance, modest in demeanour and winning of speech. In spite of his ardent desire to remain hidden, he was marked out for preferment, and, after having been Sacrist for five years and Procurator for three, he was elected Prior of the Charterhouse of Beauvale, in Nottinghamshire. Upon the death of John Batmanson a few months later, he was recalled by the unanimous vote of the brethren to become Prior of the London Charterhouse, and shortly afterwards he was nominated Visitor of the English Province of the Order.

In the summer of 1533 a royal proclamation was issued ordering the adhesion by oath of every person over the age of sixteen to the Act of Succession, which recognised Anne Boleyn as the lawful queen and her children as heirs to the throne. The cloistered monks of the Charterhouse may well have thought that, as politics were outside their province, the edict did not affect them. For about eight months they actually seem to have remained unmolested. Their great reputation, however, and the influence they wielded as directors of souls then decided the King and his officials to demand their assent. Royal commissioners accordingly presented themselves at the Charterhouse and questioned the superiors.

In his reply, the Prior, whilst disclaiming any desire or intention of interfering with the King's affairs, admitted that he could not see how the marriage with Catherine of Aragon, properly solemnised as it had been, and for so many years unquestioned, could suddenly have become invalid. On the strength of this remark he was summarily arrested and imprisoned in the Tower with his Procurator, Humphrey Middlemore. A month later, in deference to the decision of learned and devout men who deemed that the succession to the throne was not a cause for which they should sacrifice their lives, the two prisoners agreed to take the oath with the added proviso, " as far as the law of God permits." Thereupon they were allowed to return to the Charterhouse, where, after a little hesitation on the part of several of the monks, the whole community made the required declaration in its modified form. During the short period of peace which followed, the Prior was under no illusion as to his future; the night before his release from the Tower it had been revealed to him in a dream that he would return within a twelvemonth and would end his days in prison.

On February 1 of the following year there came into force another Act of Parliament—much more far-reaching than the Act of Succession. It was called the Act of Supremacy and declared it to be high treason to deny that the King was the sole and supreme head of the Church in England. That this was a very different thing from a question of mere temporal succession to the English throne, Prior Houghton fully realised. Summoning his spiritual sons to the Chapter-house, he gravely warned them that they would probably all be shortly faced with the alternative between death and apostasy. He then declared a solemn Triduum, during which they were to prepare for the approaching trial. His own heart was rent with anxiety, because he foresaw that some of the brethren—especially amongst the younger and more untried portion of the community—would not be able to hold out to the end. For their sakes he determined to make a personal appeal to Thomas Cromwell, the King's chief Secretary, in the hope of obtaining exemption from the oath of supremacy, or at least a mitigation of it. He took with him two priors who had come to London to consult him about the affairs of their monasteries : they were Robert Lawrence, a London monk, Houghton's successor at Beauvale, and Augustine Webster, trained at Sheen, but now Prior of the Charterhouse in the Isle of Axholme. Cromwell, who was aware that King Henry was greatly incensed against the Carthusians, received them roughly, and summarily cutting short Prior Houghton's opening remarks, ordered them, all three, to be committed to the Tower, although Lawrence and Webster had not opened their lips. An interrogatory at the Rolls three weeks later was followed up by a visit to the Tower of Cromwell himself and the King's Commissaries, bearing with them a copy of the oath. By this time the priors had been joined in their captivity by Richard Reynolds, a distinguished and learned Bridgettine monk from the monastery of Sion, whose singular holiness was reflected in the angelic beauty of his countenance. Cardinal Pole, who was his intimate friend, declared that he was the only religious in England well versed in the three languages " in which all liberal learning is comprised." Called upon to take the oath, the prisoners said they would do so if they might add the saving clause " as far as the law of

God allows." " I admit of no condition," was Cromwell's reply. " Whether the law of God permits or not, you must take the oath without reservation." This they absolutely refused to do, and they were accordingly committed for trial.

When, on April 29, they came before the court at Westminster Hall, they were accused of denying that Henry VIII was supreme head on earth of the Church of England. To this charge they made no defence, but the jury showed the utmost reluctance to condemn them, only consenting to declare them guilty of high treason when Cromwell appeared in person and terrified them into submission. Sentence of death was then passed upon the four monks and upon an aged secular priest, John Haile, Vicar of Isleworth, who was accused of uttering slanderous words against the King, the Queen and the Council. Their execution was fixed to take place at Tyburn on May 4, every expedient being adopted to degrade them in the eyes of the populace. They were dragged to the scaffold, lying on their backs on hurdles, and still wearing their habits—a thing hitherto unheard of in a Christian country. Arrived at the foot of the gallows, Blessed John Houghton embraced his executioner, who craved his forgiveness, and having testified that he was suffering for conscience because he was unwilling to deny a doctrine of the Church, he met his death with the utmost fortitude. After being strung up, he was cut down and disembowelled while still alive. In fact he was conscious and still able to speak when his heart was torn out. The rest of the martyrs showed the same courage. All refused a pardon proffered at the last moment at the price of acknowledging the King's supremacy. Special efforts had been made to break down the constancy of Blessed Richard Reynolds, who, as he was the last to be executed, was obliged to witness the barbarities inflicted on his companions. Their remains were parboiled, divided, and exposed in various parts of the city, an arm of Blessed John Houghton being posted over the chief entrance of his monastery.

On the very day of the execution of the Priors, one of the Commissaries visited the Charterhouse to interrogate and examine the three monks who had taken over the government, namely, Humphrey Middlemore, formerly Procurator, William Exmoor, the late Prior's confessor, and Sebastian Newdigate, once a favourite courtier in the palace of Henry VIII, but now a devout monk. Their replies were deemed unsatisfactory and three weeks later they were committed to the Marshalsea Prison, where for a fortnight they were chained to columns by the neck and feet, unable to sit or lie down, and never released for a moment. Newdigate had a special trial to undergo, for King Henry came to the prison in disguise and tried to win him over. All three came up for trial on June 12, were convicted of high treason, and were executed on June 19.

No further executions took place for some time, but the monks were not left to themselves. Resident commissioners were placed over them, their books were taken away, and in the words of Maurice Chauncy, " they never knew what it was to be free from vexation for a single hour." A monk from Sheen, who had taken the oath of supremacy, was placed over them as Prior, whilst several of the most resolute of the monks were sent to other houses. Amongst these were two priests, John Rochester and William Walworth, who were transferred to Hull. In consequence of an imprudent letter which the former addressed from there to the Duke of Norfolk, he and his brother monk were arrested, tried at York, condemned and executed on May 11, 1537, two years after the death of Blessed John Houghton.

In the meantime the constant pressure brought to bear upon the London community had been gradually breaking down the constancy of the majority, and on May 18, 1537, nineteen of the monks, besides the Prior, consented to take the oath. There still, however, remained a heroic minority of ten who continued staunch. Three of them were priests—Thomas Johnson, Richard Beer and Thomas Green or Greenwood; one was a deacon, John Davy, and the rest were the lay brothers Robert Salt, William Greenwood, Thomas Reding, Thomas Scriven, Walter Pierson and William Horn. They were imprisoned in the Marshalsea, loaded with chains and left to starve to death. For a time they were kept alive by the heroism of Sir Thomas More's adopted daughter, Margaret Clements, who, after bribing the gaoler, obtained access to the prison in the disguise of a milkmaid and fed the prisoners by placing food in their mouths. The warder, however, became alarmed when the King expressed surprise that the captives were still alive, and Margaret was refused admission. One after the other the monks died of neglect and starvation, until only William Horn remained. He was removed to the Tower, where he was treated with less inhumanity, but three years later he was attainted, condemned for denying the Royal Supremacy, and executed at Tyburn on August 4, 1540. He was the last of the eighteen who make up the roll of the English Carthusian martyrs.

Apart from the State papers in Record Office and elsewhere, all of which are calendared in the Letters and Papers, Foreign and Domestic, in the Reign of Henry VIII, our principal authority is the narrative of Dom Maurice Chauncy, Historia aliquot nostri saeculi Martyrum. Père Van Ortroy, in the

Analecta Bollandiana, vols. vi, xiv, and xxii, has studied the slight variations in the different recensions of Chauncy's work. The story is also retold with supplementary details by Dom L. Hendriks, *The London Charterhouse, etc.* (1889), and by Dom V. Doreau, *Henri VIII et les Martyrs de la Chartreuse* (1890). See also Fr. John Morris, S.J., *Troubles of our Catholic Forefathers*, vol. i, pp. 3–29, and Dom Bede Camm, *Lives of the English Martyrs*, vol. i (1904), pp. 1–46.

MAY 5

ST PIUS V, POPE

A.D. 1572

A PONTIFF of ascetic life and a great reformer, St Pius V was assuredly endowed with special grace from on high, for in the six short years that he occupied the chair of St Peter he not only succeeded in purifying the Church within by resolutely enforcing the recommendations of the Council of Trent, but he also saved her from the Mussulman peril from without, by inspiring the league which destroyed for ever the Turkish naval supremacy in the Mediterranean.

Michael Ghislieri—to give him his secular names—was born in 1504 at Bosco, in the diocese of Tortona, of well-connected parents in greatly reduced circumstances. Though destined by them for trade, he recognised even in boyhood his call to the religious life, and received the Dominican habit at the age of fourteen in the Priory of Voghera. From the commencement of his noviceship he was remarkable for his piety, his obedience and his eagerness to undertake austerities beyond those prescribed in the rule. After his ordination to the priesthood he was lector in theology and philosophy for sixteen years, and for a considerable time was employed as novice-master and in governing houses of the order—everywhere endeavouring to revive the spirit of the founder. He allowed no friar to absent himself from choir or to leave the convent without urgent necessity. He himself always travelled on foot, and though he often went to Milan to hear the confession of the governor, he would have no cloak to keep off the rain, saying that poor preachers of the gospel ought to be content with one tunic. Appointed Inquisitor for Como, Milan and Lombardy, he carried out his duties with zeal and courage—often in the teeth of bitter opposition and personal danger, many of the places within his jurisdiction having become hotbeds of heresy. Promotion came quickly. In 1551 he was made Commissary General of the Inquisition, in 1556 he was chosen Bishop of Nepi and Sutri, and the following year he was appointed Inquisitor General, and also a Cardinal—in order, as he ruefully remarked, that irons should be riveted to his feet to prevent him from creeping back into the peace of the cloister. Pope Pius IV transferred him to the Piedmontese bishopric of Mondovi—a church reduced almost to ruin by the ravages of war. Within a short time of his accession the newly appointed prelate had done much to restore calm and prosperity in his diocese, but he was soon recalled to Rome in connection with other business. Here, though his opinions were often at variance with those of Pius IV, he never shrank from openly stating his convictions. Thus, when the Sovereign Pontiff proposed to admit to the Sacred College his kinsman Ferdinand de' Medici—then only thirteen years of age—and also Frederic Gonzaga, Cardinal Ghislieri strongly opposed the suggestion on the score of their extreme youth. Again, whereas the Pope disliked the Inquisition, deprecating its severe sentences and limiting its powers, the Inquisitor General consistently upheld his tribunal as the best possible means of checking the spread of doctrines which imperilled the salvation of those who adopted them.

In December 1565 Pius IV died, and Michael Ghislieri was chosen Pope, largely through the efforts of St Charles Borromeo, who saw in him the reformer of whom the Church stood in need. The Pontiff-elect took the name of Pius V, and from the outset, made it abundantly clear that he was determined to enforce the letter as well as the spirit of the recommendations of the Council of Trent. On the occasion of his coronation, the largesses usually scattered indiscriminately amongst the crowd were bestowed upon hospitals and the really poor, whilst the money which was wont to be spent in providing a banquet for the cardinals, ambassadors and other great persons was sent to the poorer convents of the city. As a cardinal, he had bidden his dependents live as if in a monastery, and as a Pope he did his utmost to make his household a model of virtue and to purge the Curia of all irregularities. Retaining the Dominican habit under his pontifical robes, he continued the austerities and religious practices of his earlier life, taking care, at the same time, that nothing should interfere with the hours of public business.

One of his first injunctions was that all bishops should in future reside in their dioceses, and parish priests in the cures to which they had been appointed—severe penalties being imposed for disobedience. For the reform of the secular clergy, a special commission of Cardinals was formed to inquire into the competence and morals of priests. The members of the Sacred College were enjoined to keep a close watch over their households ; and the various papal departments and tribunals—notably the Dataria and the Segnatura—underwent reform and a reduction of personnel. By every means in his power,

St Pius set himself to insure the impartial administration of justice, and he appointed the last Wednesday of the month as a day on which he and his cardinals would hold a session in which to consider the grievances of those who regarded themselves as victims of injustice in other courts. The Inquisition was rebuilt on a much larger scale, a new congregation was formed for its administration, and the Pope himself often attended its meetings. Women of bad character were banished from Rome or confined to one quarter of the city on pain of corporal punishment. Bull-fights and animal-baiting were forbidden, and scandal-mongering, blasphemy and the profanation of Sundays brought severe penalties on those who indulged in them. Because the poor were often forced to borrow at exorbitant rates, he not only multiplied the Monti di Pietà, but also banished the Jews from all parts of the Papal States except Rome and Ancona. The military patrols cleared his dominions of bandits, though he indignantly refused to sanction the capture of a brigand chief by what he rightly regarded as treacherous means. In a time of famine in Rome, he imported from Sicily and France at his own expense large quantities of corn, a considerable proportion of which was distributed gratis to the poor or was sold under cost price. A determined opponent of nepotism, he kept his relatives at a distance, and although he was persuaded to follow tradition by making one of his nephews a Cardinal, he gave him little influence or power.

The Catechism which had been ordered by the Council of Trent was completed during his pontificate, and he at once ordered translations to be made into foreign tongues. Moreover, he made the catechetical instruction of the young a duty incumbent on all parish priests. To prevent the contamination of the faithful through heretical and immoral books he established the Congregation of the Index Expurgatorius. Conservative in most of his views, he was notably ahead of his contemporaries in the importance he attached to adequate instruction as a preliminary to adult baptism. In the new breviary which was published in 1568, certain saints' days and some extravagant legends were omitted and lessons from the Holy Scriptures regained their proper place, whilst the revised Missal, issued two years later, was as much a restoration of ancient usage as a revision adapted to the reviving liturgical interest of the time. To Pius the Church owed the best edition of St Thomas Aquinas which had yet appeared, and the solemn recognition of St Thomas as a Doctor of the Church. In these as in other matters, the Holy Father was greatly assisted by St Charles Borromeo. So severe were the penalties inflicted for every breach of order or morals that he was accused of wanting to turn Rome into a monastery. That he

succeeded as well as he did was largely owing to the popular veneration for his personal holiness. The very sight of his ascetic white-
bearded figure as he walked barefoot in the public processions is
said to have brought about the conversion of at least one heretic—
an Englishman of high rank. He said Mass every day and made
two long meditations on his knees. Even when he was ill and old
he fasted throughout Advent as well as through Lent, and he
prayed with such fervour that he was popularly supposed to obtain
from God whatever he asked. In the hospitals, which he visited
frequently, he loved to tend the sick with his own hands.

Reforms such as those enumerated above might seem more than
enough to engross the attention of any one man, but they were not
even the main preoccupation of St Pius V. Throughout his pontificate two menacing shadows were ever before his eyes—the spread
of Protestantism and the inroads of the Turks. To counteract these
dangers he laboured untiringly. In Italy and Spain, where the
Lutheran heresy had not taken much hold, its advance was undoubtedly checked by the stern methods of the Inquisition. In
Spain an Archbishop of Toledo was burnt at the stake, and in
Florence even a close personal intimacy with the ruling house did
not prevent Pietro Carnescechi from suffering a similar fate. The
learned Baius, whose writings were condemned, only saved himself
by recantation.

By the terms used when Pius V re-issued the Bull " In Cœna
Domini " (1568), it was made clear that as Pope he claimed a certain
suzerainty over all secular princes. This he followed up by des-
patching legates to the European courts to demand the help of
Catholic princes in suppressing heresy. To France he sent large
sums of money to assist the Holy League, in Germany he supported
the Catholics persecuted by Protestant rulers, and in the Low
Countries he furnished money and men to the Duke of Alva, of
whose atrocious cruelties he was kept in ignorance. For a long time
he cherished hopes of winning to the faith Queen Elizabeth of
England, but after five years he issued a Bull of excommunication
against her, absolving her subjects from their allegiance and for-
bidding them to recognise her as their sovereign. This was undoubtedly an error of judgement due to imperfect knowledge of
English feeling and of the conditions which obtained in that country.
Its only result was to increase the difficulties of loyal English
Catholics and to lend some appearance of justification to the
accusation of treason so frequently brought against them.

If Protestantism was the danger in Western and Northern
Europe, another peril threatened Catholic civilisation in the East

and South. The menace of the irreconcilable Turk was felt not only on the side of Hungary and Greece, but also in the Mediterranean where the Moslem corsairs had already made attacks on Malta and Cyprus. The Pope generously assisted the Knights of Malta in restoring their defences as well as in building the city of Valetta. He then set himself to form a league of defence among the Catholic rulers—a task of great difficulty owing to the petty jealousies that divided them. Eventually he persuaded Spain and Venice to join with the other Italian states and to form a great expeditionary force. To avoid dissensions, the Pope was declared chief of the league, Mark Antony Colonna was named supreme commander of the galleys, and Don John of Austria generalissimo of all the forces. Before they set out, the Pope sent his apostolic blessing, together with a promise of certain victory, provided all soldiers of evil life were disbanded. The force, which comprised 20,000 good soldiers, set sail from Corfu and came upon the Turkish fleet in the Gulf of Lepanto. There, in one of the world's greatest maritime battles, the Ottoman fleet was completely defeated and the power of the Turk in the Mediterranean permanently broken.

From the moment the expedition had started, the Holy Father had prayed for it almost unceasingly—often with uplifted hands like Moses on the mountain. He had also prescribed public devotions and private fasts and, at the very hour that the contest was raging, the procession of the Rosary in the Church of the Minerva was pouring forth petitions for victory. Meanwhile the Pope himself was conversing on business with some of his cardinals, but on a sudden he turned from them abruptly, opened a window and remained standing in front of it for some time with his eyes fixed upon the sky. Then, closing the casement, he said : " This is not a moment in which to talk business : let us give thanks to God for the victory He has granted to the arms of the Christians." To commemorate the great success he afterwards inserted the words : " Help of Christians," in the Litany of Our Lady and instituted the festival of the Holy Rosary, to be observed on the first Sunday in October. The victory was won on October 7, 1571, and in the following year the Pope was preparing to follow up this triumph by forming a league against Elizabeth of England when a painful disorder from which he had long suffered and which his austerities had aggravated carried him off on May 1, 1572, at the age of sixty-eight. His mortal remains are venerated in the great Roman basilica of Santa Maria Maggiore, within a mausoleum which was constructed for them by Pope Sixtus V, whom Pius had raised to the cardinalate.

It may not be out of place, as an illustration of the atmosphere which St Pius, by precept and example, had created in Rome, to quote a letter which Dr. Martin Azpilcueta, a near relative of St Francis Xavier, wrote in 1570 to his family in Spain. Dr. Martin, who was a famous canonist, had only come to live in Rome three years before, but he had previously seen a great deal of the world, and had dwelt in many parts of Spain, France, and Portugal. " I now know," he writes, " how much honour is due to the inhabitants of Rome. They receive us well—all of us, whatever nation we belong to—they show us respect, they offer us affection. If anyone comes to them who is unworthy of their favour they leave him alone, but they speak no evil of him unless he be himself the first to speak evil. I have seen devotion in other countries, but as for that of the Romans I am never tired of admiring it. It fills me with stupefaction, for I cannot explain such fervour, such indefatigable piety on the part of all, great, middling, and little ; men, women, and children ; rich as well as poor. How keen they are in the pursuit of Indulgences, how they love to pay honour to our Lord, our Lady, the Saints, wherever any festival summons them ! I see them come in, a distance of sixteen miles, with extraordinary piety and modesty bent upon visiting, especially during Lent, as many as four, seven or nine churches in a day, and in such crowds that in order to assist at the Holy Sacrifice and the other offices of the Church, they almost endanger their lives. Assuredly, if one wishes to know what Rome really is in this respect, as well as in many others, it is far better (I speak from experience) to see for one's self than to hear what others say. O princes and citizens of Rome, I pray that you guard very, very carefully this jewel of your piety." This was not the tone in which visitors wrote in the days of Leo X, or Paul III. The change was almost entirely due to the holy pontiff St Pius.

St Pius V played so important a part in the history of his times that anything like a full bibliography is out of the question. A list of all the older books and articles may be found in Emilio Calvi's *Bibliografia di Roma*, and the more important are cited in the eighth volume of Pastor's *Geschichte der Päpste* (and its English translation), which is entirely devoted to this pontiff. It is only necessary here to refer to the *Summarium de Virtutibus* printed in the process of Beatification for the Congregation of Sacred Rites, and to the lives by Catena and Gabutius, which are included in the *Acta Sanctorum*, May, vol. i, together with some other materials of a more miscellaneous character. A particularly valuable article by Père Van Ortroy, which includes the earliest known sketch of the life of St Pius, will be found in the *Analecta Bollandiana*, vol. xxxiii (1914), pp. 187–215. There is an excellent biography by G. Grente (1914) in the series " Les Saints," and a booklet in English by C. M. Antony (1911). It is curious to notice that in the bibliography appended to the account of St Pius V in the *Catholic*

Encyclopedia the first work mentioned is the Life by Joseph Mendham (1832). This is, in fact, a bitter indictment of the Pontiff himself, and of the Catholic Church, in the course of which we read, for example, that the Little Office of our Blessed Lady sanctioned by the Pope " is as disgusting a concentration of blasphemy and idolatry as deforms any part of the papal services," and in which complaint is also made of " the brutish bigotry and sanguinary intolerance of this pontiff."

ST BRITONIUS, Bp.

A.D. 386

St Britonius, or Brito, succeeded to the bishopric of Trèves in 382, after the death of St Bonosius. Amongst numerous ecclesiastical gatherings which he attended was an important Council at Rome, held to confirm the edicts of the Council of Nicæa. At that assembly it is alleged that in his capacity of Metropolitan or Primate of Gaul, he was reckoned the third in rank, the first and second places being occupied by Pope Damasus and St Ambrose respectively. St Britonius supported and vindicated a Spanish bishop called Ithacus, who came to Trèves in connection with the Priscillianist heresy, but who was practically driven out of the city by the magistrates in consequence of calumnies that were circulated about him. Although Britonius consistently and successfully opposed the Priscillianists in his own diocese, he never would deliver them over to the secular arm. During his episcopate St Ambrose visited Trèves, where he is said to have wrought many miracles.

Very little is known of this Saint, but a paragraph is devoted to him in the *Acta Sanctorum*, May, vol. ii. *Cf.* also Hefele–Leclercq, *Histoire des Conciles*, vol. ii, p. 68.

ST HILARY, Bp. OF ARLES

A.D. 449

The birthplace of St Hilary of Arles is not known, but he came of a noble family and was nearly related to St Honoratus, the founder and first abbot of the monastery of Lérins. Having received an excellent education and being endowed with exceptional abilities, he had the prospect of a successful career in the world. But St Honoratus, who had always loved him, was convinced that he was called to the special service of God. The holy abbot actually abandoned for a short time his island retreat to seek out his young kinsman with the object of inducing him to embrace the religious life. Hilary, however, seemed proof against all his entreaties and fears. " I will obtain from God what you will not concede ! " the monk exclaimed as they bade each other farewell. His prayers were quickly answered. Two or three days later Hilary found himself a prey to a violent interior contest. " On the one side I felt that the Lord was calling me, whilst on the other hand the seductions of the world held me back," he afterwards wrote. " My will swayed backwards and forwards, now consenting, now refusing. But at last Christ triumphed in me." Once he had definitely made up his mind, he had never looked back : he distributed to the poor the proceeds of his patrimony, which he sold to his brother, and then went to join St Honoratus at Lérins. He has left us a description of the holy, happy life led there by the monks, amongst whom, as it turned out, he was not destined to remain very long. In 426 St Honoratus was elected Bishop of Arles and being an old man, greatly desired the assistance and companionship of his favourite relation. Hilary was loth to leave Lérins, but St Honoratus went in person to fetch him and they remained together until the bishop's death. Grieved though he was at the loss of his spiritual father, the young monk rejoiced at the prospect of returning to his abbey. He had started on his journey when he was overtaken by messengers, sent by the citizens of Arles, who desired to have him for their bishop. He was obliged to consent and was duly consecrated, although only twenty-nine years of age.

In his new station, Hilary observed the austerities of the cloister, while carrying out with immense energy all the duties of his office. He allowed himself only the bare necessaries of life, wore the same cloak summer and winter, never rode a horse, but travelled everywhere on foot. Besides observing the canonical hours for prayer, he set aside stated times for manual work, the proceeds of which he gave to the poor. So great was his anxiety to ransom captives that he sold even the church plate to obtain money, contenting himself with a chalice and paten of glass. A great orator, he yet knew how to adapt his language, when necessary, so as to be understood by the most ignorant rustics. Besides building many monasteries, he was indefatigable in his visitation of them, being determined everywhere to keep up a high standard of discipline and morals amongst his suffragans and clergy. He presided over the Council of Riez, in 439, over the first Council of Orange in 441, over the Council of Vaison in 442, and over the second Council of Arles in 443. His very zeal, and, perhaps, a somewhat autocratic temper, caused him on more than one occasion to act in a way which had serious consequences for himself. The limits of his province as metropolitan of Southern Gaul had never been satisfactorily settled, and once, when he was on a visitation in debatable territory, he deposed a certain bishop called Chelidonius on the plea that before he had received holy orders he had married a widow and, as a magistrate, had passed a death sentence. Either of these charges, if substantiated, would have disqualified him for the episcopate. Chelidonius forthwith set out for Rome, where he cleared himself of the imputations to the satisfaction of Pope Leo the Great. As soon as St Hilary realised that the prelate he had deposed had gone to the Holy City, he followed him thither on foot in the middle of winter. To settle the matter a council was called, which Hilary attended—not, however, to defend his action, but to contend that the case ought to have been tried by the papal commissaries in Gaul. He did not even await the verdict. Realising that he was being kept under supervision, and fearing lest he might be forced to communicate with Chelidonius, he eluded his guards, left Rome secretly and returned to Arles. Judgement was given against him, and soon afterwards another complaint against him reached the Holy See. Whilst a French bishop called Projectus was still living—though apparently at the point of death—Hilary had hastily appointed another bishop to the see. The sick man recovered, and there were two prelates claiming the same diocese. Hilary supported his own nominee, perhaps because the other claimant was too infirm to carry out his duties, but St Leo, to whom the matter was referred, rightly judged that Hilary's proceedings had been irregular and were likely to lead to schism. He therefore censured him, forbade him to appoint any more bishops and transferred the dignity of metropolitan to the Bishop of Fréjus. Moreover, he induced the Emperor Valentinian to issue an edict in which it was declared that, for the future, nothing should be done in the Gallic Church contrary to ancient custom without the Pope's permission.

We know little about St Hilary's last years, except that he continued to labour in his own diocese with the same zeal as before, and that he died in his forty-ninth year, worn out by his labours and austerities. We are told that he made overtures of peace to the Pope, and it is clear that a reconciliation must have taken place, for St Leo, writing to his successor at Arles, shortly after his appointment, refers to the late bishop as " Hilary of sacred memory." Attempts have sometimes been made, though on very insufficient grounds, to brand St Hilary as a Semi-Pelagian. It is true that he took exception to the terms in which St Augustine stated the doctrine of predestination, but his views were strictly orthodox.

The life of St Hilary which is printed in the *Acta Sanctorum*, May, vol. ii, and is there attributed to one Honoratus, supposed to have been Bishop of

Marseilles, is probably the composition of a certain Reverentius at the beginning of the sixth century. It is a work written for edification, purporting to be the memoirs of a contemporary, but unreliable as a record of historical facts. See on all this B. Kolon, *Die Vita S. Hilarii Arelatensis* (1925) and also *cf.* Hefele–Leclercq, *Histoire des Conciles*, vol. ii, pp. 477–478, with Bardenhewer, *Altkirchlichen Literatur*, vol. iv, p. 571.

ST SACERDOS, Bp. of Limoges

c. A.D. 520 (?)

The history of St Sacerdos, Bishop of Limoges, was not written before the twelfth century, but the following particulars may be in substance correct. The son of Labanus and Mundana, natives of Bordeaux, Sacerdos was born in the Lower Périgord, about the year 470. He was educated by Bishop Capuanus at Cahors and took the habit at Calviac, of which he became prior and then abbot. After the death of Agericus he was raised to the bishopric of Limoges, being at that time thirty-nine years of age. His episcopal city, of which he is patron, honours together with him on this day his mother, Mundana, who is traditionally stated to have regained her lost sight when her blind eyes rested on the dead body of her son. She is supposed to have suffered martyrdom at the hands of the Saracens. This bishop's name appears under the variant forms of Sardon, Serdon, Sardot, Sardos, and Sadroc.

See the *Acta Sanctorum*, May, vol. ii ; Duchesne, *Fastes Épiscopaux*, vol. ii, p. 52 ; Couderc in the *Bibliothèque de l'École des Chartes*, vol. liv (1893), pp. 468–474, and a popular account by Pergot, *Vie de S. Sacerdos* (1865).

ST MAURUNTIUS (MAURONT), Ab.

A.D. 701

St Mauruntius was born in Flanders in the year 634 and was baptised by St Richarius (Requier), Abbot of Centula. The eldest son of St Adalbald and St Rictrudis, both nobles of high degree, his rank and the great abilities of which he gave proof promised him a distinguished worldly career. At the court of King Clovis II and Queen Bathildis, where he spent his youth, he occupied several important posts in the royal household. Upon the death of his father he became Lord or Duke of Douai and returned to Flanders to settle his affairs and to make arrangements for a projected marriage. But God designed him for the religious life, and the instrument by whose guidance the young man realised his true vocation was St Amandus, Bishop of Maestricht, who was, at that time, living a retired life in the monastery of Elnon. Mauruntius was so deeply moved by a sermon preached by the holy prelate that he decided to retire forthwith into the monastery of Marchiennes. There he received the tonsure from St Amandus, and a few years later he was raised to the diaconate. On his estate of Merville in the diocese of Thérouanne, he built the abbey of Breuil, or Bruel-sur-la-Lys, of which he was chosen the first abbot. When St Amatus was banished from Sens by King Theodoric (Thierry) III, he was committed to the care of St Mauruntius, who held him in such high esteem that he resigned to him the post of superior and lived under his obedience until the death of that holy bishop in 690. Mauruntius then resumed the direction of Breuil. In compliance with the dying injunction of St Rictrudis, he also retained the supervision of the double monastery of Marchiennes, where his sister, St Clotsendis, ruled as abbess over the nuns. He was actually staying at Marchiennes when he was seized with the illness of which he died.

The account of St Mauruntius in the *Acta Sanctorum*, May, vol. ii, is almost entirely derived from the biography of St Rictrudis, concerning whom see later in this volume, under May 12, p. 145.

ST AVERTINUS, Deacon

A.D. 1180 (?)

In the *Acta Sanctorum* under May 5, as well as in a number of less important collections, such as that of Butler and the *Petits Bollandistes*, we find mention of a St Avertinus, who is still commemorated on this day in the diocese of Tours. The story told of him is briefly this. St Thomas of Canterbury, in his exile and in all his troubles, was attended by a monk of St Gilbert of Sempringham, named Avertinus, whom he had raised to the diaconate. Avertinus accompanied his patron to the Synod of Tours in 1163, and after the martyrdom of the great Archbishop, he settled in Touraine, near Vençay, where he consecrated himself to the service of the poor and strangers. He seems to have ended his days as a solitary. He is invoked against dizziness and headache, and a number of *ex votos*, which were still to be seen in the church of St Avertin, near Tours, in the seventeenth century, bore witness to the existence at one time of a very considerable popular cultus.

As a curious illustration of the manner in which baseless conjecture or folk sagas come to pass for sober history, it seemed worth while to make brief mention of St Avertinus. There may well have been a hermit of that name who was venerated near Tours and in some other parts of France. But there is not a shadow of evidence for attributing to him any connection with St Thomas of Canterbury. In the vast mass of materials printed concerning the great Archbishop in the "Rolls Series" (occupying nine volumes in all) no mention can be found of an Avertinus. Neither is it likely that a devoted disciple and associate of the saint could have escaped notice in the very detailed modern Lives written by Father John Morris and Dom A. L'Huillier.

ST ANGELUS, MART.

A.D. 1220

St Angelus, who was one of the early members of the Carmelite Order, suffered martyrdom for the faith at Leocata, in Sicily. The story of his life, as it has come down to us, is not very reliable. It may be summarised as follows : The parents of St Angelus and his twin brother were Jews of Jerusalem who were converted to Christianity by a vision of our Lady. She told them that the Messias they were awaiting had already come and had redeemed His people, and she promised them two sons, who would grow up as flourishing olive-trees on the heights of Carmel—the one as a patriarch and the other as a glorious martyr. From childhood the twins displayed great mental and spiritual gifts. When, at the age of eighteen, they entered the Carmelite Order, they already spoke Greek, Latin and Hebrew. After Angelus had been a hermit on Mount Carmel for five years, our Lord appeared to him and bade him go to Sicily, where he would have the grace to offer the sacrifice of his life. The saint immediately obeyed the call. During his journey from the East, as well as after his arrival in Sicily, he converted many sinners by his teaching, no less than by his miracles. At Palermo 207 Jews sought baptism as the result of his eloquence. Similar success attended his efforts in Leocata, but he aroused the fury of a man called Berengarius, whose shameless immorality he had denounced. As he was preaching to a great crowd, a band of ruffians, headed by Berengarius, broke through the throng and stabbed him with daggers in seven places. Mortally wounded, Angelus fell on his knees, praying for the people, but especially for his murderer. He died as he uttered the words : '" In manus tuas commendo spiritum meum."

St Angelus is commemorated as a martyr in the Roman Martyrology on this day. The legend is printed from Carmelite sources in the *Acta Sanctorum*, May, vol. ii. See also the *Analecta Bollandiana*, vol. xvii (1898), p. 315, and the *Dictionnaire d'Histoire et Géographie ecclés.*, vol. iii, cc. 6–9.

ST JUTTA, WIDOW

A.D. 1260

Amongst the numerous women of high degree who were inspired by the example of St Elizabeth of Hungary, one of the most remarkable was St Jutta, or Judith, patroness of Prussia. Like her great exemplar, she was a native of Thuringia, having been born at Sangerhausen, to the south-west of Eisleben. Married at the age of fifteen to a man of noble rank, she proved an admirable wife, mother and mistress, besides being a great benefactress to the poor. Once, in a vision, Our Lord had said to her : " Follow Me " ; and she strove not only to obey Him herself, but to lead her household to do the same. In the early days of their married life, her husband, more worldly than she was, had remonstrated with her for the simplicity of her dress, but she gradually won him over to her own point of view. He was actually on a pilgrimage to the Holy Land when he died—to the great grief of his widow, who was left to bring up her children alone. As they grew up, one after another entered religious orders, and Jutta was left free to follow the call which she had long cherished in her heart. By the advice of her confessor she gave everything she possessed to the poor. Then, clad in a miserable habit, with a rope round her waist, she begged bread for herself and the poor from those who had been her dependents. Though some scoffed, others treated her with reverence, knowing what she had given up, and she resolved to go forth among strangers in order that she might be despised by all. As she wandered on, walking barefoot in summer and winter, she relieved on the road many outcasts by dressing their wounds and by feeding them with bread supplied to her in charity. At last she made her way into Prussia, the land of the Teutonic Knights, which had but lately received the Christian faith—largely as the result of the efforts of this military Order whose Grand-Master, Hanno of Sangerhausen, was a relation of her own. There she settled as a solitary in a ruinous building on the shore of a great sheet of water called the Bielcza, half a mile or so from Kulmsee. In her life, which was one of complete self-abnegation, she received wonderful graces, for besides being favoured with many visions and revelations, she was given an infused understanding of the Holy Scriptures. She herself once said that three things could bring one very near to God—painful illness, exile from home in a remote corner of a foreign land, and poverty voluntarily assumed for God's sake. The inhabitants of the neighbouring villages who passed her dwelling declared that they had often seen her raised from the ground, upheld by angels. On Sundays she attended the church at Kulmsee, and she had as her directors at first the Franciscan, Blessed John Lobedau, of Thorn, and afterwards the Dominican Provincial Henry Heidenreich. For four years she remained in her solitude, praying so fervently for the conversion of the heathen and the perseverance of the newly baptised that she often shed tears of blood. Then she was seized by a fever which proved fatal. Many miracles were recorded as having taken place at her grave, and she has been associated in the veneration of the Prussian Catholics with Blessed John Lobedau and with another female recluse, Blessed Dorothy of Marienwerder.

The very full account of this holy recluse printed in the *Acta Sanctorum* is a translation of a Polish life by Father Szembek, S.J. This claims to have been based upon a mass of materials collected for the process of canonisation, but the originals unfortunately could not be traced by the Bollandists at the date at which they wrote. See also the *Mittheilungen des Vereins f. Gesch., etc., v. Sangerhausen*, vol. i (1881), pp. 82 seq., and P. Funk, in *Festschrift für W. Goetz* (1927), pp. 81–84.

MAY 6

ST JOHN BEFORE THE LATIN GATE

A.D. 94 (?)

IN the Roman Martyrology for May 6 the first announcement takes the following form: "At Rome, of St John before the Latin Gate, who, at the command of Domitian, was brought in fetters from Ephesus to Rome, and by the verdict of the Senate, was cast into a cauldron of boiling oil before that Gate, and came forth thence more hale and more hearty (*purior atque vegetior*) than he entered it." The phrase is that of St Jerome (*adversus Jovinianum*, i, 26), and it is based upon the still earlier statement of Tertullian (*De Praescriptionibus*, ch. 36). Alban Butler, in common with the Bollandists and the most critical scholars of his time, such as Tillemont, raises no question as to the historic fact and lays stress upon it as an equivalent martyrdom. His devotional treatment of the subject may be here recapitulated.

When the two sons of Zebedee, James and John, strangers as yet to the mystery of the Cross and the nature of Christ's kingdom, had, through their mother's lips, petitioned for places of honour in the day of His triumph, He asked them if they were prepared to drink of His cup. They answered boldly, assuring their Master that they were ready to undergo anything for His sake. Our Lord thereupon promised them that their sincerity should be put to trial and that they should both be partakers of the cup of His sufferings. This was literally fulfilled in St James on his being put to death for the faith by Herod, and this day's festival records in part the manner in which it was verified in St John. It may, indeed, be said that this favourite disciple who so tenderly loved his Master, had already had experience of the bitterness of the chalice when he was present beside the Cross. But our Saviour's prediction was to be fulfilled in a more particular manner, which should entitle him to the merit and crown of martyrdom, the instrument of this trial, postponed for more than half a century, being Domitian, the last of the twelve Cæsars.

He was a tyrant, detestable in the eyes of all on account of his cruelty, and he was the author of the second general persecution of the Church. Apart from his debaucheries and his blasphemous assumption of divinity, he gloated upon the spectacle of human suffering. Tacitus says that in pitilessness he surpassed Nero, who often shunned the sight of barbarous executions, whereas Domitian was known to delight in them. He deluged Rome with the blood of its illustrious citizens, and out of a hatred to virtue banished even the philosophers such as Epictetus and Dion Chrysostom. As for the Christians, not only were their teaching and practice a standing reproach to his own vices, but the calumnies of the heathens, attributing to them all sorts of secret impieties, made them an obvious and easy prey. St John, who was the only surviving apostle and who was famous for the veneration paid to him while he governed the churches of Asia, was arrested at Ephesus and sent prisoner to Rome about the year 94. Regardless of his victim's great age and gentle bearing, the emperor condemned him to a barbarous form of death. He was probably first scourged, according to the Roman custom, and then thrown into a cauldron of boiling oil. We cannot doubt that St John exulted in the thought of laying down his life for the faith and rejoining the Master whom he loved. God accepted his oblation and in some sense crowned his desire. He conferred on him the merit of martyrdom, but suspended the operation of the fire, as he had formerly preserved the three children from hurt in the Babylonian furnace. The seething oil was changed in his regard into a refreshing bath, so that Domitian, who entertained a great idea of the power of magic, and who, it is alleged, had previously found himself baffled by some prodigy when Apollonius of Tyana was brought before him, now contented himself with banishing the apostle to the little island of Patmos. It happened, however, that only a year or two later, one of the conspiracies which were constantly being formed against this monster of cruelty proved successful. The emperor was assassinated, his statues were everywhere thrown down and his name erased from all public buildings. Under the mild rule of his successor, Nerva, St John is believed to have returned to Ephesus and there peacefully to have fallen asleep in our Lord.

More than once we read in the Gospels how our Lord's apostles ambitioned places of honour in His kingdom or contended with one another who should be the greater. " What," St Chrysostom asks, " was the answer which Christ made ? He revealed their own consciences to them and replied to the underlying thought rather than to the spoken word. Calling unto Him a little child, He said : ' Unless you be converted and become as little children, you shall not enter into the kingdom of heaven. You indeed inquire who is the greater, and dispute about the first places ; I tell you that he who has not become meeker than all the rest is not worthy even to enter into that kingdom.' Thus He brings the truth home to them in a beautiful way, and not only does He lead them to reflect, but He sets the child in the midst of them, admonishing them by the sight, and urging them to be both humble and unaffected. For a child is free from envy and from vainglory, and from the love of the first places, and he possesses the greatest of virtues—simplicity and unaffectedness and humility. It is not sufficient to have courage and prudence, but this virtue also is needed : I mean humility and simplicity. Contempt, blows, honour or praise cause a child neither resentment nor envy, nor is he thereby puffed up." No one among His disciples had taken this lesson so deeply to heart as St John, the Apostle of Love. Of all the band he came nearest to the ideal of childhood and was therefore especially beloved by his Master. The miracle of this day's feast suggests a certain tenderness in God's love for His servants. It is fully in accord with the privilege St John enjoyed of leaning his head upon our Lord's breast and hearing from His lips the words : " So will I have him remain till I come ; what is it to thee ? "

The localisation of the miracle outside the Latin Gate is certainly not historical, for the Porta Latina belongs to the walls of Aurelian, two centuries later than St John's time. This particular festival cannot be traced farther back in the Roman Church than the Sacramentary of Pope Hadrian towards the close of the eighth century. There is a church of St John at the Porta Latina, replacing an older one which owed its existence to that Pontiff. See Duchesne, *Liber Pontificalis*, vol. i, pp. 508 and 521. Mgr Duchesne suggests that the choice of this date (May 7) is connected with the occurrence in the Byzantine calendar of a feast on May 8, commemorating a miracle of St John at Ephesus. In the so-called *Missale Gothicum* there is a Mass of St John the Evangelist which must have fallen in May, not long after the Invention of the Cross. The incident of the boiling oil seems originally to have belonged to certain apocryphal but early " Acts of John," of which we now only possess fragments. On the general question see Kellner, *Heortology* (Eng. trans.), p. 298.

ST EVODIUS, Bp. of Antioch

c. A.D. 64 (?)

We learn from Origen and from Eusebius that the predecessor of St Ignatius in the see of Antioch was Evodius, who had been ordained and consecrated by the Apostles themselves—doubtless when St Peter was about to leave Antioch for Rome. Later writers have tried to identify Evodius with the Evodias or Evodia mentioned by

St Paul in his epistle to the Philippians—though this person was almost certainly a woman—and have also described him as a martyr. According to tradition, he was one of the seventy disciples sent out by Our Lord to preach. He is supposed to have coined the word " Christian," which, as we know from the Acts of the Apostles, was first used in Antioch to denote members of the Church of Christ. This is stated by the chronicler Malalas, who wrote in the latter part of the sixth century, and we further learn from him that St Peter happened to be passing through Antioch at the time when St Evodius died, and that the Apostle thereupon consecrated St Ignatius to be bishop in his room. If this is true, Evodius must have died before A.D. 64.

There is a short notice in the *Acta Sanctorum*, May, vol. i ; but consult also G. Salmon in the *Dictionary of Christian Biography*, vol. ii, p. 428, and Harnack, *Chronologie d. Altchrist. Literatur*, vol. i, p. 94, as well as *Die Zeit des Ignatius* by the same author.

ST EADBERT, Bp.
A.D. 698

The Venerable Bede, writing of St Eadbert, Bishop of Lindisfarne, states that he was remarkable for his knowledge of the Holy Scriptures, as well as for his faithful observance of the divine precepts. All his life long he was extremely generous to the poor, for whose benefit he invariably set aside a tenth part of his possessions. Ordained successor to St Cuthbert in the see of Lindisfarne, he governed wisely for eleven years, and covered with lead St Finan's great wooden cathedral church which had previously been thatched only with reeds—Scottish fashion. He made it a practice to retire twice a year for forty days of solitary prayer to the retreat—probably the tiny island known as St Cuthbert's Isle—where his great predecessor had spent some time before finally withdrawing to Farne. It was during one of these absences, though with his entire sanction, that his brethren elevated the body of St Cuthbert, eleven years after his death, in consequence of the great number of miracles that took place at his grave. When the relics were found to be incorrupt, some of the monks hastened to impart the joyful news to St Eadbert, taking with them the garments which had covered the saint. The bishop, after he had devoutly kissed them, gave instructions that the sacred body should be put into a new coffin which was to be raised above the pavement for greater veneration.

He added that the space below, which had been sanctified by containing the relics of St Cuthbert, would not long remain empty. Scarcely had his orders been carried out when he was seized with a fever which proved mortal, and his own remains were laid in the empty grave.

All our information is, practically speaking, derived from Bede in his *Hist. Eccles.*, bk. iv. C. Plummer in his notes, Canon Raine in the *Dict. Chr. Biog.*, the *Acta Sanctorum*, May, vol. i, and Symeon of Durham add very little. There is no evidence of liturgical cultus, though St Eadbert's relics shared the wanderings of those of St Cuthbert, and ultimately rested with them at Durham.

ST PETRONAX, ABBOT

A.D. 747

The second founder of the Abbey of Monte Cassino, St Petronax, was a native of Brescia. When on a visit to Rome he seems to have been induced by Pope Gregory II to make a pilgrimage to the tomb of St Benedict in the year 717. There, among the ruins of the old monastery which had been destroyed in 581, he found a few solitaries, who elected him their superior. Other disciples soon gathered round them. Through the generosity of prominent nobles, chief amongst whom was the Lombard Duke of Beneventum, and with the strong support of three Popes, he succeeded in rebuilding Monte Cassino, which, under his long and vigorous rule, regained its old eminence. St Willibald, afterwards Bishop of Eichstätt, received the habit at his hands. St Sturmius, the founder of the Abbey of Fulda, spent some time at Monte Cassino learning the primitive Benedictine rule, and great men of all kinds, princes as well as ecclesiastics, stayed within its hospitable walls. St Petronax ruled over the community until his death, the date of which was probably 747. Recent investigation has shown that St Willibald himself, during the ten years he spent at Monte Cassino, contributed much to the restoration of primitive Benedictine discipline and to the general development of this great abbey.

The more relevant texts in Paul Warnefrid's *Historia Longobardorum* have been extracted by the Bollandists and by Mabillon in the *Acta Sanctorum O.S.B.*, vol. iii, part 1, pp. 693–698. But see especially Abbot J. Chapman, " La Restauration du Mont Cassin par l'Abbé Petronax " in the *Revue Bénédictine*, XXI (1904), pp. 74–80, and Dom H. Leclercq in the *Dictionnaire d'Archéol.*, etc., vol. xi, cc. 3451–3468.

~ BLESSED BONIZELLA PICCOLOMINI, Widow

A.D. 1300

The dioceses of Siena and Pienza hold in great veneration the memory of Blessed Bonizella Cacciaconti. She was connected by birth with the old Umbrian nobility, and married Naddo, one of the Piccolomini of Siena. Upon being left a widow, she retired into the district of Belsederio and devoted herself and her possessions to relieving the sick and poor. After her death it was noticed that bees, though they generally avoid the dead, alighted upon the hand which had dispensed so generously to the afflicted. We are told, indeed, that it was through the bees resorting in swarms to the spot that the tomb of Blessed Bonizella at Trequanda was discovered many years later, when her body was found to be intact—as was also that of her infant nephew Guy, who lay at her feet. The Bollandists complain of the lack of documents concerning the life of Blessed Bonizella, but it was explained to them by the local clergy that a fire at the cathedral had destroyed them all. Her cultus seems to rest entirely upon the preservation of her body from all decay, and upon the rumour of striking miracles. It is alleged that a thief who tried to steal a gold ring which may be seen on one of her fingers was stricken with blindness, but healed again when he restored what he had taken.

See the *Acta Sanctorum*, May, vol. ii.

BLESSED PRUDENTIA, Virg.

A.D. 1492

The life of Blessed Prudentia seems to have been quite uneventful, and her fame rests entirely upon the miracles she is reported to have wrought after her death. A member of the noble Milanese family of the Casatori, she joined the Order of the Hermits of St Augustine in the Convent of St Martha, in her native city. She was promoted to be superior of the Convent of St Mark at Como, and succeeded in settling the dissensions which were dividing the two communities. Her zeal was displayed not only amongst her nuns, whom she ruled with great prudence, but also in bringing about the restoration of the Church of the Visitation at Como. Full of years, labours and merits, she passed to her eternal reward after she had governed the house at Como for thirty-eight years.

It was generally believed that her body, after it had been placed on the bier, rose up and paid a last obeisance to the Blessed Sacrament.

Here again the Bollandists, apparently with good reason, complain of the lack of materials, though the Augustinian historiographer, Father A. Torelli, had done his best to help them. Their account is printed in vol. ii for May.

BLESSED EDWARD JONES AND BLESSED ANTONY MIDDLETON, MM.

1590

Edward Jones was a Welshman from St Asaph, and Antony Middleton was a Yorkshireman. Both were educated at the Douai College in Rheims, raised to the priesthood and chosen for the English Mission. Middleton came to London in 1586, and owing to his juvenile appearance and small stature was able to labour for a considerable time without rousing suspicion. Jones, who followed two years later, at once made a name for himself among the Catholics as a fervent and eloquent preacher. They were tracked down by spies who professed to be Catholics, and they appear to have been hanged before the doors of the houses in Fleet Street and Clerkenwell within which they had been arrested, the words " For Treason and Foreign Invasion" being posted up in large letters as an explanation of this summary justice which, as attested by witnesses present at the trial, was full of irregularities. Middleton, whose request that he might address the people was refused, called God to witness that he died simply and solely for the Catholic faith and for being a priest and preacher of the true religion. He then prayed that his death might obtain the forgiveness of his sins, the advancement of the Catholic faith and the conversion of heretics. According to the testimony of eye-witnesses, he was flung off the ladder, cut down, and disembowelled while still alive. They died on May 6, 1590.

The account originally given by Challoner (*Memoirs of Missionary Priests*, ed. Pollen, pp. 162–163) is not altogether accurate. See the fuller narrative printed by the Catholic Record Society, vol. v, pp. 182–186, and *cf.* Pollen, *Acts of English Martyrs*, pp. 308–309 and 315–317. It appears that Bd. Edward Jones was sentenced in virtue of his own confession that he was a priest, made under torture.

MAY 7

ST STANISLAUS, Bp.

A.D. 1079

THE cultus of St Stanislaus is widespread in Poland—especially in his episcopal city of Cracow, which honours him as principal patron and preserves the greater part of his relics in a silver coffer in the cathedral. His biography, written some four hundred years after his death, by St Casimir's tutor, the historian John Dlugosz, seems to be an uncritical compilation from various earlier writings and from oral tradition, for it contains several conflicting statements, besides a certain amount of matter which is obviously purely legendary.

Stanislaus Szczepanowski was born on July 26, 1030, at Szczepanow, in the diocese of Cracow. He came of noble parents, who had been childless for many years until this son was vouchsafed to them in answer to prayer. They devoted him from his birth to the service of God, and encouraged in every way the piety which he evinced from early childhood. He was educated at Gnesen and afterwards " at the University of Paris " (!) where he studied philosophy, the arts, theology and canon law. At the close of seven years he qualified for a master's degree, but from humility refused to receive it. After his return to Poland upon the death of his parents, he distributed the whole of his inheritance to the poor. He was then ordained priest by Lampert Zula, Bishop of Cracow, who gave him a canonry in the cathedral and subsequently appointed him his preacher and vicar-general. The eloquence of the young priest and his saintly example brought about a great reformation of morals amongst his penitents—clergy as well as laity flocking to him from all quarters for spiritual advice. Bishop Lampert wished to resign the episcopal office in his favour, but Stanislaus refused to consider the suggestion. However, upon Lampert's death, he could not resist the will of the people seconded by an order from Pope Alexander II, and he was consecrated bishop in 1072. He proved himself a zealous apostle, indefatigable in preaching, strict in maintaining discipline, and regular in his visitations. His house was always crowded with the poor, and he kept a list of widows and other distressed persons to whom he systematically distributed doles.

Poland at that epoch was ruled by Boleslas II, a prince who had distinguished himself greatly in war against the Russians, but whose finer qualities were completely eclipsed by his unbridled lust and savage cruelty. None of his attendants dared oppose him in any way for fear of arousing his ungovernable temper. Stanislaus alone ventured to beard the tyrant and to remonstrate with him at the scandal his conduct was causing. At first the King endeavoured to vindicate his behaviour, but when pressed more closely he expressed regret and made some show of repentance. The good effects of the admonition, however, soon wore off : Boleslas relapsed into his evil ways. There were acts of rapacity and political injustice which brought him into conflict with the bishop and at length he perpetrated an outrage which caused universal indignation. A certain landowner in the palatinate of Sirad had a wife who was very beautiful. Upon this lady Boleslas cast lustful eyes, and when she repelled his advances, he caused her to be carried off by force and lodged in his palace. The Polish nobles called upon the Archbishop of Gnesen and the prelates who frequented the court to expostulate with the monarch. Fear of offending the King closed their lips and the people openly accused them of conniving at the crime. St Stanislaus, when appealed to, had no such hesitation : having commended himself and his cause to God, he went again to Boleslas and rebuked him for his sin. He closed his exhortation by reminding the prince that if he persisted in his evil courses he would bring upon himself the censure of the Church with the sentence of excommunication. The threat roused the King to fury. He declared that a man who could address his sovereign in such terms was more fit to be a swineherd than a shepherd of souls, and cut short the interview with sinister threats. He first had recourse to calumny—if we may believe a story related by the saint's later historians. St Stanislaus, we are told, had bought some land for the Church from a certain Peter, who died soon after the transaction. It was suggested to the deceased man's nephews that they should claim back the land on pretence that it had not been paid for. The case came up before the King : no witnesses for the defence were allowed to be heard and the verdict seemed a foregone conclusion, when, in answer to a dramatic appeal from St Stanislaus, the dead man appeared before the court in his grave-clothes and vindicated the bishop. If we can credit this story we are further asked to believe that the marvel produced no permanent change of heart in Boleslas whose barbarity and lust had only increased with time. At last, finding all remonstrance useless, St Stanislaus launched against him a formal sentence of excommunication.   The tyrant professed to disregard the ban, but when he entered the cathedral of Cracow he found that the church offices were at once suspended by order of the bishop.   Furious with rage, he pursued the saint to the little chapel of St Michael, outside the city, where he was saying Mass, and ordered some of his guards to enter and slay him.   The men, however, returned, saying that they could not kill the saint as he was surrounded by a heavenly light.   Upbraiding them for cowardice, the King himself entered the building and dispatched the holy bishop with his own hand. The guards then cut up the body into pieces and scattered them abroad to be devoured by beasts of prey.   Protected, it is said, by eagles, the sacred relics were rescued three days later by the cathedral canons and privately buried at the door of the chapel in which the saint had been martyred.   Ten years later the remains were solemnly translated to the Cathedral of Cracow.   Pope Gregory VII laid Poland under an interdict, and the people rose up against Boleslas, who was driven from the kingdom and died in exile.   The saint was canonised by Pope Innocent IV in 1253.

The long life of St Stanislaus by John Dlugosz is printed in the *Acta Sanctorum*, May, vol. ii.   Two other shorter biographies, both written by Dominicans at an earlier date, have since been discovered and published. For fuller details see Poncelet, *Bibliotheca Hagiographica Latina*, nn. 7832–7842.   The action of Pope St Gregory VII has been studied in the seventh volume of Gfrörer's *Kirchengeschichte*, devoted to Gregory VII and his times, pp. 557 *seq.*   Considerable discussion was caused in Poland by the publication in 1904 of a work on Poland in the eleventh century by Professor Wojchiechowski.   He maintained that Stanislaus had been guilty of treason, had plotted to dethrone his sovereign, and had therefore rightly been put to death.   To this charge Professor Miodonski and other Catholics replied with vigour.   Polish biographies of the Saint are numerous, but little seems to have been written in other languages.

ST DOMITIANUS, Bishop of Maestricht

c. A.D. 560

The principal patron of Huy on the Meuse is St Domitianus, whose relics still repose in a beautiful mediæval reliquary in the Church of Notre Dame.   A native of France, the saint was elected Bishop of Tongres, but his episcopal seat was afterwards removed to Maestricht.   At the Synod of Orleans in 549 he distinguished himself for the skilful manner in which he refuted the doctrines of the heretics. He evangelised the Meuse valley, converting numerous pagans besides building churches and hospices in his diocese. When, towards the close of a severe famine, the well-to-do were ceasing to relieve their poorer neighbours lest they themselves should suffer from shortage, the holy Bishop made an eloquent and successful appeal to their generosity, rebuking their lack of faith and prophesying a plentiful harvest. Tradition attributes to St Domitianus the slaying of a terrible monster, which was causing great distress by poisoning the drinking-water of Huy. A procession still takes place to the place beside a spring where the saint overcame the real or metaphorical dragon. St Domitianus is invoked against fever.

The formal biographies of St Domitianus printed in the *Acta Sanctorum*, May, vol. ii, are all very late. A few notices in the *Gesta Ep. Leodiensium* (see Pertz, *M. G. Scriptores*, vol. vii, p. 178, and vol. xxv, pp. 26–27) are more reliable. See also Duchesne, *Fastes Épiscopaux*, vol. iii, p. 189.

ST SERENICUS, ABBOT, AND ST SERENUS, HERMIT

c. A.D. 669

Serenicus, or Cerenicus, and his brother Serenus, or Seneridus, were young patricians from Spoleto who abandoned their family and their possessions at the bidding—it is said—of an angel, and betook themselves to Rome. The tombs of the apostles were at that time under the care of the Benedictines, with whom the two strangers were brought into contact and from whom they received the habit. For some time they lived the community life in Rome, edifying their brethren by their youthful piety, but before long they withdrew, still under angelic guidance, to seek a new home beyond the Alps in France. On the site of the present town of Château Gontier, in the diocese of Angers, and subsequently in the forest of Charnie, near the village of Saulge in Maine, they led a life of extreme self-abnegation as solitaries. But, desirous though they were of remaining lost to the world, the fame of their sanctity began to attract visitors who disturbed their solitude. So strongly did Serenicus feel the call to greater seclusion that he bade farewell to his brother from whom he had never previously been parted and struck out into the unknown region of Hyesmes, accompanied by a child whom he had baptised and who would not leave him. On a spot surrounded by boulders, situated over the river Sarthe and approached only by a narrow path, he determined to make his abode. He was soon

to discover that solitude was not for him.   Disciples gathered round
him unbidden, and he became the head of a community of 140
monks, whom he taught to recite the full psalmody, consisting of
the complete Roman use in addition to all the Benedictine offices.
He continued to rule over the monastery he had founded until his
death which occurred when he was very old.

In the meantime his brother Serenus had remained in his
hermitage at Saulge, his fasts and austerities winning for him
many graces, including visions, ecstasies and miracles.   When the
countryside was stricken by pestilence, famine and drought, following
on the horrors of civil war, St Berarius, Bishop of Le Mans, besought
the intercession of the holy recluse.   The cleansing rain which
cleared away the infection and refreshed the earth was attributed
by the grateful people to the prayers of St Serenus, whose reputation
as a wonder-worker was greatly enhanced.   Like St Serenicus,
he lived to old age, and as he lay dying, sounds of celestial music
are said to have been plainly heard by those who were near him at
the time.

The not very convincing narrative, compiled seemingly in the eighth
century, which is here summarised, has been printed both by the Bollandists and in Mabillon, *Acta Sanctorum O.S.B.*, vol. ii, pp. 572–578.

<hr/>

ST JOHN OF BEVERLEY, Bp. of York

A.D. 721

Few native saints enjoyed a greater reputation in Catholic
England than St John of Beverley, Bishop of York, whose shrine
was one of the favourite places of pilgrimage until the Reformation.
The learned Alcuin had an extraordinary devotion to him and celebrated his miracles in verse, whilst Athelstan ascribed to him his
victory over the Scots and Henry V his defeat of the French at
Agincourt.   At the instance of the latter a synod in 1416 ordered
the feast of St John of Beverley to be kept throughout England.
The saint was born at Harpham, a village in the province of Deira
which comprised Yorkshire, Lancashire and the portion of Northumbria south of the Tyne.   As a young man, he was attracted to
Kent by the famous school of St Theodore in which he became a
distinguished student under the holy abbot Adrian.   Upon his
return to his own country, he entered the great double abbey of
Streaneshalch, or Whitby, then under the rule of the Abbess Hilda.

His exceptional abilities marked him out for preferment, and early in the reign of King Alcfrid, after the death of Eata, he was appointed Bishop of Hexham. Whatever time he could spare from the duties of his office he devoted to heavenly contemplation, retiring for that purpose at stated periods to a cell beside the church of St Michael beyond the Tyne, about a mile and a half from Hexham. Often he would be accompanied by some poor person, whom he would serve, and once, at the beginning of Lent, he took with him a youth who seems to have suffered from a loathsome form of ringworm and who had never been able to speak. On the second Sunday, after the Bishop had traced the sign of the Cross on the young man's tongue, he taught him to say " Gae "—the Anglo-Saxon equivalent for " Yes." From this beginning he led him on to pronounce the letters of the alphabet and then to enunciate syllables and words. In this manner the youth gradually acquired the use of speech and was at the same time cured of the malady which disfigured him. When St Wilfrid returned from exile, the bishops of the sees into which his province had been divided were dispossessed, and St John vacated Hexham, but he was probably reinstated when Wilfrid was driven out once more. After the death of Bosa, St John was appointed Bishop of York, Hexham and Ripon being subsequently ceded to St Wilfrid. The Venerable Bede, who received holy orders from St John when Bishop of Hexham, refers to him at some length in his Ecclesiastical History, giving ample testimony to his sanctity, and recounting several miracles which had been described to him by such reliable eye-witnesses as Bercthun, Abbot of Beverley and Herebald, Abbot of Tynemouth. After St John had been translated to York he continued his practice of a periodical retirement from the world for spiritual refreshment. He chose for his retreat an abbey which he had built at Beverley, then a forest, now a market town, twenty miles from York. This monastery, a double one, intended for the use of both sexes, he placed under the rule of his disciple Bercthun, who became the first Abbot of Beverley, or, as it was then called, Endeirwood—wood of the Deiri. In 717, when he was much worn by age and fatigue, St John resigned his bishopric to his chaplain, St Wilfrid the Younger, and retired to Beverley, where he spent the four last years of his life in the faithful performance of all monastic duties. He died on May 7, 721.

The *Ecclesiastical History* of Bede is our most reliable source of information. More than three centuries later Folcard, a monk of St Bertin, but then resident in England, wrote a life of John of Beverley, followed by a long series of miracles. This, together with other documents, has been edited by Canon James Raine for the Rolls Series in *The Historians of the Church of York*, vol. i. See also Canon Raine's two volumes on Hexham in the Surtees Society publications. Entries in the Calendars (for which consult Stanton's *Menology*, p. 201) give evidence of a widespread cultus of St John of Beverley from an early date in England. Stanton's *Menology* (p. 676) speaks of the discovery of certain relics of St John of Beverley as late as the year 1664.

MAY 8

THE APPARITION OF ST MICHAEL

A.D. 492 (?)

IT cannot be disputed that in the apocryphal literature, which, both before and after the coming of Christ, was so prevalent in Palestine and among the Jewish communities of the Diaspora, the archangel St Michael (Michael=who is like to God ?) played a great part. A starting-point may be found in the authentic Scriptures ; for the tenth and twelfth chapters of the Book of Daniel speak of Michael as " one of the chief princes," the special protector of Israel, and describe how at that time shall Michael rise up, "the great prince who standeth for the children of thy people " (Dan. xii 1). In the *Book of Henoch*, which is regarded as the most important and influential of all the Old Testament apocrypha, Michael comes before us repeatedly as "the great captain," "the chief captain," he "who is set over the best part of mankind," *i.e.* over the chosen race who are the inheritors of the promises. He is merciful, and it is he who will explain the mystery which underlies the dread judgements of the Almighty. Michael is depicted as ushering Henoch himself into the divine presence, but he is also associated with the other great archangels, Gabriel, Raphael and Phanuel, in binding the wicked potentates of earth and casting them into a furnace of fire. The merciful conception of the leader's office is, however, especially emphasised in the *Testaments of the Twelve Patriarchs* and in the *Ascension of Isaias* (c. A.D. 90 ?) in which last we read of "the great angel Michael always interceding for the human race," but in this same work he is further presented as the scribe who records the deeds of all men in the heavenly books.

In New Testament times it is written in the Apocalypse of St John (xii 7-9) that "there was a great battle in heaven. Michael and his angels fought with the dragon, and the dragon fought and his angels ; and they prevailed not, neither was their place found any more in heaven. And that great dragon was cast out, that old serpent who is called the devil and Satan, who seduceth the whole world : and he was cast unto the earth, and his angels were thrown down with him." Still more significant of the close association of a cult of St Michael with Jewish traditions or folk-lore is the mention of his name in the Epistle of St Jude (v 9) : "When Michael the archangel, disputing with the devil, contended about the body of Moses, he durst not bring against him the judgement of railing speech, but said : 'The Lord rebuke thee.'" Whether this is a direct quotation from the apocryphal writing known as *The Assumption of Moses* may be disputed, because we do not possess the text of the latter part of that work ; but Origen expressly states that it is a quotation and names this book. The story there recounted seems to have been that when Moses died, "Samael" (*i.e.* Satan) claimed the body on the ground that Moses, having killed the Egyptian, was a murderer. This blasphemy kindled the wrath of Michael, but he restrained himself, saying only : "The Lord rebuke thee, O slanderer (*diabole*)." What seems certain is that *The Assumption of Moses* did give prominence to the part played by St Michael in the burial of Moses, and also that this same book was cited by certain Fathers at the Council of Nicæa in A.D. 325.* It was probably of pre-Christian origin, but we find in the *Shepherd of Hermas*, dating from the early part of the second century A.D., an illustration of the veneration in which St Michael was held by those who were undoubtedly Christians. In the eighth "Similitude" we have the allegory of the twigs cut from the great willow tree, some of which sprout into vigorous life when planted and watered, while others droop or wither away. An angel of majestic aspect presides over the awards when these twigs are brought back for inspection and judgement is passed upon them. This, we are told, is "the great and glorious angel Michael who has authority over this people and governs them ; for this is he who gave them the law and implanted it in the hearts of believers ; he accordingly super-intends them to whom he gave it to see if they have kept the same."

The *Shepherd of Hermas* was treated by some of the early Fathers as if it formed part of the canon of Scripture, but it hardly seems to have been so widely popular as a very extravagant apocryphal writing of Jewish origin known as the *Testament of Abraham*, which is probably not very much later in date. In this the archangel Michael throughout plays almost the leading part. His difficult task is to reconcile Abraham to the necessity of death. Michael is presented to the reader as God's Commander-in-Chief, the organiser of all the divine relations with earth, one whose inter-vention is so powerful with God that at his word souls can be rescued

* See Mansi, *Concilia*, vol. ii, p. 844 ; and S. Székely, *Bibliotheca Apocrypha*, vol. i, pp. 244 and 253.

even from Hell itself. We have, for example, passages like the following :

"And Abraham said to the chief-captain [*i.e.* St Michael], 'I beseech thee, archangel, hearken to my prayer, and let us call upon the Lord and supplicate His compassion and entreat His mercy for the souls of the sinners whom I formerly in my anger cursed and destroyed, whom the earth swallowed up and the wild beasts tore in pieces and the fire consumed through my words. Now I know that I have sinned before the Lord our God. Come then, O Michael, chief-captain of the hosts above, come let us call upon God with tears, that He may forgive my sins and grant them to me.' And the chief-captain heard him and they made entreaty before the Lord, and when they had called upon Him for a long space there came a voice from Heaven, saying : 'Abraham, Abraham, I have hearkened to thy voice and to thy prayer, and forgive thee thy sin, and those whom thou thinkest that I destroyed I have called up and brought them into life by My exceeding kindness, because for a season I have requited them in judgement and those whom I destroy living upon earth I will not requite in death.'"

Whether this and similar *apocrypha* were based on Jewish traditions or not, there can be no doubt that they were read by Christians. In most of them there is nothing so glaringly unorthodox as to stamp them as attacks upon the Christian faith. What is more, the thinly disguised fictional element, which is predominant in most of the hagiographical literature, even of the early centuries, must infallibly have dulled the critical sense of the great majority of readers, however piously inclined. To this we may safely attribute the fact that these apocryphal writings were very widely circulated and that we find echoes of them even in a canonical epistle like that of St Jude and still more in several of the early Greek Fathers. The liturgy itself was imperceptibly coloured by them. A most conspicuous example is the still existing Offertory chant, *Domine Jesu Christe, Rex gloriæ*, etc., in Masses for the dead : "O Lord Jesus Christ, king of glory, deliver the souls of all the faithful departed from the pains of hell and from the deep pit ; deliver them from the mouth of the lion that hell may not swallow them up and that they may not fall into darkness, but may the standard-bearer Michael introduce them to the holy light ; which Thou didst promise of old to Abraham and his seed. We offer to Thee, O Lord, sacrifices and prayers ; do Thou receive them in behalf of those souls whom we commemorate this day. Grant them, O Lord, to pass from death to that life, which Thou didst promise of old to Abraham and to his seed."

There are many reminiscences here of the type of apocryphal literature which has just been spoken of. The association of St Michael with Abraham is full of significance for anyone who is acquainted with the so-called *Testament of Abraham*. To enter into details would here be out of place, but it must suffice to point out that from the prominence thus given to St Michael, further developments followed very naturally. When the popular mind had familiarised itself with the idea that he was not only the chief captain of the heavenly army and the great protector, but also the arbiter of man's destinies on the threshold of the world to come, some public and external manifestation of the appeals made to this beneficent influence in private could not long be delayed. Any nucleus provided by an alleged miraculous happening would awaken ready response and would suffice to crystallise into one determined form the latent devotion of the crowd. There are indications of an early cult of St Michael, connecting him with the wonders wrought by the hot springs of Phrygia, notably at Hierapolis, and it seems certain that already in the fourth century a church was dedicated to him near Constantinople, possibly in the lifetime of the first Christian Emperor, Constantine. This impulse came from the East, though there is evidence that a basilica in honour of St Michael was constructed near Rome at the sixth milestone along the Via Salaria at an early date. Several Masses, apparently connected with this shrine, or possibly with others bearing the same dedication within the city, are provided in the earliest Roman Mass-book, the so-called *Leonianum*, and are assigned to the end of September. Whether the dedication on Mount Garganus, in Apulia, where Greek influences were dominant, is older than this cannot be easily determined. According to the written legend, still summarised in the Breviary, it occurred in the time of Pope Gelasius (492–496). A bull which had strayed from the herd of a certain rich land-owner found its way into a cave near the summit of the eminence called Mount Garganus. In the search which was made for it portents occurred by which the great archangel manifested his desire that this spot should be consecrated in his honour. Numberless miracles were believed to have been wrought in the cave or crypt, where a spring trickled which was accredited with a marvellous healing virtue. That the fame of this shrine soon spread all over the West is manifested by the fact that Mount Garganus is mentioned in one of the oldest manuscripts of the *Hieronymianum* in connection with the feast of St Michael on September 29. Even in England the Anglo-Saxon collection of sermons called the *Blickling Homilies*, written before the end of the tenth century, supplied an account of

Mount Garganus and its crypt chapel, from which, to quote a modern English version, we may learn that : " There was also from the same stone of the church roof, at the north side of the altar, a very pleasant and clear stream issuing, used by those who still dwell in that place. Beside this piece of water was a glass vessel hung on a silver chain, which received this joy-giving tide, and it was the custom of this people when they had been houselled (*i.e.* had received holy Communion) that they by steps should ascend to the glass vessel and there take and taste the heavenly fluid." This is an interesting piece of evidence for the fact that long before Communion under both kinds was abolished for the laity, it was customary to take a draught of water after receiving the Precious Blood, or more probably, under Greek influences, after receiving the dipped Host, which is still the Oriental manner of administering the Sacrament of the Eucharist.

The full text of the legend is printed in Ughelli, vol. vii, *cc.* 1107–1111, and in the *Acta Sanctorum*, September, vol. viii ; on which *cf.* Ebert, *Geschichte der Literatur des Mittelalters*, ii, p. 358. See also Kellner, *Heortology* (Eng. trans.), pp. 328–332, and Leclercq in *Dictionnaire d'Archéologie, etc.*, vol. xi, *cc.* 903–907. There can be little doubt that the story of the foundation of Saint-Michel au Péril de Mer, the famous Mont Saint-Michel near Avranches in Normandy, which is traditionally dated 709, was based on the legend of Monte Gargano. At what date the crag, now known as St Michael's Mount, near Marazion in Cornwall, received its name, does not seem certain. The statement that a church or chapel was built there in the fifth century is more than questionable, but there is evidence that in 1088 it was made over as a priory to the Norman abbey of Mont Saint-Michel.

ST VICTOR MAURUS, Mart.

A.D. 303

St Ambrose says of St Victor that he was one of the patrons of Milan, and as such he associates him with St Felix and St Nabor. A native of Mauretania, he was called Maurus to distinguish him from other confessors of the name of Victor. He is stated to have been a soldier in the Pretorian guard, a Christian from his youth, and to have been arrested for the faith when quite an old man. After enduring severe tortures, he suffered martyrdom by decapitation under Maximian in Milan about the year 303. His body was buried by order of the bishop of the diocese, St Maternus, beside a little wood, and a church was afterwards built over his remains. St Gregory of Tours tells us that God honoured his tomb by many miracles. St Charles Borromeo caused the sacred relics to be translated in 1576 to the new church in Milan which had then been recently built by the Olivetan monks and which still bears St Victor's name.

In the *Passio* of this martyr—it is printed in the *Acta Sanctorum*, May, vol. ii—we have the usual fantastic accumulation of torments. He is said, for example, to have been basted with molten lead, which instantaneously cooled on touching his flesh, and did him no sort of harm. Nevertheless, the fact of his martyrdom and early veneration at Milan is beyond doubt. There is quite a considerable literature concerning him, for which see the references in Delehaye's commentary on the *Hieronymianum*, p. 238. Consult especially F. Savio, *I santi Martyri di Milano* (1906), pp. 3–24 and 59–65.

ST ACACIUS, or AGATHUS, MART.

A.D. 303 or 305

With the exception of St Mucius, St Acacius, or Agathus, is the only genuine ancient martyr of Byzantium. He was a Cappadocian, a centurion in the Martian cohort who perished for the faith during the persecution under Diocletian and Maximian. He suffered alone, and the seventy-seven companions who are commonly associated with him must be referred elsewhere. According to his so-called Acts, which, however, are not trustworthy, he was denounced by the tribune Firmus at Perinthus in Thrace, where he was cruelly tortured under the judge Bibienus. He was then taken to Byzantium, publicly scourged and finally beheaded.

Constantinople contained two, if not three, churches dedicated to St Acacius, one of which was built by Constantine the Great. It was nicknamed "the Walnut," because, built into its structure, was the walnut tree upon which the saint was said to have been suspended for his flagellation. The church was afterwards restored by the Emperor Justinian, who overlaid it with marble of such dazzling whiteness that Greek writers compared it to a snow palace. The Calabrian town of Squillace claims to possess the saint's relics, which are supposed to have been miraculously transported from Greece to Italy.

The Greek text of the Acts of Acacius is printed in the *Acta Sanctorum*, May, vol. ii, and there is also an ancient Syriac version edited by Bedjan. See what has been written concerning this martyr by Père Delehaye in the *Analecta Bollandiana*, vol. xxxi (1912), p. 228, as well as in his *Origines du Culte des Martyrs*, pp. 268–271, and in his commentary on the *Hieronymianum*, p. 239. This martyr's name is found both in the ancient Syriac *Breviarium* of *c.* 412, and in the Spanish calendar of Carmona. *Cf.* also Salaville, " Les Églises de St Acace " in *Échos d'Orient*, vol. xi (1909), pp. 105 *seq.*

ST GIBRIAN, HERMIT

c. A.D. 515

Towards the end of the fifth century—so we are told—there arrived in Brittany from Ireland a pious family consisting of seven brothers and three sisters, all of whom had abandoned their native land that they might serve God more freely in a strange country. The men were St Gibrian, St Helan, St Tressan, St German, St Veran, St Abran and St Petran, and the women's names were Francla, Pomptia and Posemna. St Gibrian, who was the eldest and a priest, was their leader. They eventually settled as solitaries in the forest land near the Marne, living alone, but not so far apart that they could not visit each other for spiritual consolation from time to time. Gibrian's hermitage was at the junction of the Côle and the Marne. He died in his retreat, after a life of prayer and austerity, and an oratory was erected over his tomb. To preserve his relics from the ravages of the Normans they were afterwards removed to the Abbey of St Remigius at Rheims, where they remained until the French Revolution, when they were scattered and lost.

The Bollandists deal with this alleged family of saints in the *Acta Sanctorum*, May, vol. ii, printing what purports to be their story from a medieval MS. at Reims. A collection of reputed miracles worked at the shrine after the translation to Reims is to be found in an appendix to the seventh volume for May. Dom Gougaud, in his *Gaelic Pioneers of Christianity*, p. 4, seems to be right in treating the account as legendary, but these saints are still liturgically commemorated in some French dioceses, notably at Reims itself. See also O'Hanlon, *Lives of Irish Saints*, vol. v, p. 129.

ST DESIDERATUS, BP. OF BOURGES

c. A.D. 550

St Desideratus was one of a holy trio, his two brothers, Desiderius and Deodatus, being locally venerated as saints, although there is no mention of any one of the three in the Roman Martyrology. They were the sons, we are told, of Auginus and Agia, a worthy couple of Soissons, who not only devoted their time and possessions to relieving the poor, but practically turned their house into a hospital. Desideratus attached himself to the court of King Clotaire, to whom he became a sort of secretary of state, and over whom he exercised a most salutary influence. In the midst of the splendours by which he was surrounded he lived a mortified life, always wearing a hair shirt under the sumptuous attire that befitted his position. He used the great powers with which he was entrusted to stamp out heresy and to punish simony.   On various occasions he expressed a desire to retire into a monastery, but the proposal was always vetoed by the King and his suite, who declared that he ought rather to consult the public weal than to indulge his own private inclinations.   Upon the death of St Arcadius in 541, Desideratus was chosen Bishop of Bourges, and during the nine years of his episcopate he acquired a great reputation as a peacemaker and wonder-worker.   From a visit to Rome he brought back to his diocese many relics of the saints.   The holy bishop took part in various synods—notably in the fifth Council of Orleans and the second Council of Auvergne, both of which dealt with the errors of Nestorius and Eutyches, besides providing for the restoration of ecclesiastical discipline. In his old age St Desideratus obtained as vicar a young priest named Flavian, whose untimely death hastened his own end.   He died on May 8, probably in the year 550.

The narrative printed in the *Acta Sanctorum*, May, vol. ii, is of late date and unreliable ; but there can be no question of the historical existence and pious activity of St Desideratus.   See Duchesne, *Fastes Épiscopaux*, vol. ii, p. 28.

ST BONIFACE IV, Pope

A.D. 615

Not very much is known to us about the saintly Pope who ruled the Church for six years under the title of Boniface IV.   He was the son of a physician and a native of the " city " of Valeria in the Abruzzi.   He is supposed to have been a pupil of St Gregory the Great at St Sebastiano, in Rome, and the Benedictines accordingly claim him as a member of their order.   His reign was signalised by the conversion of the Pantheon—the temple erected by Marcus Agrippa in honour of all the Roman deities—into a Christian church, dedicated to Our Lady and the holy Martyrs.   The building was bestowed by the Emperor Phocas upon the Roman pontiff, who purified it and consecrated it on May 13, 609.   At a synod of all the Italian bishops, summoned primarily for the restoration of ancient discipline, St Boniface IV is said to have conferred with St Mellitus, Bishop of London, then on a visit to Rome, about the affairs and organisation of the English Church.   On his return he brought letters from the Pope to King Ethelbert.   St Boniface IV was the recipient of a famous and much-discussed letter from the great St. Columbanus, which combines remarkable expressions of devotion and loyalty to the Holy See, with altogether unwarrantable insinuations of laxity in the matter of doctrine. On his death this holy Pope was buried in the portico of St Peter's, but his remains were afterwards transferred to the interior of the basilica.

In the *Acta Sanctorum* Boniface is noticed on May 25 (May, vol. vi), but a more up-to-date account of his pontificate will be found in Mann, *The Lives of the Popes*, vol. i, pp. 268–279. See also Duchesne, *Liber Pontificalis*, vol. i, pp. 317–318 ; and Laux, *Der hl. Kolumban* (1919), or in an earlier English form, G. Metlake, *The Life and Writings of St Columban* (1914).

ST WIRO, CONF.

SEVENTH CENTURY

With respect of the birthplace of St Wiro we can only say that it was somewhere in the British Isles, for whereas Alcuin asserts that he was a Northumbrian, certain other writers declare that he was a Scotsman and others that he was a native of County Clare in Ireland. We read that from his earliest youth he modelled himself upon St Patrick, St Cuthbert and St Columban. After his ordination he went with another priest, St Plechelm, and the deacon, St Otger, to Rome, where he and St Plechelm are said to have been consecrated by the Pope to be regionary bishops. When they had laboured for some time in their native land, the three friends—perhaps at the suggestion of St Willibrord—passed over to the Netherlands, where they spent part of their time in evangelising the lower valley of the Meuse, and the rest in retirement and prayer. Pepin of Heristal gave them the Mount of St Peter, afterwards called St Odilia, or Odilienberg, at a league's distance from Ruremond, and there they built several cells as well as a church which they dedicated to Our Lord and His Holy Mother. Pepin is said to have held St Wiro in such great veneration that he appointed him his director and made it a rule to repair to him barefoot every Lent, and often at other times, to receive penance from him or from St Plechelm. St Wiro died in extreme old age, and a monastery was erected on the site of the cells occupied by the three friends.

A medieval biography of St Wiro is printed in the *Acta Sanctorum*, May, vol. ii, but it is late and unreliable. See rather Van der Essen, *Étude critique et littéraire sur les vitæ des saints merovingiens*, pp. 105–109 ; J. Snieders, " L'Influence de l'hagiographie irlandaise," etc., in the *Revue d'Histoire Ecclésiastique*, vol. xxiv (1928), pp. 849–850 ; and J. F. Kenney, *The Sources of the Early History of Ireland*, p. 509.

ST BENEDICT II, POPE
A.D. 685

Pope St Benedict II was brought up from infancy in the service of the Church and became at an early age proficient in the Holy Scriptures, as also in ecclesiastical chant, for which he was an enthusiast. A Roman by birth, he took part, after his ordination, in the government of the Church under Popes Agatho and Leo II. After the death of the latter in 683, he was elected to the chair of St Peter, his virtues, his liberality, and his intellectual abilities marking him out as specially suited to fill that sacred office. In accordance with ancient custom, the Popes were at that time still chosen by the clergy and people of Rome, the consent of the Christian Emperor being also required. The embassies between Rome and Constantinople necessary before this sanction could be obtained frequently entailed not only inconvenience, but also delay, and nearly a year elapsed between the death of Pope Leo and the coronation of Benedict II. One of the first successful efforts of the new Pontiff was to induce the Emperor Constantine Pogonatus to issue a decree enacting that, for the future, the suffrages of the clergy, the people and the soldiery of Rome should suffice for the election of the Pope. So great was the Emperor's regard for St Benedict that he sent him locks of the hair of his two sons, Justinian and Heraclius—thus signifying to him, according to the symbolism of the time, that they were the Holy Father's spiritual sons. St Benedict did much to enforce the general acceptance of the decrees of the Council of Constantinople against the Monothelites. Moreover, when the pronouncements of the Council of Toledo appeared to him ambiguous in regard to that heresy, he obtained the summoning of another council which restated the views of the members in terms which left no doubt as to their orthodoxy. With great earnestness he strove to win back to the true faith Macarius, Bishop of Antioch, who had been deposed for heresy. In his short pontificate of eleven months, he found time to restore several of the Roman churches and to labour for the conversion of heretics. He was also interested in the English Church, stoutly upholding the cause of St Wilfrid of York. St Benedict II died on May 8, 685, and was buried in St Peter's.

The *Acta Sanctorum* treat Pope St Benedict II under May 7 (vol. ii). The *Liber Pontificalis* (Duchesne, vol. i, pp. 363–365) is our principal authority ; but see also Muratori, *Annales*, ad. ann. 684, and Hefele–Leclercq, *Histoire des Conciles*, vol. iii, pp. 549 *seq.* Mgr Mann in his *Lives of the Popes*, vol. i, part 2, pp. 54–63, has gathered up all the available information.

∙ ST PETER, ABP. OF TARENTAISE
A.D. 1175

St Peter of Tarentaise, one of the glories of the Cistercian Order, was born near Vienne in the French province of the Dauphiné. He early displayed a remarkable memory, coupled with a great inclination for pious studies, and at the age of twenty he entered the Abbey of Bonnevaux which had been founded by St Bernard as an offshoot of Clairvaux. With great zeal he embraced the austerities of the primitive rule, edifying all who came into contact with him by his charity, his humility and his modesty. His parents, after the birth of their four children, had agreed to live in perpetual continence and had made their house a refuge for the destitute to whom they yielded up their own beds, contenting themselves with sleeping upon straw. After a time, the father and the other two sons followed Peter to Bonnevaux, whilst the mother, with the only daughter, entered a neighbouring Cistercian nunnery. Besides these members of his own family, no less than seventeen men of high rank were led by the example of Peter to become monks at Bonnevaux. He was not quite thirty when he was chosen superior of a new house built at Tamié, or Tamiens, in the desert mountains of the Tarentaise. It overlooked the pass which was then the chief route from Geneva to Savoy, and the monks were able to be of great use to travellers. There, with the help of Amadeus III, Count of Savoy, who held him in high esteem, he founded a hospice for the sick and for strangers, in which he was wont to wait upon his guests with his own hands. In 1142 the Count procured his election to the Archbishopric of Tarentaise, and Peter was compelled by St Bernard and the General Chapter of his order, though much against the grain, to accept the office. He found the diocese in a deplorable state, due mainly to the mismanagement of his predecessor, an unworthy usurper named Idrael, who had eventually to be deposed. Parish churches were in the hands of laymen, the poor were neglected, and the clergy, who ought to have stemmed the general tide of iniquity, too often promoted irregularity by their evil example. In place of the Cathedral clergy whom he found lax and careless, he substituted the Canons Regular of St Augustine, and he soon made his chapter a model of good order. He undertook the constant visitation of his diocese ; recovered for the Church the property which had been alienated ; appointed good priests to various parishes ; made excellent foundations for the education of the young and the relief of the poor ; and everywhere provided for the due celebration of the services of the Church. The author of his life, who was his constant companion at this period, testifies to numerous miracles which he wrought, mainly in curing the sick and multiplying provisions in time of famine. Apprehension at finding himself honoured as a wonder-worker, and the natural longing of a monk for solitude turned his mind back to the cloister and in 1155, after he had administered the diocese for thirteen years, he suddenly disappeared, leaving no trace behind. Actually he had made his way to a remote Cistercian convent in Switzerland, where, being quite unknown, he was accepted as a lay brother. Great was the dismay throughout the diocese of Tarentaise when the departure of the archbishop became known, and diligent was the search made for him throughout the religious houses of the neighbouring provinces. Not until a year later was he discovered by a young man who had been trained by him and who had vowed to continue his search until it was rewarded with success. His identity having been revealed to his new superiors, Peter was obliged to leave them and to return to his see, where he was greeted with great demonstrations of joy. He now took up his duties more zealously than ever. The poor were ever his first consideration : twice in bitterly cold weather he gave away his own habit at the risk of his life. He rebuilt the hospice of the Little St Bernard and founded other similar refuges for travellers in the Alps. He also inaugurated a practice, kept up until the French Revolution, of making a free distribution of bread and soup during the months preceding the harvest, when food was scarce in many parts of his hilly diocese. The dole came to be called " May bread." All his life he continued to dress and to live like a Cistercian, replacing manual labour by the spiritual functions of his office. Essentially a man of peace, he had a singular gift for allaying seemingly implacable enmities and on several occasions averted bloodshed by reconciling contending parties. His chief political efforts, however, were directed to supporting the cause of the true Pope Alexander III against the pretensions of the Anti-pope Victor IV, who, though elected by three Ghibelline Cardinals only, had behind him the powerful backing of the redoubtable Emperor Frederick Barbarossa. At one time, indeed, it seemed as though the Archbishop of Tarentaise was the only subject of the Empire who dared openly to oppose the pretender, but it soon became apparent that he carried with him the whole of the great Cistercian Order. To establish the claims of the true Sovereign Pontiff, St Peter preached in Alsace, Lorraine, Burgundy and many parts of Italy, the effect of his words being enhanced by numerous miracles of healing. He also spoke out fearlessly in various councils and even in the presence of the Emperor himself, who was so far impressed by his sanctity and courage as to permit in him a freedom of speech he would endure from no one else.

It was not granted to the saint to die amongst his mountain flock. His reputation as a peacemaker led Alexander III to send him in 1174 to try to effect a reconciliation between King Louis VII of France and Henry II of England. St Peter, though he was old, set out at once, preaching everywhere on his way. As he approached Chaumont in the Véxin, where the French Court was being held, he was met by King Louis and by Prince Henry, the rebellious heir to the English throne. The latter, alighting from his horse to receive the Archbishop's blessing, asked for the saint's old cloak, which he reverently kissed. Both at Chaumont and at Gisors where he interviewed the English King, St Peter was treated with utmost honour, but the reconciliation for which he laboured did not take place until after his death. As he was returning to his diocese he was taken ill in the road near Besançon and died as he was being carried into the Abbey of Bellevaux.

Our most copious and trustworthy source of information is the Life written by the Cistercian, Geoffrey of Auxerre, Abbot of Hautecombe, in response to the request of Pope Lucius III. It is printed in the *Acta Sanctorum*, and we know that it was completed before 1185, that is, within ten years of the death of the saint. But there are besides this many references to St Peter in the correspondence, chronicles, and hagiographical literature of the time. Even a man like Walter Map, who was prone to write of the Cistercians with the utmost bitterness, speaks with profound reverence of St Peter of Tarentaise. See *The Life of St Hugh of Lincoln* (Quarterly Series), pp. 625–626, and in the same work an account of the relations between St Hugh, the Carthusian, and his Cistercian brother bishop (pp. 60–64, etc.). Consult further Le Couteulx, *Annales Ordines Cartusiensis*, vol. ii *passim*; Chevray, *Vie de S. Pierre de Tarentaise*; and G. Müller, *Leben des hl. Petrus von Tarentaise* (1892).

MAY 9

ST GREGORY NAZIANZEN
Bp., Doctor of the Church
A.D. 390

IN view of his resolute defence of the truths promulgated by the Council of Nicæa, St Gregory Nazianzen has been declared a Doctor of the Church and has also been surnamed "the Theologian"—a title which he shares with the Apostle St John. Born about the year 329 at Arianzus in Cappadocia, he was the son of St Nonna and of St Gregory the Elder, a wealthy landowner and magistrate, who, after being converted to Christianity by his wife, had been raised to the priesthood and for forty-five years was Bishop of Nazianzus. The younger Gregory and his brother, St Cæsarius, received the best education available. Having studied together for a time at Cæsarea, in Cappadocia, where they made the acquaintance of St Basil the Great, Gregory, who was intended for the law, went on to Cæsarea, in Palestine, which had a famous rhetorical school, and then went on to join his brother at Alexandria. It was usual for scholars to pass from one great educational centre to another, and Gregory, after a short stay in Egypt, decided to complete his training in Athens. As the vessel which bore him rolled tempest-tossed for days, the young man realised with terror the danger he ran of losing not only his body, but also his soul, because he was still unbaptised. But he probably shared the views of many pious men of that period with regard to the difficulty of obtaining forgiveness for post-baptismal sin, for he does not appear to have been baptised until many years later. During the greater part of the ten years Gregory spent in Athens he enjoyed the companionship of St Basil, who became his most intimate friend. Another but far less congenial fellow-student was the future Emperor Julian, whose affectations and extravagances even then disgusted the serious young Cappadocians. Gregory was thirty when he left Athens, having learnt all that its masters could teach him, and being desirous of seeing his parents and his friend Basil, from whom he had been separated for some time. It is not clear with what plans Gregory returned to Nazianzus ; if he had intended to practise law or to teach rhetoric, he soon changed his mind. He had always been earnestly devout, but about this time he was led to adopt a much more austere mode of life—apparently as the result of a great religious experience, possibly his baptism. Consequently, when Basil, who was living the life of a solitary at Pontus, on the Black Sea, invited him to join him, Gregory responded eagerly to the call. In a wildly beautiful spot which Basil has described in graphic language, the two friends spent a couple of fruitful years in prayer, mortification and study, compiling a collection of extracts from Origen and drawing up that Basilian code which was to form the basis of all Christian monastic rule until the days of St Benedict.

From this peaceful existence Gregory was called home to assist his father—then over eighty years old—in the management of his diocese and estate. Not content, however, with the help his son could give him as a layman, the aged Bishop, with the connivance of certain members of his flock, ordained him priest more or less by force, in the cathedral on a festival day. Taken by surprise and terrified at finding himself invested with a dignity from which he had always shrunk in the consciousness of his own unworthiness, he acted on the impulse of the moment and fled away to his friend Basil. Ten weeks later, however, he returned to shoulder his responsibilities in obedience to what he realised was a call from on high. The apology he wrote for his flight is a noble treatise on the priesthood which has been drawn upon by countless writers on the same subject from St John Chrysostom and St Gregory the Great down to our own day. An incident was soon to show how much his assistance was needed. The old prelate, like many others, had been led to give his assent to the decisions of the Council of Rimini in the hope of conciliating the Semi-Arians. This gave great offence to many of the most zealous Catholics—especially the monks—and it was entirely due to Gregory's tact that a schism was averted. His oration on the occasion of the reconciliation is still extant, as are also two funeral discourses he delivered at that period of his life, the one, in 369, on his brother, St Cæsarius, who had been the Imperial physician at Constantinople, and the other on his sister, Gorgonia.

In the year 370 Basil was elected Metropolitan of Cæsarea, in succession to Archbishop Eusebius, who had ordained him priest six years previously. At that period the Emperor Valens and the procurator Modestus were doing their utmost to introduce Arianism into Cappadocia and were finding Basil the chief obstacle in their way. To diminish his influence, Cappadocia was divided into two, Tyana being made the capital of a new province. Anthimus,

Bishop of Tyana, promptly claimed archiepiscopal jurisdiction over the recently-established province, whilst St Basil maintained that the civil division did not affect his own authority as metropolitan. It seems to have been solely to consolidate his position by settling a friend on disputed territory that he nominated Gregory to a new bishopric which he established at Sasima, a miserable, unhealthy town on the borderland between the two provinces. Gregory did, indeed, very reluctantly submit to consecration, but he never went to Sasima, the governor of which was an open adversary. In reply to the reproaches of St Basil, who accused him of slackness, he declared that he was not disposed to fight for a church. He was deeply hurt at the treatment he had received, and although he became reconciled to St Basil, the friendship was never again the same. He actually remained at Nazianzus, acting as coadjutor until his father's death the following year. He had long ardently desired to live the solitary life, but was induced to carry on the government of Nazianzus until a new bishop was appointed. His health, however, broke down in 375 and he withdrew to Seleucia, the capital of Isauria, where he spent five years.

The death of the persecuting Emperor Valens brought peace once more to the Church, and it was decided to send learned and zealous men to those cities and provinces where the faith had suffered the greatest set-back. It was realised that the Church of Constantinople was of all others the most desolate, having been dominated by Arian teachers for between thirty and forty years, and being without a church in which to assemble the few Catholics who remained in it. At the suggestion of several bishops, an invitation was sent to St Gregory to come and rebuild the faith. To the sensitive peace-loving recluse the prospect of being plunged into that whirlpool of intrigue, corruption and violence must, indeed, have seemed appalling, and at first he declined to leave his solitude. Eventually, however, he was induced to consent, but his trials were to begin with his entrance into Constantinople, for as he made his appearance, poorly clad, bald, and prematurely bent, he was ill received by a populace accustomed to dignity and splendour. At first he lodged with relations in a house which he soon converted into a church and to which he gave the name of Anastasia—the place where the faith would rise again. In this small building he preached and taught his little flock, and it was here that he delivered the celebrated Orations on the Trinity, which won for him the title of Theologian—meaning in effect one who apprehends aright the Divinity of Our Lord. Gradually his audience increased and the fame of his eloquence spread. On the other hand, the Arians and Apollinarists pursued him unrelentingly with calumnies, insults, and even personal violence. They broke into his church : they pelted him in the streets and dragged him before the civil magistrates as a brawler. He comforted himself by reflecting that if his adversaries were the stronger party, he had the better cause : though they had the churches, God was with him : if they had the populace on their side, the angels were on his. Moreover, he won the esteem of some of the greatest men of the age : St Evagrius of Pontus came to serve him as his archdeacon, and St Jerome, arriving in Constantinople from the deserts of Syria, was glad to sit at his feet and learn of him.

Yet trials of all sorts continued to beset the Catholic champion from his own party as well as from heretics. A certain Maximus, an adventurer in whom he had believed and whom he had publicly praised, actually tried to supersede him by obtaining consecration from some passing bishops and causing himself to be proclaimed while St Gregory was ill. The would-be usurper was promptly driven out, but St Gregory himself was greatly chagrined and mortified—especially as Maximus had won the ear of some whom Gregory had regarded as his friends.

Early in the year 380 the Emperor Theodosius was baptised by the Catholic bishop of Thessalonica and shortly afterwards he promulgated an edict to his Byzantine subjects, bidding them observe the Catholic faith as professed by the Pope of Rome and the patriarch of Alexandria. This he followed up, when he came to Constantinople, by giving the Arian patriarch the option of subscribing to the Nicene faith or leaving the city. The prelate selected the latter course and Theodosius immediately determined to instal Gregory in his place. Hitherto he had been a bishop in Constantinople, but not the Bishop of Constantinople. The nomination having been confirmed synodically, St Gregory was solemnly installed in the Cathedral of St Sophia with great pomp and amid the acclamations of the people. He did not, however, retain the seat for many months. His old enemies rose against him, and fresh hostility was aroused by his decision in the matter of the vacant see of Antioch. The validity of his election was contested, and attempts were actually made upon his life. Always a lover of peace, and fearing lest the unrest should lead to bloodshed, Gregory determined to lay down his office. " If my tenure of the see of Constantinople is leading to disturbance," he cried out in the assembly, " I am willing, like Jonas, to be thrown into the waves to still the tempest, although I did not raise it. If all followed my example, the Church would enjoy uninterrupted tranquillity. This dignity I never desired : I assumed the charge much against my

will. If you think fit, I am most ready to depart." Having obtained
the Emperor's reluctant consent, he then prepared to leave the city,
after delivering a dignified and touching farewell to the citizens.
His work there was done : he had rekindled the torch of the faith
in Constantinople when it was well-nigh extinguished and had kept
it burning at the Church's darkest hour. It was characteristic of
his magnanimity that he always maintained cordial relations with
his successor Nectarius, a man who, in every respect but birth, was
his inferior.

For some time after leaving Constantinople, Gregory divided
his time between his parental estate upon which he was born and the
city of Nazianzus, which was still without a bishop, but after the
year 383, when, through his efforts, his cousin Eulalius was appointed
to fill the vacant see, he retired completely into private life, leading
a secluded existence and taking much delight in his garden with its
fountain and a shaded grove. Yet he practised at the same time
severe mortifications, never wearing shoes or seeing a fire. Towards
the end of his life he wrote a number of pious poems, partly for
his own pleasure, partly for the edification of others. They have
considerable biographical and literary interest, because in them he
recounts his life and sufferings, and they are written in graceful
verses which occasionally rise to sublimity. Upon them, upon
his orations and upon his excellent letters, his reputation as a
writer has rested through the centuries. He died in his retreat
in the year 390, and his remains, which were first translated
from Nazianzus to Constantinople, now repose at St Peter's in
Rome.

St Gregory greatly loved to dwell upon the condescension of
God to men. "Admire the excessive goodness of God," he writes
in one of his letters. "He vouchsafes to accept our desires as
though they were a thing of great value. He burns with an ardent
longing that we should desire and love Him, and He receives the
petitions we send up for His benefits as though they were a benefit
to Himself and a favour we did Him. He gives with a greater joy
than the joy with which we receive. Only let us not be too apathetic
in our petitions or set too narrow bounds to our requests : nor let
us ask for frivolous things which it would be unworthy of God's
magnificence to propose that He should grant us."

St Gregory's own letters and writings (notably the long poem, *De Vita
Sua*, of nearly two thousand verses) are the principal source of information
regarding his life. Unfortunately the great Benedictine edition of his
works suffered many setbacks at the time when it was being prepared for the
press. Successive editors died, and the first volume, containing the sermons,

only appeared in 1778. Hence before the second volume was ready the French Revolution had occurred, and it did not see the light until 1840. The Academy of Cracow has undertaken a new critical edition, which is appearing slowly, but is not yet completed. Many of the earlier manuscripts of St Gregory Nazianzen, some of which belong to the ninth century, are embellished with miniatures. On these the article of Dom Leclercq, which reproduces many of the drawings, may conveniently be consulted. See the *Dictionnaire d'Archéologie, etc.*, vol. vi, cc. 1667–1710. For English readers Cardinal Newman's essay in his *Historical Sketches*, vol. iii, pp. 50–94, and the article of H. W. Watkins in the *Dictionary of Christian Biography*, vol. ii, pp. 741–761, will always be of value. See also A. Benoît, *S. Grégoire de Nazianze* (2nd ed.), 1885 ; Duchesne, *Histoire Ancienne de l'Église* (Eng. trans.), vol. ii ; E. Fleury, *Grégoire et son Temps* (1930) ; and Th. Disdier in *Échos d'Orient*, vol. xxxiv (1931), pp. 485–497. A fuller bibliography is provided by Bardenhewer both in his *Patrologie* and in his *Geschichte der altkirchlichen Literatur*, vol. iii (2nd ed.), pp. 162–188 and 671.

ST BEATUS, Hermit

A.D. 112 (?)

St Beatenberg, above the Lake of Thun, derives its name from St Beatus, a hermit who, at an early date, is said to have occupied a cave on its slope and died there—supposedly about the year 112. A whole legendary history afterwards grew up about him. It was believed that he had been baptised in England by the Apostle St Barnabas, and that he had been sent to evangelise Switzerland by St Peter, who ordained him priest in Rome. His cave, where he was reputed to have slain a dragon, became a favourite place of pilgrimage, until it was closed by the Zwinglians. His cultus was then transferred to Lungern, in Oberwalden, and St Peter Canisius did much to revive and propagate it. Modern research, however, has revealed that the tradition of St Beatus as the Apostle of Switzerland is a late one, extending back no further than the middle of the eleventh century—if as far.

The Swiss St Beatus is often confused with a namesake, honoured on the same day, *viz.*, St Beatus of Vendôme, who preached the gospel first on the shores of the Garonne, then at Vendôme and Nantes and who is stated to have died at Chevresson, near Laôn, about the close of the third century. This St Beatus seems to have a better claim to be regarded as historical, for his name undoubtedly was entered on this day in the *Hieronymianum* and his legend has seemingly supplied much that is attributed to the Swiss Beatus.

Both these legends are dealt with in the *Acta Sanctorum*, May, vol. ii. The cultus of the Swiss St Beatus is apparently still active, and he is regarded

as a sort of national patron. See, on the relations between these two supposed
hermit missionaries, the *Analecta Bollandiana*, vol. xxvi (1907), pp. 423–453 ;
O. Scheiwiller in the *Zeitschrift f. Schweitzer. Kirchengeschichte*, vol. v
(1911), pp. 21–52 ; and on the folklore aspects Bächtold–Stäubli, *Handwörterbuch des deutschen Aberglaubens*, vol. i, pp. 964–966.

ST PACHOMIUS, THE ELDER, ABBOT

A.D. 346

   Although St Anthony is often reckoned the founder of Christian
monasticism, that title belongs more properly to St Pachomius, for he
was the first—not, indeed, to gather round him communities of
Christian ascetics on a large scale—but to organise them and draw up
in writing a rule for their common use.   He was born of heathen
parents in the Upper Thebaïd about the year 292, and when he was
twenty was conscripted for the Emperor's army.   As he and other
recruits were being conveyed down the Nile under wretched conditions, they received great kindness from the Christians of Thebes, who
were moved with compassion for them.   This disinterested charity
Pachomius never forgot, and as soon as the army was disbanded, he
made his way to a town in the Thebaïd where there was a Christian
church and enrolled himself among the catechumens.   After his
baptism, his one preoccupation was how best to correspond with the
grace he had received.   Having heard that an old hermit called
Palæmon was serving God with great perfection in the desert, he
sought him out and begged him to receive him as a disciple.   The
old man set before him the hardships of the life, but Pachomius was
not to be deterred.   Having promised obedience, he received the
habit.   The life they led together was one of extreme austerity ;
their diet was bread and salt ; they drank no wine and used no oil ;
they always watched half the night and frequently passed the whole
of it without sleep.   Sometimes they would repeat the entire psalter
together ; at other times they would occupy themselves in manual
labour accompanied by interior prayer.
   One day, when Pachomius was visiting, as he occasionally did,
a vast uninhabited desert on the banks of the Nile called Tabenna,
or Tabennisi, he is said to have heard a voice bidding him erect a
monastery there, and about the same time he had a vision of an angel
who gave him certain instructions regarding the religious life.
These revelations he imparted to Palæmon, who accompanied him
to Tabenna about the year 318, helped him to construct a cell and
remained with him for some time.

The first disciple to receive the habit at Tabenna from St Pachomius was his own eldest brother John : others followed, and within a comparatively short time the number of his monks exceeded one hundred. He led them to an eminent degree of perfection, mainly through his own fervent spirit and example. He passed fifteen years without ever lying down, taking his short rest sitting on a stone, and from the moment of his conversion he never ate a full meal. Yet his rule for others was graduated according to their capacity, for he refused no applicant on the score of age or weakliness. He built six other monasteries in the Thebaïd, and from the year 336 resided often at Pabau, or Pboou, near Thebes, which became a larger and even more famous community than Tabenna. By the advice of Serapion, Bishop of Tentyra, he built for the benefit of the poor shepherds a church, in which for some time he acted as lector, but he could never be induced to offer himself for the priesthood, or to present any of his monks for ordination, although he was always prepared to give the habit to men who were already priests. He zealously opposed the Arians, and in 333 was favoured by a visit from St Athanasius. For the benefit of his sister whom, however, he never would see, he built a nunnery on the opposite side of the Nile. Cited to appear before a council of bishops at Latopolis, to answer certain accusations, he displayed such humility in his replies to his calumniators that all present marvelled. Humility and patience were indeed virtues which he practised in a heroic degree and which he inculcated on his followers. When some of the monks, knowing that miracles of healing often took place at his intercession, suggested that he should intervene on behalf of his favourite disciple Theodore, who was afflicted with constant headaches, he replied : " Though abstinence and prayer are of great merit, yet sickness suffered with patience is of much greater." The saint was also endowed with the gift of prophecy, and foresaw with great grief the eventual decay of monastic fervour in his order. He died of a painful epidemic disease which had already carried off one hundred of his brethren. He had lived to see seven thousand monks in the various monasteries under his charge. Cassian tells us that the larger his communities were, the more perfect was the observance of discipline, all obeying the superior more readily than any single person could be found to do elsewhere. The order subsisted in the East till the eleventh century, for Anselm, Bishop of Havelburgh, writes that he saw five hundred monks of that institute in a monastery at Constantinople.

The story of the angel who appeared to Pachomius, bidding him gather young monks about him at Tabennisi, has not everywhere found acceptance ; and still more difficulty has been raised over the brass tablet which the angel is supposed to have brought him and which is said to have been inscribed with a summary of the rule he was to follow.   None the less, such an account of its contents as we read in the *Lausiac History* of Palladius cannot have been a mere burlesque of the practices observed by the monks.   The source of the rule may be legendary and it may be difficult to determine what its authentic provisions actually were.   But there is a fair measure of resemblance among the texts handed down in Greek or in Ethiopic when compared with the amplified Sahidic original which St Jerome translated by means of an interpreter and which we only know through this translation.   There is probably some foundation for that mitigation of austerity according to the capacity of the subject which Palladius makes so prominent.   The angel-borne tablet is said to have enjoined : " Thou shalt allow each man to eat and drink according to his strength ; and proportionately to the strength of the eaters appoint to them their labours.   And prevent no man either from fasting or eating.   However, assign the tasks that need strength to those who are stronger and eat, and to the weaker and more ascetic such as the weak can manage."   So, too, we have probably a glimpse of the practice actually followed, when Palladius quotes further : " Let them sleep not lying down full length, but let them make sloping chairs easily constructed and put their legs on them and thus sleep in a sitting posture," or again : " As they eat, let them cover their heads with their cowls, lest one brother see another chewing.   A monk is not allowed to talk at meals, nor let his eye wander beyond his plate or the table."   What is certain is that St Benedict's rule, which has shaped nearly all surviving monasticism in the West, borrowed a good deal from Pachomius. Abbot Cuthbert Butler, in his edition of the *Regula S. Benedicti*, makes thirty-two references to St Jerome's *Pachomiana*.

Of all the early saints of the East it is St Pachomius who seems of recent years to have attracted most attention. New discoveries have been made especially of Coptic (*i.e.* Sahidic) texts, though for the most part these unfortunately are only fragmentary. Other MSS. previously neglected have now been collated in many different redactions and languages. The older generation of Bollandists (in the *Acta Sanctorum*, May, vol. iii) did a great deal, but in the seventeenth century no exhaustive research of Oriental sources was possible. Their modern representatives, however, have recently published a thoroughly satisfactory edition of *St Pachomii Vitæ Græcæ* (1932), edited by Père F. Halkin, S.J. With this great advance may be associated the not less important study of L. T. Lefort, *S. Pachomii Vitæ Sahidice Scriptæ*, which has been published in two parts in the *Corpus Scriptorum Christianorum Orientalium* (1933 and 1934), as also in the same series Lefort's edition of a Bohairic Life of Pachomius (1925). Another recent piece of research is that of Dom A. Boon, O.S.B., *Pachomiana Latina*, an essay on St Jerome's translation of the Rule with an appendix on the Greek and Coptic versions. Amongst a multitude of somewhat older studies the essay of F. Ladeuze, *Le Cénobitisme Pakhômien*, deserves special mention, and Dom H. Leclercq, in his long article " Monachisme," in the *Dictionnaire d'Archéologie et de Liturgie*, vol. xi (1933), especially in *cc.* 1807–1831, has brought together a number of valuable bibliographical references. There are also biographies, with slight variations, in Syriac and Arabic. M. Amélineau, who was among the first to take account of the Coptic texts, published in 1887 an *Étude historique sur S. Pachôme*. Some rationalist critics, laying stress upon the fact that the saint is said before his baptism to have resided in a little temple of Serapis, have sought to draw the inference that the whole monastic idea was an importation from paganism ; but, as Ladeuze and others have pointed out, Pachomius lived there after his thoughts had been turned to Christianity. The building referred to was probably only an abandoned shrine. In spite, however, of the research bestowed upon the subject, the life and work of St Pachomius still remain very much of a problem, as such an authority as Père Peeters (see the *Analecta Bollandiana*, vol. lii, 1934, pp. 286–320) is the first to confess.

ST GERONTIUS, Bp.

A.D. 501

All that is known of St Gerontius is that he was Bishop of Cervia (Ficocle) in the archdiocese of Ravenna, and that he was murdered by " ungodly men "—presumably bandits—at Cagli, on the Flaminian Way, near Ancona, as he was returning from a synod in Rome, presided over by Pope Symmachus. A Benedictine Abbey, dedicated to him, was afterwards erected on the spot where he fell, and the Church honours him as a martyr.

What the Bollandists are able to tell us regarding St Gerontius has much more to do with his cult than with his personal history. See the *Acta Sanctorum*, May, vol. ii, and Ughelli, *Italia Sacra*, vol. ii, *c.* 486. The saint is locally held in great honour.

BLESSED NICHOLAS ALBERGATI, Cardinal

A.D. 1443

Even before 1744, when his cult was formally approved, Blessed Nicholas Albergati was held in great veneration by the Carthusians and by the Augustinians. A Bolognese of good family, he had begun to study for the law, but decided, at the age of twenty, to enter the Carthusian Order. He rose to be superior of several houses, and in

1417 the clergy and citizens of Bologna chose him for their bishop—a dignity which only the express command of his superiors could induce him to accept. He always retained his monastic austerity, lived simply in a small house and sought out the poor in their homes. Pope Martin V and his successors in the Chair of St Peter charged him with important diplomatic missions which he accomplished with conspicuous success. In 1426 he was raised to the dignity of a cardinal. Thomas Parentucelli of Sarzana, whom he had educated, chose the name of Nicholas when he was elected Pope, out of gratitude and veneration for his generous patron. So great was the Cardinal's reputation as a mediator where feuds had broken out that he was sent as papal legate to foreign courts as well as to Italian states that were at variance, and received the surname of "the Angel of Peace." In the capacity of papal legate he took part in the Council of Bâle, and he also opened the Council of Ferrara where, and at Florence, he had much to do with the reconciliation of the Greeks. Pope Eugenius IV held him in the highest esteem ; he consulted him in almost all things, made him Grand Penitentiary, and came to see him frequently when he was ill.

Blessed Nicholas died in Siena, when visiting a house belonging to the Augustinians, whose Protector he was. Although it was an unprecedented thing for a Pope to attend the obsequies of a cardinal, Eugenius IV took part in the funeral services for his Grand Penitentiary at Bologna, being present also at his actual burial. Cardinal Albergati was a great patron of learning and the author of several literary works.

A full biography as well as a panegyric will be found in the *Acta Sanctorum*, May, vol. ii, and another panegyric in the *Analecta Bollandiana*, vol. vii (1888), pp. 381–386. A long account is also given in Le Couteulx, *Annales Ordinis Carthusiani*, vol. vii. See further Pastor, *Geschichte der Päpste*, vol. i.

MAY 10

ST ANTONINUS, Abp.

A.D. 1459

OF all the numerous prelates who through many centuries
have ruled the diocese of Florence, no one has ever gained
so great and lasting a hold upon the loving veneration of
the Florentines as St Antoninus. His father, a citizen of good
family, who was notary to the republic, was called Nicholas Pierozzi,
and he himself received in baptism the name of Anthony. The
diminutive, *Antonino*, which clung to him all his life, was given him
in childhood because of his small stature and gentle disposition.
A serious boy, much addicted to prayer, he loved to listen to the
sermons of Blessed John Dominic, then Prior of Santa Maria
Novella, and when he was fifteen he asked the friar to admit him
to the Dominican Order. The saintly Prior, judging him too
weakly for the life, tried to put him off by bidding him study on for
a time and learn the *Decretum Gratiani*, but when, within a year, the
lad returned, having committed the whole of the treatise to memory,
he was received without further hesitation. He was actually the
first postulant to take the habit in the new Priory at Fiesole, which
Blessed John Dominic had built. For the noviciate Antonino was
sent to Cortona, where he had as novice master Blessed Lawrence of
Ripafratta and as companions Blessed Peter Capucci and the future
great artist Fra Angelico da Fiesole. Antoninus early gave evidence
of exceptional gifts as a scholar and as a leader of men. He was
chosen, when very young, to govern the great convent of the Minerva
in Rome; and afterwards he was successively prior at Naples,
Cajeta, Cortona, Siena, Fiesole and Florence. As Superior of the
reformed Tuscan and Neapolitan Congregations and also as Provincial of the whole Roman province he zealously enforced the measures
initiated by Blessed John Dominic with a view to restoring the
primitive rule. At Florence in 1436 he founded the famous Convent
of San Marco in buildings taken over from the Silvestrini, but
practically rebuilt by him after designs by Michelozzi and decorated
with the frescoes of Fra Angelico.

The adjacent late thirteenth-century church was rebuilt with great magnificence by Cosimo de' Medici, "the father of his country," to serve the new Dominican house. In addition to his official duties, St Antoninus preached often and wrote works which made him famous among his contemporaries. He was consulted from Rome and from all quarters, especially in intricate cases of canon law. Pope Eugenius summoned him to attend the General Council of Florence, at which a reconciliation was effected between the Catholic and Eastern Churches, and he assisted at all its sessions. He was occupied with reforming houses in the province of Naples when he learnt, to his dismay, that the Pope had nominated him to be Arch-bishop of Florence. In vain did he plead incapacity, ill-health and advancing years ; the Holy Father was inflexible and left him no freedom of choice. He was consecrated in March 1446 amid the rejoicings of the citizens.

In his new capacity St Antoninus continued to practise all the observances of his rule—as far as his duties would permit. The most rigid simplicity reigned where he resided : his household consisted of six persons only : he had no plate or horses : even the one mule which served the needs of the whole establishment was often sold to assist the poor, but as often bought back by some well-to-do citizen and restored to its charitable owner. He gave audience daily to all comers whilst declaring himself especially the protector of the poor, at whose disposal he kept his purse and granaries. When these were exhausted he gave away his furniture and his clothes. To assist the needy who were ashamed to beg, he established the College of St Martin, which has been the means of supporting thousands of families in reduced circumstances.

Although naturally gentle, the saint was firm and courageous when the honour of God demanded it. He put down all gambling in his diocese, was the determined foe of both usury and magic, and reformed abuses of all kinds. In addition to preaching nearly every Sunday and festival, he visited his whole diocese once a year—always on foot. His reputation for wisdom and integrity was such that he was unceasingly consulted by those in authority, laymen as well as ecclesiastics ; and his decisions were so judicious that they won for him the title of "the Counsellor." When Pope Eugenius IV was dying, he summoned Antoninus to Rome, received from him the last sacraments and died in his arms. Nicholas V sought his advice on matters of Church and State, forbade any appeal to be made to Rome from any of the Archbishop's judgements and declared that Antoninus in his lifetime was as worthy of canonisation as the dead Bernardino (da Siena), whom he was about to raise to the altars of the Church. Pius II nominated him to a small commission charged with reforming the Roman court. In no less esteem was he held by the Florentine government, who charged him with important embassies on behalf of the republic and would have sent him as their representative to the Emperor if illness had not prevented him from leaving Florence. During a severe epidemic of plague which lasted over a year, the saintly archbishop laboured untiringly to assist the sufferers, inspiring by his example the clergy regular and secular to do the same. Very many of the friars of Santa Maria Novella, Fiesole and San Marco were carried off, and religious to fill the convents had to be procured from the houses of the Order in Lombardy. As usual, famine followed upon the heels of the epidemic. The saint stripped himself of almost everything and obtained substantial relief for the victims from the Pope, who never refused him any request. For two or three years from 1453 Florence was shaken by frequent earthquakes and a violent storm wrought havoc in one quarter of the city. St Antoninus maintained the most distressed of the victims, rebuilt their houses and gave them a fresh start. He also cured a number of sick persons, for all knew that he possessed the gift of miracles. Cosimo de' Medici publicly asserted that the preservation of the republic from the dangers which threatened it was largely due to the merits and prayers of the holy archbishop. God called him to his reward on May 2, 1459, in his seventieth year, and Pope Pius II, who was in Florence at the time, assisted at his funeral.

In the *Acta Sanctorum*, May, vol. i, there is printed a Life of St Antoninus by Francis Castiglione, one of the Archbishop's household, together with a supplement by Leonard de Seruberti, O.P., and some extracts from the process of canonisation. There are a good many other sources of information in the chronicles, correspondence, diaries, etc., of the period, few of which were accessible in the seventeenth century. By far the best attempt to utilise these materials is that made by the Abbé Raoul Morçay in his substantial work, *Saint Antonin, fondateur du couvent de Saint-Marc, archévêque de Florence*, 1914. This is a very satisfactory biography, embodying many details which were recorded by the Archbishop's notary, Baldovino Baldovini, in a memoir which has only come to light in recent years. A shorter account of the Saint has been contributed to the series " Les Saints " by A. Masseron in 1926. See also the many references to St Antoninus in vol. i of Pastor's *Geschichte der Päpste* (vol. ii of the English translation) and also in Père Mortier's *Histoire des Maîtres Généraux O.P.* On the literary work of the Saint the *Dictionnaire de Théologie* may be consulted (vol. i, *cc.* 1451–1453), and also J. B. Walker, *The Chronicles of St Antoninus* (1933), who covers rather more ground than Schaube, the first and more scholarly explorer in this field. For a fuller bibliography dealing with the early literature see Taurisano, *Catalogus Hagiographicus O.P.*

ST CALEPODIUS, Mart.

A.D. 222

The reputed founder of the Roman cemetery which bears his name, St Calepodius was a Roman priest who, according to the legendary Acts of Pope Callistus, suffered martyrdom during the reign of Alexander Severus as the result of a fanatical attack by the populace upon the Christians. He was decapitated and his body was cast into the Tiber, from whence it was rescued and brought to Pope Callistus by a fisherman who had caught it in his net. Amongst a number of companions who are said to have perished in the same outbreak were the consul Palmatius, his family and forty-two members of his household, the senator Simplicius, with sixty-eight of his dependents, and a couple named Felix and Blandina. The reputed relics of St Calepodius are to be found in the Roman churches of St Maria in Trastevere and San Pancrazio, as well as in the cathedral of Taranto.

There was undoubtedly a small catacomb which bore the name of Calepodius situated on the Via Aurelia, three miles from the city, and there is early and trustworthy evidence that Pope St Callistus I was buried there. Beyond that we know very little. See Duchesne, *Liber Pontificalis*, vol. i, pp. 141–142 ; Delehaye's commentary on the *Hieronymianum* (for November 13), pp. 555–556 ; and Dom Leclercq in *Dictionnaire d'Archéologie*, vol. ii, cc. 1593–1595.

SS. ALPHIUS and Companions, Marts.

A.D. 251

The principal patrons of Vaste in the diocese of Otranto, and of Lentini, in Sicily, are SS. Alphius, Philadelphus and Cyrinus, who were martyred at the latter place and were probably natives of the former. The various accounts of them which have come down to us are conflicting and quite unreliable. According to one legend, they and their sister St Benedicta, after being well instructed in the Christian faith by their father and a certain Onesimus, were apprehended with a number of companions during the Decian persecution and were taken to Rome. There they endured severe torture and were then removed to Pozzuoli, near Naples, where Onesimus and some of the party suffered martyrdom. The rest were transferred to Sicily and again tried and tortured. Their bold confession of faith caused the conversion of many spectators, including twenty soldiers.

Eventually Alphius, who was twenty-two, died as the result of having his tongue torn out, Philadelphus, who was twenty-one, was roasted to death, and Cyrinus, who was nineteen, was boiled to death in a vessel full of hot pitch. In 1517 three bodies were discovered, and being identified with these saints, were elevated with great pomp at Lentini—a town seventeen miles south-west of Catania.

Although these alleged martyrs are duly entered in the Roman Martyrology, and their story occupies altogether some sixty folio pages in the *Acta Sanctorum* (May, vol. ii), there is no reliable evidence of early cultus. Their " Acts " must be regarded as nothing better than a pious Greek romance. See *Dictionnaire d'Hist. et Géog. eccles.*, vol. ii, c. 676.

SS. GORDIAN AND EPIMACHUS, MARTS.

A.D. 250 AND 362 (?)

Practically speaking, all the martyrologies, etc., of the Western Church from the sixth century onwards make mention of SS. Gordian and Epimachus, who are also commemorated in the Roman Martyrology on this day. Epimachus is said to have been thrown into a lime kiln at Alexandria in 250 with a certain Alexander, after they had endured cruel tortures for the faith. The body of St Epimachus was subsequently taken to Rome. In the reign of Julian the Apostate, St Gordian was beheaded in Rome and his body was placed with that of St Epimachus in the same tomb. The greater part of their remains were afterwards given by Bd. Hildegard, Charlemagne's wife, to the Abbey of Kempten, in Bavaria, which she had restored. The so-called " Acts " of these two saints are spurious.

In contrast to the martyrs last mentioned, the historic existence and cult of SS. Gordian and Epimachus can raise no doubts. The epitaph of Pope Damasus on St Gordian is still preserved to us, and describes the martyr as little more than a boy, whereas the legendary " Acts " present him as having been the " vicarius," the responsible minister, of the Emperor Julian. See on the whole matter the text and notes of Père Delehaye's Commentary on the *Hieronymianum*, May 10, p. 244. The Acts are printed in the *Acta Sanctorum*, May, vol. ii. There seems no sufficient reason to suppose, as Butler does, that the two martyrs were separated by a century in time. *Cf.* J. P. Kirsch, *Der Stadtrömische christliche Festkalender*, pp. 54–55.

ST COMGALL, ABBOT

c. A.D. 601

St Comgall is commonly reckoned one of the four founders of Irish monasticism, the others being St Columbkill, St Mochuda and St Ailbhe. He was born in Ulster of noble parents about the year 516, and spent some years under the direction of St Fintan in the monastery of Cluain Eidnech or Clonenagh at the foot of the Slieve Bloom range. He was ordained priest by a certain Bishop Lugid, who is said to have deterred him from dedicating himself to missionary work in Great Britain. For a time he retired to an island in Lough Erne where he and some companions practised such austerities that seven of them died of hunger and cold. In response to the remonstrances of Bishop Lugid, Comgall relaxed his rule for his disciples, though not for himself. Emerging from his retreat, he founded the great Abbey of Benchor, or Bangor, which became the largest and most famous monastery in Ireland. No less than three thousand monks are said to have lived under the government of St Comgall at Bangor and in its daughter houses. Dividing their time between their religious exercises and manual work, they led a most mortified life in accordance with a rule composed by St Comgall on the model of that of St Basil. The holiest men of the age sought the friendship of the Abbot of Bangor and great saints owed their training to him—notably St Columbanus, who afterwards carried the tradition of Bangor to France and Italy. St Comgall seems to have carried out his early missionary aspirations by accompanying St Columbkill, the apostle of Caledonia, and St Cainnech on an expedition to Iona and Inverness where they preached the Gospel to a Pictish chieftain called Brude. On his way home he is stated to have visited Wales and to have founded there a monastery in a place called the Land of Heth. St. Comgall continued to rule Bangor until his death, although during the last years of his life he endured terrible sufferings—apparently as the result of his great austerities. He also became totally deaf. He died in 601 after receiving the holy viaticum from St Fiachra of Congbuil.

There is a Latin life of St Comgall which is printed in the *Acta Sanctorum*, May, vol. II, and also in C. Plummer's *Vitæ Sanctorum Hiberniæ*, vol. ii, pp. 3–21. The rule attributed to St Comgall, or what purports to be a metrical version of it, has been edited by J. Strachan in the periodical *Eriu*, vol. i (1904), pp. 191–208. See also J. Ryan, *Irish Monasticism* (1931), and Dom Gougaud, *Christianity in Celtic Lands* (1933), in both of which works many references to St Comgall and his monks will be found in the index. In A. P. Forbes' *Kalendars of Scottish Saints* there is a lengthy

account of St Comgall (pp. 308–310) drawn largely from the legends of the
Aberdeen Breviary. A curious alphabetical hymn in honour of the saint
(" *Hymnus sancti Comgilli Abbatis nostri* ") occurs in the *Bangor Antiphonary*
(H. Bradshaw Society, 1895, vol. ii, pp. 16–19, and notes). The D stanza
runs thus :

> Doctus in Dei legibus : divinis dictionibus,
> Dilatus sanctis opibus, Deo semper placentibus,
> Dedicatus in moribus : Dei Stephanus hagius
> Docebat sic et cæteros : Dicta docta operibus.

The date of this MS. can be accurately fixed as between A.D. 680 and 691.
One living word of St Comgall's seems to have been preserved in a gloss
upon the *Félire* of Œngus ; in reference to the death of his confessor, he
remarked : " My soul-friend has died and I am headless, and ye, too, are
headless, for a man without a soul-friend is a body without a head."

ST CATALDUS, Bp. of Tarentum

c. A.D. 685 (?)

St Cataldus was a learned Irish monk who for some time presided
over the great school of Lismore after the death of its founder,
St Carthach. Resigning his post with a view to seeking greater
retirement, he undertook a pilgrimage to Jerusalem. On his way
home he was chosen bishop of Tarentum or Taranto, not in the sixth
century as certain Italian writers have asserted, much less in the
second, but towards the close of the seventh. He is said to have
restored the faith—possibly the Roman rite—after the expulsion of
the Greeks in 671. St Cataldus is titular saint of Taranto cathedral,
being reckoned the second bishop of the diocese.

This is another of those cases in which we know next to nothing of the
life of the saint, but have long accounts of the veneration paid to what were
believed to be his relics. See the *Acta Sanctorum*, May, vol. ii ; O'Hanlon,
Lives of the Irish Saints, vol. v, p. 185, and Ughelli, *Italia Sacra*, vol. ix,
cc. 162–168. He was honoured also at Seurre and Auxerre in France (where
he is called " St Cartault ") because some portion of his relics are said to
have been brought there. On the obscure question of the date at which he
lived, consult Kenney, *The Sources for the Early History of Ireland*, vol. i,
p. 185.

ST SOLANGIA, Virg. and Mart.

A.D. 880

St Solangia, who is sometimes called the St Geneviève of Berry,
is also the patroness of that province of France. The child of

pious vine-dressers, poorly endowed with this world's goods, she was born at Villemont, near Bourges. She dedicated herself to God from early childhood and took a vow of chastity at the age of seven. Her occupation was to mind her father's sheep as they grazed on the pasturages. It is said that she was always attended by a guiding star which shone over her head with special brilliancy as the hour of prayer approached. Besides having a great power over animals, she was endowed with the gift of healing and effected many cures. Reports of her beauty and sanctity reached the ears of Bernard, one of the sons of the Count of Poitiers, and he came on horseback to make advances to her as she was alone with her flock. When she resisted, he caught her up and set her in the saddle before him, but she succeeded in slipping from his horse, sustaining serious injury in her fall. The young man then despatched her with his sword or with his hunting-knife. According to the legend, the girl afterwards arose and carried her head in her hands as far as the Church of St Martin-du-Cros, in the cemetery of which an altar was erected in her honour about the year 1281. A field near her home in which she liked to pray received the name of " Le Champ de Sainte Solange." The martyr is specially invoked in times of drought.

That St Solangia (Solange) has enjoyed much popular veneration in Bourges and surrounding districts is made clear by the number of devotional brochures published about her. See, for example, the *Vie de S. Solange*, written by Joseph Bernard, which has appeared in more than one edition. There is an account of this martyr in the *Acta Sanctorum*, May, vol. ii, but the evidence there furnished is very unsatisfactory.

BLESSED BEATRICE OF ESTE, Virg.

A.D. 1226

The childhood of Blessed Beatrice of Este cannot have been a happy one. Her mother died when she was an infant, her father the Marchese Azzo of Este, when she was six; and her elder brother, Aldobrandinus, who was her natural protector, was poisoned when she was ten. The charge of the little girl devolved partly on her stepmother and partly on a paternal aunt. From the time of her father's death Beatrice would only wear the simplest clothes, absolutely refusing to put on the adornments which belonged to a girl of her rank. As she approached a marriageable age her relations, desirous of extending the power of the great house of Este, began to consider a suitable match for her, in spite of her protestations that she wished to live the religious life. Despairing of overcoming the opposition of her surviving brother, Beatrice secretly left home and made her way to the Benedictine Abbey of Solarola, where she received the habit at the age of fourteen. A year and a half later, she and ten other sisters were transferred to Gemola, a quiet place less exposed to warlike attacks and worldly interruptions. There Beatrice spent the remainder of her short life, dying when she was in her twentieth year. In 1578 her relics were translated to Padua, where they are held in great veneration. Her cult was approved in 1763.

A life by a contemporary, one Albert of the Holy Ghost, a religious at Verona, was printed for the first time by G. Brunacci in 1767. The narrative in the *Acta Sanctorum* is translated from the Italian of Bishop Tomasini who wrote in the middle of the seventeenth century. See also P. Balan, *La Beata Beatrice d' Este* (1878).

BLESSED JOHN OF AVILA, CONF.

A.D. 1569

Amongst the great religious leaders of sixteenth century Spain, one of the most influential and certainly the most eloquent was Blessed John of Avila, the friend of St Ignatius Loyola and the spiritual adviser of St Theresa, St John of God, St Francis Borgia, St Peter of Alcantara and of Luis of Granada who became his biographer. He was born in New Castile at Almodovar-del-Campo of wealthy parents, who sent him, at the age of fourteen, to Salamanca University to prepare to take up law. A worldly career, however, had no attraction for the boy and he returned home where for three years he gave himself up to devotional exercises and austerities. Then, at the suggestion of a mendicant Franciscan who was greatly impressed by his piety, he went to Alcalà to study philosophy and theology. There he had as his master the celebrated Dominican Soto : there also he laid the foundation of a life-long friendship with Peter Guerrero, afterwards Archbishop of Granada. His parents died while he was still at Alcalà, leaving him their sole heir, but no sooner had he been ordained priest than he distributed the proceeds of his inheritance to the poor. From the moment he began to preach it was clear that he possessed extraordinary oratorical powers, and when he expressed a desire to go as a missionary to Mexico, the Archbishop of Seville bade him remain in Spain and evangelise his fellow countrymen. Appointed missioner for Andalusia he laboured indefatigably for nine years in this great province. Rich and poor, young and old, learned and unlearned, saints and sinners—all flocked to hear him. Countless souls were brought by him to penance and amendment of life, whilst many were led into the path of perfection under his direction. When he preached, he spoke like one inspired and, indeed, the only preparation he ever made for his sermons was his daily meditation of four hours. To a young priest who asked him how to become a good preacher, he replied that the only way he knew of was to love God very much.

By his fearless denunciation of vice in high places, he made for himself some bitter enemies who actually succeeded in obtaining his imprisonment by the Inquisition at Seville on a charge of preaching rigorism and the exclusion of the rich from the Kingdom of Heaven. The accusation could not be substantiated, and his first public appearance after his release was made the occasion for an extraordinary popular ovation. When his time in Andalusia was completed, Blessed John devoted himself to giving what were practically missions in all parts of Spain, but especially in the cities. Moreover, he kept up a vast correspondence with his spiritual children and with other persons who desired his advice. For the last seventeen years of his life he was in constant pain which he bore with unflinching patience. Of his writings the most celebrated are a collection of his letters and a treatise entitled *Audi Filia* which he drew up for Doña Sancha Carillo, a rich and beautiful young woman who, under his direction, had given up great worldly prospects at court to lead a life of prayer and solitude under her father's roof.

Our best sources of information are the *Summarium de Virtutibus* in the process of beatification ; the writings of Blessed John himself and the sketch of his life written by his friend and contemporary, Luis de Granada. His writings may most conveniently be consulted in the bulky work—there are 2199 pages—*Obras del B. Maestro Juan de Avila*, published at Madrid in 1927. His spiritual letters are regarded as one of the classics of Spanish literature and were reprinted as such in the series of *Classicos Castellanos*, by Don Vincente Garcia de Diego, in 1912. The preface of this last-named volume is also a valuable contribution, especially from the point of view of chronology, to the biography of this master of the spiritual life. Ever since his beatification in 1924 the Society of Jesus has kept his feast almost as that of one of her own members, and indeed, as Don Vincente Garcia shows, Blessed John had fully determined at the age of fifty-nine to enter the Society, but was deterred by the rigorism and rather extravagant attitude of Father Bustamente, the then Provincial of Andalusia. His devotion to the Order and its Founder, however, did not in any way slacken. He was attended by a Jesuit Father in his last hours and left his body to be buried in their church at Montilla. His Life, by Father degli Oddi, S.J., has been translated into English (1898). A more recent Life, by Père J. M. De Buck, S.J., appeared at Louvain in 1927. Finally a small collection of his letters was translated by the Benedictine nuns of Stanbrook and published in 1904 with a preface by Cardinal Gasquet. Blessed John's gifts as a sacred orator cannot fairly be judged by his extant sermons, which for the most part are merely imperfect reports taken down by his auditors.

MAY 11

ST MAMERTUS, Archbishop of Vienne

c. A.D. 475

WE do not know much about the life of St Mamertus. He was the elder brother of Claudianus, the poet, author of *De Statu Animæ*, whom he ordained priest, and both brothers seem to have enjoyed a deserved reputation for learning as well as piety. Claudianus is also said to have helped him as Vicar General in the discharge of his episcopal duties. In 463 trouble arose in connexion with the consecration of a bishop to the see of Die, which Pope Leo not long before had transferred from the province of Vienne to that of Arles. The Burgundian King Gondioc complained to Pope Hilary that Mamertus, without justification, had consecrated a new bishop for Die. By order of the Pope, a council of twenty bishops was held at Arles to inquire into the matter and a report was sent to Rome. Though Hilary wrote rather severely and declared that Mamertus deserved to be deposed for this usurpation, no change was, in fact, made, and the new Bishop of Die was allowed to retain his see after confirmation from Arles. Somewhat later than this we learn that Mamertus translated to Vienne the remains of the holy martyr Ferreolus who had been put to death in that part of the country a century or two earlier (see under September 18). But that which more than anything else has made the name of St Mamertus famous in ecclesiastical history is his institution of the penitential processions on what we now call the " Rogation Days," the three days preceding the feast of the Ascension. These are the *Litaniæ Minores*, which in the time of Pope Leo III (795–816), were adopted in Rome itself, Frankish influence, under the Emperor Charlemagne, thus making itself felt throughout the whole of Western Christendom.

That St Mamertus was the real author of the Rogation processions is proved by an abundance of early testimony. We have a letter addressed to Mamertus himself by St Sidonius Apollinaris, in which he speaks of these supplications which the Archbishop had instituted and which had proved so efficacious a remedy in the panic which had seized upon all the populace. He enlarges at the same time on the courage this true shepherd of his people had shown by standing his ground when others were taking to flight. St Avitus, who himself became Archbishop of Vienne only fifteen years after Mamertus's death and who, as a child, had received baptism at his hands, preached a homily, still preserved to us, on one of the occasions when the Rogation processions came round. From him we learn in some detail of the tribulations with which the country had been afflicted at the time of their institution. He speaks of shocks of earthquake, of repeated conflagrations and of the wild deer taking refuge in the busy haunts of men. Very naturally, according to the ideas of the period, St Mamertus had interpreted these calamities as the judgement of God upon the sins of the people, and the remedy he proposed was entirely of a penitential character. He obliged all to fast and to join in a long and laborious procession of young and old to the cathedral during which many psalms were sung. What is certain is that the example set at Vienne was almost immediately followed in other parts of France and in time became universal in the West. At the first council of Orleans, held in 511, the twenty-seventh decree prescribes that all the churches are to celebrate these three Rogation days before the feast of the Ascension. A strict fast is to be kept on all three days as in the time of Lent, no work is to be done, even by those of servile condition, in order that they may be free to be present in church and take part in the processions ; in particular all clerics who absent themselves from these offices are to be punished as the bishop in each case may direct. From the writings of contemporaries or of such historians as St Gregory of Tours, it is clear that Mamertus was looked upon not only as a holy and self-sacrificing pastor of souls, but also as a leader who possessed both tact and courage. St Avitus, in his homily, is full of admiration for the sound judgement he displayed in reconciling both the secular officials and the people to an observance which imposed so heavy a tax upon their good will.

St Avitus, in the sermon just referred to, shows himself to have been an orator of real power. He paints with admirable force the advantages of collective prayer. The weak take courage from their contact with the strong ; the timid are no longer self-conscious when they are units in a crowd all animated with the same purpose. He insists that we must be bold in our appeal for help ; we must take Heaven by storm. It is our Lord Himself who has said : " Ask and you shall receive, seek and you shall find, knock and it shall be opened to you." Finally he concludes in his peroration : " You must clamour in the accents of supplication ; and if while the danger increases He still remains deaf, you must knock with unsparing

hands. You must say to Him : 'Arise, why sleepest Thou,
O Lord ? arise and cast us not off at the end. Why turnest Thou
Thy face away, and forgettest our want and our trouble ? ' No doubt,
when He is awakened, He will only say : ' Why art thou fearful,
O thou of little faith ? ' But if He does but restore you to safety
again, let Him scold your faint-heartedness as much as He will.
If our faith is weak because we dread earthly perils, still the fact
that we have recourse to Him shows that some glimmer of faith is
there. Wherefore if we have not said to Christ : ' Watch Thou,
while we watch with Thee,' at least let us say : ' Wake up, for our
sakes.' We forgot to ask Him not to leave us, let us appeal to
Him to come back and not desert us on this blundering passage of
ours, until He calms the winds and the waves, and by a speedy
ending stills the mad turbulence of the world around us.''

In the *Acta Sanctorum*, May, vol. ii, nearly all the early references to
St Mamertus will be found collected. As to the Rogation Days, see Kellner,
Heortology (English translation), pp. 189–194, but Mr. Edmund Bishop does
well to point out (*Liturgica Historica*, pp. 128–130), that we must be on our
guard against attaching to the word '' Litanies,'' as used in connection with
the Rogations, the meaning which it bears now. '' So far as I can read,'' he
says, '' there is no indication whatever that litanies were at the first institution sung on these three days at all.'' '' In a word,'' he adds, '' so far as the
original testimonies go, the substance of the devotion of the Rogations was
psalm-singing, with, perhaps, the prayers or collects which in some quarters
accompanied the singing of psalms.'' Cf. also Abbot Cabrol's article
'' Litanies,'' in the *Dictionnaire d'Archéologie*, etc., as well as what has
previously been said in earlier volumes of this present work—February,
pp. 31–36, and April, p. 285.

ST GENGULPHUS, Conf.

A.D. 760

St Gengulphus, or Gengoul, was a noble Burgundian knight, so
greatly beloved by Pepin the Short, at that time Mayor of the Palace,
that he used to sleep in the great man's tent during his campaigns.
Gengulphus is said to have been married to a woman of rank in
whom for a long time he trusted, but she proved scandalously
unfaithful to him. Finding remonstrances and appeals useless, he
quietly withdrew from her to a castle of his in Burgundy after making
suitable provision for her maintenance. There he spent his time
in penitential exercises and his money in alms. He died—so the
legend avers—from a wound inflicted by his wife's lover who, at
her instigation, broke in upon him one night to murder him as he

lay in bed. The fame of St Gengulphus afterwards spread to
Holland, Belgium and Savoy as the result of the distribution of his
relics and the miracles with which he was credited.

The short biography printed in the *Acta Sanctorum*, May, vol. ii, seems
to be largely fabulous ; it has been critically edited by W. Levison in the
Monumenta Germaniæ, Scrip. rer. Meroving., vol. vii, pp. 142 *seq.* The
famous nun, Hroswitha of Gandersheim, at the close of the tenth century,
wrote an account of the martyrdom in elegiac verse (see Winterfeld's edition
of her works, 1902, pp. 32 *seq.*). The cultus of St Gengulphus was widespread both in France and Germany. For his representation in art consult
Künstle, *Ikonographie*, vol. ii, pp. 258–259, and for the folk-lore which has
gathered round his name Bächtold-Stäubli, *Handwörterbuch des deutschen
Aberglaubens*, vol. iii, pp. 289–290.

ST MAJOLUS (MAIEUL), Abbot

A.D. 994

Provence in the early part of the tenth century suffered terribly
from the incursions of the Saracens, and St Majolus, who at an
early age was left heir to large estates near Riez, was obliged to take
refuge with relatives of his who lived at Mâcon, in Burgundy.
There he received the tonsure and a canonry from his uncle Bishop
Berno, by whom he was afterwards sent to Lyons to study philosophy
under a celebrated master, Antony, Abbot of L'Isle Barbe. Upon
his return to Mâcon he was made archdeacon, although he was still
young, and when the see of Besançon fell vacant, he was selected to
fill it. To avoid being forcibly consecrated to a dignity for which he
felt himself unfitted, he fled to the Abbey of Cluny, to which his
father had been a great benefactor. There he received the habit
and was appointed by the Abbot Aimard librarian and apocrisarius.
In this double capacity he not only had direction of the studies
and care of the treasury, but he also conducted all important business
outside the monastery. In the course of the various journeys he was
obliged to make, he won golden opinions for his humility and wisdom.
As St Berno*, the first abbot of Cluny, had chosen St Odo to be his
coadjutor, and St Odo in his turn had selected Aimard, so Aimard,
when he lost his sight, raised St Majolus to the dignity of joint abbot.
His wisdom and virtue gained him the respect of all the princes of
the age. The Emperor Otto the Great placed entire confidence in
him and gave him supervision over all the monasteries in Germany

---

* Berno was not then an uncommon name, and it may be well to point
out that Berno, first Abbot of Cluny, was quite a different person from the
Berno, Bishop of Mâcon, mentioned above.

and other parts of the empire. The Empress St Adelaide and her son Otto II had no less esteem for the holy Abbot, who succeeded in reconciling them when they were at variance. By virtue of the immense privileges bestowed through him upon the Congregation of which he was the head, he was able to reform a great number of monasteries, many of which adopted the Cluniac rule. The Emperor was anxious that he should be chosen Pope, but could not overcome his opposition. To all that could be urged he replied that he knew how little fitted he was to fill so high an office and how different his manners were from those of the Romans. A man of great scholarship, he did much to foster true learning. Three years before his death he appointed St Odilo as his coadjutor and from that time gave himself up to the exercises of penance and contemplation. He could not, however, disregard the express request of Hugh Capet, King of France, that he would undertake a journey to settle reforms in the Abbey of St Denis, near Paris. On the way thither he fell ill and died at the Abbey of Souvigny on May 11, 994. At his funeral which took place in the church of St Peter at Cluny, the King of France himself was present.

There is abundant material for the life of St Majolus. Three separate biographies of early date are printed in the *Acta Sanctorum*, May, vol. ii, a compendious account of which is furnished in the *Bibliotheca Hagiographica Latina*, nn. 5177–5187. Upon the complicated problem of the relations of these lives a valuable note was contributed by L. Traube to the *Neues Archiv.*, vol. xvii (1892), pp. 402–407. See also J. H. Pignot, *Histoire de l'Ordre de Cluny*, vol. i, pp. 236–303 ; E. Sackur, *Die Cluniazenser*, vol. i, pp. 205–256 ; S. Hilpisch, *Geschichte des Ben. Mönchtums*, pp. 170 *seq.* A hymn written by St Odilo on St Majolus has been printed by Dom G. Morin in the *Revue Bénédictine*, vol. xxxviii (1926), pp. 56–57.

ST ANSFRIDUS, OR ANFRID, BISHOP OF UTRECHT

A.D. 1008 OR 1010

In early life St Ansfridus was a distinguished warrior, noted for his success in suppressing brigands and pirates, and for this reason high in the favour of the Emperors Otto III and Henry II. He was a Count of Brabant and when the see of Utrecht fell vacant at the death of Bishop Baldwin the Emperor suggested that he should be appointed to succeed him. In spite of his opposition he was consecrated bishop in 994. He founded a convent for nuns at Thorn near Liége and the Abbey of Hohorst, or Heiligenberg, to which he retired when blindness came upon him. It was there also he died. At the time of his burial a number of the citizens of Utrecht came to Heiligenberg, and seizing their opportunity when the people of the neighbourhood were busily engaged in extinguishing a conflagration which had accidentally (?) broken out at that moment, took possession of the venerated remains and carried them off. When the Heiligen monks discovered their loss, a fierce pursuit was on the point of taking place, but the Abbess of Thorn, by her prayerful entreaties, succeeded in preventing the threatened rescue by force of arms. St Ansfridus accordingly was peacefully interred in his own episcopal cathedral at Utrecht.

What is printed in the *Acta Sanctorum*, May, vol. i, as a fragmentary life of St Ansfridus is in reality merely an extract from the *De Diversitate Temporum* of the Benedictine monk Albert or Alpert of St Symphorian at Metz. He was a contemporary who wrote in 1022, and though he does not tell us very much, the substance of what he says is trustworthy.

ST WALTER (GUALTERIUS or GAUTIER), Abbot

A.D. 1070

St Walter was born at the Castle of Conflans on the Vienne, the chief seat of his family, which was one of the foremost in Aquitaine. For his education he was sent to the Augustinian Canons at Dorat where he had Blessed Israel as his master and where he received the habit. The ill-will of an unreasonable superior led him to retire to Conflans, but he was soon afterwards elected Abbot of L'Esterp— a position he held for thirty-eight years. He had an ardent zeal for souls, and his influence spread far beyond the walls of his monastery. So great was his reputation for converting sinners that Pope Victor II granted him special faculties for dealing with penitents—including the right to excommunicate and to restore to communion. For the last seven years of his life he was blind, but he continued his activities until his death. His biographer tells us that while yet a young monk St Walter made a pilgrimage to Jerusalem in the course of which journey rumour seems to have credited him with some remarkable miracles. Driven to land on a desolate shore, he and his companions had nothing to eat, but a strange bird flew over them and dropped at his feet a fish which was so large that Walter by himself could not even lift it from the ground. So again this gentle saint's compassion for human infirmity and error was unbounded, and when his companions, absorbed in external tasks, forgot that the day was Friday and had prepared a meal of meat, he not only allowed them to eat it, saying that they might count on the indulgence of the great St Martin whose feast it was, but he set them the example by partaking of it himself. One of the company, scandalised and rigorist, hotly denounced this concession, but immediately after lost the whole sum of money he was carrying in his purse, a calamity which the writer treats as a divine rebuke to his self-righteousness.

The biography, ascribed to the famous Bishop Marbod, who was a contemporary, is printed in the *Acta Sanctorum*, May, vol. ii. What is in any case certain is that Abbot Walter is repeatedly referred to by the chroniclers of that age as a man of outstanding holiness, whose undertakings were marvellously blessed by Heaven.

BLESSED ALBERT OF BERGAMO, CONF.

A.D. 1279

Blessed Albert of Bergamo was a peasant farmer who lived an exemplary life amongst his neighbours in the Valle d'Ogna and became a Dominican tertiary. His time was divided between religious exercises and manual labour. Though married he had no children, and he had much to bear from a shrewish wife as well as from other relations who resented his liberality to the poor. In later life he went on pilgrimages to Rome and Jerusalem and is said to have visited Compostella eight times, always supporting himself on the way by the work of his hands. Eventually he settled in Cremona where he became closely associated with another holy man—Blessed Homobonus—and where he died in the year 1279. He was famous in Cremona for his miracles. Some of the wonders which he is said to have worked in his lifetime are certainly of a very remarkable and unusual character. For example, in the *Short Lives of Dominican Saints*, edited by Fr. John Procter, O.P., we read : " One day he was carrying a barrel of wine to the house of a poor woman, when it accidentally slipped from his shoulder and broke to pieces on the road. ' King of Glory, come to my assistance,' exclaimed the holy man, according to his wont in all difficulties. Then he gathered up the broken pieces of wood, adjusted them in their proper places, and collected the spilt wine in his hands so that not a drop was lost."

In the Prato edition of the *Opera Omnia* of Pope Benedict XIV, vol. vi (1842), pp. 35–36, will be found a summary of the evidence presented to establish the fact of the immemorial cultus paid to Blessed Albert of Bergamo. The documents submitted at that time were printed for the Congregation of Rites, and the decree of confirmation is dated May 9, 1748. See also the *Année Dominicaine*, V, (1891), pp. 375–381. A short notice of Blessed Albert will also be found in the *Acta Sanctorum*, May, vol. ii, under May 7.

BD. VIVALDUS, or UBALDO, Hermit

A.D. 1300

St Vivaldus, or Ubaldo, was a disciple and fellow townsman of Blessed Bartolo of San Gemignano whom he nursed for twenty years through a particularly distressing form of leprosy. Afterwards he lived as a solitary inside a hollow chestnut-tree at Montajone, in Tuscany. One day as a huntsman was seeking game in the mountains, his hounds discovered the hermit, who was kneeling in his retreat in an attitude of prayer, but was quite dead. It is stated that at the moment his soul passed to God the bells of Montajone began ringing of themselves and never ceased pealing until the huntsman came in with the news of the discovery of the holy remains. St Vivaldus had been attached to the Third Order of St Francis, and the Observants built a convent on the site where he had lived and died.

The brief account printed in the *Acta Sanctorum*, May, vol. i, seems to contain all that has been recorded of Bd. Vivaldo. The decree by which Pius X, in 1908, confirmed his cultus may be read in the *Analecta Ecclesiastica* for 1908, p. 145, but it adds nothing material to the facts mentioned above. Neither is anything further to be learnt from the article of Father Ghilardi in the *Miscellanea Storica della Valdesa*, vol. xi (1903), pp. 38–42.

BLESSED JULIANUS a VALLE, Conf.

EARLY FOURTEENTH CENTURY (?)

At Valle, in Istria, three feasts are held annually in honour of Blessed Julianus Cesarello a Valle, a local Franciscan whose tomb is greatly venerated. He is principal patron of Castel della Valle and his cultus was confirmed in 1910, but beyond the fact that he was a priest and a very active missionary, nothing is known of his history.

In the decree confirming his cultus which will be found in the *Acta Apostolicæ Sedis*, vol. ii (1910), pp. 159–162, it is freely admitted that the circumstances of his life and the date of his death cannot now be discovered. On the other hand, there are abundant memorials of the veneration paid to him in the district which was the scene of his labours. As the name of this Father Julian is mentioned among other servants of God in a document entitled *Provinciale Ordinis Fratrum Minorum*, which was written about 1343, he must have died at latest in the early part of that century.

BLESSED BENINCASA, HERMIT

A.D. 1426

Blessed Benincasa, a member of one of the great Florentine families, entered the Servite Order at a very early age and when only twenty-five was permitted to embrace the life of a hermit on the mountain of Montagnata, near Siena. There he gave himself up to prayer, but was greatly tried by diabolical assaults. Through a little window he gave spiritual advice to the men who resorted to him—with women he would have no dealings—and healed the sick by the sign of the cross or by holy water. Realising, however, that the devil was tempting him to pride, he retired to another spot much more difficult of access. His death is said to have been announced to the people in the plain by the spontaneous ringing of the church bells and by a light which streamed from his cave.

An account of Bd. Benincasa is given in the *Acta Sanctorum*, May, vol. vii, supplement. This is almost entirely based on Father A. Giani, *Annales Ordinis Servorum*. In the seventeenth century the local veneration of Bd. Benincasa at Montechielo, where he was buried, seems almost to have died out. This was explained at the time by the fact that a rumour was in circulation that his authentic relics had been stolen. The cultus of this Beato was, however, officially sanctioned by Pope Pius VIII in 1829. There is a short modern Life by L. Raffaelli (1927).

BLESSED ALOYSIUS RABATA, CONF.

A.D. 1490

Few incidents seem to have marked the life of Blessed Aloysius Rabata. Admitted to the Carmelite Order as a young man at Trapani, in Sicily, he was afterwards Prior of the friary at Randazzo. He lived on bread and water and was remarkable for his humility, his patience and his zeal for souls. As Superior he insisted upon performing the most lowly tasks, such as road-mending and begging for alms. He took the sins of his penitents so much to heart that when a poor man confessed to a theft for which he was unable to make restitution, his ghostly father himself approached the injured party and with tears continued to implore forgiveness until it was granted. He died from the after-effects of a blow on the head inflicted by a scoundrel whom he refused to bring to justice. He would not even disclose the identity of the perpetrator of the outrage.

A tolerably full notice of this Beato is printed in the *Acta Sanctorum*, May, vol. ii. It is mainly derived from the materials which were collected in 1533 and 1573 with a view to his canonisation. The beatification only took place in the nineteenth century under Pope Gregory XVI.

BLESSED LADISLAUS OF GIELNIOV, Conf.

A.D. 1505

One of the principal patrons of Poland, Galicia and Lithuania is Blessed Ladislaus of Gielniov, a Pole born in the year 1440, who, after being educated in the University of Warsaw, entered the Franciscan Convent of the Strict Observance founded in that city by St John Capistran. He was several times elected Provincial and drew up a revised constitution which received the approbation of the Commissary General at the General Chapter held in Urbino in 1498. At the request of Duke Alexander, grandson of Ladislaus Jagello, he sent out a picked body of friars to evangelise Lithuania. Before they started he warned them that the example of personal holiness must always precede the preaching of the gospel. The mission was greatly blessed : not only were thousands of pagans baptised, but many schismatics were reconciled. Blessed Ladislaus himself was an ardent missioner and a man of great eloquence, and when he was relieved of his office of Provincial and became Guardian of Warsaw he was in great request as a preacher. He delivered sermons in every part of Poland, and wrote both in Latin and in Polish. He also composed hymns which were sung by the people at evening services. His favourite topic was the Passion and his best-loved text " Jesus of Nazareth, the King of the Jews." In 1498 Poland was in great danger : the Tartars had made a league with the Turks and were advancing with an army of 70,000 men. Ladislaus called upon the panic-stricken population to pray and to put their trust in God, who alone could deliver them. The invading army was encamped between the Pruth and the Dniester when suddenly the waters of both rose up in flood, inundating the country. This was followed by an intense frost and then by a blinding snowstorm. Thousands of the enemy's men and horses were drowned, thousands more perished of cold, and the miserable remnant were easily defeated and almost exterminated by the Wallachian Prince Stephen. The victory was generally ascribed to the prayers of Blessed Ladislaus, whose prestige was enormously enhanced. His brethren often beheld him raised from the ground in ecstasy and on the Good Friday before his death, as he was preaching on the Scourging of Our Lord to an immense congregation, he was seen by all to be lifted up into the air and to hang there as though crucified. Afterwards when he slowly sank to the ground he was so weak that he had to be carried to the convent infirmary, where he died a month later, mourned by the whole city.

A very ample Life, published in Latin by the Franciscan Father Vincent Morawski, at the beginning of the seventeenth century, has been reprinted in the *Acta Sanctorum*, May, vol. i. There is also a brief account by Fr. Léon in his *Auréole Séraphique* (Eng. Trans.), vol. iii, pp. 335-337. The *Lexikon für Theologie und Kirche* mentions two modern writers, P. Cz. Bogdalski, and K. Kantak, who, in recent works dealing with the Franciscan missions in Poland, have specially called attention to Bd. Ladislaus. These books, however, are written in Polish.

ST FRANCIS JEROME, Conf.

A.D. 1716

A boundless zeal for the conversion of sinners and a tender love for the poor, the sick and the oppressed were the outstanding characteristics of St Francis Jerome, the eloquent Jesuit missioner whom the inhabitants of the Two Sicilies venerate to this day as, in a special sense, the Apostle of Naples. The eldest of a family of eleven, he was born in 1642 at Grottaglie, near Taranto, in Apulia, and from infancy gave evidence of extraordinary piety. After he had made his first communion at the age of twelve, he was received into the house of some secular priests in the neighbourhood who lived together a community life under the patronage of St Gaetano. The good fathers were not slow to perceive that their young charge was no ordinary boy; from leaving him in charge of their church they promoted him to teaching the catechism and brought him to the notice of the Archbishop of Taranto, who gave him the tonsure when he was barely sixteen. In Taranto, where he studied the humanities, he received minor orders. Then, with a view to learning canon and civil law, he went to Naples in the company of an artistic brother who desired to study under an eminent painter. In 1666 Francis was ordained priest for which a dispensation had to be obtained as he was not yet twenty-four. For the next five years he taught at Naples in the Jesuit Collegio dei Nobili. The impression he made there upon his pupils may be gauged from the fact that the boys habitually spoke of him among themselves as " the holy priest." At the age of twenty-eight, having overcome the opposition of his parents, he entered the Society of Jesus, to which he felt specially called. During the first year of the noviciate he was subjected to exceptionally severe tests by his superiors, who were so completely satisfied that at its close they sent him to help the celebrated preacher Father Agnello Bruno in his mission work. From 1671 till 1674, the two holy priests laboured untiringly and with great success, mainly amongst the simple peasants of the province of Otranto. At the close of that mission Francis was recalled to Naples where he completed his theological studies and was professed. He was now appointed preacher at the Neapolitan church known as the Gesù Nuovo. It was his ardent desire to be sent to Japan, when there was talk of attempting a new missionary effort in that land which had ruthlessly exterminated every Christian teacher who landed on its shores, but he was told by his superiors that he must regard the Kingdom of Naples as his India and Japan. It was, indeed, to be the scene of his untiring activities for the remaining forty years of his life. From the outset his preaching attracted huge congregations and was rewarded by such excellent results that in the Jesuit Mother-house in Naples he was set to train other missionaries. In the provinces he conducted altogether at least 100 Missions, but the people of Naples would never allow him to be long absent from their city, so that this continued to be his headquarters. Wherever he went, men and women hung upon his lips and crowded to his confessional. Innumerable souls were converted by him and led on to amendment of life. It was confidently asserted that at least four hundred hardened sinners were annually reclaimed through his efforts. Not satisfied with preaching in the churches, he would visit the prisons, the hospitals and even the galleys, in one of which— a Spanish one—he brought to the faith twenty Turkish prisoners. Moreover, he did not hesitate to track down sinners to the very haunts of vice, in which it sometimes happened that he was very roughly handled. Often he would preach in the streets—occasionally on the spur of the moment. Once, in the middle of a stormy night, he felt irresistibly moved to turn out and preach in the dark in an apparently deserted part of the town. The following day there came to his confessional a young woman who had been living a sinful life but had been conscience-stricken when through her open window she had heard his stirring appeal of the previous evening. Amid his numerous penitents of all classes, perhaps the most remarkable was a woman, French by birth, called Marie Alvira Cassier. She had murdered her father and had afterwards served in the Spanish army, disguised as a man. Under the direction of St Francis Jerome she not only was brought to penitence, but attained to a high degree of holiness. The effects of the preaching of the holy Jesuit were enhanced by his reputation as a wonder-worker, but he consistently disclaimed any extraordinary powers, attributing the numerous cures which attended his ministrations to the intercession of St Cyrus, an African martyr for whom he had a special veneration.* St Francis Jerome died at the age of seventy-four, after much suffering, and his remains were interred in the Jesuit Church of Naples where they still lie.

Besides the testimony of witnesses collected in the *Summarium de Virtutibus* presented for the Beatification, there is a valuable report drawn up by the saint himself to acquaint his superiors with the more striking manifestations of God's grace during fifteen busy years of his missionary labours. These " Brevi Notizie " have been printed by Father Boero in his book *S. Francesco di Girolamo e le sue Missioni dentro e fuori di Napoli* (1882). We have also two Italian Lives written by fellow Jesuits who had known the saint intimately in his lifetime. That by Stradiotti appeared in 1719, and that by Bagnati in 1725. Among more modern contributions to the subject, the *Vita di San Francesco di Girolamo*, by Father degli Oddi, has been, perhaps, the most widely circulated, but Père J. Bach's *Histoire de S. François de Geronimo* (1867), is the most complete. See further the convenient *Raccolta di Avvenimenti singolari e Documenti autentici*, collected by Canon Alfonso Muzzarelli (Rome, 1806), as well as the Life by C. de Bonis. In English there is a biography by A. M. Clarke which appeared in the " Quarterly Series " in 1891, and an admirable article by the Bollandist Father Van Ortroy in the *Catholic Encyclopedia*.

---

* On this St Cyrus see the January volume of this series, pp. 396–394.

MAY 12

SS. NEREUS, ACHILLEUS and DOMITILLA, Marts.
First Century (?)

THE cultus of SS. Nereus and Achilleus is very ancient, going back, we may say with certainty, to the fourth century. It was on the occasion of their festival, which was observed with some solemnity in Rome two hundred years later that St Gregory the Great delivered his twenty-eighth homily. "These saints, before whom we are assembled," he says, "despised the world and trampled it under their feet when peace, riches and health gave it charms." The church in which he spoke was erected over their tomb in the cemetery of Domitilla, on the Via Ardeatina. A new church was built by Leo III about the year 800 and this lay in ruins when Baronius, who derived from it his title as Cardinal, rebuilt it and restored to it the relics of SS. Nereus and Achilleus which had been removed to the church of St Adrian.

Nereus and Achilleus were pretorian soldiers—as we know from the inscription Pope Damasus placed on their tomb—but their legendary "Acts" suppose them to have been attached as eunuchs to the household of Flavia Domitilla and to have shared her banishment. Of this lady, who was the great-niece of the Emperor Domitian,* Eusebius writes : " In the fifteenth year of Domitian, for professing Christ, Flavia Domitilla, the niece of Flavius Clemens, one of the consuls of Rome at that time, was transported with many others to the island of Pontia," i.e. Ponza. St Jerome describes her banishment as one long martyrdom. Nerva and Trajan were perhaps unwilling to restore the relations of Domitian when they recalled the other exiles. The " Acts " report that Nereus, Achilleus and Domitilla were removed to the island of Terracina, where the

* The opinion now more generally accepted holds that there were two Christian ladies who bore the name Flavia Domitilla. The elder was the daughter of a sister of Domitian and Titus, and she, as the wife of Flavius Clemens, was banished to the island of Pandatania. We learn this from Dion Cassius. The second Domitilla was a niece by marriage of the first, and it is she who was banished to Ponza, a fate which St Jerome seems to regard as equivalent to martyrdom.

first two were beheaded during the reign of Trajan, whilst Domitilla was burnt because she refused to sacrifice to idols. This story probably found its starting-point in the fact that the bodies of the two former martyrs were buried in a family vault, which burying-place later became known as the cemetery of Domitilla. The excavations of de Rossi in that catacomb in 1874 resulted in the discovery of their empty tomb in the underground church constructed by Pope Siricius in 390.

All, therefore, that we can with any confidence affirm regarding SS. Nereus and Achilleus is what we can gather from the inscription which Pope Damasus wrote in their honour towards the close of the fourth century. The text is known from the reports of travellers who read it when the slab was still entire, but the broken fragments which de Rossi found in his excavation of the cemetery of Domitilla in the last century are sufficient to identify it beyond possible doubt. Its terms, in English, run as follows : " The martyrs Nereus and Achilleus had enrolled themselves in the army and exercised the cruel office of carrying out the orders of the tyrant, being ever ready through the constraint of fear to obey his will. O Miracle of the Faith ! Suddenly they cease from their fury, they become converted, they fly from the camp of their wicked leader ; they throw away their shields, their armour and their blood-stained javelins. Confessing the Faith of Christ, they rejoice to bear testimony to its triumph. Learn now from the words of Damasus what great things the glory of Christ can accomplish."

The legendary story of Nereus and Achilleus, and the discovery of the cemetery of Domitilla with which it is connected, have given rise to a considerable literature. The " Acts," printed in the *Acta Sanctorum*, May, vol. iii, have been since edited or commented upon by such scholars as Wirth (1890) ; Achelis, in *Texte und Untersuchungen*, vol. xi, pt. 2 (1892) ; Schaefer, in the *Römische Quartalschrift*, vol. viii (1894), pp. 89–119 ; P. Franchi de' Cavallieri, in *Note Agiographiche* no. 3 (1909), etc. Cf. also J. P. Kirsch, *Die römischen Titelkirchen* (1918), pp. 90–94 ; Huelsen, *Le Chiese di Roma nel medio evo*, pp. 388–389, etc., and Delehaye's commentary on the *Hieronymianum*, p. 249. Abundant references to the archæological literature devoted to the cemetery of Domitilla will be found in Dom Leclercq's article in the *Dict. d'Archéologie, etc.*, vol. iv (1921), cc. 1409–1443.

ST PANCRAS, MART.

A.D. 304 (?)

We have no reliable information concerning St Pancras whose martyrdom is celebrated on this day. The story, as it is usually told,

is based upon his so-called " acts " which were fabricated long after
his death and contain serious anachronisms.   He is supposed to
have been a Syrian or Phrygian orphan who was brought by an
uncle to Rome where both were converted to Christianity.   Pancras
was still only in his fourteenth year when he was beheaded for the
faith under Diocletian.   He was buried in the cemetery of Calepodius,
which afterwards took his name, and about the year 500 a basilica was
built or rebuilt over his tomb by Pope Symmachus.   St Augustine
dedicated to him the first church he erected in Canterbury and some
fifty years later Pope St Vitalian sent to Oswy, King of Northumber-
land, a portion of the martyr's relics, the distribution of which seems
to have propagated his cultus in England.   St Gregory of Tours,
who called St Pancras " the Avenger of Perjuries," asserted that
God, by a perpetual miracle, visibly punished false oaths made in
the presence of his relics.

The " Acts," which exist both in Latin and in Greek and in more than
one recension, may be read in the *Acta Sanctorum*, May, vol. iii.   They are
discussed with the Greek text by P. Franchi de' Cavalieri in *Studi e Testi*,
vol. xix, pp. 77–120.   Pancras's tomb was near the second milestone
along the Via Aurelia, and the church of Pope Symmachus was very
handsomely restored by Pope Honorius (625–638), the inscription commemorating the fact is known to us.   Pope St Gregory the Great had previously built a monastery for Benedictines under his invocation, and it seems
likely that the dedication of the church erected by St Augustine at Canterbury may have been suggested by a remembrance of the Roman community
in which he had lived.   In the calendar of St Willibrord St Pancras is
commemorated on May 12, but not SS. Nereus and Achilleus.

ST EPIPHANIUS, Bp. of Salamis

A.D. 403

St Epiphanius was born at Besanduk, a village near Eleutheropolis in Palestine about the year 310.   In order to qualify himself
for the study of the Holy Scriptures he acquired in his youth a
knowledge of Hebrew, Coptic, Syriac, Greek and Latin.   Frequent
interviews with holy solitaries, whom he used to visit, gave him a
strong inclination to the religious life, which he embraced very young.
Even if, as one of his biographers asserts, he made his first essay of
monasticism in Palestine, it is certain that he soon went to Egypt
to perfect himself in ascetical discipline by staying with one or more
of the desert communities.   He returned to Palestine about the year
333, was ordained priest and built at Eleutheropolis a monastery, of

which he became superior. The mortifications he practised seemed
to some of his disciples to overtax his strength, but in answer to their
expostulations he would always say : " God gives not the Kingdom
of Heaven except on condition that we labour : and all we
can do bears no proportion to the crown we are striving for."
To his bodily austerities he added an indefatigable application to
prayer and study, and most of the books then current passed through
his hands. Nevertheless, during the cruel persecution under
Constantius, he frequently found time to leave his cell in order to
comfort the afflicted Catholics. In his great zeal for orthodoxy
he considered himself bound to break off communion with his own
diocesan Eutychius, who had adopted the views of the heretic
Acacius. In the course of his reading, he was also shocked by the
errors he detected in the writings of Origen. His reaction was violent
and he ever afterwards regarded Origen as the fountain-head of all the
heresies that were afflicting the Catholic Church. Epiphanius, in
his monastery, came to be regarded as the oracle of Palestine and the
neighbouring countries ; it was asserted that no one ever visited him
without receiving spiritual comfort. Indeed, his reputation spread
to more distant lands, and in the year 367 he was chosen Bishop of
Salamis, or Constantia, as it was then called, in Cyprus. He continued,
however, to wear the monastic habit and to govern his community at
Eleutheropolis which he visited from time to time. His charity
to the poor is described as boundless and many pious persons made
him the dispenser of their alms. The holy widow St Olympias, in
order to obtain his blessing, bestowed upon him a valuable gift of
land and money for that purpose. The veneration which all men had
for his sanctity exempted him from the persecution of the Arian
Emperor Valens in 371 ; and he was almost the only Catholic bishop
on the eastern shores of the Mediterranean who was not molested
during that reign. In 376 he undertook a journey to Antioch in a vain
endeavour to convert Vitalis, the Apollinarist bishop ; and six years
later he accompanied St Paulinus from that city to Rome where they
attended a council summoned by Pope Damasus. They stayed in
the house of St Jerome's friend, the widow St Paula, whom St
Epiphanius was able to entertain in Cyprus for ten days, three years
afterwards, when she was on her way to Palestine to rejoin her
spiritual father.

Saint though he was, the bishop was a violent partisan and his
prejudices led him, as an old man, to take action in ways which were
—to say the least—regrettable. Thus, after having stayed as an
honoured guest with John the Patriarch of Jerusalem, he had the
bad taste to preach a sermon in the metropolitan church, attacking

his host whom he suspected of sympathy with Origenism. Then, having withdrawn to Bethlehem, he proceeded to commit the ecclesiastical offence of ordaining, in a diocese not his own, Paulinianus, the brother of St Jerome. The complaints of the patriarch, and the scandal caused, however, obliged him to take the newly-ordained priest back with him to exercise his ministry in Cyprus. On another occasion, being incensed at the sight of a picture of our Lord or of a saint on the curtain over the door of a village church, he tore it to pieces, recommending that it should be used as a shroud. It is true that he subsequently replaced the curtain by another, but we are not told what the villagers thought of the exchange. Finally, he allowed himself to be used as a mere tool by Theophilus, the unscrupulous Patriarch of Alexandria, and to appear in his stead at Constantinople to impeach the four " Tall Brothers," (ἀδελφοὶ μακροί) who had escaped from the persecution of Theophilus and had appealed to the Emperor. Epiphanius, on his arrival, refused the proffered hospitality of St John Chrysostom because he had protected the fugitive monks, but, when he was brought face to face with the Tall Brothers and asked to state his charges against them, he was obliged to make the unpardonable and humiliating admission that he had read none of their books and knew nothing whatever of their doctrines ! In a somewhat chastened spirit he set out shortly afterwards to return to Salamis, but he died on the voyage home.

The fame of St Epiphanius rests chiefly upon his writings, the principal of which are (i) The *Anchoratus*—a treatise designed to confirm unsettled minds in the true faith. (ii) The *Panarium*, or medicine-chest against all heresies. (iii) The book of Weights and Measures, which depicts many ancient Jewish customs and measures. (iv) An essay on the Precious Stones set in the breastplate of the High Priest. These works, which were formerly much esteemed, show the writer to have amassed a vast amount of information, but to the modern mind he seems to be regrettably lacking in judgement and the gift of clear exposition. Well might St Jerome describe him as " a last relic of ancient piety ! "

The so-called biography of St Epiphanius attributed to a supposed Bishop Polybius is historically worthless and has not been printed in the account given of the saint in the *Acta Sanctorum*, May, vol. iii. For our knowledge of his life we have to go to the Church historians, such as Sozomen and the controversialists who occupied themselves with the writings of Origen and with the history of St John Chrysostom. A critical edition of the works of Epiphanius, for which the Prussian Academy of Sciences has undertaken the responsibility, makes but slow progress. For more detailed information regarding the saint's life and writings, see the *Dictionnaire de*

Théologie, vol. v. (1913), *c.c.* 363–365 ; Bardenhewer, *Geschichte der alt-kirchlichen Literatur*, vol. iii, pp. 293–302 ; and P. Maas in the *Byzantinische Zeitschrift*, vol. 30 (1930), pp. 279–286. There is an excellent article on St Epiphanius in the *Dictionary of Christ. Biog.*, vol. ii, p. 149–156, by R. A. Lipsius

ST MODOALDUS, Bp.

c. A.D. 640

Aquitaine was the birthplace of the holy bishop of Trèves, St Modoaldus, who is also known as Modowaldus and Romoaldus. He seems to have belonged to a family of high rank which was prolific in saints, for one of his sisters was St Severa and the other was St Iduberga, the wife of Pepin of Landen and the mother of St Gertrude of Nivelles and of St Begga. By reason of his aristocratic connections Modoaldus came to be frequently received at the court of King Dagobert, where he met St Arnold of Metz and St Cunibert of Cologne, with whom he formed a close friendship. King Dagobert esteemed the young ecclesiastic so highly that he nominated him to the vacant bishopric or archbishopric of Trèves, but this mark of favour did not prevent the saint from constantly remonstrating with his royal patron for his personal licentiousness and the loose morals of his court. In the course of time his strictures touched the King's heart : he became sincerely penitent and tried to make amends for the past. Not only did he take St Modoaldus as his spiritual father and adviser, but he also gave him large grants of land and money with which to make religious foundations. Amongst these may be mentioned the nunnery of Oeren, near Trèves, over which Dagobert's daughter, St Irmina, was given rule ; the church of St Martin at Münster–Maienfeld, the convent of Pfalzl, or Palatiolum, previously a royal villa on the Moselle, and the abbey of St Symphorianus at Trèves, to which the bishop's sister, St Severa, was appointed abbess. Few incidents in the life of St Modoaldus have come down to us, and even the dates of his consecration and death are doubtful. However, he was certainly present at the Council of Rheims in 625. He ordained the martyr St Germanus of Grandval, whom he had brought up, and gave hospitality to St Desiderius of Cahors—as may be gathered from the letter of thanks afterwards written to him by his late guest. St Modoaldus died after an episcopate which the Bollandists conjecture to have extended approximately from 622 to 640. By his own wish he was buried beside St Severa in the abbey church of St Symphorianus. The building was afterwards destroyed by the Normans, but the head of St Modoaldus was long preserved in the archiepiscopal chapel at Trèves.

During his life and after his death the saint was regarded as a special protector of the poor.

The very sketchy biography of St. Modoaldus, written more than 400 years after his death by Stephen, Abbot of the monastery of St James at Liége, is of no particular historical value. It is printed with the usual introduction and commentary in the *Acta Sanctorum*, May, vol. iii.

ST RICTRUDE (RICTRUDIS), ABBESS

A.D. 688

The family of St Rictrude was one of the most illustrious in Gascony, and her parents Ernold and Lichia were very devout as well as wealthy. In her father's house when she was a young girl Rictrude met one who was to be her director for a great part of her life. This was St Amandus, then an exile from the territory of King Dagobert, whose licentious conduct he had condemned. The prelate was occupied in evangelising the Gascons, many of whom were still pagans, and was received as an honoured guest by Ernold and his wife. Later on there arrived another distinguished visitor in the person of St Adalbald, a young French nobleman in great favour with King Clovis. He sought and obtained from his hosts the hand of Rictrude in spite of the opposition of relations who viewed with disfavour any alliance with a Frank. The home to which Adalbald took his bride was Ostrevant, in Flanders, where he had great possessions, and there four children were born to them— Maurontius, or Mauront, Eusebia, Clotsind and Adalsind—all of whom, like their parents, were destined to be honoured in later times as saints. After his return from exile St Amandus would come now and then to stay with this remarkable family, whose holy and happy life is described in glowing terms by the tenth-century compiler of the life of St Rictrude. She had been married sixteen years when Adalbald, on occasion of a visit he made to Gascony, was murdered by some of her relations who had never forgiven him for his successful wooing. The blow, though a terrible one to St Rictrude, proved the means of weaning her heart entirely from the world. She told St Amandus that she wished to retire into a convent, but he advised her to wait until her son was old enough to take up his residence at court. This delay entailed on her a severe trial in later years, when King Clovis II suddenly made up his mind to give her in marriage to one of his favourites—for she was still attractive and very wealthy. The King's commands in such cases were law, and Rictrude pleaded with him in vain. Eventually, however, St Amandus persuaded the monarch to allow her to follow her vocation, and Rictrude joyfully set out for Marchiennes, where she had in past years founded a double monastery for men and women. There she received the veil from St Amandus. Her two younger daughters, Adalsind and Clotsind, accompanied her, but Eusebia remained with her paternal grandmother, St Gertrude, at Hamage. After a few years at court Maurantius decided that he too wished to abandon the world and it was at Marchiennes, in his mother's presence, that he received the tonsure. Adalsind died young, but Clotsind lived to become Abbess of Marchiennes when St Rictrude passed to her eternal reward at the age of seventy-six.

The Life of St Rictrudis, which was written by Abbot Hucbald of Elnon in 907, seems to represent a very sincere attempt to arrive at historical truth, however greatly the biographer was hampered by the lack of materials, most of which are said to have perished when Marchiennes was raided and burnt by the Normans in 881. See the admirable discussion of the subject by L. van der Essen in the *Revue d'Histoire ecclésiastique*, vol. xix (1923), especially pp. 543–550 ; and in the same author's *Étude critique des Saints mérovingiens* (1907), pp. 260–267. Hucbald's Life, with other materials, may be read in the *Acta Sanctorum*, May, vol. iii. W. Levison, in the *M.G.H. Scrip. rer. merov.*, vol. vi, has only re-edited the Prologue.

ST GERMANUS, PATRIARCH OF CONSTANTINOPLE

A.D. 732

St Germanus was the son of a prominent senator of Constantinople named Justinian, who, having been implicated in the conspiracy which led to the murder of Constans II, father of Constantine Copronymus, paid the forfeit with his life. Germanus had been educated for the priesthood and was for some time attached to the metropolitan church, but after his father's death, at a date which is not recorded, he was appointed Bishop of Cyzicus. Nicephorus and Theophanes assert that he countenanced the attempts made by the Emperor Philippicus to spread the Monothelite heresy and that he was one of the signatories to the decrees of the schismatical assembly at Constantinople, which in 712 denounced the Sixth General Council. This, however, seems inconsistent with the bishop's subsequent unflinching defence of orthodoxy, and the encomiums passed upon him by the Second Œcumenical Council of Nicæa. Under the successor of Philippicus, Anastasius II, who

was an orthodox Catholic, the heretical patriarch John was deposed
and Germanus was translated from Cyzicus to the see of Constantinople. Within a year of his accession he called a synod of 100 bishops
at which the doctrine of the two wills and two operations in Our
Lord was once more enunciated and a sentence of anathema passed
against those who had been leaders of the Monothelite heresy.
After Leo the Isaurian had ascended the imperial throne in 717,
St Germanus, at his request, crowned him in the Cathedral of St
Sophia. During the ceremony, which was enacted with great
splendour, the Emperor solemnly swore to preserve the Catholic
faith undefiled and he afterwards wrote to Pope Gregory II asking
to be received into communion. Ten years later, when Leo declared
himself in sympathy with the Iconoclasts and set himself against the
cultus of images, St Germanus reminded him of the solemn vow he
had made. In spite of this remonstrance, the Emperor issued an
edict prohibiting the outward display of reverence to religious statues
and pictures, all of which were to be raised to a height which precluded the public from kissing them. A later and still more drastic
decree ordered the general destruction of sacred images and the white-
washing of church walls. The people were greatly perturbed by
these measures, and when it became known that Leo had commanded
the demolition of a much venerated statue of Our Lord which stood
over the gate of the palace, their anger burst forth. As the official
charged with the task struck the figure with his axe, women shook the
ladder on which he stood, and when he fell the multitude clubbed
him to death. This unfortunate incident brought upon the Catholics
a terrible persecution which entailed in many cases mutilation,
confiscation of property and banishment. The patriarch, though
a very old man, spoke out fearlessly in Constantinople in defence of
the cultus of sacred images and wrote letters upholding the Catholic
tradition to bishops inclined to favour the Iconoclasts. In one of
these which he sent to Thomas of Claudiopolis he says : " Pictures
are history in figure and tend to the sole glory of the heavenly Father.
When we show reverence to representations of Jesus Christ we do
not worship the colours laid upon the wood : we are venerating the
invisible God who is in the bosom of the Father : Him we adore
in spirit and in truth." In reply to an epistle he addressed to Pope
Gregory II, St Germanus received an answer, still preserved to us,
in which the Holy Father expresses his deep appreciation of the
patriarch's vindication of Catholic doctrine and tradition.

Over and over again did Leo attempt to win over the aged
prelate, but finally, in 730, realising that his efforts remained fruitless, he called a synod at which he practically compelled St Germanus

to relinquish his office. The saint then retired to his paternal home at Platanium, where he spent the remainder of his life in monastic seclusion, preparing for his death which took place when he was over ninety. Of his writings, the greater part of which have perished, the most famous was an Apology for St Gregory of Nyssa against the Origenists. Baronius described them as having kindled a beacon which illuminated the whole of the Catholic Church.

A medieval life of St Germanus in Greek was edited by A. Papadopoulos Kerameus in 1881, but it is of little value. The statement, for example, that the Patriarch, to escape from the resentment of the Emperor Leo, took refuge in a convent of nuns at Cyzicus, and wearing their habit was quite unrecognisable because he already looked like a wizened old woman, can hardly be credited. Our surest source of information is to be found in such letters of the period as have been preserved, and in the proceedings of the councils. There is an excellent article on St Germanus in the *Dictionnaire de Théologie*, vol. vi (1920), cc. 1300–1309 ; to this a full bibliography is appended, as also in Bardenhewer, *Geschichte der altkirchlichen Literatur*, vol. v, pp. 48–51. See also Hefele-Leclercq, *Histoire des Conciles*, vol. iii, pp. 599 *seq.*

ST DOMINIC DE LA CALZADA, Hermit

c. A.D. 1109

St Dominic de la Calzada—of the Causeway—was so called from the road which he made for pilgrims on their way to Compostella. He was a native of Villoria in the Spanish Basque country, and as a young man had made several unsuccessful attempts to become a Benedictine, his uncouth appearance and his ignorance causing him to be rejected wherever he applied. He then went to live as a solitary in a hermitage of his own construction surrounded by a garden which he cultivated with care. When St Gregory of Ostia came to preach in North-eastern Spain, Dominic attached himself to his person and remained with him until St Gregory's death. Bereft of his master, Dominic was again cast upon his own resources. Not far from his former hermitage lay the wilderness of Bureba through which many of the pilgrims had to pass to reach the shrine of St. James. It was virgin forest and was dangerous not only because no proper road traversed it, but also because the thick undergrowth and trees afforded a lurking place for bandits. Here Dominic took up his abode. Having built himself a cabin and an oratory which he dedicated to Our Lady, he set about felling trees and building a good road. So successful were his efforts that settlers began to gather round him. With their help he was able to construct also a hospice and a bridge. He died about the year

1109, and his grave, which he had made himself, became famous for miracles. The town of St Domingo de la Calzada which grew up round his shrine was at one time important enough to be the seat of a bishopric—now transferred to Calahorra.

The account in the *Acta Sanctorum*, May, vol. iii, is derived mainly from a set of breviary lessons and from a Life compiled by Louis de la Vega in 1606. See also the *Encyclopedia Europeo-Americana*, vol. xviii, p. 1846.

BLESSED FRANCIS PATRIZZI, Conf.

A.D. 1328

Among the holy men who have shed lustre on the Servite Order, not the least notable was Blessed Francis Arrighetto, descended from a branch of a noble Sienese family, the Patrizzi, by which last name he is more commonly spoken of. He was drawn to God while still only a boy on listening to a sermon preached by the Dominican Blessed Ambrose Sansedoni. Francis had a great desire to hide himself in some desert place, but he felt that duty required him to remain with his mother who was a widow and blind. After her death he, at the age of twenty-two, was received into the Order of Servites by St Philip Benizi (A.D. 1285) and became in a short time very famous as a missioner and preacher. His confessional was crowded, and the popularity he thus enjoyed seems to have caused some jealousy and criticism amongst his brethren. Sensitive and perplexed, for fear he was giving scandal, he besought the guidance of our Blessed Lady, and was thereupon afflicted with sudden deafness. This infirmity was not permanent, but he took it as a sign that it was by the use of his tongue and not of his ears that God wished to be served. He had a wonderful gift for preaching most moving sermons with little or no preparation, and he was indefatigable in exercising it. Though relentless in inflicting pain upon his body by taking the discipline and in other ways, he held that it was a mistake to starve himself ; he needed all his strength to do the work committed to him. He foresaw that he would die on the feast of the Ascension, 1328, but he went out to preach on that day as he had been asked to do. He collapsed by the roadside as he went. The touching story of his end is told by his biographer in great detail. His whole life was spent in Siena, where he is still much venerated.

All that is likely to be known concerning Bd. Francis may be read in the text and annotations of the life edited in the *Analecta Bollandiana*, vol. xiv (1895), pp. 167–197, by Father Soulier, O.S. The author of this biography was Father Christopher de Palma, a contemporary.

BLESSED GEMMA, Virg.

A.D. 1429

Solmona, in the Abruzzi, which was Ovid's native place, has also given birth to a very different type of character in the person of Blessed Gemma, a holy recluse who lived and died there and whose relics are still venerated in the Church of St John. Gemma's parents were devout peasants who encouraged their little girl's precocious piety and set her to mind the sheep—an occupation which gave her ample leisure for prayer and contemplation. According to tradition, when she was twelve years old, her beauty attracted the notice of a local count called Roger, who sent his servants to kidnap her. Brought into his presence, God lent a marvellous power to her words, and she succeeded in so greatly impressing him that he undertook to build her a hermitage. Whatever truth there may be in that story, it is clearly established that she lived a holy life for forty-two years in a cell adjoining the church. The cultus which continued uninterrupted after her death was formally approved in 1890.

A short notice of this Beata will be found in the *Acta Sanctorum*, May, vol. iii. The decree which amounts to an equivalent beatification may be read in the *Acta Sanctæ Sedis*, vol. xxiii (1890), p. 48. Also a little book about the holy anchoress was published by B. Silvestri at Prato in 1896.

BLESSED JANE OF PORTUGAL, Virg.

A.D. 1490

Blessed Jane of Portugal came into the world heiress to the throne of her father, Alphonsus V, and although a brother was born three years later, the little boy's delicacy and the untimely death of the children's mother, Elizabeth of Coïmbra, made it seem not unlikely that the young Infanta would eventually become Queen. She was accordingly brought up in royal state and no pains were spared to fit her for the high position she might be called on to fill. Nevertheless, from childhood Jane took little pleasure in earthly things, caring only for what concerned the service of God. Unknown to all but two or three pious members of her suite, she wore a hair-shirt, used the discipline and spent long hours of the night in prayer. When, at the age of sixteen, she found that her father was making plans for her marriage she asked him to permit her to embrace the religious life, but was met by a point-blank refusal. He did not, however, for the moment, press her to marry and allowed her to lead a secluded life in the palace. She had a great devotion to Our Lord's Passion, meditating especially on the Crown of Thorns which she caused to be added to her escutcheon and embroidered on her tapestries. In 1471 King Alphonsus and Prince John started on a punitive expedition against the African Moors, leaving Jane, then nineteen years of age, as Regent during their absence. The campaign was successful : and in the midst of the public rejoicings which followed their return, the Infanta again asked permission to retire into a convent. She obtained from her father a conditional consent, and, though it was for a time suspended owing to the objections of Prince John, Blessed Jane, the moment she felt secure, took prompt action. She distributed her personal effects and set out for the Bernardine Convent of Odivellas on her way to her ultimate objective, the Dominican Priory of Aveiro, which had been founded by a widow, Brites de Leitoa, some fifteen years before. Jane entered the Priory on August 4, 1472, but she was never allowed by her family to take full vows, or to give up control of her property. For a long time she did not even dare to receive the habit. Nevertheless, as far as she could, she led the life of a simple sister, always seeking to perform the most lowly tasks. Her income she devoted to charity —especially to redeeming captives. Her peace was repeatedly disturbed by her relations, who could never resign themselves to her refusing the brilliant matches which continued to be suggested for the Infanta. Maximilian, King of the Romans, and Richard III, King of England, are said to have been amongst the suitors. Moreover, Jane's family seem to have been genuinely concerned about her health, and they insisted upon making her leave Aveiro—never a salubrious place—when the plague was raging there. She died at the age of thirty-eight, of a fever supposed to have been contracted from contaminated or poisoned water given to her on her way home after a visit to Court, by a woman of position whom she had banished from the town of Aveiro because of her scandalous life.

The most authentic account of the life of Blessed Jane is that by Margaret Pineria, who had been one of her ladies in waiting. It was written in Portuguese, but in the *Acta Sanctorum*, May, vol. vii, it is accessible in a Latin translation. See also a popular French Life, by de Belloc, with a number of engravings which appeared in 1897 ; M. C. de Ganay, *Les Bienheureuses Dominicaines* (1913), pp. 279–304 ; and a brief sketch in Procter, *Lives of Dominican Saints*, pp. 122–126. Her cultus was authorised in 1693.

BLESSED JOHN STONE, Mart.

(?) A.D. 1539

Beyond the fact that he was an Augustinian friar, a Doctor of Theology, and that he died a martyr, not very much is known about Blessed John Stone, though his portrait and name may be found in old engravings representing the English martyrs as formerly depicted on the walls of the Church of St Thomas in the English College at Rome. It was at first conjectured that he suffered about May 12 in the year 1538, and this date was accepted on the authority of the Augustinian Luigi Torelli in his *Historia Ecclesiastica della Revoluzione d'Inghilterra*, but an account book of the City Chamberlain of Canterbury seems to indicate December 1539 as the time when Blessed John Stone received the martyr's crown. It was, therefore, to him in all probability that Ingworth, one of the King's visitors, was referring when he complains in December 1538 of the insolence of a prisoner at the Austin Friars of Canterbury, and mentions how he " still held and still desired to die for it, that the King may not be head of the Church of England."

See Camm, *Lives of the English Martyrs*, vol. i, pp. 269–273 ; and Stanton's *Menology*, pp. 228 and 647.

MAY 13

ST ROBERT BELLARMINE, Cardinal, and Doctor
of the Church
A.D. 1621

ONE of the greatest polemical theologians the Church has ever produced, and her foremost controversialist against the doctrines of the Protestant Reformation, was Robert Francis Romulus Bellarmine, whose feast is kept upon this day. Born at Montepulciano, in Tuscany, of a noble but impoverished family, he was the son of Vincenzo Bellarmine and of Cynthia Cervini, half-sister to Pope Marcellus II. Even as a young boy Robert showed great promise. He knew Virgil by heart, he wrote good Latin verses, he played the violin, and he could hold his own in public disputations —to the great admiration of his fellow-citizens. Moreover, he was so deeply devout that in 1559, when Robert was seventeen, the Rector of the Jesuit College at Montepulciano described him in a letter as " the best of our school, and not far from the kingdom of heaven." It was his ambition to enter the Society of Jesus, but he had to encounter strong opposition from his father, who had formed great worldly plans for his clever son. Robert's mother, however, was on his side, and eventually he obtained the permission he desired. On September 19, 1560, he went to Rome to present himself to the General of the Order, by whom his noviciate was curtailed to enable him to pass almost immediately into the Roman College to enter upon the customary studies. Ill-health dogged his steps from the cradle to the grave, and his delicacy became so pronounced that, at the close of his three years of philosophy, his superiors sent him to Florence to recruit his strength in his native Tuscan air, whilst at the same time teaching boys and giving lectures on rhetoric and on the Latin poets. Twelve months afterwards he was transferred to Mondovi in Piedmont. There he discovered that he was expected to instruct his pupils in Cicero and Demosthenes. He knew no Greek except the letters of the alphabet, but with characteristic obedience and energy he set to work to study at night the grammar lesson he was expected to deliver the next day. Within a short time he had got so far ahead of those he was teaching that he was able to expound to them the most abstruse of all the writers of Greek prose. In addition to teaching he also preached sermons, which attracted vast crowds. Indeed, even the cathedral could not contain all his would-be hearers. Amongst the congregation on one occasion was his Provincial, Father Adorno, who promptly transferred him to Padua that he might prepare himself in that famous university town to receive ordination. Again he studied and preached, but before the completion of his course he was bidden by the General of his Order, St Francis Borgia, to proceed at once to Louvain in Belgium to finish his studies there, and to preach on Sundays in Latin to the undergraduates with a view to counteracting the dangerous heretical doctrines which were being propagated by Dr. Michael Baius the Chancellor, and others. It is interesting to note that on his journey he had as companion for part of the way the Englishman, William Allen, afterward to become like himself a cardinal. From the time of his arrival at Louvain until his departure seven years later, his sermons were extraordinarily popular, although they were delivered in Latin, and although the preacher had no physical advantages to commend him, for he was small of stature and he had to stand on a stool in the pulpit to make himself seen and heard. On the other hand, men declared that his face shone with a strange light as he spoke and that his words seemed like those of one inspired.

After his ordination at Ghent in 1570, he was given a professorship in the University of Louvain—the first Jesuit to hold such a post—and began a course of lectures on the *Summa* of St Thomas Aquinas, which were at the same time brilliant expositions of doctrine and a vehicle through which he could, and did, controvert the teachings of Dr. Michael on such matters as grace, free will, and papal authority. In contrast to the controversial tactics of the time he never made personal attacks on his enemies or mentioned them by name. Not content with the great labour entailed on him by his sermons and lectures, St Robert, during his stay at Louvain, taught himself Hebrew and embarked upon a thorough study of the Holy Scriptures and of the Fathers. To assist the studies of others he also made time to write a Hebrew grammar which became extremely popular.

A serious breakdown in health, however, necessitated his recall to Italy, and there, in spite of the efforts of St Charles Borromeo to secure his services for Milan, he was appointed to the recently established Chair of Controversial Theology at the Roman College. For eleven years, from 1576, he laboured untiringly, giving lectures and preparing the four great volumes of his *Disputations* on the controversies of the Christian faith which, even three hundred years later, the great ecclesiastical historian Hefele described as " the most complete defence of Catholic teaching yet published." It showed such profound acquaintance with the Holy Scriptures, the Fathers, and all the heretical writers, that many of his opponents could never bring themselves to believe that it was the work of one man. They even suggested that his name was an anagram covering a syndicate of learned and wily Jesuits. The work was one urgently needed at that particular moment, because the leading Reformers had recently published a series of volumes purporting to show, by an appeal to history, that Protestantism, not Catholicism, truly represented the Church of the Apostles. As these were published at Magdeburg, and as each volume covered a century, the series became known as the " Centuries of Magdeburg." The answer which Baronius set out to furnish in the field of history, St Robert Bellarmine supplied in the field of dogmatics. The success of his Controversies was instantaneous : laymen and clergy, Catholics and Protestants, read the volumes with avidity, and even in Elizabethan England, where the work was prohibited, a London bookseller declared, " I have made more money out of this Jesuit than out of all the other divines put together."

In 1589 he was separated for a while from his books to be sent with Cardinal Gaëtano on a diplomatic embassy to France, then in the throes of war between Henry of Navarre and the League. No tangible results came of the mission, but the party had the experience of being in Paris for eight months during the siege, when, to quote St Robert's own words, they " did practically nothing though they suffered a very great deal." As opposed to Cardinal Gaëtano, who had Spanish sympathies, St Robert was openly in favour of trying to make terms with the King of Navarre if he would become a Catholic, but within a very short time of the raising of the siege, the members of the mission were recalled to Rome by the death of Sixtus V. Soon afterwards we find St Robert taking the leading part on a papal commission appointed by Pope Clement VIII to edit and make ready for publication the new revision of the Vulgate which had been called for by the Council of Trent. An edition had indeed already been completed during the reign of Sixtus V and under that Pope's immediate supervision, but it contained many errors due to defective scholarship and to a fear of making important alterations in the text. Moreover, it was never in general circulation. The revised version, as produced by the commission and issued with the imprimatur of Clement VIII, is the Latin Bible as we have it to-day, with a preface composed by St Robert himself. He was then living at the Roman College, where, as official spiritual director to the house, he had been brought into close contact with St Aloysius Gonzaga, whose death-bed he attended and to whom he was so deeply attached that in his will he asked to be buried at the feet of the youthful saint, " once my dear ghostly child." Recognition of Bellarmine's great qualities followed quickly. In 1592 he was made Rector of the College ; in 1594 he was elected Provincial of Naples ; and three years later he returned to Rome in the capacity of theologian to Clement VIII, at whose express desire he wrote his two celebrated Catechisms, one of which is still in general use throughout Italy. These catechisms are said to have been translated more frequently than any other literary work except the Bible and the Imitation. In 1598, to his great dismay, he was nominated a Cardinal by Clement VIII on the ground that " he had not his equal for learning." Though obliged to occupy apartments in the Vatican and to keep up some sort of an establishment, he relaxed none of his former austerities. Moreover, he limited his household and expenses to what was barely essential : he lived on bread and garlic—the food of the poor ; and he denied himself a fire even in the depth of winter. Practically all the money that came to him from the Holy See he distributed to the poor, to whom he was accessible at all times.

In 1602 he was, somewhat unexpectedly, appointed Archbishop of Capua, and within four days of his consecration he left Rome to take up his new charge. Admirable as the holy man appears in every relation of life, it is perhaps as shepherd of his immense flock that he makes the greatest appeal to our sympathy. Laying aside his books, the great scholar, who had no pastoral experience, set about evangelising his people with all the zeal of a young missionary, whilst initiating the reforms decreed by the Council of Trent. He preached constantly, he made visitations, he exhorted the clergy, he catechised the children, he sought out the necessitous, whose wants he supplied, and he won the love of all classes. He was not destined, however, to remain long away from Rome. Paul V, who was elected Pope three years later, at once insisted upon retaining Cardinal Bellarmine by his side, and the Archbishop accordingly resigned his see. From that time onwards, as head of the Vatican Library and as a member of almost every congregation, he took a prominent part in all the affairs of the Holy See. When Venice ventured arbitrarily to abrogate the rights of the Church, and was placed under an interdict, St Robert became the Pope's great protagonist in a pamphlet contest with the Republic's theologian, the famous Servite, Fra Paolo Sarpi. A still more important adversary was James I of England. Cardinal Bellarmine had remonstrated with his friend, the Archpriest Blackwell, for taking the oath of allegiance to James—an oath purposely so worded as to deny to the Pope all jurisdiction over temporals. King James, who fancied himself as a controversialist, rushed into the fray with two books in defence of the oath, both of which were answered by Cardinal Bellarmine. In the earlier rejoinder, St Robert, writing in somewhat lighter vein, made humorous references to the monarch's bad Latin, but his second treatise was a serious and crushing retort demolishing all his adversary's arguments and covering every point in the controversy. Standing out consistently and uncompromisingly as a champion of the Pope's supremacy in all things spiritual, the Cardinal nevertheless held views on temporal authority which were displeasing to extremists of both parties. Because he maintained that the Pope's jurisdiction over foreign rulers was indirect, he lost favour with Sixtus V, and because in opposition to the Scotch jurist, Barclay, he denied the divine right of kings, his book, *De Potestate Papæ*, was publicly burnt by the Parliament of Paris.

The saint was on friendly terms with Galileo Galilei, who dedicated to him one of his books. He was called upon, indeed, to admonish the great astronomer in the year 1616, but his admonition, which was accepted with a good grace, amounted to a caution against putting forward, otherwise than as a hypothesis, theories not yet fully proved. Well would it have been for Galileo if he had continued to act in accordance with that advice ! It would be impossible in limited space even to enumerate the various activities of St Robert during these later years. He continued to write, but his works were no longer controversial. He completed a commentary on the Psalms and wrote five spiritual books, all of which, including the last, on the *Art of Dying*, were soon translated into English. When it became clear that his days were drawing to a close, he was allowed to retire to the Jesuit novitiate of St Andrea. There he died, at the age of seventy-nine, on September 17, 1621—on the day which, at his special request, had been set aside as the Feast of the Stigmata of St Francis of Assisi.

It hardly needs saying that the sources of information for such a career are far too copious to be specified in detail. The mere fact that the beatification was opposed, and in this way retarded, by a certain school of theologians who did not find themselves in harmony with Bellarmine's views, has had the result of multiplying to a quite unusual extent the printed documents connected with the process. Besides these quasi-official materials and the seventeenth century Lives, notably those by Fuligatti (1st edition 1624) and Daniel Bartoli (1678), it will be sufficient to call attention to the brief autobiography of the saint written in 1613 at the pressing instance of Father Mutius Vitelleschi. This may most conveniently be consulted in the valuable work of Père Le Bachelet, *Bellarmin avant son Cardinalat* (1911). Père Le Bachelet supplemented this with another important collection of documents entitled *Auctarium Bellarminianum* (1913). For English readers the work which supersedes all others and which is as exhaustive in its range as it is attractive in treatment, is the *Life of Blessed Robert Bellarmine*, by Father James Brodrick, S.J., published in 1928 in two volumes. Since then the holy Cardinal has been canonised and declared a Doctor of the Universal Church. In connection with this last distinction the Congregation of Sacred Rites has issued an imposing volume, *De S. Roberto Bellarmino Univ. Eccl. Doctore* (1931), setting out the grounds upon which the declaration was based. This includes (pp. xxi–xxxii) what is in effect a very full bibliography.

ST GLYCERIA, VIRG. AND MART.

c. A.D. 177

The Greek Acts, which are our sole authority for the life of St Glyceria, are unfortunately quite unreliable, and all that can be asserted definitely is that she was a Christian maiden who suffered martyrdom at Heraclea in the Propontis towards the close of the second century. The legend follows conventional lines : She is said to have been the daughter of a Roman official of senatorial rank living at Trajanopolis in Thrace. She openly avowed her faith in the presence of Sabinus the prefect, who caused her to be led to the temple of Jupiter that she might sacrifice. Instead of doing so, she threw down the statue of the god and broke it. She was suspended by the hair and beaten with iron rods, but sustained no harm. Deprived of food by her jailors in prison, she was fed by an angel. When placed in a hot oven the fire was promptly extinguished. Her hair was then dragged out and she was exposed to wild beasts, but she died before they could reach her. A splendid church was erected to her honour at Heraclea, where her head is still venerated. The rest of her relics were taken to the island of Lemnos.

In his *Origines du Culte des Martyrs* (p. 281), Père Delehaye remarks that nothing could be more clearly demonstrated than the early cultus of St Glyceria at Heraclea. The Emperor Maurice visited the shrine in 591 and Heraclius in 610, while there is mention of St Glyceria's tomb as a centre of devotion in the " Passion " of the Forty Martyrs of Nicomedia. On the other hand the story printed with the Greek text in the *Acta Sanctorum*, May, vol. iii, is, as stated above, no more than a pious fiction. *Cf.* also the *Byzantinische Zeitschrift*, vol. vi (1897), pp. 96–99.

ST MUCIUS, OR MOCIUS, MART.

A.D. 304

St Mucius, or Mocius, was a Christian priest who suffered at Constantinople during the persecution of Diocletian, and his cultus goes back to very early times. This is all we know for certain about the saint, for his so-called Acts are undoubtedly spurious. In them we read that St Mucius was an eloquent Christian preacher at Amphipolis in Macedonia, and that, on the occasion of the feast of Bacchus, he overthrew the deity's altar, casting the votive offerings on the ground. The crowd would have rent him to pieces had not the Proconsul interfered to have him arrested. The tribunal which tried him condemned him to be burnt alive, but he walked unscathed in the flames accompanied by three strangers, whilst the prefect and nine attendants were consumed by the fire. The martyr was then sent to Heraclea, where he was tortured on the wheel and afterwards exposed to the wild beasts, which refused to touch him. Eventually he was conveyed to Constantinople and there beheaded.

Père Delehaye, in the *Analecta Bollandiana*, vol. xxxi (1912), pp. 163–187 and 225–232, devotes considerable space to St Mocius. He first prints the best text of the " Acts " together with the panegyric of a certain Michael, and then points out that the obviously fictitious acts do not detract from the historic character of the martyrdom itself. There undoubtedly was a church dedicated to Mocius in Constantinople at the end of the fourth century, and this may have been built by the Emperor Constantine. Further, it is pretty certain that the martyr is mentioned at about the same date in the ancient Syriac martyrology, though his name, one knows not how, has been transformed into " Maximus." He is also mentioned in the *Hieronymianum*.

ST SERVATIUS, OR SERVAIS, BP. OF TONGRES

A.D. 384

It is recorded of St Servatius, supposed to be an Armenian by birth, that he gave hospitality to St Athanasius during his banishment, and that he defended the great patriarch's cause and the Catholic faith at the Council of Sardica in 343 or 344. He also took part in an alleged synod at Cologne, which deposed the Arian bishop of that city. After the murder of Constans, the usurper Magnentius sent him and another bishop as envoys to Alexandria to plead his cause with the Emperor Constantius. Nothing came of the embassy, but Servatius was able, while in Egypt, to renew his intercourse with St Athanasius. In the year 359 we find the Bishop of Tongres at the

Council of Rimini, valiantly holding out, together with St Phœbadius, Bishop of Agen, against the Arian majority. Before the assembly broke up they were indeed beguiled into signing, under a misapprehension, the formulary set forth by the council, but when, on their return to France, they were enlightened by a warning from St Hilary of Poitiers, they at once denounced the council and repudiated its enactments in unequivocal terms.

St Gregory of Tours relates that St Servatius foretold the invasion of Gaul by the Huns, and that he strove to avert the calamity by watching, fasting, and prayer as well as by a pilgrimage to Rome. This penitential journey he undertook with the object of commending his flock to the care of the two great apostles. But he was informed by revelation, whilst he was in the holy city, that God was determined to punish the sins of the nation—though the calamity would not occur during his lifetime. Almost immediately after his return to Tongres, he contracted fever and died, either in his episcopal city or, according to some authorities, in Maestricht. That same year Tongres was plundered and partially destroyed in a raid by an unfriendly tribe. It was not, however, till seventy years later, when Attila with his Huns overran and ravaged the country, that the prophecy was completely fulfilled.

The cultus of St Servatius was very considerable during the Middle Ages in the Low Countries, and many legends grew up about him. His relics are preserved in a beautiful ancient reliquary at Maestricht, where his staff, his drinking cup, and his silver key are also treasured. According to tradition the key was given to him when in Rome by St Peter in a vision, but it is actually one of the " Claves Confessionis S Petri," which popes have from time to time bestowed on those they wished to honour and which contained filings from the chains of St Peter. The drinking cup, on the other hand, was popularly supposed to have been the gift of an angel, and to have the property of healing fever. The bishopric of Tongres was transferred to Maestricht after the death of St Servatius.

The " Acts " of St Servatius, printed in part in the *Acta Sanctorum*, May, vol. iii, are only a compilation of Herigerus, Abbot of Lobbes, in the tenth century. Several older texts, however, have since been discovered and have been edited in the *Analecta Bollandiana*, vol. i (1882), pp. 88–112, and in G. Kurth, *Deux Biographies de St Servais* (1881). See also G. Kurth, *Nouvelles Recherches sur S. Servais* (1884). A. Proost, *Saint Servais* (1891) ; F. Wilhelm (1910), G. Gorris (1923), and Duchesne, *Fastes Episcopaux*, vol. iii, p. 188. There has undoubtedly been a very widespread cultus of St Servais and the literature is considerable. On St Peter's keys, *cf. Dict. d'Archéologie, etc.*, vol. iii, c. 1861.

ST JOHN THE SILENT, Hermit
A.D. 558

St John derived the surname by which he is always designated from his great love of silence and recollection. He was born in the year 454, at Nicopolis in Armenia, of an illustrious family which had, in the past, supplied generals and governors for that part of the empire. After the death of his parents he built, with part of his patrimony, a church in honour of Our Lady as well as a monastery in which, at the age of eighteen, he shut himself up with ten companions. Here, under the direction of their youthful superior, the little community led a most edifying life of devotion and asceticism, filling up with manual work the hours not occupied in public prayer and other necessary duties. The great reputation St John acquired for sanctity and leadership led the Archbishop of Sebaste to consecrate him Bishop of Colonia in Armenia, much against his will, when he was only twenty-eight. For nine years he exercised his episcopal functions, zealously instructing his flock, depriving himself of even the necessaries of life that he might relieve the poor, and continuing to practise as far as possible all the austerities of his former life. His brother and nephew, who filled honourable posts in the Emperor's palace, were moved by his example to despise the world amid the luxuries by which they were surrounded. It was far otherwise with his brother-in-law, the Governor of Armenia, who oppressed the Church so cruelly that John, after many vain remonstrances, was impelled to seek justice from the Emperor Zeno at Constantinople. He obtained the redress he sought, but his inability to remedy certain other evils, combined with a strong desire for a secluded life, had by this time decided him to lay down his charge. Instead of returning to Armenia he quietly went to Jerusalem—uncertain as to his future vocation. His biographer assures us that whilst he was watching one night in prayer he saw before him a bright cross in the air and heard a voice which said : " If thou desirest to be saved, follow this light." The cross then moved before him, and at length directed him to the " laura " (monastery) of St Sabas. Convinced that he now knew God's will for him, St John immediately betook himself to the laura, which then contained one hundred and fifty monks, all animated with the spirit of their holy founder and superior. St John was then thirty-eight years old. St Sabas at first placed him under the steward to fetch water, carry stones, and serve the workmen in building a new hospital. John came and went like a beast of burden, remaining ever recollected in God, always cheerful and silent. After this test, the experienced superior set him to receive and entertain strangers. The holy man served everyone as though he were serving Christ Himself. By this time St Sabas recognised that his novice was already on the road to perfection and, in order to allow him opportunities for uninterrupted contemplation, he allowed him to occupy a separate hermitage—a privilege he accorded only to a very few. During five consecutive days of the week, which he passed fasting, John never left his cell ; but on Saturdays and Sundays he attended public worship in church. After three years spent in this eremitic life, he was made steward of the laura. The worldly business which this office entailed was no distraction to him : so great was his love for God that his mind was fixed on Him continually and without effort. Four years later St Sabas, who had kept him under observation, thought him worthy of the priesthood and decided to present him to the patriarch Elias. Upon their arrival at the church of Mount Calvary, where the ordination was to take place, John said to the patriarch : " Holy father, I have something to impart to you in private : afterwards, if you judge me suitable, I will receive holy orders." The patriarch granted him a private interview, and St John, when he had bound him to secrecy, said : " Father, I have been consecrated bishop : but on account of my many sins I have fled and have sought out this desert to await the coming of the Lord." The patriarch was startled, and having summoned St Sabas, declared : " I cannot ordain this man because of certain particulars he has communicated to me." St Sabas returned home deeply grieved because he feared that John must have committed some terrible crime, but in answer to his earnest prayer the truth was made known to him by revelation. He was, however, directed not to divulge the secret to others. After this episode John remained for four years in his cell, speaking to no one except to the person who brought him the necessaries of life. In the year 503, the factious spirit of certain turbulent monks obliged St Sabas to leave his laura. St John at the same time withdrew into a neighbouring desert, where he spent six years conversing only with God and subsisting on the wild roots and herbs he found growing there. When St Sabas was recalled to his community he went out into the wilderness to seek St John, who returned to the laura and shut himself up in one cell for forty years. Experience had taught him that a soul accustomed to speak to God alone finds only bitterness and emptiness in all worldly intercourse. Moreover his love of obscurity and his humility made him desire more than ever to live unknown. Nevertheless the fame of his sanctity made it impossible for him to realise his ambition, and he now no longer refused to give audience to those who resorted to him for spiritual advice. Amongst these was Cyril of Scythopolis, who wrote the saint's life when he had reached the great age of 104, whilst still preserving the vigour of mind and the amiability which had always characterised him. Cyril relates that he himself in early manhood had consulted the hermit, then ninety years old, as to his choice of a career. St John advised him to enter the monastery of St Euthymius. Instead of following the holy man's counsel, Cyril went to a small monastery on the bank of the Jordan. There he at once contracted a fever of which he nearly died. But in the night St John appeared to him in his sleep and, after a gentle reprimand, told him that if he repaired at once to St Euthymius he would regain his health and win God's favour. The next morning, after partaking of the Blessed Eucharist, he set out for the aforesaid monastery of St Euthymius, and found that he had entirely recovered. The same author also describes how, in his presence, St John exorcised an evil spirit from a child by making on its forehead the sign of the cross with holy oil. Both by example and precept St John led many souls to God, and continued in his hermitage to emulate, as far as this mortal state will allow, the glorious employment of the heavenly spirits in an uninterrupted exercise of love and praise. He passed to their blessed company in A.D. 558—having lived in the desert for a period of seventy-six years, interrupted only by the nine years of his episcopate.

St John's astonishing austerity, love of silence, and gift of contemplation stand in strange contrast to our worldliness and unmortified spirit. Interior recollection is the essence of Christian virtue : without it the most active zeal and devotion can only be superficial. A love of Christian silence—a silence not of stupidity or sullenness but of virtue and choice—is a proof that the soul makes it her chief delight to be occupied with God, finding no comfort comparable to that of conversing with Him. This is the earthly paradise of all who are truly devout.

Cyril of Scythopolis, the biographer from whom we derive all our knowledge of St John, had been impressed even as a boy by a casual meeting with St Sabas. He seems to have entered the monastery of St Euthymius in 544 and to have passed on to the laura at Jerusalem in 554. Though credulous, like all men of his generation, and delighting in marvels, he was a conscientious reporter of what he believed to be the truth. The biography he wrote is printed in the *Acta Sanctorum*, May, vol. iii. See also Ehrhard in the *Römische Quartalschrift*, vol. vii (1893), pp. 32 *seq.*

BLESSED IMELDA, Virg.
A.D. 1333

The patroness of fervent first communion, Blessed Imelda, came of one of the oldest and wealthiest families in Bologna. Her father was Count Egano Lambertini, and her mother was Castora Galuzzi. Even as a tiny child she showed unusual piety, taking delight in prayer and constantly retiring to a quiet corner of the house, which she adorned with flowers and sacred pictures to make it into a little oratory. When she was nine she was placed, at her own wish, in the Dominican Convent of St Mary Magdalen in Val di Pietra, to be trained there by the nuns. Her sweet disposition soon endeared her to all, whilst the zeal with which she entered into all the religious exercises of the house greatly edified the sisters. Her special devotion was to the Eucharistic presence of Our Lord at Mass and in the tabernacle. To receive Our Lord in Holy Communion became the consuming desire of her heart, but the custom of the place and time had fixed twelve as the earliest age for a first communion. After meditating on the immeasurable condescension of God in thus bestowing Himself to men, she would sometimes exclaim : " Tell me, can anyone receive Jesus into his heart and not die ? "

When she was eleven years old she was present with the rest of the community at the Ascension Day Mass. All the others had received their communion : only Imelda was left unsatisfied. The nuns having made their thanksgiving were preparing to leave the church when some of them were startled to see what appeared to be a Sacred Host hovering in the air above Imelda, as she knelt before the closed tabernacle absorbed in prayer. Quickly they attracted the attention of the priest, who hurried forward with a paten on which to receive It. In the face of such a miracle he could not do otherwise than give to Imelda her first communion, which was also her last. For the rapture with which she received her Lord was so great that it broke her heart. She sank unconscious to the ground, and when loving hands upraised her, it was found that she was dead.

The Bollandists in the *Acta Sanctorum*, May, vol. iii, inserted a notice of Blessed Imelda on the ground of a long-established cultus, though the formal papal confirmation did not occur until 1826. Many devotional booklets—notably those by Lataste (1889), Corsini (1892), Wilms (1925), and T. Alfonsi (1927)—have been published concerning her. But see more especially M. C. de Ganay, *Les Bienheureuses Dominicaines* (1913), pp. 145–152. There is also a short account in Procter, *Lives of Dominican Saints*, pp. 259–262, and a small French devotional sketch, R. Zeller, *Imelda Lambertini, vierge dominicaine*, 1923.

BLESSED (?) JULIAN OF NORWICH, Recluse

c. A.D. 1423

Apart from the autobiographical details given in the *Revelations of Divine Love*, history has preserved few records of the holy woman usually known as Blessed Julian, or Dame Juliana of Norwich. She lived as a strict recluse in the anchoress-house attached to the old church of St Julian, and had, even in her lifetime, a reputation for great sanctity. She is said to have survived to an advanced age, having two maids to wait upon her when she was old, but the actual date of her death is unknown—as is also her parentage. That she was certainly living at the age of seventy appears from a notice prefixed to an ancient manuscript of her book purporting to have been transcribed by a contemporary, and now in the British Museum. It runs : " Here is a vision schewed be the goodenes of God to a deuoute Woman and hir Name is Julyan that es recluse atte Norwyche and yit ys in lyfe. Anno dni millmo CCCCXIII°. In the whilke Vision er fulle many comfortabylle wordes and gretly styrrande to all thaye that desyres to be crystes looverse."

At the beginning of her book Julian states that before she received what she calls the " shewings," she had desired three gifts from God —that He would grant her a greater realisation of Christ's sufferings, that He would send her a severe illness which would bring her to death's door and detach her from earthly things, and that He would give her the three wounds of " very contrition," of "kind compassion," and of "wilful longing towards God." The first two aspirations in course of time passed from her mind, but the third remained ever with her.

When she was thirty and a half years old she actually did contract a malady so serious that her life was despaired of. On the fourth day she received the last sacraments, and on the seventh she seemed to be sinking. All she had strength to do was to keep her eyes fixed on the crucifix. Then, quite suddenly, all her pains left her, and between four and nine o'clock in the morning of May 8, or the 13th, 1373, she had a succession of fifteen distinct visions or shewings, concluded by a sixteenth during the night after the following day. These visions for the most part presented different aspects of Our Lord's Passion, which, while producing in her the compunction she had desired, brought her wonderful peace and joy, although their full significance did not unfold itself until long afterwards. " And from that time that it was shewed," she writes, " I desired oftentimes to learn what was Our Lord's meaning. And fifteen years after and more I was answered in ghostly understanding, saying thus : ' Wouldst thou learn thy Lord's meaning in this thing ? Learn it well : love was His meaning. Who shewed it thee ? Love. Wherefore shewed it He ? For love. Hold thee therein and thou shalt learn and know more in the same. But thou shalt never know nor learn therein other thing without end.' Thus was I learned that Love was Our Lord's meaning." Elsewhere she speaks of being inwardly instructed for twenty years all but three months. At the time when the visions came she was, according to her own account, " a simple creature that colde no letters," in other words, illiterate, but in the years that elapsed before she wrote her book she must have acquired a considerable knowledge of the Christian mystics, for while her style and her message are her own she often uses their terminology and adopts their distinctions. A modern writer, Professor Edmund Gardner, has pointed out one passage which indicates familiarity with the letters of her great contemporary, St Catherine of Siena, and there are several others which appear to have been suggested by the teaching of Eckehart. It would have been strange indeed if she had remained uninfluenced by the spiritual revival on the Continent, for Norwich, as the second largest city in England, and the centre of the woollen trade, was in close and constant communication with the Low Countries. Anchoresses, although they never left their houses, could and did hold intercourse through a window with the outside world, and one who like Julian was famous as a saint and a visionary, would undoubtedly receive many visits from pious strangers—ecclesiastics and layfolk. The book which she eventually produced remains perhaps the most beautiful and certainly the tenderest exposition of Divine Love that has ever been written in the English language. From beholding God's charity as exhibited to mankind in the Passion of Our Incarnate Lord, she rises to the contemplation of His eternal, all-embracing, all-directing, all-creating love. Even what had been a sore perplexity to her—lapses into sin on the part of those called to be saints—she sees to be somehow " behovable " because God has permitted them, and because such failures can be translated through contrition into increased love and humility. To a distressful world Julian sought to pass on words of consolation with which Our Lord had comforted her own soul : " I can make all thing well : I will make all thing well : I shall make all thing well : and thou shalt see thyself that all manner of thing shall be well."

Four manuscripts are known of Mother Julian's *Revelations of Divine Love*. That dated 1413 is shorter than the others which were all copies made at a much later period It is difficult to be sure whether the fifteenth century manuscript represents a primitive text which was subsequently expanded by her, or whether it is an abridgement of what Julian originally wrote. The first printed edition was produced by the Benedictine Dom Serenus Cressy in 1670. Since then Father Tyrrell, Miss Grace Warrack, D. Harford and others have edited the text afresh, and there has also been a French translation. See further R. H. Thouless, *The Lady Julian, a Psychological Study*, 1924

ST PETER REGALATUS, CONF.

A.D. 1456

St Peter Regalatus came of a noble family settled at Valladolid in Spain. He lost his father in infancy, and when he was in his thirteenth year he obtained, though with difficulty, his mother's permission to enter the Franciscan convent of his native city. He soon became distinguished amongst his brethren for his extraordinary fervour. When Peter Villacretios, after initiating a rigorous reform at Aguilar in the diocese of Osma, founded another convent at Tribulos on the Douro, which seemed to most people more like a prison than a monastery, our saint at his own earnest request was allowed to form one of the community. By the austerity of his penances, his assiduity in prayer, and his frequent ecstasies, in which he is said to have been often raised from the ground, he seems to have equalled the most eminent saints of his order. The sufferings of Our Lord were the principal subject of his meditations, and he lived in constant union with God. Upon the death of Father Villacretios he succeeded him in the government of his reformed congregation, and died at Aguilar on March 30, 1456, in the sixty-sixth year of his age. He was called Regalatus on account of the zeal with which he enforced the rule.

The Bollandists, who treat of St Peter Regalatus on March 30 (*Acta Sanctorum*, March, vol. iii), print only a Latin translation of the Spanish Life by Antony Daza (1627), with some extracts from the process then instituted before the Auditors of the Rota. Several Spanish biographies have since appeared, notably one by J. Infantes (1854). See also the Bull of canonisation issued by Benedict XIV, and many references in that Pontiff's great treatise *De Beatificatione etc. Sanctorum* ; with Léon, *Auréole Séraphique* (Eng. trans.), vol. ii, pp. 150–159.

ST ANDREW HUBERT FOURNET, Conf.

A.D. 1834

In studying the lives of those who have been raised to the altars of the Church, we find many instances of men and women who, from childhood, have felt drawn to the mode of life they afterwards adopted, but occasionally we come across individuals who began by experiencing a positive aversion from what subsequently proved to be their vocation. To this latter category belonged St Andrew Hubert Fournet. He was born on December 6, 1752, at Maillé, near Poitiers, of devout and well-to-do parents. Possibly his good mother rather overdid her pious instructions and her laudation of the priestly office, for little Andrew was frankly bored by religion : he wished neither to pray nor to learn : all he wanted to do was to amuse himself. In a book belonging to him when a lad, and preserved as a relic, may be read the following words written in his childish hand-writing : " This book belongs to Andrew Hubert Fournet, a good boy, though he is not going to be a priest or a monk ! " At school his idleness and frivolity led him into many scrapes, and one day he ran away—only to be brought back in disgrace and to receive a thrashing. Later on he went to Poitiers, ostensibly to study philosophy and law, but his main study was to get as much pleasure out of life as possible. Once he enlisted and was bought out. Then his mother tried to obtain some secretarial work for him : his handwriting, however, was too bad. Almost in despair his family sent him to an uncle, a parish priest in a lonely, poverty-stricken parish. This was the turning-point in his life. The uncle was a holy man who won his nephew's confidence and who succeeded so well in drawing out the good that underlay his frivolity, that before long Andrew appeared a changed character. He set himself to study theology, was ordained priest, and became his uncle's curate. After serving a second and more strenuous cure he was nominated parish priest in his native town of Maillé in 1781. His liberality to the poor and his winning personality soon endeared him to the whole parish. For a time he continued to enter-tain friends at a well appointed table, but the casual criticism of a beggar led him to give away all his silver and every article of furniture that was not absolutely necessary. From that time forward he and his mother, his sister, and a curate led an almost conventual life in the presbytery. His simplicity soon extended itself from his manner of life to his speech. " Your Reverence used to preach so finely that no one understood you," his sacristan remarked one day. " Nowadays we can all follow every word you say."

This peaceful, happy existence came to an end with the outbreak of the French Revolution. St Andrew refused to take the oath which the new Government required of the clergy, and was consequently outlawed. Only by stealth could he minister to his flock—now in the woods, now in a barn, now in a humble cottage—and always at the risk of his life. Towards the end of 1792, at the bidding of his bishop, he retired to Spain, but after an absence of five years he decided that he could no longer leave his flock unshepherded. Secretly he made his way back to his parish, which he entered at the dead of night. The news of his return spread like wildfire and his ministrations were sought on all hands. The danger, however, was greater than ever : the pursuivants were constantly on his track : and on several occasions he only escaped by the skin of his teeth. Once, as he was sitting by a cottage fire, the bailiffs entered in search of him. The good woman of the house promptly boxed his ears for an idle churl and bade him give his place to the gentlemen while he went off to mind the cattle. The ruse succeeded, but in telling the story St Andrew was wont to add : " She had a heavy hand : she made me see stars ! " Another day he eluded capture by feigning to be a corpse. The officials sent in search of him drew back at the sight of a shrouded figure on a bed surrounded by candles and kneeling women.

The accession to power of Napoleon Bonaparte brought relief to the faithful, for the First Consul soon realised that it was politic to make terms with the Church. Fournet openly took control of his parish and presbytery, and set himself to rekindle the embers of religion. He gave many missions, and was untiring in the pulpit and confessional. In all his efforts he was ably seconded by a noble lady of the neighbourhood, Elisabeth Bichier des Ages, who, under his guidance, formed a congregation of devoted women pledged to teach children and to look after the sick and poor. St Andrew directed the Sisters and drew up their rule. Their rapidly increasing numbers compelled them before very long to move to larger quarters in some disused old conventual buildings near La Puye. They became known as the Daughters of the Cross, but the foundress liked to call them Sisters of St Andrew.

When Abbé Fournet had reached the age of sixty-eight, fatigue and increasing infirmities induced him to resign his parish work at Maillé and to retire to La Puye. Here he not only devoted himself to the new community but also gave assistance in the adjoining parishes, and became spiritual adviser to many souls—clergy as well as layfolk. In the process of beatification some remarkable evidence was given of the miraculous multiplication of food, and especially of grain, effected by the prayers of St Andrew when the nuns among

whom he resided needed bread for themselves and their children.
He died on May 13, 1834, and was canonised on June 4, 1933.

The most copious and reliable source of information are the documents
printed for the Congregation of Sacred Rites in the process of beatification.
A biographical summary in some detail is included in the Bull of canonisation.
It may be found in the *Acta Apostolicae Sedis*, vol. xxv (1933), pp. 417–428.
See also L. Rigaud, *Vie de A. H. Fournet* (1885) ; an anonymous Italian
life, *Il beato Andrea Uberto Fournet* (1885) ; and Rigaud, *La beata Elisabetta
Bichier des Ages* (1934).

MAY 14

ST BONIFACE OF TARSUS, Mart.

(?) A.D. 306

THE martyr, St Boniface of Tarsus, seems to have found no
public cultus before the ninth century, although he is said
to have suffered in 306, and his reputed acts, even if they
contain a substratum of truth, are obviously embellished with fictitious details. The story may be summarised as follows : There
was living in Rome about the beginning of the fourth century a
wealthy young woman named Aglæ, beautiful, well-born, and so
fond of attracting attention that on three occasions she entertained
the city with public shows at her own expense. Her chief steward was
a man called Boniface, with whom she lived on terms of undue intimacy. He was dissolute and given to intemperance, but, on the
other hand, he was liberal, hospitable, and extremely kind to the poor.
One day Aglæ summoned him and bade him go to the East and
fetch the relics of some of the martyrs. " For," she said, " I have
heard tell that they who honour those that suffer for Jesus Christ will
have a share in their glory. In the East His servants daily suffer
torments and lay down their lives for Him." Boniface prepared to
obey, and, having collected a considerable sum of money, he bade
farewell to Aglæ, adding, " I will not fail to bring back relics of
martyrs if I find any, but what if my own body should be brought
to you as one of them ? " From that time he was a changed man,
and during his long voyage he neither ate meat nor drank wine, spending much of his time in prayer and fasting. The Church at that
period enjoyed peace in the West, but in the East the persecution,
inaugurated under Diocletian, was being continued under Galerius
Maximianus and Maximinus Daza. It raged most fiercely in Cilicia
under an inhuman governor of the name of Simplicius. Boniface
accordingly directed his steps to Tarsus, the capital of that province.
On arriving at the city he alighted, and sent his servants with the
horses to the inn, whilst he himself went straight to the court of the
governor. Simplicius was found sitting on the judgement-seat, and
twenty Christians were being cruelly tortured before him. Boniface

ran towards them, exclaiming: " Great is the God of the Christians !
Great is the martyrs' God ! and you, servants of Jesus, pray for me
that I may join with you in fighting the devil ! " The angry governor
caused him to be arrested and ordered that sharpened reeds should be
thrust under his nails and molten lead poured down his throat.
The people, revolted by so much cruelty, began to cry out, " Great
is the God of the Christians ! " Simplicius, in some alarm, hastily
withdrew, fearing a tumult, but the following day he called for Boniface again and condemned him to be cast into a cauldron of boiling
pitch from which, however, he emerged unscathed. Finally, a soldier
cut off the martyr's head with his sword. The body was bought by
his servants for five hundred pieces of gold, embalmed and conveyed
back to Italy. Half a mile from Rome, on the Latin Way, it was
met by Agläe, accompanied by a procession of priests and of other
persons bearing lighted torches. In that place she erected a church
to enshrine the sacred relics, and when she herself died, after leading
a penitential life for fifteen years, her remains were laid beside his.
In 1603 their reputed relics were found, with those of St Alexius,
in the church which formerly bore the name of St Boniface, but is
now known as St Alessio.

The account here given, abbreviated from Alban Butler, was published
by him, apparently without the least misgiving, as a narrative derived from
" the authentic Acts " of the martyr. Père Delehaye, and other modern
authorities, pronounce the story to be no more than a pious fiction (see his
Légendes Hagiographiques, p. 113). The " Acts " are to be found in the
Acta Sanctorum, May, vol. iii. See further Duchesne, *Mélanges d'Archéologie*, 1890, pp. 2–10, and the *Nuovo Bulletino di Archeologia crist.*, vol. vi
(1900), pp. 205–234. The story was very popular in the Middle Ages and
gave rise to much folklore ; on which consult Bächtold-Stäubli, *Handwörterbuch des deut. Aberglaubens*, vol. i, pp. 1475, *seq.*

SS. VICTOR AND CORONA, MARTS.

(?) SECOND CENTURY

The martyrdom of St Victor and St Corona appears to belong
to the second century, but time, place, and circumstances are equally
doubtful. The Roman Martyrology following the ancient *Hieronymianum* names Syria as the country where they suffered ; the older
copies of the so-called " Acts " speak of Egypt. According to one
tradition Victor was a native of Damascus, a soldier in the army of
Antoninus Pius. As he made no secret of being a Christian, his
superior officer, Sebastian by name, called upon him to burn incense

to the gods. He refused and was subjected to appalling tortures. His fingers were crushed and then torn out joint by joint : he was cast into a fiery furnace : he was made to eat poisoned food : he was sprayed with boiling oil : he was singed with flaming torches : he was suspended by the feet : he had a mixture of vinegar and chalk thrust into his mouth. From all these torments he came forth unhurt and was finally killed by blows from a hatchet. The courage displayed by the martyr so wrought upon the feelings of a young woman of sixteen, the wife of a soldier, that she broke out into loud expressions of admiration and sympathy. She also declared that she saw two crowns falling from heaven—the one for Victor and the other for herself. On being arrested she avowed herself to be a Christian. She was torn asunder by being tied by her hands and feet to two trees, the branches of which had been forcibly brought near each other and were then suddenly released.

In his paper on The Martyrs of Egypt (*Analecta Bollandiana*, vol. xl, 1922), Père Delehaye has dealt with the legend of Victor and Corona (pp. 117-118). In spite of the long elogium devoted to them in the Roman Martyrology, all that can be said in their favour is that the story was widely circulated in the Western Church from an early date.

ST PONTIUS, Mart.

(?) Third Century

St Pontius, an illustrious primitive martyr, suffered in the persecution of Valerian about the year 258 at Cimella, a city afterwards destroyed by the Lombards but rebuilt in modern times as Cimiez on the French Riviera, near Nice. According to his legendary history he was the son of a Roman senator, and was instructed in the Christian faith as a lad by Pope Pontianus. Upon the death of his father, he gave away his inheritance to the poor, devoting himself to good works. He was greatly esteemed by the Emperor Philip and by his son—both of whom he converted to Christianity. After the murder of his royal patron he fled to Cimella, but was arrested as a Christian and condemned to be tortured and exposed to the wild beasts. As the creatures would not attack him, the governor ordered him to be beheaded.

Here again we find in the Roman Martyrology a name which in Alban Butler's time was reputed to be that of " an illustrious primitive martyr." On the other hand modern hagiography, as represented by the doyen of the Bollandists, Père Delehaye, tells us that the " Acts " (printed in the *Acta*

Sanctorum, May, vol. iii) are historically worthless and cannot be of older date than the sixth century, though they pretend to have been written by a contemporary, an eye-witness of the martyrdom. Neither in this case is there any adequate evidence of early cultus. See *Analecta Bollandiana*, vol. xxv (1906), pp. 201–203.

ST CARTHACH MOCHUDA, ABBOT

A.D. 637

St Carthach appears to have adopted the name of his master, St Carthach the Elder, who, for his part, called his disciple Mochuda, or my Chuda—Chuda, or Chudd, being presumably the younger man's actual name. A native of Kerry, and of royal race, he is said to have been employed as a swineherd when he came under the care of St Carthach the Elder, from whom he received his monastic training, and by whom he was afterwards ordained priest. About the year 580, he went to live as a hermit at a place called Kiltallagh, but the jealousy of two neighbouring bishops caused him to withdraw, and he spent a year at Bangor under the direction of St Comgall. He then returned to Kerry, where he preached and built churches. By the advice of St Colman Elo, with whom he made some stay, he decided to establish himself at Rahan, or Rathin, in Westmeath. There, about the year 590, he founded a monastery in which he gradually assembled over eight hundred monks. For these disciples he drew up a rule which is still extant, and remains one of the great treasures of the Irish Church. It is in the form of a metrical poem, 580 lines long, and is divided into nine sections. His monks, who subsisted entirely on the vegetables they cultivated themselves, led a most austere life, very similar to that afterwards adopted by the Trappists. Besides having the charge of this monastery, St Carthach seems to have ruled as bishop over the Fircall district. The community had been settled at Rahan for over forty years when they were expelled by King Blathmac. On Easter Day, 635, St Carthach set out from Rahan accompanied by 800 monks to seek a new home. After some wandering, the great party arrived at the banks of the River Blackwater, where the Prince of the Nandesi, or Decies, gave them a tract of land for a new monastery. St Carthach remained with them for two years, laying the foundation for the great abbey and school of Lismore, which was to become famous throughout Christendom. He then retired to a cave near the place now known as St Carthach's Well, and spent the last few weeks of his life preparing himself for death. He died on May 14, 637. St Carthach is regarded as the founder of the episcopal see of Lismore, which was united to that of Waterford by Pope Urban V in 1363, at the request of King Edward III. From the lustre shed upon it by the sanctity and miracles of St Carthach, Lismore came to be regarded in after-ages as a holy city—a reputation well sustained by its great school and monastery. One half of it was closed to women, being entirely occupied by cells and other monastic buildings. Thither flocked from all parts of Ireland and England crowds of eager young students, and many older men who desired to end their days within its hallowed walls. As recently as 1891 the burial-place of St Carthach was discovered by Dr. Grattan-Flood.

Materials for the life of St Carthach are relatively speaking abundant. There are two Latin lives, both of which are printed in the *Acta Sanctorum*, May, vol. iii, while the longer has been re-edited by C. Plummer in his *Vitæ Sanctorum Hiberniæ*, vol. i, pp. 170–199. There is also an Irish life (not a direct translation of either of these) which may be found in C. Plummer's *Bethada Náem nÉrenn*, vol. i, pp. 291–299, with an English translation in vol. ii. The Rule mentioned above has been printed with an English translation by Mac Eclaise in the *Irish Ecclesiastical Record* for May, 1910, pp. 495–517. See also Kenney, *Sources for the Early History of Ireland*, vol. i, pp. 473–475 ; Gougaud, *Christianity in Celtic Lands, passim* ; and especially C. Plummer's Preface to his *Vitæ S. H.*, pp. xlv–xlviii.

ST EREMBERT, Bp. of Toulouse

c. A.D. 672

Amongst the many pious men who received the Benedictine habit at Fontenelle Abbey from the hands of its founder St Wandrille, one of the most distinguished was a youth called Erembert, a native of Waucourt near Poissy, in the department of Seine et Oise. He was not, however, suffered to remain undisturbed in his monastic retreat, for King Clotaire III summoned him to become Bishop of Toulouse. One incident in his episcopal life alone has come down to us. He was on a visit to his brother Gamardus in his birthplace when a fire broke out which threatened to destroy the town. St Erembert prostrated himself in prayer in the Church of St Saturninus and then emerged holding his pastoral cross erect. Immediately the wind veered, the flames died down, and the people flocked to the church praising God. Ill-health induced St Erembert to resign office in the year 668. He retired to Fontenelle, then under the rule of St Lambert, and there he remained until his death. His brother Gamardus, with his two sons, afterwards entered Fontenelle, upon which they bestowed all the family estates.

A Latin life compiled at Fontenelle a century and a half later is not historically of much value. It has been printed by Mabillon and in the *Acta Sanctorum*, May, vol. iii, and it was re-edited in 1910 by W. Levison in the *M. G. H. Scrip. rer. meroving.*, vol. v, pp. 652 *seq.* See also Duchesne, *Fastes épiscopaux*, vol. i, p. 307.

ST PASCHAL I, POPE

A.D. 824

Paschal I became Pope at a time when the occupants of St Peter's chair were being greatly harassed by a strong anti-papal party led by influential vassals of the Church, who inflamed the Roman populace and everywhere fomented disaffection. In 815, they had plotted to depose and kill Leo III; and his successor, Stephen IV, found himself constrained to seek assistance and protection at the court of Louis the Pious. Paschal was a Roman who had been educated in the Lateran school, and had come into prominence as Abbot of St Stephen's—a post which entailed on him a general charge of the pilgrims in Rome. In 817, on the very day after the death of Stephen IV, the clergy and people of Rome proceeded to elect Paschal, very much against his will, and without waiting for the Emperor's sanction. He, however, lost no time in entering into relations with Louis, who in due course sent him the usual *pactum confirmationis*. In 823 the Emperor's son, Lothair, came to Rome, and Pope Paschal is said to have crowned him King of Italy and of the Rhine provinces. Peace was maintained so long as the Imperial soldiers remained in the Holy City, but no sooner had they withdrawn than the old feuds broke out again, the opposition leaders maintaining that the Emperor, not the Pope, was suzerain of Rome and the Papal States. Because they favoured this view, two important officials, Theodore, Primicerius of the Church, and Leo, the Nomenclator, were seized by members of the Papal household, blinded and then beheaded. By a solemn expurgatorial oath, taken in the presence of fifty bishops and of the Imperial commissioners, Pope Paschal cleared himself of the charge of having been privy to the murder, but he refused to deliver up the perpetrators to justice, alleging, in the first place, that they were not amenable to secular courts, and in the second that their victims had been guilty of treason, and were consequently outside the pale of the law. In that same year he gave to Ebbo, Archbishop of Rheims, plenipotentiary powers authorising him to undertake the evangelisation of Denmark. His sympathy extended to the Oriental Christians, then suffering persecution at the hands of the Iconoclastic Emperor,

Leo ; he wrote letters on their behalf to Constantinople and, although his efforts in that direction were fruitless, he was able to afford generous assistance to such fugitives as came to Rome. For the use of Greek monks he left and endowed the monastery of S. Prassede, the church of which he had embellished with mosaics and had enlarged by the addition of the oratory of St Zeno to serve as a burial-place for his mother. In the catacomb of St Callixtus he discovered the body of St Cecilia, which he translated to the church bearing her name, just then in process of reconstruction. He also removed from the catacombs to Roman churches the relics of many other saints, including Popes Lucius I and Urban I, as well as the holy martyrs Processus, Martinianus, Maximus, Valerianus, and Tiburtius. Other churches in the city were restored or adorned by him, and in the mosaic which decorates the apse at S. Maria della Navicella may still be seen his portrait—a very small figure prostrate at the feet of Our Lady in glory. St Paschal I reigned seven years and three months, dying most probably on February 11, 824.

The *Liber Pontificalis* contains little but a record of the Pope's building operations and benefactions. For his history we have to turn to the scanty correspondence preserved to us, and to the chroniclers. There has not, of course, ever been any question of a formal canonisation, and the grounds upon which Pope Paschal's name has been included in the Martyrologium (now under February 11) are somewhat obscure. There is a notice devoted to Pope Paschal in the *Acta Sanctorum*, May, vol. iii, but see especially Mgr Mann, *Lives of the Popes*, vol. ii, pp. 122–135.

ST HALWARD, Mart. (?)

A.D. 1043 (?)

In Norway St Halward, or Hallvard, was formerly held in great honour, and its capital, Oslo, is still under his patronage. His true history is shrouded in obscurity, even the date at which he lived being doubtful, but tradition has supplied us with an account of his death. He is said to have been the son of Thornez, sister to King Olaf the Fat, and to have been engaged in trading with the various Baltic islands. He was about to embark on his homeward voyage after one of his expeditions, when he was accosted by a woman who besought him to receive her into his ship and save her from her enemies. As she appeared to be in terrible distress and was obviously soon to become a mother, he chivalrously acceded to her request. Before they could start, three men came running down to the shore demanding the surrender of the woman, whom they accused of theft.

She denied the charge, and Halward refused to deliver her over to their vengeance, though he said he was willing to give them the value of what she was accused of stealing. Thereupon one of the men drew his bow and shot the saint dead. After they had attached a heavy stone to his neck, they flung his body into the sea, but it floated on the water and drifted to the coast of Gothland. St Halward's relics were afterwards taken to Oslo where a stone church was built to enshrine them early in the twelfth century.

However slight and legendary the account may seem which is printed in the *Acta Sanctorum*, May, vol. iii, and in Storm, *Monumenta historica Norvegiæ, etc.*, there can be no question that the church of St Halward at Oslo was held in great honour. In the Icelandic " Saga of Hacon," of the middle of the thirteenth century, this church is many times mentioned, and we learn, for example, that King Sigurd and the younger King Hacon were buried there. See the *Hacon Saga* (Rolls Series), § 288.

BLESSED GILES OF PORTUGAL, CONF.

A.D. 1265

During the reign of Sancho the Great, King of Portugal, one of the monarch's most trusted counsellors was Rodrigues de Vagliaditos, the governor of Coïmbra. This nobleman had several sons, of whom the third, Giles, or Egidius, by name, was destined for the Church in accordance with the tradition then prevalent in aristocratic families. With that object in view he was sent to the University of Coïmbra, where he at once attracted attention by his brilliant abilities. The king, who was greatly interested in him, bestowed upon him a canonry and other benefices, but the young man himself was far more concerned with experimental science than with theology. He therefore elected to go to the University of Paris to qualify for a medical degree. He had started on his journey and had proceeded but a little way when he fell in with a stranger, whom he afterwards considered to be the devil incarnate. The man induced him to go to Toledo instead of to France. In that city Giles took up his abode, and not only studied alchemy and physics but also became deeply interested in necromancy and the Black Arts. He appears to have plunged headlong into every form of evil, and he so completely turned his back upon religion that he drew up a document which purported to be a pact with Satan and sealed it with his blood. After seven years in Toledo Giles reverted to his original design. He took his doctor's degree in Paris, and then practised there as a physician with considerable success. Before very long, however, his conscience began to prick him. One night he had an alarming dream in which a gigantic spectral warrior threatened him, crying out, " Amend your life." Upon awaking he tried to disregard the warning as being a mere nightmare, but the vision was repeated a night or two later. This time the spectre shouted, " I shall kill you unless you amend your life ! " " I *will* amend it ! " exclaimed Giles as he awoke, and he kept his word. Without delay he burnt his magical books, destroyed the phials which contained his potions and set out on foot to return to Portugal. After a long and weary journey he arrived, footsore and weary, at Valencia in Spain, where he was hospitably received by the Dominican friars, then engaged in building themselves a priory. There Giles sought absolution for the sins of the past and there he received the habit. The rest of his life was edifying in the extreme. He had indeed to face fierce trials from the powers of darkness, and the memory of his iniquitous pact often tempted him to despair of salvation, but he persevered in prayer and mortification. After seven years he was granted a vision in which Our Lady restored to him the sinister document, and his anxiety on that score was allayed for ever.

Soon after his profession Blessed Giles was sent to Santarem in Portugal : at a later date he spent some time in the Parisian house of the Order, where he contracted a warm friendship with Blessed Humbert de Romans, the future Master-General of the Friars Preachers. Because of his learning and sanctity Giles was elected Provincial for Portugal, but he soon laid down the charge on the score of age. In his last years, which were spent at Santarem, the holy man was favoured with frequent ecstasies, and showed himself to be endowed with the gift of prophecy.

The resemblance which this story bears to such popular legends as that of Cyprian and Justina (see the September volume, pp. 321–323), not to speak of Faust and other fictions of similar purport, renders its more sensational elements very open to question. The lengthy narrative which the Bollandists (*Acta Sanctorum*, May, vol. iii) have borrowed from Father Resendio seems to lack any reliable corroboration. The same type of story is to be found in Procter, *Lives of Dominican Saints*, pp. 130–133.

BLESSED PETRONILLA OF TROYES, Virg.

A.D. 1355

Very little seems to be known about Blessed Petronilla except that she belonged to the family of the Counts of Troyes, and that she was the first abbess of the convent of Moncel, founded by King

Philip le Bel when he was staying in the neighbouring town of Pont-Saint-Maxence. In his charter he expressed his desire to establish a community of Poor Clares where the nuns should pray continually for himself, his successors, the state, and the souls of his deceased relations; but although he laid the foundation, the house was not completed for occupation until the reign of Louis of Valois. On July 17, 1336, Queen Jane of Burgundy placed there twelve nuns drawn from three different houses, and the new community was soon enriched by liberal donations of land and money. During the captivity of King John the convent sold its jewels, together with the gold and silver vessels bestowed on it by Louis of Valois, in order to contribute towards the monarch's ransom. Down to the time of their dispersion at the French Revolution, the Poor Clares of Moncel regarded Blessed Petronilla as their special protector and patroness. In 1793 the abbey church was destroyed, and the monastic buildings passed into secular hands. Blessed Petronilla is commemorated in the Franciscan Martyrologium, and her feast is also kept by the Capuchins.

See H. L. Fautrat, " L'Abbaye du Moncel," in *Mémoires com. archéo. Senlis*, vol. vi (1892), pp. 1–24 ; *Gallia Christiana* (nova), vol. ix, pp: 852–856.

BLESSED MICHAEL GARICOÏTS, Conf.

A.D. 1863

Towards the close of the eighteenth century, and in the early part of the nineteenth, there was living in the Lower Pyrenees, at the hamlet of Ibarra, a family of poor peasants named Garicoïts. Their cottage was humble enough to human eyes, but God's blessing must have rested upon it because its hospitable door was always open to receive the proscribed priests who, from time to time during the French Revolution, and the years immediately following, came to minister in secret to the faithful. Here on April 15, 1797, there was born to Arnold and Gratianne Garicoïts their eldest son Michael. Life is hard in those mountain regions, and the boy was a mere child when he was hired out to be shepherd boy to a farmer. His own often expressed desire was to be a priest, but his parents always replied, " No, we are too poor." The old grandmother thought otherwise. One day she went to talk the matter over with the parish priest of St Palais, who in times past had often found a hiding-place in the Garicoïts' cottage. Through his efforts the boy was received first into the College of St Palais and afterwards at Bayonne, arrangements having been made that he should be no charge upon his parents but should earn his expenses by working out of school hours for the priests and in the bishop's kitchen. It was a strenuous time for the young peasant, but he was clever and healthy. Moreover, he was working to attain his heart's desire. Philosophy he studied at Aire and theology in the *grand séminaire* at Dax, where he was nicknamed " Our Aloysius Gonzaga." Whilst still a seminarist he took a class in a preparatory school near by, and in December 1823 he was ordained priest in Bayonne Cathedral by Bishop d'Astros. His first parochial experience was gained at Cambo, whither he was sent to act as *vicaire* to the *curé*, who was in feeble health. In the two years he remained there he did much to revive religion, combating Jansenism by the custom of frequent communion as well as by introducing Sacred Heart devotions. He tackled freethinkers with so much fervour that one of them was heard to exclaim, " That devil would give his life to save the soul of an enemy ! " Father Garicoïts' next call was to a professorship in the Great Seminary for priests at Bétharram, and then to be superior—a congenial post which he filled with conspicuous ability and success. The bishop, however, suddenly decided to merge the seminary with that of Bayonne, and Blessed Michael found himself with two other priests left alone to carry on the services. During this period, when he was more or less stranded, there began to take shape in his mind a scheme for training priests to do mission work among the people. With two or three companions he started to live a community life, and then, in order that he might better know God's will, he went to Toulouse to attend a Retreat given by Father Le Blanc—a Jesuit. To this good priest he opened his heart, and was encouraged to persevere. " You will be the father of a congregation that will be our sister," said the Jesuit, and Father Garicoïts drew up in 1838 a constitution largely based on that of the sons of St Ignatius. Like them, his missionaries were to take life vows and to spread far and wide. Associates gathered round him at Bétharram, and all seemed promising when a check came from an unexpected quarter. The bishop who had been his patron and had ordained him was replaced by another, who viewed with disapproval his idea of founding a new congregation. His constitutions were subjected to a fundamental revision, he was told to confine himself to the diocese, and to work only under the direction of the bishop. Not till 1852 was the community allowed to choose its own superior, and even then it was tied down by regulations which hampered its activity. Father Garicoïts submitted, but with a heavy heart. " What pangs accompany the birth of a congregation ! " he once said to one of his sons ; but generally he bore his trials in silence. He died on Ascension

Day, May 14, 1863, at Bétharram. Fourteen years later, in September 1877, the Institute of Auxiliary Priests of the Sacred Heart was approved in Rome, and sanctioned as a separate congregation on the lines Blessed Michael had laid down.

The brief of beatification, which contains a detailed biographical summary, will be found in the *Acta Apostolicæ Sedis*, vol. xv (1923), pp. 263–269. Lives of Blessed Michael have been written in French by B. Bourdenne (1921), and by the Abbé Bordacher (1926). See also Ph. Mazoyer, *Lourdes et Bétharram* (1895), especially pp. 272 *seq.*

MAY 15

ST JOHN BAPTIST DE LA SALLE, Conf.

A.D. 1719

THE founder of the Institute of the Brothers of the Christian Schools was born at Rheims on April 30, 1654. His parents, Louis de la Salle and Nicolle Moët, were both of noble family, and his father held the office of presiding councillor of the Court of Appeal. From the instructions of a devout mother, the boy, John Baptist, early gave evidence of such remarkable piety that he was designated for the priesthood. He received the tonsure when he was only eleven, and became a member of the Cathedral chapter of Rheims at the age of sixteen, an uncle having resigned a canonry in his favour. His early studies he pursued in his native city, but in 1670 he entered the seminary of St Sulpice in Paris. His parents died when he was twenty, and after his ordination he took charge of his three younger brothers. A young man of striking appearance, well connected, refined, and scholarly, he seemed assured of a life of dignified ease or of high preferment in the Church. But God in His providence had other designs for him—of which he himself had no presentiment. His attention seems first to have been drawn to the education of the poor when one of his fellow-canons on his deathbed committed to his care the spiritual direction of a girls' orphanage and school as well as of the Sisters of the Holy Infant Jesus who conducted it. Even then he does not seem to have been especially interested, for when a suitable occasion presented itself a few years later he passed on the work to other hands. He had, however, through the orphanage come into touch with a wealthy woman, a relation of his own, who, after assisting the nuns in their labours for girls, desired to found something similar for boys. She entrusted the establishment of a school to a layman called Adrien Nigel, an enthusiast in the cause of education, and gave him an introduction to Canon de la Salle. By their joint efforts a school was started in the parish of St Maurice, and soon afterwards another in the parish of St James. Gradually the young canon became more and more drawn into the work and grew interested in the seven masters who taught in these schools. He rented a house for them, fed them with food from his own table, and tried to instil into them the high educational ideals which were gradually taking shape in his own mind. After a time, though their uncouth manners repelled him, he decided to invite them to live in his own home that he might have them under his constant supervision. The result must have been a great disappointment. Not only did two of his brothers indignantly leave his house— a step he may have apprehended—but five of the schoolmasters themselves soon took their departure, unable or unwilling to submit to an almost monastic discipline for which they had never bargained. The reformer waited, and his patience was rewarded. Other men of a better type presented themselves, knowing what would be expected of them, and these formed the nucleus of what was to prove a new community. To house them more suitably the saint gave up his paternal home, and moved with them to more suitable premises at the entrance to the Rue Neuve. As the movement became known, requests began to come in from outside for schoolmasters trained on the new method, and De la Salle found his time fully engrossed. Partly for that reason and partly because he realized the contrast his disciples drew between his well-paid, assured official income and their own uncertain position he decided to give up his canonry. This he did against the wishes of all his friends, and even of the Archbishop of Rheims. The next question for consideration was the use he should make of his private fortune, which he no longer wished to retain for his own use. Should he employ it for the infant community, or should he give it away? He went to Paris to consult Father Barré, a saintly man who was greatly interested in education, and whose advice had helped him in the past. Father Barré was strongly opposed to the idea of endowment. " Si vous fondez, vous fondrez " (" If you endow, you will founder "), he said, and the saint, after fervent prayer for light, determined to sell all he had and to distribute the proceeds to the poor—who at that time were in the direst need, as a famine was raging in Champagne. So completely did the saint divest himself of all that when, shortly afterwards, he had occasion to visit the Duc de Mazarin at Rethel, he had to beg his bread on the journey. His life from that time became even more austere. He had naturally a very delicate palate, but he deliberately starved himself until the pangs of hunger enabled him to swallow any food, however coarse or ill-prepared. Eventually he so completely lost the sense of taste, that he once ate quite unknowingly and unconcernedly a dish of wormwood the cook had sent in by mistake.

As the institute grew and postulants of all classes presented themselves, the question of a regular rule necessarily arose. The saint held a conference with twelve of his older disciples and, after consideration, it was decided to make a provisional code, the vows taken to be yearly renewable until vocations became certain. At the same time a name was decided upon for members of the community. They were to be called the Brothers of the Christian Schools. They were to wear the soutane without a belt, a broad-brimmed hat and thick shoes. For an outer garment they were to adopt—at the suggestion of the mayor—the long cloak with hanging sleeves which was usually worn in Champagne during the winter.

The first serious trial that befell the Institute came in the form of illness amongst the brothers, several of whom died between the years 1681 and 1688. Our saint seems to have attributed this visitation to his own incapacity to rule, and he consequently persuaded his disciples to elect another superior. No sooner, however, did this become known than the Archiepiscopal Grand Vicar ordered him to resume his office. His wisdom and his guiding hand were indeed necessary, for external pressure was about to cause unforeseen developments in the new congregation—developments which would greatly widen its field of operation. Hitherto recruits had been full-grown men, but now applications began to be received from boys between the ages of fifteen and twenty. To reject promising lads at a malleable age might mean losing them altogether, and yet they were not old enough to be subjected to a rule framed for adults. De la Salle accordingly decided to set up a Junior Noviciate. He lodged the youths in an adjoining house, gave them a simple order of the day, and entrusted their training to a wise Brother, whilst retaining supervision of them himself. But soon there appeared another class of candidate who also, like the boys, could not well be refused and who likewise required to be dealt with apart. These were young men of good character who were sent by their parish priests to the saint with a request that he would train them as Catholic schoolmasters, and send them back to teach in their own villages. He accepted them, found them a domicile, undertook their training, and thus founded the first Normal School for teachers.

All this time the work of teaching poor boys had been steadily going on, although hitherto it had been restricted to Rheims. In February 1688 our saint, at the request of M. de la Barmondière, the Curé of St Sulpice in Paris, took over a school in that parish. It was the last of seven free schools founded by M. Olier, which had eventually been compelled to close down for lack of satisfactory teachers. The Brothers were so successful that a second school was opened in the same district. The control of these Paris foundations was entrusted to Brother l'Heureux, a most gifted and capable man whom the Saint designed to be his successor, and whom he was about to present for ordination. It had been his intention to have priests in his institution to take charge of each house, but Brother l'Heureux's unexpected death made him doubt whether his design had been according to God's will. After much prayer it was borne in upon him that if his order was to confine itself strictly to the work of teaching, for which it had been founded, and to remain free from caste distinctions, the Brothers must continue to be laymen. He therefore laid down the statute—perhaps the most self-denying ordinance which could ever be imposed upon a community of men—that no Brother of the Christian Schools should ever be a priest, and that no priest should ever become a member of the Order. That regulation is in force to this day. Certain troubles which had affected the work during the founder's absence in Paris led him afterwards to take a house at Vaugirard to serve as a Retreat where his sons could come as need arose to recruit both body and spirit. It also became the Novice house of the Order. Here in 1693 the saint drew up the matured rule which gave permission for the first time for the taking of life vows. Here also he wrote his *Manual for Christian Schools*, in which he sets forth the system of education to be carried out— a system which revolutionised elementary education, and is successfully pursued at the present day. It replaced the old method of individual instruction by class teaching, it insisted on silence while the lessons were being given, and it taught in French and through French—not through Latin. Up to this period the schools opened by the Brothers had all been intended for poor children, but a new departure was made at the request of King James II of England, then an exile in France. He wanted a college for the sons of his Irish adherents, and at his request the saint opened a school for fifty boys of gentle birth. They naturally required a higher form of education, and the saint himself assisted in their instruction. About the same time he started for the benefit of boys of the artisan class the first French Sunday School. In it technical instruction was combined with religious teaching and exercises, and it at once became extremely popular.

As may be imagined, St John Baptist de la Salle had not been able to carry out all these schemes without experiencing many trials. He had heartrending disappointments and defections amongst his disciples, and bitter opposition from the secular schoolmasters, who resented his intrusion into what they regarded as their special preserves. At one time the very existence of the Institute seems to have been jeopardised through the injudicious action of two Brothers occupying posts of authority. Complaints of undue severity towards novices reached the Archbishop of Paris, who sent his Vicar-General to make investigations. The Brothers unanimously exonerated their superior from blame in the matter, but the Vicar-General was prejudiced and drew up an unfavourable report. The result was that St John Baptist was told to regard himself as deposed—a verdict he received without a murmur. When, however, the Vicar attempted to impose on the Brothers a new Superior—an outsider from Lyons— they indignantly exclaimed that M. de la Salle was their Superior, and that they would one and all walk out of the house rather than accept another. Though the saint afterwards induced them to make a formal submission, the fresh appointment was allowed to lapse, and the founder remained in charge of his congregation. Somewhat later than this the removal of the Noviciate from Vaugirard to larger premises inside Paris, together with the opening of new schools in connection with it, almost immediately led to a violent organised attack on the Paris schools in which the lay schoolmasters were joined by the Jansenists, and by those who, on principle, were opposed to education other than manual for the children of the poor. They enlisted the help of the police, who raided the Christian schools, hampered the work in every way, and summoned the Brothers to appear before the Courts. St John Baptist found himself involved in a series of law-suits, and obliged to close all his Parisian schools and houses. Eventually, however, the storm, having spent itself, died down, the persecution ended as suddenly as it had begun, and before long the Brothers were able to resume and even extend their educational work in the capital without any disturbance resulting.

Elsewhere the Institute had been steadily developing. As early as 1700 Brother Drolin had been sent to found a school in Rome, and in France schools were started successively at Chartres, at Calais, in Languedoc, in Provence, at Rouen, and at Dijon. In 1705 the Noviciate was transferred to St Yon in Rouen. There a boarding-school was opened, and an establishment for troublesome boys, which afterwards developed into an industrial school. Soon afterwards the founder made another attempt to retire from active participation in the government of the Institute, but he was soon recalled to Paris to defeat attempts to alter the fundamental rules of the Society. He was wholly successful in this, but in 1716 decided finally to resign, and summoned all the directors of the various houses to elect a new Superior. From that moment he would give no orders, and lived like the humblest of the Brothers. He taught novices and boarders, for whom he wrote several books, including a Method of Mental Prayer.

In Lent, 1719, he suffered a good deal from asthma and rheumatism, but would give up none of his habitual austerities. Then he met with an accident, and gradually grew weaker. He passed away on Good Friday, April 7, 1719, in the sixty-eighth year of his age. His last words, uttered in reply to the question if he accepted all his sufferings with joy : " Yes, I adore in all things the designs of God for me."

In a sketch of the life of St John Baptist de la Salle, written as far back as 1891,* Francis Thompson, the poet, speaks as follows : " Were education indeed free, and indeed education, then were half the social question solved. No scheme will avail to save more than a fraction—may it be a large fraction !—out of that drift of adult misery wherewith the iniquitous neglect of our forefathers has encumbered the streets. But the children ! There is the chance ; there, alas, also is the fear. Think of it. If Christ stood amidst your London slums, He could not say, ' Except ye become as *these* little children.' Far better your children were cast from the bridges of London than they should become as those little ones. Could they be gathered together and educated in the truest sense of the word ; could the children of the nation at large be so educated as to cut off future recruits to the ranks of Darkest England ; then it would need no astrology to cast the horoscope of to-morrow. ' *La tête de l'homme du peuple,*' nay rather *de l'enfant du peuple*, around *that* sways the conflict. Who grasps the child, grasps the future. The grim old superstition was right. When man would build to a lasting finish, he must found his building over a child." The example of St John Baptist de la Salle may well lead everyone of us to ask himself : " What have I done to help and to encourage this most necessary and divine work ? What sacrifices am I prepared to make that the Christian education of our children may be carried on in spite of all the hindrances and hostilities which beset it ? "

There is no lack of excellent Lives of St John Baptist de la Salle, especially in French. The foundation of all is the biography by Blain, the intimate friend of the Saint, which appeared in 1733. Of modern works the most important is probably that of J. Guibert, priest of Saint Sulpice, *Histoire de St Jean Baptiste de la Salle*, which runs to nearly 800 pages and was brought out on occasion of the canonisation in 1900. Two excellent appreciations of minor bulk are those of A. Delaire, *St Jean-Baptiste de la Salle* (1900), in the series " Les Saints," and of F. Laudet, *L'Instituteur des Instituteurs, St J. B. de la Salle* (1929). In English, besides the sketch already mentioned, by Francis Thompson, there is an American volume by Brother Leo, *Story of St John Baptist de la Salle* (1921).

---

* It was republished by Burns and Oates in 1911, and, short though it is, it furnishes an admirable appreciation of the Saint and his work.

ST TORQUATUS AND COMPANIONS, MARTS.
(?) FIRST CENTURY

The first Christian missionaries to attempt the evangelisation of Spain are said to have been seven holy men who had been specially commissioned by St Peter and St Paul, and sent forth for that purpose. According to the legend the party kept together until they reached Guadix in Granada, where they encamped in a field whilst their servants went into the town to buy food. The inhabitants, however, came out to attack them, and followed them to the river. A miraculously-erected stone bridge enabled the Christians to escape, but it collapsed when their pursuers attempted to cross it. Afterwards the missionaries separated, each one selecting a different district in which he laboured and was made bishop. Torquatus chose Guadix as the field of his labours, and is honoured on this day in association with his companions, all six of whom, however, have also special feasts of their own. St Torquatus and the other bishops appear to have suffered martyrdom.

For this story we have only the authority of a set of medieval breviary lessons, printed in the *Acta Sanctorum*, May, vol. iii. There is no trace of early cultus to confirm it. See J. P. Kirsch, *Kirchengeschichte*, vol. i, p. 307, n. 25.

ST ISIDORE OF CHIOS, MART.
(?) A.D. 251

The saint Isidore named in this day's martyrologium appears to have been a native of Alexandria. We are told that he was a commissariat officer in the army of the Roman Emperor Decius, and went to Chios with the fleet, which was under the command of the leader Numerius. Whilst he was staying in the island he was discovered to be a Christian and was denounced to Numerius by his captain, Julius. Placed on trial he showed great constancy, threats and promises proving equally unavailing. As he refused to sacrifice, his tongue was cut out and he was beheaded. His body was sunk in a well, but it was recovered by pious Christians. It was then interred by a soldier called Ammianus, who was afterwards martyred at Cyzicus, and by a holy woman, St Myrope, who is said to have been flogged to death because of her charity in giving Christian burial to martyrs. The well became famous for its healing properties, and over the tomb of St Isidore a basilica was erected. In the fifth century, as the result of a vision, or dream, St Marcianus, who was at that time treasurer of the Cathedral of Constantinople, dedicated to St Isidore a chapel in a church he was building in honour of St Irene. From Constantinople the cultus of St Isidore spread to Russia. In 1525 Christian merchants conveyed the relics of St Isidore to San Marco in Venice, where they are said to be still preserved in a marble tomb.

It is to be feared that in this case again the *Passio* (printed in the *Acta Sanctorum*, May, vol. iii) is no better than a pious romance. But the cultus is relatively early and identified with Chios. St Isidore was known even to St Gregory of Tours. See Delehaye, *Origines du Culte des Martyrs*, pp. 261, 275, 457; and *Recueil des historiens des Croisades, Occident*, vol. v, pp. 321–334.

ST PETER AND COMPANIONS, OF LAMPSACUS, MARTS.

A.D. 251

During the persecution under Decius there was living at Lampsacus on the Hellespont a young Christian of lofty character and noble appearance called Peter. Brought before Olympius, the proconsul, and bidden to sacrifice to Venus, he refused, and made a spirited attack upon the worship of so licentious a deity, the words of which are quoted in his "Acts." He was tortured on the wheel and then beheaded. Immediately afterwards at Troas the same proconsul had to deal with three other Christians, whose names were Nicomachus, Andrew, and Paul. They declared themselves to be Christians, but under torture Nicomachus abjured his faith. Dionysia, a girl of sixteen, who was present, exclaimed in horror at his defection, bewailing his lack of constancy. She was promptly arrested, and on being questioned avowed herself to be a Christian. As she refused to sacrifice, she was condemned like Andrew and Paul to die on the morrow. In the meantime she was given over for the night to the tender mercies of two young men, who were allowed to insult her as they would. But by the mercy of God she was protected from harm. The following morning Andrew and Paul were taken from prison, delivered to the mob, and stoned outside the city walls. Dionysia followed, desiring to die with them, but by order of the proconsul she was brought back and beheaded within the city.

Whatever be thought of this rather suspicious document (printed in the *Acta Sanctorum*, May, vol. iii), these martyrs found their way into the *Hieronymianum*. See Père Delehaye's commentary, p. 256. The fact that they, or at least one of the group, suffered at Lampsacus can hardly be doubted.

ST HILARY, or HILARUS, Abbot of Galeata
A.D. 558

A copy of St Paul's epistles, which came into the hands of St Hilary of Galeata when he was twelve years old, first inspired him to abandon the world in order to serve God in solitude. Shortly afterwards he heard that gospel read in church, in which Our Lord says that if anyone would be His disciple he must hate father, mother, and his own life. Uncertain as to the exact meaning of the words he consulted a pious old man, who hesitated to expound this counsel of perfection to a lad of his years. But the boy insisted, and received the explanation he sought. Confirmed in his previous conviction, Hilary immediately forsook his Tuscan home, crossed the Apennines, and took up his abode in a hermitage beside the river Ronco. Afterwards he fashioned a cell for himself, with an oratory on a neighbouring mountain peak. Gradually disciples gathered round, and for their sake he built a monastery on land granted by Olybrius, a rich nobleman of Ravenna whom he had freed from an evil spirit, and who had been converted, together with his household of ninety persons. This abbey, which he named Galeata, was subsequently called after him, St Ilaro. He gave his monks no written rule, but they continued to observe the way of life instituted by him—a round of praise, prayer, and manual work. According to a popular legend, he was always visibly protected by his guardian angel in times of danger—notably when Theodoric the Goth threatened to destroy him and his monastery because he refused to pay him tribute. The conqueror was certainly favourably impressed by the saint, for he not only besought his prayers but also gave him territory for the enlargement of his abbey. St Hilary died in 558, at the age of eighty-two, and his body was reverently translated in 1488, when the monastery passed into the hands of the Camaldolese Order.

There seems no reason to doubt that the short Life, which purports to be written by Paul, a disciple of St Hilarus, is a substantially faithful record. It is printed in the *Acta Sanctorum*, May, vol. iii.

SS. DYMPNA and GEREBERNUS, Marts.
(?) *c.* A.D. 650

In the town of Gheel, twenty-five miles from Antwerp, great honour is paid to St Dympna, whose body, and that of St Gerebernus, buried in two ancient marble sarcophagi, were discovered, or re-discovered, there in the thirteenth century. Widespread interest was taken in them because the elevation of the relics of St Dympna was followed, it is alleged, by the restoration to normal health of a number of epileptics, lunatics, and persons under malign influence who visited her shrine. Ever since then she has been regarded as the patroness of the insane, and the inhabitants of Gheel have been distinguished by the kindly provision they have made for those so afflicted. As early as the close of the thirteenth century an infirmary was built for their accommodation and at the present time the town possesses a first-class state sanatorium for the care and supervision of mental defectives, the greater number of whom lead contented and useful lives as boarders in the homes of farmers or other local residents whom they assist by their labour, and whose family life they share. The body of St Dympna is preserved in a silver reliquary in the church which bears her name. Only the head of St Gerebernus now rests there, his other remains having been removed to Sonsbeck in the German diocese of Münster.

The true history of these saints is probably lost, but popular belief, reaching back to the date of the finding of their relics, has attached to them a story which, with local variations, is to be found in the folk-lore of many European countries. Briefly summarised, it runs as follows. Dympna was the daughter of an Irish, British or Armorican King—a pagan—and of a Christian princess who died when their child was very young, though not before she had been instructed in the Christian faith and baptised. As she grew up, her extraordinary resemblance to her dead mother whom he had idolised awakened an unlawful passion in the King, her father. Consequently, by the advice of St Gerebernus, her confessor, she fled from home to avoid further danger. Accompanied by the priest and attended by the court jester and his wife, she embarked in a ship which conveyed them to Antwerp. From thence they made their way south-east, through a tract of wild forest country, until they reached a little oratory dedicated to St Martin and built on a site now covered by the town of Gheel. Here they settled, intending to live as holy solitaries. In the meantime, however, Dympna's father had started in pursuit and in due time arrived at Antwerp, from whence he sent out spies who discovered the refuge of the fugitives. The clue by which they were traced was the use of strange coins similar to those which the spies themselves proffered in payment. Coming upon them unawares, the King first tried by cajolery to persuade his daughter to return with him. She refused, and as she was supported by St Gerebernus, the pagan tyrant ordered his attendants to kill them both. The men promptly despatched the priest, but hesitated to attack the princess. Thereupon the unnatural father struck off his daughter's head with his own sword. The bodies of the saints, which were left exposed on the ground, were afterwards buried by angelic or human hands in the place where they had perished.

This story is treated by Père Delehaye in his *Légendes Hagiographiques* (Eng. trans., pp. 9, 105, 157) as an almost typical example of the infiltrations of folklore into hagiography. The text of the legend is in the *Acta Sanctorum*, May, vol. iii. See further Van der Essen, *Étude critique sur les Vies des Saints méroving.*, pp. 313–320 ; Künstle, *Ikonographie*, vol. ii, pp. 190–192 ; and Janssens, *Gheel in Beeld en Schrift* (1903). An interesting feature in the case is the fact that lunatics who go to Gheel to be healed are made to pass through an archway immediately underneath the shrine of the saint. One finds many early examples, even at Jerusalem itself, in which the squeezing through some narrow aperture is believed to be a condition for obtaining special favour.

ST RUPERT AND ST BERTHA, HERMITS

c. A.D. 840 (?)

The history of St Rupert and St Bertha was written and their cultus popularised some three hundred years after their death, by St Hildegard, "the Sibyl of the Rhine," who spent the latter part of her life on the Rupertsberg. According to this account, Rupert was the son of a pagan father and of a Christian mother called Bertha who came of the family of the Dukes of Lorraine and owned in her own right much property beside the Rhine and the Nahe. Her husband having been killed in battle when their son was still an infant, Bertha devoted herself entirely to his education. So eagerly did the boy respond to the Christian instruction he received that the rôles of teacher and pupil were practically reversed. "Look, mother ! those are all your children ! " he would say as ragged little beggars gathered round them, and once, in reply to his mother's suggestion of building a church, he exclaimed : " But first of all we must obey God and give our bread to the hungry and clothe the naked." These words produced such a profound impression on St Bertha that she immediately erected several hospices for the poor. When Rupert was twelve, he and his mother went to Rome to visit the tombs of the apostles. Upon their return they made several religious foundations and gave away the rest of their possessions. Accompanied by his mother, Rupert then retired to live as a hermit in the hilly country near Bingen, which was afterwards called the Rupertsberg. There he gave himself up entirely to prayer and penance. He was only twenty years of age when he contracted a fever of which he died. St Bertha continued to serve God in the same place for another twenty-five years, and when she, too, passed away, she was buried beside her son in a convent which they had built beside the Nahe.

The text of St Hildegard's narrative is in the *Acta Sanctorum*, May, vol. iii. See also P. Bruder, *St Rupertus Büchlein*, 1883.

ST NICHOLAS MYSTICUS, PATRIARCH OF CONSTANTINOPLE

A.D. 925

After the death of St Anthony Cauleas, Nicholas, a member of the Emperor's privy council, was appointed Patriarch of Constantinople. He was a man both able and pious, but he incurred the displeasure of the Emperor Leo the Wise by refusing to sanction his fourth marriage. When the archbishop proceeded to excommunicate his sovereign, he was deposed and banished to the monastery he had founded at Galacrenos. Leo recalled him when he lay on his deathbed. After his return to Constantinople St Nicholas was reinstated in the patriarchate as well as in the council and was held in great esteem by Constantine Porphyrogenitus, whom he had baptised, and by the two co-regent Emperors Alexander and Romanus Lecapenus, the latter of whom he crowned. It was in virtue of his position as President of the " mystic " or privy council of the Byzantine court that the saint acquired the surname of " Mysticus " by which he is generally known. He is mentioned in the Greek *Menæa*, but no great cult seems to have been paid to him either in the eastern or western Church.

There is a notice in the *Acta Sanctorum*, May, vol. iii, and see Nilles, *Kalendarium Utriusque Ecclesiæ*, vol. i, p. 212 ; as well as S. P. Lambros, in *Byzantinische Zeitschrift*, vol. i (1890), pp. 551–554.

ST ISIDORE AGRICOLA, CONF.

A.D. 1130

The patron of Madrid, St Isidore the Labourer, was born in the Spanish capital of poor, but very devout parents, and was christened Isidore after the celebrated Archbishop of Seville. Although unable to procure educational advantages for their son, his father and mother early instilled into his mind a great horror of sin and a love of prayer. As soon as he was old enough to work, Isidore entered the service of John de Vergas, a wealthy resident of Madrid, as a day labourer on his estate outside the city, and with that one employer he remained all his life. He married a girl as poor and as pious as himself, but after the birth of one son, who died young, they agreed to serve God in perfect continence. Isidore's whole life was a model of Christian perfection lived in the world. He would rise early to go to church, often after having spent the greater part of the night in prayer, and all day long, whilst his hand guided the plough, he would be communing with God, with his guardian angel or with the holy saints. Public holidays he would spend in visiting the churches of Madrid and the neighbouring districts. Kind and helpful though he always was to others, he did not escape the malice of detraction. His fellow workmen, jealous of the favour with which his employer regarded him, complained that his attendance at church caused him to be late in starting work. To test the truth of this accusation, de Vergas hid himself in the hollow of a tree to watch. He saw that Isidore did actually arrive after his fellow labourers, and he was advancing to upbraid him for this irregularity when he was surprised, we are told, to see a second team of snow-white oxen led by unknown figures ploughing beside that driven by Isidore. As he stood watching, rooted to the ground, the strange team disappeared and he realised that supernatural help had supplied all that was lacking. Other people also reported having seen angels assisting Isidore in his labours, and John de Vergas came to revere his pious servant who, it is said, worked several miracles for the benefit of his employer and his family.

The saint's liberality to the poor was so great that he was wont to share his meals with them, often reserving for himself only the scraps they left over. On one occasion, when he had been invited to a confraternity dinner, he remained so long in church absorbed in prayer that the feast was nearly over before he made his appearance—followed by a train of beggars. His hosts expostulated, saying that they had reserved for him his portion, but that they could not possibly feed the whole crowd. St Isidore replied that there would be ample for himself and for Christ's poor. So, indeed, it happened, for when the food was produced, there was enough and to spare for them all. Amongst the numerous stories told of the holy man is one which illustrates his love for dumb animals. On a snowy winter's day, as he was carrying a sack of corn to be ground, he saw a number of birds perched disconsolately on the bare branches, obviously unable to find anything to eat. Isidore opened the sack and, in spite of the jeers of a companion, poured out half its contents upon the ground. When, however, they reached their destination the sack proved to be still quite full and the corn, when ground, produced double the usual amount of flour. St Isidore died May 15, 1130, and was buried in the cemetery of St Andrew's Church. His wife survived him for several years and, like him, is honoured as a saint. In Spain she is venerated as Santa Maria de la Cabeza, because her head (Sp. *cabeza*) is often carried in procession in times of drought. Forty years after the death of St Isidore his body was transferred to a more honourable shrine, and a great impetus was given to his cultus by the report of many miracles worked through his intercession.

In the year 1211, St Isidore is said to have appeared in a vision to King Alphonsus of Castile, then engaged in fighting the Moors in the Pass of Navas de Tolosa, and to have shown him an unknown path by means of which he was able to surprise and defeat the enemy. More than four hundred years later, King Philip III of Spain, on his return from Lisbon, was taken so ill at Casaribios del Monte that his life was despaired of by the physicians. Thereupon the shrine of St Isidore was carried in solemn procession from Madrid to the chamber of the sick monarch. At the hour the relics were removed from the Church of St Andrew, the fever left the King, and when they were brought into his presence, he recovered completely. The following year the saint's body was placed in a rich new shrine which cost one thousand six hundred gold ducats. The Spanish royal family had long desired to have St Isidore formally enrolled amongst the saints, and in March 1622 he was duly canonised together with St Ignatius, St Francis Xavier, St Theresa and St Philip Neri. In Spain this holy quintet are commonly spoken of as " The Five Saints."

The foundation document upon which our knowledge of the saint is almost entirely based is a life by " John the Deacon," probably identical with the Franciscan writer Johannes Ægidius of Zamora. It is printed in the *Acta Sanctorum*, May, vol. iii, but as it was compiled a century and a half after St Isidore's death, it cannot be regarded as a very trustworthy record. A critical edition of this Latin text was published by Father F. Fita, S.J., in the *Boletin de la Real Academia de la Historia*, vol. ix (1886), 102–152. Lives in Spanish (including several poetical settings by Lope de Vega) and in Italian are numerous. The best biography is said to be that by Father J. Bleda, O.P. (1622), and there is a more modern account in French by J. P. Toussaint (1901). But by far the most satisfactory treatment of the points of interest in the history of St Isidore is that published by Fr. Garcia Villeda in *Razón y Fe*, January to May, 1922. He in particular supplies very full details regarding the preservation of the body of the saint. It is mummified, but still entire.

BD. MAGDALEN ALBRICI, or ALBRIZZI, Virg.

A.D. 1465

The Albrici or Albrizzi family to which Blessed Magdalen belonged ranked among the nobility, and her father was a distinguished citizen of her native city Como. From early childhood the little girl surprised and edified those about her by her piety, but during the lifetime of her parents she remained at home, devoting herself specially to relieving the poor for whom she had a great love. After the death of her father and mother, however, she decided to retire from the world. With the consent of her three brothers, she selected the Convent of St Margaret, a house at Como, which had been founded by two sisters Liberata and Faustina, and which was considered suitable for a woman of her rank. She had actually reached the door and was about to apply for admission when she distinctly heard a voice say to her three times : " Magdalen, turn your steps to Brunate : that is where you must go." There existed, as she well knew, a very poor convent situated in an isolated spot up in the mountains at Brunate, and thither, with her confessor's sanction, she now betook herself. It was dedicated to St Andrew and contained only a few nuns, but after Blessed Magdalen's reception the numbers increased considerably. She was soon chosen Superior and through the support of Blanche, Duchess of Milan, was able to affiliate the community to the Hermits of St Augustine, a special Bull of ratification having been granted by Pope Nicholas V. Lack of the bare necessaries of life sometimes obliged the nuns to make begging expeditions into Como, where they were liable to be detained for the night when bad weather made it difficult for them to get back into their mountain fastness. To obviate the undesirable necessity of their having to accept casual hospitality from strangers, and also to provide a hospice for young women stranded in Como without a home, Blessed Magdalen, after a time, founded a kind of daughter-house in the city, though she herself remained at Brunate. Hers was a hidden life, but she was endowed with supernatural gifts which precluded her from remaining as unknown as she could have wished. She healed the sick and foretold the future, while her trust in God was so perfect that many miracles were wrought in immediate response to her prayers. She also was animated by a deep devotion to Our Lord's Eucharistic Presence, constantly urging her nuns to frequent communion. It was her practice to divide the night into three watches. The first she would place under the care of St Michael, whilst she meditated on the justice of

God : the midnight watch she would entrust to the patronage of St Gabriel as she prayed for some special soul or souls : and the third she would commend to all the holy angels whilst she made her plans for the ensuing day. She appears to have died on May 15, 1465, at an advanced age, after a long and painful illness.

The account printed in the *Acta Sanctorum*, May, vol. iii, is a transcript from the Life written by Father Paul Olmo in 1484. The cult of Bd. Magdalen was confirmed by Pope Pius X in 1907 and the decree may be read in the *Analecta Ecclesiastica*, vol. xvi (1908), pp. 19–20. A Life by G. B. Melloni was published at Bologna in 1764.

MAY 16

ST JOHN NEPOMUCEN, Mart.

A.D 1393

ST JOHN NEPOMUCEN was born in Bohemia—probably between the years 1340 and 1350. The appellation by which he is always distinguished is derived from his native town of Nepomuk, or Pomuk, but his family name was actually Wölflein, or Welflin. From early childhood he had been consecrated by his parents to the service of God and he studied with a view to the priesthood at Staab, at Saatz, and finally at the University of Prague which had recently been founded by the Emperor Charles IV, King of Bohemia, on the lines of the Universities of Paris and Padua. Later on we find him occupying the posts of notary in the imperial chancery and proto-notary to the Archbishop. In 1387 he took his degree at Padua as doctor of canon law and two years afterwards was made a canon in the collegiate church of the Wyschehrad in Prague, and then Vicar-General of the archdiocese. In 1390 he resigned the benefice of St Gallus to become archdeacon of Saatz— a dignity which admitted him to the metropolitan chapter of St Veit. The Emperor Charles IV had died at Prague in 1378 and had been succeeded by his son Wenceslas IV at the age of sixteen. The prince had already been completely demoralised by flattery and power, and young though he was, had sunk into degrading vices which earned for him the nicknames of "the Slothful" and "The Drunkard." At times he gave way unrestrainedly to fits of rage or caprice in which he would perpetrate acts of savage cruelty. The great reputation of St John Nepomucen induced the monarch to appoint him Lenten preacher to the court, and his discourses are said to have had, for a time, a salutary effect upon his royal master. The saint received from Wenceslas the offer of the bishopric of Leitomischl, which he is said to have refused. There seems no evidence for this, or for the statement that he was appointed court almoner and confessor to Queen Sophia, the daughter of Duke John of Bavaria, who was the King's second wife. She was a beautiful and pious princess who sorely needed the consolations of religion, for she had much to bear from her barbarous husband. Shamelessly unfaithful himself, Wenceslas was intensely jealous, and harboured unworthy suspicions of his young wife whose conduct was irreproachable. A tradition, widely credited in Bohemia to this day, attributes the martyrdom of St John Nepomucen to the resentment aroused in the King by the holy man's uncompromising refusal to reveal to him the substance of the queen's confessions. On the other hand, no mention of this appears in the contemporary documents, and several incidents which occurred afterwards might easily account for the monarch's subsequent vengefulness.

It happened one day that the tyrant, finding a fowl brought to his table not roasted to his satisfaction, gave an order surpassing, if possible, the extravagances of Caligula or Heliogabalus. He commanded that the cook should immediately be spitted and roasted alive at the same fire before which the fowl had been cooked. His officials proceeded forthwith to carry out the cruel sentence and had already pierced the poor servant with several spits when St John rushed into the dining-hall to intercede for the victim. Wenceslas, however, would listen neither to his appeals nor to his threats of divine vengeance. He only lost his temper and caused the holy man to be imprisoned for several days.

In 1393 Wenceslas resolved to found a new diocese at Kladrau, in S.W. Bohemia, in order to give a bishopric to one of his favourites. To furnish a cathedral and endowment he proposed to confiscate the church and revenues of the ancient Benedictine Abbey of Kladrau as soon as the abbot, who was very old, should die. This proposal was strenuously opposed by Archbishop John of Jenstein and by St John Nepomucen as his Vicar General. Acting under instructions from them, the monks, immediately after the abbot's death, proceeded to the election of a new superior. The archbishop and his two vicars-general ratified the appointment so promptly that the King was informed at the same moment of the death of the one abbot and the institution of the new. Such incidents greatly strained the relations between Wenceslas and the heads of the Bohemian clergy, but an open breach came when the court attempted to interfere with clerical prerogatives. It was the law in Bohemia as in other Christian countries that criminous clerics should be dealt with by the ecclesiastical courts. Nevertheless, when two priests were found guilty of a grave crime, they were summarily executed by order of the royal chamberlain, instead of being brought before the ecclesiastical court, presided over by St John Nepomucen. The archbishop felt himself in duty bound to resist this encroachment on the rights of the Church, and launched an excommunication against the chamberlain. Wenceslas was furious. In vain did his councillors attempt to bring about a reconciliation : the king thirsted for vengeance. He summoned or invited the archbishop, the vicars-general, and other prominent dignitaries to come before him, and after striking the aged dean Boheslas on the head with the handle of his dagger, until the blood streamed, he ordered that all the party should be bound and imprisoned. The Archbishop escaped—perhaps by the connivance of the officials—and this circumstance seems to have incensed the King still more against the rest. It was evening, and by the light of torches they were tied hand and foot and cruelly tortured by the executioner. Wenceslas, it is said, with his own hand, wreaked his fury on St John and his coadjutor Nicholas Puchnik, by applying a burning torch to their sides. Though he eventually released the others after binding them by an oath to secrecy and forcing them to declare themselves to be on his side, he reserved a very different fate for the saint. His feet were fastened to his head, his hands were tied behind him, and a piece of wood as a gag was forced into his mouth to prevent him from uttering a sound. Half dead, he was then borne secretly through the streets to the bridge and was cast into the Moldau. The cruel deed did not long remain undiscovered. Over the spot where the martyr sank appeared strange lights resembling seven stars or luminous flames, and in the morning the body was washed ashore. It was immediately recognised and the secret was divulged by the executioners. The cathedral canons took up the sacred relics, which were solemnly deposited first in the Church of the Holy Cross, and afterwards in the Cathedral, where they are venerated to this day, having—in a wonderful way—escaped profanation by the Hussites and the Calvinists. When the tomb was opened in 1719 the saint's tongue was found to be dried, but incorrupt. On the old bridge the place from which he was thrown is marked by a metal plate adorned with seven stars—the saint's emblem in art.

Some years later Wenceslas was forced to resign his kingdom and to yield the imperial crown to his brother Sigismund. He continued to live a life of indolence and debauchery until he died of an attack of apoplexy, without having made his peace with God. St John Nepomucen is principal patron of Bohemia, where he is invoked against floods and against calumnies, as well as for help to make a good confession.

The account which the *Acta Sanctorum*, May, vol. iii, furnish of St John Nepomucen is not altogether trustworthy. The Bollandists were not permitted to have access to the archives at Prague, and they have followed Balbinus and the materials which, from unsatisfactory sources, were first

presented for the confirmation of cultus. Even in the Bull of canonisation the death of this martyr is alleged to have taken place in 1383, whereas
it certainly occurred in 1393. On the other hand there is no solid reason
for supposing that there were two different Johns, Canons of the cathedral,
who have been confused. But the controversy, which has been conducted
with much acrimony, is too intricate to be discussed here at length. A
convenient statement of the whole question is available in the little volume
of J. Weisskopf, *S. Johannes von Nepomuk* (1931) and also in W. A. Frind,
Der heilige Johannes von Nepomuk (1929). A good bibliography and discussion
of the earlier writers on the question will be found in the *Kirchenlexikon*,
vol. vi, pp. 1725–1742.

ST PEREGRINUS, Bp. of Auxerre, Mart.

c. A.D. 261

An accepted legend states that the first Bishop of Auxerre,
St Peregrinus, was consecrated by Pope Sixtus II and was sent from
Rome at the request of the Christians resident in that part of Gaul.
Landing at Marseilles, in the company of Marsus a priest,
Corcodamus a deacon, and two lectors, Jovianus and Jovinianus,
he preached the gospel in that city, as well as in Lyons on his way.
During his episcopate the greater part of the inhabitants of Auxerre
are said to have been converted to Christianity. He built a church
on the banks of the Yonne and evangelised all the surrounding
country. In the mountainous district of the Puisaye, some ten
leagues or more S.W. of Auxerre, stood the town of Interanum—
the present Entrains—at a point where several roads met. The
Roman prefect had a palace there and the place had become a great
centre for the worship of Roman deities. On the occasion of the
dedication of a new temple to Jupiter, St. Peregrinus went to the
town and appealed to the populace to abandon idolatry for the one
true God of the Christians. He was seized, brought before the
governor and condemned to death. After being cruelly tortured
he was beheaded.

This account is based upon two texts, one of which is printed in the
Acta Sanctorum, May, vol. iii, while the other may most conveniently be
consulted in Migne, *P. L.*, vol. 138, *cc.* 219–221. There is no reason to
doubt the fact of the martyrdom, for the *Hieronymianum* commemorates it
on this day and informs us that the tragedy took place at the " vicus Baia-
cus " (Bouky), where Peregrinus was buried. See also Duchesne, *Fastes
Épiscopaux*, vol. ii, p. 431.

ST POSSIDIUS, Bp.

c. A.D. 440

Except that he was a native of proconsular Africa and a pupil of St Augustine's at Hippo, nothing is known of the early history of St Possidius. It seems to have been about the year 397 that he was made bishop of Calama in Numidia—a diocese greatly disturbed by the factions of the Donatists as well as by pagan opposition. He was closely associated with St Augustine in his struggles against heresy and suffered personal violence in an attempt made upon his life by the extremists amongst the Donatists. For the energy he displayed against Pelagianism at the synod of Mileve in 416, he was commended by Pope Innocent I. He made a religious foundation at Calama on the lines of St Augustine's monastery at Hippo and obtained for Calama part of the relics of St Stephen.

When in 429 the Vandals under King Genseric passed over from Spain into Africa, they quickly made themselves masters of Mauritania, Numidia, and the proconsular province except the strong fortresses of Carthage, Cirta, and Hippo. Calama was destroyed, and Possidius took refuge with his lifelong friend St Augustine, who died not long afterwards in his arms whilst the barbarians were besieging Hippo. Prosper, in his chronicle, states that Possidius and two other bishops were driven from their sees by the Arian Genseric. The saint died in exile: he was alive in 437, but the date of his death is unknown. Tradition reports that he spent the close of his life in Italy, dying at Mirandola. St Possidius wrote a short life of St Augustine and left an Index or Catalogue of his writings.

What we know of St Possidius is gathered from miscellaneous sources, but especially from the works of St Augustine. See the *Acta Sanctorum*, May, vol. iv. There is a good notice of Possidius in the *Dict. of Christ. Biog.*, vol. iv, pp. 445–446.

ST CARANTOCK, CARANTOG, OR CARANNOG, Ab.

SIXTH CENTURY

St Carantock was a Welsh abbot, formerly greatly venerated in Cardiganshire where he founded the church of Llangrannog. He also lived for some time in Ireland, but returned to Great Britain and made a religious settlement at a place called Chernach that may have been either Carhampton in Somerset, or the Cornish village of

Crantock, which still preserves the saint's holy well and celebrates Crantock Feast on May 16. At a later date he is said to have passed over to Brittany. This is confirmed by a statement in the *Life of St Guenael* to the effect that when that holy man returned to Brittany from England, after collecting a number of companions and books, he proceeded at once to pay a visit to St Carantock. Moreover there is in Brittany a widespread cultus of St Carantock, sometimes alone, sometimes in association with his disciple, St Tenenan. Eventually, however, he came back to Britain where, according to the Homily in *The Cambro-British Saints*, he died " in his illustrious city,* the best of all his cities, which is called the city of Chernach."

For the most reliable information available concerning St Carantoc the reader must consult the brochure of Canon Doble and C. G. Henderson (1928), in the series of Cornish Saints for which the former is mainly responsible. The text printed with interpolations from a Cottonian manuscript in the *Acta Sanctorum*, May, vol. iii, is of very doubtful historical value. A better text is that given in an appendix to J. T. Evans' volume on the Church Plate of Cardiganshire. But see also Dean Armitage Robinson in the *Downside Review*, vol. 46 (1928), pp. 234–243. He shows that the saint was closely connected with Carhampton in West Somerset.

ST FIDOLUS (PHAL), ABBOT

c. A.D. 540

Whilst Clovis I was endeavouring to consolidate his position in Poitou and Aquitaine, he sent his son Theodoric (Thierry) to subjugate the mountainous district of the Auvergne. The prince's army devastated the province, taking many prisoners, amongst whom was a lad called Fidolus, the son of a local governor. The ransoming and liberation of captives was a work of mercy widely practised by the pious in the Middle Ages ; and Fidolus, as he was being conveyed with others through Troyes, was purchased by Aventinus, a holy man who, after being cellarer and almoner to St Camelianus of Troyes, had retired to live as a solitary in the island of Aumont but had been obliged to take direction of a community formed of his numerous disciples. From the first Aventinus treated the stranger like a son, and Fidolus not only returned his affection, but proved an exemplary monk—humble, obedient, devout, and mortified. He was raised to the office of Prior, and when, after a

---

* *Civitas*, as Mr. Wade Evans has pointed out (*Life of Saint David*, p. 106), in these early Celtic documents commonly means a religious community, *i.e.* a monastery.

number of years, Aventinus felt once again the call to retire into solitude, he knew that he could safely leave his community in the charge of his spiritual son. Fidolus accepted with reluctance the office of abbot, but he retained it until his death, treading the path of perfection himself and leading his brethren to follow in his footsteps. At a later date the monastery took the name of St Phal.

The best of the two or three not very satisfactory accounts preserved of St Fidolus has been edited by Bruno Krusch in the *M. G. H. Scrip. rer. meroving.*, vol. iii, pp. 428–432. The others will be found in Mabillon and in the *Acta Sanctorum*, May, vol. iii. It seems highly probable that some confusion has arisen between the Aventinus mentioned above and another Aventinus, who, at about the same period, died as Bishop of Chartres.

ST GERMERIUS, Bp. of Toulouse

(?) A.D. 560

St Germerius was only thirty years old when he became Bishop of Toulouse, and is said to have occupied the see for fifty years. Although a native of Angoulême, he had been educated at Toulouse whither he had migrated in early boyhood. Very shortly after his consecration he was summoned to the court of Clovis, the first Christian King of France, and was treated with great respect by the monarch, who entertained him for three weeks. Before he left, Clovis loaded him with gifts for his churches—gold and silver vessels and crosses, as well as fine linen. He also bestowed upon him, free of all charges, the district of Dux (?) near Toulouse and as much land for a cemetery as seven yoke of oxen could till in a day. At Dux, Germerius built a church with three altars which he placed under the patronage of St Saturninus, the first bishop of Toulouse. We read that, on the day of its dedication, it was lighted by three hundred wax candles and that a number of sick persons were restored to health. At a later period the holy bishop founded a monastery at Dux, besides a second church or oratory which he dedicated to St Martin. A great lover of the poor, he appointed almoners whose special work it was to assist the needy. In all his good works St Germerius was ably seconded by his two favourite disciples, Dulcidius and Pretiosus.

The saint died and was buried in his monastery at Dux, but his relics together with those of his two companions were afterwards translated to the neighbouring church of St James at Muret, where they still lie in a crypt beneath the sanctuary. The cultus of St Germerius goes back to a very early date.

There is every reason to be distrustful of the life printed in the *Acta Sanctorum*, May, vol. iii. No Germerius can be found in the episcopal lists of Toulouse. See Duchesne, *Fastes Épiscopaux*, vol. i, p. 397. As against C. Douais, *Mémoires Soc. Antiq. France*, 1890, pp. 1–134, see L. Saltet in *Annales du Midi*, xiii (1901), pp. 145–175.

ST BRENDAN, Abbot of Clonfert

A.D. 577 or 583

There is hardly any Irish saint whose name is more widely known than that of St Brendan, though it is to be feared that this exceptional prominence is due rather to the popularity of the saga, called his *Navigatio* (sea-voyage), admittedly a fiction, than to the tradition of his saintliness. His life is preserved to us in several varying texts, Latin and Irish, but even when we eliminate the extravagances of the *Navigatio*, which have been incorporated in some of these accounts, the residue is far from producing the impression of a sober historical record. The early Bollandists who, like other scholars of that generation, were indulgent in their attitude towards the marvellous, decided against printing the full biography in their *Acta Sanctorum*, on the ground that it was " fabulous." On the other hand, it is certain that St Brendan was a real personage and that he exercised great influence amongst his contemporaries in the sixth century. He was probably born near Tralee on the west coast of Ireland, and Findluagh is given as his father's name. For five years as a tiny child he was committed to the care of St Ita (see January 15 in this series, Vol. I, p. 192), and after that he was watched over by Bishop Erc who had already baptised him as an infant and who was in due time to ordain him priest. St Jarlath of Tuam is also named as one of the holy men whom he visited with the view of obtaining edification and counsel.

To determine the chronological sequence of events is quite impossible, but we should be led to infer that shortly after being raised to the priesthood, St Brendan assumed the habit of a monk and gathered followers around him in a settled community. How he could have left these behind to start off with sixty chosen companions in skin-covered coracles to discover the isles of the blessed is a difficulty which does not seem to have troubled his biographers. One or other of these speaks of two separate voyages, though the first expedition is said to have lasted for five or seven years. At the same time, while it is ridiculous to suppose, as some fervent advocates of the legend have done, that the abbot sailed to the

Canaries or travelled north-west to the coast of Greenland, so competent an authority as Dr. J. F. Kenney states : " It is reasonably certain that Brendan himself made a voyage to the Scottish isles and perhaps to the Strathclyde, Cumbria, or Wales." We know at any rate that Adamnan, writing little more than a century after St Brendan's death, describes him as visiting St Columba in the little island of Hinba, Argyllshire. The biographers, whose narratives are probably later in date, discourse at considerable length of a visit he also paid to St Gildas in Britain and of the marvels which happened on that occasion.

The most reliable fact which we can connect with the life of St Brendan is his foundation of a monastic community at Clonfert (in 559 ?). His biographers speak of his governing a community of three thousand monks. He is also said to have had a rule of life dictated to him by an angel. We know nothing of its nature, but we are told that the rule was followed " down to the present day " by those who succeeded him in the office of abbot. There seems, again, no sufficient reason for questioning the statement that he did not die at Clonfert, but that God called him to his reward when he was paying a visit to his sister, Brig, who governed a community at Enach Duin. After offering Mass, he said : " Commend my departure in your prayers," and Brig replied : " What do you fear ? " " I fear," he said, " if I go alone, if the journey be dark, the unknown region, the presence of the King, and the sentence of the Judge." Foreseeing that attempts would be made to detain his body, he directed that his death should be kept secret for a time, while his remains were taken back to Clonfert in a cart, disguised as luggage he was sending on in advance of his own return.

The biographical materials, which are relatively abundant, consist principally of two Latin lives, edited by C. Plummer in his *Vitæ Sanctorum Hiberniæ*, vol. i, pp. 90–151, and vol. ii, pp. 270–292 ; that edited by P. Grosjean, S.J., in the *Analecta Bollandiana*, vol. xlviii (1930), pp. 99–121 ; an Irish life edited by Whitley Stokes in the *Lismore Lives*, pp. 99–115, and a second Irish life edited by Plummer in his *Bethada Náem nÉrenn*, vol. i, pp. 44–95. Professor Plummer has also provided a valuable discussion of the problems arising from these texts, see the prefaces of the two works mentioned and also the *Zeitschrift für Celtische Philologie*, vol. v (1905), pp. 124–141. The literature occasioned by the story of St Brendan, and especially by the *Navigatio*, which in the Middle Ages was translated into almost all European languages, and has (see Goeje, Leiden, 1890) points of contact with the sagas current in Arabic, is very extensive. Consult further J. F. Kenney, *Sources for the early history of Ireland*, i, pp. 408–412 ; Nutt and Meyer, *The Voyage of Bran* (1897) ; Schirmer, *Zur Brendanus Legende* (1888), *etc.* An attractive little illustrated volume is that of J. Wilkie, *S. Brendan the Voyager and his Mystic Quest* (1916).

ST DOMNOLUS, Bp. of Le Mans

A.D. 581

The various accounts we have of the career of St Domnolus are somewhat conflicting, and it seems clear that our sources of information are unreliable. He was probably abbot of a monastery in Paris when he attracted the favourable notice of King Clotaire I who offered him the see of Avignon. This he refused, but the King afterwards bestowed upon him the bishopric of Le Mans, which he held for twenty-one years. He built several churches and a hospice on the Sarthe for poor pilgrims. Attached to it was a monastery with a church, to the dedication of which he invited his special friend, St Germanus of Paris. We find him taking part in the Council of Tours in 566. St Domnolus is duly commemorated on this day in the Roman Martyrology.

St Gregory of Tours speaks of Domnolus as having reached a high pitch of sanctity and working many miracles, and we have also two apparently authentic charters of his. On the other hand, the biographical materials supplied by the *Vita* (printed in the *Acta Sanctorum*, May, vol. iii), and by the *Actus Pont. Cenom.* (*ibid.*), are altogether untrustworthy and are almost certainly compilations fabricated by the chorepiscopus David more than two centuries later, though they profess to be written by a contemporary. See on all this, Havet, in the *Bibl. de l'École des Chartes*, vol. 54, pp. 688–692 ; Celier, in *Revue historique et archéol. du Maine*, vol. 55 (1904), pp. 375–391 ; A. Poncelet, in the *Analecta Bollandiana*, vol. xxiv (1905), pp. 515–516, and Duchesne, *Fastes Épiscopaux*, vol. ii, p. 337.

ST HONORATUS, Bp. of Amiens

c. A.D. 600

The famous Faubourg and Rue St Honoré in Paris derive their name from St Honoratus who was Bishop of Amiens at the close of the sixth century. History has little to tell us about him except that he was born at Port-le-Grand or Ponthieu in the diocese of Amiens where he also died, and that he elevated the relics of SS. Fuscianus, Victoricus, and Gentianus which a priest called Lupicinus had discovered after they had been forgotten for three hundred years. The cultus of St Honoratus received a great impetus and became widespread in France in consequence of a number of remarkable cures which followed the elevation of his own body in 1060, and which were attributed to his agency. In 1204 Reynoldus Cherez and his wife Sybilla placed under his patronage the church they built in Paris. Nearly a hundred years later another Bishop of Amiens, William of Mâcon, dedicated to his saintly predecessor the Charterhouse he was building at Abbeville. St Honoratus is generally regarded in France as the patron of bakers, confectioners, corn chandlers and of all trades that deal with flour, and his appropriate emblem in art is a baker's peel.

Although St Honoratus is mentioned on this day in the Roman Martyrology, the materials for his history, printed in the *Acta Sanctorum*, May, vol. iii, are altogether late and unreliable. See, however, Duchesne, *Fastes Épiscopaux*, vol. iii, p. 125 ; and H. Josse, *La Légende de S. Honoré* (1879).

ST UBALDUS, Bp. of Gubbio

A.D. 1160

We are fortunate in possessing an excellent and reliable biography of Ubaldus Baldassini, Bishop of Gubbio, compiled by Theobald, his immediate successor. The saint, descended from a noble family in Gubbio, became an orphan at an early age and was educated by his uncle, also bishop of the same see, in the cathedral school. Having completed his studies in the seminary of St Secundus, he was ordained priest and was appointed dean of the cathedral, young though he was, that he might reform the canons amongst whom grave irregularities were rampant. The task was no easy one, but he succeeded before long in persuading three of the canons, better disposed than the rest, to join him in the pious observances of a common life. Then, that he might obtain experience in the management of a well-conducted household, he resided for three months with a community of regular canons which had been established by Peter de Honestis in the territory of Ravenna. The rule which they followed he brought back to Gubbio, and within a short time it was accepted by the whole chapter. A few years later, after their house and cloisters had been burnt down, Ubaldus thought it a favourable moment to retire from his post into some solitude. With this object in view he made his way to Font Avellano where he communicated his intention to Peter of Rimini. That great servant of God, however, regarded the plan as a dangerous temptation and exhorted him to return to the post in which God had placed him for the benefit of others. The saint accordingly returned to Gubbio, rebuilt the cloisters and rendered his chapter more flourishing than it had ever been before. In 1126 St Ubaldus was unanimously chosen bishop of Perugia ; but he hid himself so that the deputies from that city could not find him, and after they had retired, he went to Rome, threw himself at the feet of Honorius II and begged with many tears that he might be excused. His request was granted, but when, two years later, the see of Gubbio fell vacant, the Pope himself directed that the clergy of that city should proceed to elect Ubaldus. At the beginning of 1129 Honorius consecrated him with his own hands. In his new office the saint displayed all the virtues of a true successor to the apostles, but perhaps his most distinguishing characteristic was a mildness and patience which made him appear insensible to injuries and affronts. On one occasion the workmen engaged upon repairing the city wall encroached upon his vineyard and were injuring his vines. He gently drew their attention to this and requested them to desist. Thereupon the overseer, who probably did not recognise him, became abusive and pushed him so roughly that the saint, who had previously suffered from a fractured thigh, fell into a pool of liquid mortar. He rose up, splashed all over with lime and dirt, and without a word of expostulation returned to his house. Eye-witnesses, however, reported the incident and the citizens clamoured loudly that the overseer should be banished for his offence and his goods confiscated. So great was the popular indignation that a severe sentence seemed a foregone conclusion, when St Ubaldus appeared in court and claimed that since the offence had been committed against an ecclesiastic, it came under his jurisdiction as bishop. Then, turning to the culprit, he bade him give him the kiss of peace in token of a perfect reconciliation, and, after a prayer that God would forgive him that and all his other trespasses, he directed that the man should be set at liberty.

The saint often defended his people in public dangers. Hearing one day that a fierce encounter between rival factions had broken out in the street, he threw himself between the combatants, and there fell to the ground. The rioters at once laid down their weapons, fearing that they had killed their beloved bishop, but he soon reassured them as to his safety, only giving thanks to God that their strife was at an end. The Emperor Frederick Barbarossa during his wars in Italy had sacked the city of Spoleto and threatened to subject Gubbio to a similar fate. Ubaldus, moved by solicitude for his flock, met the Emperor on the road and in the course of a single interview, diverted the tyrant from his purpose. During the last two years of his life, the holy bishop suffered from a complication of painful diseases which he bore with heroic patience. On Easter Day 1160, although very ill, he rose to say Mass, and, that he might not disappoint his people, preached and gave them his blessing.

He was carried back to his bed from which he never rose again. On the vigil and feast of Pentecost, as he lay dying, the whole population of Gubbio filed past his couch, anxious to take a last farewell of one whom each individual regarded as his dear father in God. The saint died on May 16, 1160, and the people who flocked to his funeral from far and wide were eye-witnesses of the many miracles God performed at his tomb. In the devotion thus engendered, a wonderful spirit of charity was infused into all hearts, animosities were extinguished, injuries were forgotten, and cities which had long been at variance were reconciled.

The Life by Bishop Theobald is printed in the *Acta Sanctorum*, May, vol. iii, and there is a further collection of miracles in vol. vii. A modern Italian biography was published by Gianpaoli in 1885. On the curious confusion between St Ubaldus and the " St Theobald " who is honoured as the patron of Thann,.in Alsace, see H. Lempfrid in *Mittheilungen d. Gesellschaft f. Erhalt. d. gesch. Denkmäler im Elsass*, vol. xxi (1903), pp. 1–128.

ST SIMON STOCK, Conf.

A.D. 1265

Although St Simon Stock was undoubtedly a very active member of the Carmelite Order at a critical period of its history, and although his alleged connection with the brown scapular revelation (or promise) has made his name familiar to all pious Catholics, we know very little in detail of his life and character. When he died at Bordeaux on May 16, 1265, he is said to have been a hundred years old, but this statement of John Grossi, writing a century and a half after the event, is hardly sufficient to establish a longevity so unusual. It is hard to believe that he could have been elected General of the Order at the age of eighty-two, travelling afterwards not only to many different parts of England, but to Sicily, Bologna, and Gascony. In the same authority, Grossi, we read that St Simon being a strict vegetarian, when a cooked fish was on one occasion set before him, he told them to throw it into the river again, whereupon it swam away fully restored to life. Neither can we attach much more importance to another statement in the same context that Simon was called Stock because as a boy he had adopted the life of an anchoret, making his home in the hollow trunk of a tree. All that has to do with the saint before the year 1247 is conjectural. It is probable enough, as Father Benedict Zimmerman supposes, that after a short period spent as a hermit in England, he made his way to the Holy Land, and having there come into contact with some of the primitive Carmelites whose original profession was eremitical, he joined their organisation as a religious. When the hostility of the Saracens made life impossible for the brethren, we know that their settlements in the East were broken up and that nearly all returned to Europe. In these circumstances St Simon seems to have come back to his native Kent, and being evidently a man of vigour as well as of exceptional holiness, he was elected superior-general, in succession to Alan, when a chapter was held at Aylesford in 1247. His period of rule was marked by wonderful developments of the Order. As Father Benedict notes : " St Simon established houses in four University towns, Cambridge, Oxford, Paris, and Bologna, with the result that a very large number of young, and probably immature, men joined the Order. A considerable number of foundations were made in England, Ireland, perhaps also in Scotland, in Spain, and in various countries on the Continent." We have every reason to believe that about the same time the rule which was originally drafted for hermits primarily intent upon their own individual perfection, had to be substantially modified now that the members of the Order were becoming mendicant friars, busied with preaching and the work of the ministry. This revision was carried through and a preliminary approval was granted by Pope Innocent IV in the year 1247 itself. In 1252 a letter of protection was obtained from the same pontiff to secure them from the molestations of certain of the clergy, for the success of the White Friars had provoked jealousy and hostility in many quarters. It was also at this time of stress and trial, that our Lady is believed to have honoured St Simon with a singular proof of her favour. We are told that the Queen of Heaven appeared to him holding the scapular of the Order in her hand, and that she said : " This shall be a privilege unto thee and all Carmelites ; he who dies in this habit shall be saved." This is not the place to embark upon the discussion of a controversy which has lasted for centuries. It must be admitted that the evidence adduced in favour of this celebrated vision is not entirely satisfactory. There is no contemporary or quasi-contemporary document which attests it. On the other hand the wearing of the brown scapular of the Carmelites has become a widespread devotion in the Church and has been enriched with great indulgences by many different Popes. St Simon's devotion to our Lady is exemplified by two antiphons, the *Flos Carmeli* and the *Ave stella matutina*, which are unhesitatingly attributed to his authorship and which are employed liturgically by the Calced Carmelites. The saint has never been formally canonized, and his name is not inserted in the Roman

Martyrology, but his feast by permission of the Holy See is kept in the Carmelite Order, and we are told that after his death many miracles were wrought beside his grave at Bordeaux.

Almost everything which is evidential in connection with the life of St Simon will be found cited in the *Monumenta Historica Carmelitana* (1907), of Father Benedict Zimmerman, O.C.D., and to this should be added the same writer's articles in the *Irish Ecclesiastical Record*, May 1901 and February to April 1904, as also in *The Month* for October 1927. With regard to the scapular controversy the conservative Carmelite position is presented by P. E. Magennis in his book *The Scapular and some Critics* (1914), and in the articles by J. P. Rushe in the *Irish Ecclesiastical Record* for 1911. On the other side see the *Irish Ecclesiastical Record*, July 1904, and May and June 1911 ; also *The Month*, June and July 1927.

MAY 17

ST PASCHAL BAYLON, Conf.

A.D. 1592

THE notice of St Paschal Baylon in the Roman Martyrology tells us not only that he was a man of wonderful innocence and austerity of life, but also that he has been proclaimed by the Holy See patron of all Eucharistic Congresses and confraternities of the Blessed Sacrament. It is a striking fact that a humble friar, of peasant birth, who was never even raised to the priesthood, and whose name in his own day was hardly known to any but his townsfolk in a corner of Spain, should now from his heavenly throne preside over those most imposing assemblies in which eminent prelates as well as the lay-folk of the Catholic Church are found gathered together in vast multitudes.

Thanks mainly to his fellow-religious, superior and biographer, Father Ximenes, we are well informed regarding Paschal's early days. He first saw the light at Torre Hermosa, on the borders of Castile and Aragon, on a Whit Sunday, and to that accident he seems to have owed his Christian name, for in Spain, as well as in Italy, the term *Pascua* is given to other great feasts of the year besides Easter. So the little son born to Martin Baylon and his wife Elizabeth Jubera was called Pascual, just as we are told that the famous Cervantes was christened Miguel because he came into the world on St Michael's day. The pious couple possessed little in the way of worldly goods, but they owned a flock of sheep, and from his seventh to his twenty-fourth year, Paschal first as the deputy of his own father, and then serving other employers, led the life of a shepherd or goat-herd. Some of the incidents ascribed to that time are probably legendary, but one or two certain facts stand out : for example, that this poor shepherd lad, who never had any schooling, taught himself to read and write, being determined to recite the Little Office of our Blessed Lady, the central feature of the *Horae B. Mariæ Virginis*, then the prayer-book universally in use among all lay-folk. It was noticed with surprise that he went barefoot despite the briars and rough, stony mountain tracks, lived on the poorest fare, fasted often, and wore under his shepherd's cloak some sort of imitation of a friar's habit. He could not always get to Mass, but when he was unable to leave his charge in the early morning, he knelt for long spaces of time, absorbed in prayer, his eyes fixed upon the distant sanctuary of Nuestra Señora de la Sierra where the holy sacrifice was being offered. Fifty years afterwards an aged shepherd who had known Paschal in those days deposed that on such occasions the angels more than once brought the Blessed Sacrament suspended in the air above a chalice to the pious lad that he might gaze upon it and venerate it. He is also alleged to have had a vision of saints, identified by conjecture with St Francis and St Clare, who directed him to offer himself to God in the Order of Friars Minor discalced. More convincing than this testimony is the evidence given of his scrupulous sense of justice. The damage which his beasts, in spite of all his efforts, occasionally caused to the vines or growing crops was to him a continual source of worry. He insisted that compensation should be made to the owners and often paid for it out of his own slender wage. In that matter his fellows, though they respected him for it, thought he went to absurd lengths.

When Paschal, seemingly about the age of eighteen or nineteen, first sought admission among the discalced Friars Minor, St Peter of Alcantara, the author of the reform, was still living. The austerity of the rule which he had revived was only equalled by the fervour of those who practised it. Probably the friars of the Loreto convent, knowing nothing of the young shepherd who came from a district two hundred miles away, doubted his fortitude. At any rate, they put him off, but when they admitted him some few years later, they soon realised that God had committed a treasure to their keeping. The community lived at the level of the first fervour of the reform, but Brother Paschal even in this ascetical atmosphere was recognised as being pre-eminent in every religious virtue. One is apt to regard with some distrust the extravagant eulogiums of hagiographers, but no discerning reader can make himself acquainted with the description which Father Ximenes has left of his friend without realising that we have here no conventional panegyric, but a straight-forward statement of his own inmost conviction. In charity towards all, especially the poor, in humility, modesty, patience, uninterrupted labour and the practice of an almost extravagant poverty ; in joyous equanimity, despite a penitential life which was incredibly austere, Paschal was a marvel even to those mortified men who shared the same hard external conditions and were bound by the same rule. In what he deemed to be matters of conscience he was inflexible. One likes the story of the ladies who when Paschal was porter came to the door to ask the Father Guardian to come down to hear their confessions. "Tell them," said the Guardian, "that I am out." "I will tell them," amended Paschal, "that your Reverence is engaged." "No," the Guardian insisted, "tell them that I am not at home." "Forgive me, Father," objected the brother very humbly and respectfully, "I must not say that, for that would not be the truth and would be a venial sin"; and thereupon he returned to the door in perfect peace of mind. It is such little flashes of independence which relieve the monotony of the catalogue of virtues and enable us to see something of the human element in a soul so exalted and purified.

It is pleasant, too, to read of the little devices by which Paschal schemed to secure special delicacies for the sick, the poor, and those whom he regarded as exceptionally deserving, as well as of the tears sometimes seen in the eyes of this austere man, who normally repressed all signs of emotion, when he was brought into contact with some pathetically hard case. Although, it seems, he never laughed, still he was gay, and there was nothing gloomy about his devotion or even his spirit of penance. Ximenes tells us how on one occasion when Paschal was refectorian and had shut himself in to lay the tables, another friar peeping through the buttery-hatch caught sight of the good brother executing an elaborate dance, like a second *tombleur de Notre Dame*, leaping high and moving rhythmically backwards and forwards, before the statue of our Lady which stood over the refectory door. The intruder withdrew noiselessly, but coming in again a few minutes later with the customary salutation, "Praised be Jesus Christ," he found Paschal with so radiant a countenance that the memory of the scene was a spur to his devotion for many days afterwards. It is no small tribute that Father Ximenes, who was himself a Provincial of the Alcantarines, within little more than half a century of their inauguration, says of St Paschal: "In no single case do I remember to have noted even the least fault in him, though I lived with him in several of our houses and was his companion on two long journeys; such journeys being commonly an occasion when a man, worn out with fatigue and the monotony, allows himself some indulgence which is not entirely free from blame."

It is, however, as the Saint of the Eucharist that St Paschal is best remembered outside his own native country. Many years before the great work of annual Eucharistic Congresses was instituted and our saint was nominated its patron, the title-page of Father Salmeron's Spanish biography bore the heading *Vida del Santo del Sacramento S. Pascual Bailon*. The long hours which he spent before the tabernacle, kneeling without support, his clasped hands held up in front of, or higher than, his face, had left a deep impression upon his brethren who over and over again had watched him praying in this attitude. No wonder that he was for them the " Saint of the Blessed Sacrament." The recognition of this special characteristic goes back to his earliest biographer. Ximenes tells us how the good brother, whenever he had a moment free from his other duties, invariably made his way to the church to honour the presence of our Lord, how it was his delight to serve Mass after Mass in succession beginning with the very earliest, how he stayed behind in choir when at the conclusion of Matins and Lauds the rest of the community had retired again to sleep, and how the dawn found him there still on his knees, eager as soon as the bell rang to descend from the choir to the church in order to visit the altars at which the Holy Sacrifice was to be offered.

Father Ximenes prints some specimens, too lengthy unfortunately to quote, of the simple but very devotional prayers recited by Paschal at the time of Communion. Whether they were his own composition, as his biographer supposes, is not so clear. The Saint had long kept what he himself calls a *cartapacio* (a home-made scrap-book, formed, it seems, out of odds and ends of paper which he had rescued from the rubbish-heap—such was his practice of poverty) and in this he noted down in a beautiful handwriting certain prayers and pious reflections which he had either come across in his reading or had composed himself. One at least of these books —there seem to have been two—is still preserved. Shortly after Paschal's death some of these prayers were brought to the notice of Blessed Juan de Ribera (he was beatified in 1796), then Archbishop of Valencia and titular Patriarch of Antioch. He was so impressed that he begged to have a relic of this holy lay-brother who, it seemed to him, had achieved so perfect an understanding of spiritual things. When a relic was brought him by Father Ximenes, this Father tells us that the Archbishop said to him : " Ah ! Father Provincial, what are we to do ? These simple souls are wresting heaven from our hands. There is nothing for it but to burn our books." To which Ximenes answered : " My Lord, it is not the books that are in fault, but our own pride. Let us burn that."

St Paschal, the Saint of the Eucharist, had, it appears, some experience in his own person of the ferocity with which Protestant reformers manifested their hatred of the sacraments, and their malevolence against all faithful sons of the Church. He was on one occasion sent into France as the bearer of an important communication to Father Christopher de Cheffontaines, the very learned Breton scholar who at that time was Minister General of the Observants. For a friar wearing the habit of his Order the journey across France at that time, when the wars of religion had reached their most acute phase, was extremely dangerous, and the choice for such an errand of a simple lay-brother, who certainly did not know any French, remains a mystery. Perhaps his superior believed that his simplicity and trust in God would carry him through where more diplomatic methods would fail. He succeeded in his mission, but was very roughly handled ; on several occasions barely escaping with his life. At one town in particular, where he was stoned by a party of Huguenots, he seems to have sustained an injury to his shoulder which was a cause of suffering for the rest of his days. At Orleans, we are told by most of his biographers, even by Ximenes, that he was questioned as to his belief in the Blessed Sacrament of the Altar, and that, when he unhesitatingly made profession of his faith, the heretics instituted a sort of formal disputation in which they were worsted by the good brother who was preternaturally aided from on high. Here again in their fury the heretics stoned him, but he escaped, because all their missiles fell wide of the mark. It seems, however, a little difficult to believe in such a disputation in argumentative form with citation of authorities.

St Paschal died, as he was born, on a Whit Sunday, in the friary dedicated to Our Lady of the Rosary at Villareal. He was fifty-two years old. It was held to be significant of his life-long devotion to the Blessed Sacrament that with the holy name of Jesus on his lips he passed away just as the bell was tolling to announce the Elevation at the High Mass. He had long been honoured as a saint, owing to the miracles of all kinds attributed to him in life, especially in his dealings with the sick and poor, and these miracles were multiplied beside his bier. There can be little doubt that the unusually great number of remarkable cures, reported then and later, influenced ecclesiastical authorities to take unwontedly speedy action in the matter of his beatification. He was in fact beatified before St Peter of Alcantara, the author of the Reform to which he belonged, though St Peter had died thirty years earlier than he. Perhaps a bizarre factor which intervened in the case, causing considerable popular excitement, contributed to this result. It was universally believed that curious knockings (*golpes*) proceeded from Paschal's tomb, which knockings were invested with portentous significance. This phenomenon is said to have continued for a couple of centuries, and his later biographers devote much space both to the *golpes* and their interpretation.

Our information concerning St Paschal comes almost entirely from the Life by Father Ximenes and from the process of beatification. A Latin version of Ximenes' biography, somewhat abridged, is printed in the *Acta Sanctorum*, May, vol. iv. Lives in Spanish, Italian and French are numerous, *e.g.* those by Salmeron, Olmi, Briganti, Beaufays, Du Lys, and L. A. de Porrentruy. This last has been translated from the French by O. Staniforth, under the title of *The Saint of the Eucharist* (1908). See also Léon, *Auréole Séraphique* (Eng. trans.), vol. ii, pp. 177-197. Probably the best modern life is that written in German by Father Grötcken (1909).

ST RESTITUTA, VIRG. MART.
(?) *c.* A.D. 257

St Restituta was an African virgin martyr who suffered during the reign of Valerian or during that of Diocletian at a place which in some texts is called Ponizara, but which is elsewhere stated to have been Carthage. At her trial before the judge Proculus, she boldly confessed that she was a Christian and poured scorn upon the heathen deities. She was cruelly tortured, and, if we may believe her so-called Acts, was placed in a boat which having been filled with pitch and other inflammable substances was set adrift after it had been towed out to sea and ignited. The little vessel was carried by the winds and currents to the shores of the island of Ischia near Naples. There the martyr's remains were rescued and recognised. The relics were subsequently translated to Naples to be placed under the high altar of a new church dedicated to the saint. That basilica became the old cathedral, but is now a side chapel in the present cathedral. Carthage also had a church called after the martyr St Restituta.

Despite the abnormally long elogium devoted to this martyr in the Roman Martyrology, the evidence is very inadequate. The " Acts " are printed in the *Acta Sanctorum*, May, vol. iv.

ST MADRON, OR MADERN, HERMIT
(?) FIFTH OR SIXTH CENTURY

There is considerable difference of opinion as to the identity of St Madron, who has given his name to a large parish near the Land's End and also to its beautiful old church—the mother church of Penzance. According to some authorities, Madron was St Medran, brother to St Ohdran and a favourite disciple of St Kieran of Saighir (or St Piran), whom he accompanied to Cornwall in 491. The Welsh on the other hand claim him as being their St Padarn or Badarn, who was buried at Llanbadarn near Aberystwith. A third theory is that he is Macron or Madron, a Cornishman who went with St Tugdual and his companions to Brittany in 545 and was buried at Tréguier at his master's feet.

Out on the open moor—about a mile north-east of Madron Churchtown—lie the picturesque ruins of St Madron's Oratory or Baptistery where the saint is said to have ministered and where he may have lived as a hermit. The remains of what appears to have been a stone altar together with the grassy hillock attached to it became known as " St Madron's bed." About fifty yards away is St Madron's Well from which water was conveyed through the chapel. The oratory and the well were at one time famous for miracles, one of which is attested by Dr. Joseph Hall, the Protestant Bishop of Exeter, as having been investigated by himself in 1641. In a treatise on " The Invisible World," he wrote : " The commerce which we have with the good spirits is not now discerned by the eyes, but is, like themselves, spiritual. Yet not so, but that even in bodily occasions, we have many times insensible helps from them : in such manner as that by the effects we can boldly say : ' Here hath been an angel, though we see him not.' Of this kind was that (no less than miraculous) cure which at St Madern's in Cornwall was wrought upon a poor cripple, John Trelille whereof (besides the attestation of many hundreds of neighbours) I took a strict and personal examination in that last visitation which I either did or ever shall hold. This man, that for sixteen years together, was fain to walk upon his hands, by reason of the close contraction of his legs (upon three admonitions in a dream to wash in that well) was suddenly so restored to his limbs that I saw him able to walk and get his own maintenance. I found here was no art nor collusion : the thing done, the author invisible." A more detailed description of the same cure is given by another writer, Francis Coventry by name, in a book entitled *Paralipomena Philosophiæ*. Religious services are held beside St Madron's Well in May and on the Sunday after the Nativity of St John Baptist by the Wesleyans and the Anglicans respectively. They are of comparatively recent institution, but an old custom of visiting the spring on the first Sunday in May for purposes of divination goes back to pagan times—perhaps to the Stone Age.

See Baring-Gould and Fisher, *Lives of the British Saints*, vol. iii, p. 396.

BD. RATHO, or RASSO, Count of Andechs, Conf.

A.D. 953

The famous pilgrimage-place of Grafrath in Bavaria derives its name from Blessed Ratho, " Graf " of Andechs, who is buried there and whose intercession is sought at his shrine by countless invalids —especially by those suffering from hernia and stone. The beatus, whose name is also written Ratto, Rasso, Rago, and Rapoto, is popularly known as St Grafrath. His father was Count of Diessen and Andechs, and he had one brother who died on a pilgrimage to the Holy Land, and a sister, Halta, who became the mother of St Conrad, Bishop of Constance. He himself embraced the profession of arms and was remarkable for his great stature and for his prowess in all knightly exercises. He also distinguished himself in battle as leader of the Bavarians against the Hungarians. In 942, with Bertold I, he fought the foes of his country, and when they returned six years later he assisted Henry I in driving them back over the frontier. Peace having been restored, he laid aside his weapons to undertake pilgrimages to Rome and to the Holy Land from which he brought back numerous relics—the greater part of which are now at Andechs. On what was then an island in the Amper, under the shadow of the height crowned by the castle afterwards known as the Rassoburg, he built a monastery for twelve Benedictine monks to which he gave the name of Wörth. The church was consecrated to Our Lady and the Apostles Philip and James by St Ulric on May 1, 951. The following year Ratho assumed the habit at Wörth and in 953 he died there. Although shortly after his death the monastery and church were destroyed by the Hungarians, the relics of Blessed Ratho were saved, and his tomb escaped the ravages of that period. At a later date his body was stolen and stripped of its costly adornments ; but it was recovered and replaced in its original burial-place.

It is very difficult to decide what historical value attaches to the narrative compiled by I. Keferlocher from earlier materials. There has been of late a reaction against the complete discredit into which all the Andechs story had fallen. The text is in the *Acta Sanctorum* (for June 19). See also Rader, *Bavaria Sancta*, vol. i, pp. 161–5 ; Blattmann, *Der Hl. Rasso* (1892) ; R. Bauerreiss, *Fuss-Wallfahrt zum hl. Berg Andechs* (1927).

ST BRUNO, Bp. of Würzburg.

A.D. 1045

St Bruno of Würzburg was the son of Conrad, Duke of Carinthia, and of Baroness Matilda, niece of St Bruno-Bonifatius, the second apostle of Prussia, after whom his great-nephew was named. Having embraced the ecclesiastical state, the younger Bruno became Bishop of Würzburg in 1033 and ruled his diocese successfully for eleven years. The whole of his patrimony he spent in building the magnificent cathedral of St Kilian and in restoring or embellishing the other churches under his rule. A wise man and a profound scholar, he became the counsellor of two Emperors and wrote various books, including commentaries on the Holy Scriptures, the Paternoster, the Apostles' Creed and the Creed of St Athanasius. He accompanied his kinsman, Conrad II, to Italy, and is said to have persuaded him to abandon the siege of Milan and to make terms with its inhabitants, as the result of a warning he received in a vision from the great St Ambrose, Bishop of Milan. When the Emperor Henry III, "the Black," marched against the Hungarians in 1045, he took St Bruno in his suite. On their way through Pannonia the royal party put up for a night at the castle of Bosenburg or Porsenberg on the Danube, opposite the present town of Ips in Upper Austria. The building seems to have been in a dilapidated condition, for, while the court was at dinner, the banqueting gallery suddenly collapsed. By grasping at a window, the Emperor almost miraculously escaped disaster, but all the rest—courtiers and soldiers alike —were more or less injured, several of them being killed outright. St Bruno, though in a dying state, lingered on for seven days. His body was taken back to Würzburg where it was buried with great pomp in the basilica he had erected.

There seems to be no proper biography, but there is a notice in the *Acta Sanctorum*, May, vol. iv. See also H. Bresslau, *Jahrbücher der dtsch. Geschichte unter Konrad II* (1884); and J. Baier, *Der hl. Bruno von Würzburg* (1893).

ST THETHMAR, or THEODEMAR, Conf.

A.D. 1152

St Thethmar, also known by the names of Theodemar and Thiadmer, was born at Bremen, and at an early age became a canon in his native city. Another member of the chapter at that time was

St Vicelinus, of whom he had been the favourite pupil and with whom he was to be constantly associated. When in 1123, St Vicelinus went to France to pursue higher studies, he took his disciple with him, and when, three years later, he set out as a missionary to evangelise the Wagrian Wends, Thethmar accompanied him to share his arduous labours. Afterwards the Abbey of Falstera or Neumünster which Vicelinus founded became St Thethmar's headquarters, but towards the close of his life he went to Hagorsdorf in Holstein where he died—two years before his master. From the fact that St Vicelinus was ordained by St Norbert and that his monks followed the rule of St Augustine, it seems almost certain that St Thethmar belonged to the Premonstratensian Order. The holy man's body was preserved at Neumünster until the monastery was moved to Bordesholm in 1328. The monks then took the sacred relics with them.

A short notice will be found in the *Acta Sanctorum*, May, vol. iv.

BLESSED ANDREW ABELLON, CONF.

A.D. 1450

The birthplace of Blessed Andrew Abellon was St Maximin, the ancient Provençal town which for the last seven hundred years has claimed to possess the relics of St Mary Magdalene and has been visited by countless pilgrims, amongst others by St Louis, King of France, in 1254. Blessed Andrew received the Dominican habit in his native town and became Prior of the Royal Monastery of St Mary Magdalene at a time when the great church which is supposed to enshrine the head of its holy patroness was slowly approaching completion : it was begun in 1295, but not finished until 1480. Blessed Andrew was distinguished for his piety and for the zeal with which he enforced regular observance. In addition to labouring as a missioner, he exercised his talents as an artist in many of the Dominican churches of the South of France. He died in 1450 and was beatified in 1902.

Not much seems to be known about the life of Bd. Andrew. The decree of Confirmation of Cultus is printed with some other matter in the *Analecta Ecclesiastica*, vol. x (1902), pp. 443–448 ; but most of this space is taken up with the proof that the Beato after his death was held in great veneration. There is also an account of Bd. Andrew, by Father H. Cormier (Rome, 1903), and sundry references in Fr. Mortier's *Histoire des Maîtres Généraux O.P.*, vol. iv. It need hardly be pointed out that the sanctity of Bd. Andrew is

in no way prejudiced by the fact that historical evidence is lacking to establish
the genuineness of the relics in which he so devoutly believed. On this
question of the authenticity of the St Mary Magdalene legend, see the July
volume of this series, pp. 315–316, and the Irish quarterly magazine, *Studies*,
vol. xxiii (1934), pp. 110–123. It may be noticed that on the last page of this
article, " Saint-Marcellin," by a regrettable oversight, has been misprinted
for Saint-Maximin.

MAY 18

ST VENANTIUS, Mart.

(?) A.D. 257

IT is necessary to devote a notice to St Venantius because he is commemorated on this day with Mass and office under the rite of a double throughout the universal Church. Moreover, the fictitious history of this youth of seventeen is narrated in three long lessons in the Breviary and emphasised by a set of hymns written expressly for the feast. The honour thus paid to the martyr of Camerino is due to the personal action of Pope Clement X, who after having held the see of Camerino for close on forty years was elected Sovereign Pontiff at the age of eighty (1670–1676). There is but the slenderest evidence of any cultus of this martyr. The fact that the name of Venantius appears in church dedications, or was attached to relics, proves little, because there was an authentic St Venantius who was the first bishop of Salona near Spalato (Split) in Dalmatia, on the shore of the Adriatic. The apocryphal "Acts" of the martyr of Camerino narrate that this youth came before the judge to profess himself a Christian, that he was scourged, seared with torches, suspended head downward over fire and smoke, had his teeth knocked out and his jaw broken, was thrown to the lions who only licked his feet, was precipitated without suffering any injury from a high cliff, and finally had his head cut off, with a number of other martyrs who had declared themselves Christians after witnessing the spectacle of his constancy. All this was attended with supernatural apparitions, with the death of two judges who successively presided over the tribunal before which he appeared, and finally with earthquakes and a portentous storm of thunder and lightning.

The text in which all these things are recorded is printed in the *Acta Sanctorum*, May, vol. iv (see also May, vol. vii, appendix), but with a commentary emphasizing its unhistorical character. It seems, in fact, to be of no earlier date than the twelfth century and to be a mere imitation of the equally spurious "Acts" of St Agapitus of Præneste. It is possible that some earlier fiction which grew up round the authentic martyr St Venantius, Bishop of Salona, may have influenced both. See Karl Bihlmeyer in the *Kirchliches Handlexikon*, vol. ii, c. 2563.

SS. THEODOTUS, THECUSA, AND COMPANIONS, MARTS.

(?) A.D. 304

Like many other narratives which have found more or less authoritative acceptance both in the Eastern and Western Church, the story of SS. Theodotus, Thecusa, and their companions is not historical fact, but a pious romance. Shorn of many picturesque details, the tale runs as follows : Theodotus was a charitable and devout Christian who had been brought up by a pious virgin called Thecusa and who plied the trade of an innkeeper at Ancyra in Galatia. The faithful in this province, during the persecution of Diocletian, suffered terribly at the hands of a particularly cruel governor. Theodotus fearlessly assisted the imprisoned Christians and buried the martyrs—though at the risk of his life. He was bearing back the relics of St Valens, which he had rescued from the river Halys, when he encountered, near the town of Malus, a party of Christians who had recently regained their liberty through his exertions. They were overjoyed at the meeting, and sat down to an *alfresco* meal to which they invited Fronto, the local Christian priest. In the course of conversation Theodotus remarked that the place would be an ideal site for a Confession or chapel for relics. " Yes," was the priest's reply, " but you must first have the relics." " Build the church," said Theodotus, " and I will provide the relics." With these words he gave Fronto his ring as a pledge.

Soon afterwards there occurred in Ancyra an annual feast to Artemis and Athene, during the course of which, statues of the goddesses were washed at a pond in which women consecrated to their service bathed in full view of the public. There happened to be at that time imprisoned in the town seven Christian virgins, amongst whom was Thecusa. The governor, who had been unable to shake their constancy, condemned them to be stripped, to be carried naked and erect in an open chariot after the idols and then to be drowned in the pond unless they consented to wear the garlands and robes of the priestesses. As they indignantly refused to do this, the sentence was carried out, stones having been attached to the necks of the martyrs to prevent their bodies from rising. However, Theodotus rescued them one tempestuous night while the guards were sheltering from the storm, and gave them Christian burial. The secret was betrayed by an apostate, and Theodotus, after being subjected to appalling tortures, all of which he survived, was finally decapitated.

Now it came to pass on the day of his friend's death that the priest Fronto had occasion to come to Ancyra with his ass to sell his wine. Night had fallen when he arrived, and, as the gates were closed, he gladly accepted the proffered hospitality of a little band of soldiers encamped outside the city. In the course of conversation he discovered that they were guarding the pyre on which the body of the dead Theodotus was to be burnt on the morrow. Thereupon he plied them with his wine till they were completely intoxicated and, after replacing the ring on its former owner's finger, he laid the body of Theodotus across the back of his ass which he set at liberty, well knowing that it would return home. In the morning he loudly bewailed the theft of his ass and thus escaped suspicion. The animal, as he had anticipated, bore its sacred burden back to Malus, and there the Confession which Theodotus had desired was built to enshrine his own remains.

It might be said without exaggeration that the attitude adopted by modern Catholic scholars towards the story of Theodotus is typical of the change which has come over the whole science of hagiography. Alban Butler, following the footsteps of such generally sound authorities as Ruinart, the early Bollandists and Tillemont, believes that this narrative was written by one Nilus, " who had lived with the martyr, had been his fellow prisoner and was an eye-witness of what he relates." But there are grave reasons for believing that Nilus has merely been invented by an artifice common to all fiction, and that the story, with its reminiscences of a tale occurring in Herodotus, must be treated as a pious romance written by an author possessing rather more literary skill than we commonly find in such cases. See Delehaye in the *Analecta Bollandiana*, vol. xxii (1903), pp. 320–328 ; and vol. xxiii (1904), pp. 478–479. The texts are best given in P. Franchi de' Cavalieri, *Studi e Testi*, no. 6 (1901), and no. 33 (1920). See also the *Acta Sanctorum*, May, vol. iv, and the *Revue des Questions historiques*, vol. xviii (1904), pp. 288–291.

ST POTAMION, Bp. of Heraclea, Mart.

c. A.D. 340

St Potamion was Bishop of Heraclea in Egypt. St Athanasius says that he was doubly a martyr, inasmuch as he suffered cruel persecution first for vindicating the Catholic faith before the heathens and then for defending the divinity of Our Lord before the Arians. When Maximinus Daia persecuted the Christians in 310, St Potamion made a bold confession, and was subjected to savage tortures which entailed permanent lameness as well as the loss of an eye. These marks of his sufferings rendered him a conspicuous figure at the Council of Nicæa in 325, where he took a vigorous part against the Arians. Ten years later he accompanied St Athanasius to the

Council of Tyre and nobly defended that champion of the faith. Under the Arian Emperor Constantius, the prefect of Egypt, Philagrius, and the heretical priest Gregory who had usurped the see of Athanasius, travelled over all Egypt, tormenting and banishing the Catholics. Foremost among their victims was St Potamion, whose uncompromising attitude had specially incurred their animosity. By their order he was arrested and beaten with clubs until he was left for dead. The tender care of those who rescued him enabled him to make a partial recovery, but he died soon afterwards as the result of the ill-treatment he had received.

The available information, gathered almost entirely from SS. Epiphanius and Athanasius, is set out in the *Acta Sanctorum*, May, vol. iv. See also Hefele-Leclercq, *Conciles*, vol. i, pp. 658–659.

ST ERIC, KING AND MART.

A.D. 1160

St Eric was descended through his father from a good old Swedish family, whilst on his mother's side he was of royal race. He married Christina, daughter of Inge IV, King of Sweden and, upon the death of King Sverker II, was chosen on account of his exceptional merits and placed upon the throne by the election of the states—according to the ancient laws of the land. Pious from his early youth, Eric IX continued as a king to keep a strict watch over his own soul and conduct. He treated his body with great severity, fasting and watching much, in order to subdue the flesh and to fit himself for that intercourse with God by prayer upon which he relied for guidance. He was the father and the servant of his people. With indefatigable zeal he administered justice to all, but especially to the poor, to whose complaints his ears were ever open and whose grievances he investigated and redressed. He often visited in person the sick poor, besides relieving them with bountiful alms. Content with his own patrimony, he levied no taxes. He did much to establish Christianity in Upper Sweden and built or completed at Old Upsala the first large church to be erected in his country. He earned the title of the Lawgiver by the wise regulations he made to restrain and civilise his half-savage subjects. The ancient laws and constitutions of the kingdom were by his orders collected into one volume which became known as King Eric's Law or the Code of Upland. These remained part of the Swedish constitution until the close of the thirteenth century, when they were revised by King Magnus Ladulas (Barn-lock) and incorporated by him in another Code entitled the Gardsraette. Although St Eric was a great lover of peace, he found himself constrained to take up arms against the pagan Finlanders who were making frequent descents upon his territories and pillaging the country. He vanquished them in a great battle; but after the victory he wept bitterly at the sight of the dead bodies of his enemies lying on the field, because they had died unbaptised. At his expressed desire, St Henry, Bishop of Upsala, who had accompanied him on the expedition, remained in Finland to evangelise the people after their subjugation. The holy king's zeal for the faith was far from pleasing to some of his pagan nobles. At first they contented themselves with ridiculing his piety, but after a time they entered into a conspiracy with Magnus, the son of the King of Denmark, who coveted the Swedish crown. St Eric was hearing Mass on the day after the Feast of the Ascension when news was brought that a Danish army, swollen with Swedish rebels, was marching against him and was close at hand. He answered calmly : " Let us at least finish the sacrifice : the rest of the feast I shall keep elsewhere." After the Mass was over, he recommended his soul to God, made the sign of the cross, and, to spare the blood of his followers who were ready to defend his life at the expense of their own, marched forth alone in advance of his guards. The conspirators rushed upon him, beat him down from his horse, heaped indignities upon him in derision of his faith and cut off his head. His death occurred on May 18, 1160. Although St Eric was never formally canonised, he was regarded as the principal patron of Sweden until the Protestant Reformation. His banner, which was always carried in battle, has played a great part in Swedish history and was regarded as a portent of victory. The king's relics are preserved in the Cathedral of Upsala, and his effigy appears in the arms of Stockholm.

The principal source for the life of St Eric is the biography written more than a century and a half after his death by the Dominican Israel Erlandson. It is printed with annotations in the *Acta Sanctorum*, May, vol. iv. In the *Lexikon für Theologie und Kirche*, vol. iii, *c.* 753, references are given to some more modern authorities in Swedish who deal with the events of St Eric's reign.

<hr>

BD. WILLIAM OF TOULOUSE, HERMIT
A.D. 1369

At a very early age Blessed William de Naurose joined the Hermits of St Augustine in his native city of Toulouse. Young though he was, he had already begun to tread the path of perfection, and with the triple promise he made at his profession he dedicated himself to the Holy Trinity. With the vow of obedience he offered himself to the Father under whom all things are in subjection, with the vow of poverty to the Son who for our sake became poor, and with the vow of chastity to the Holy Ghost, the Spouse of Our Lady and all pure souls. After his ordination he was sent to pursue his higher studies at the University of Paris—then the educational centre of Christendom. His course completed, he was entrusted with mission work and soon became celebrated as a preacher and as a director of souls. A great promoter of prayer for the holy souls in Purgatory, he was once visited by a wealthy woman who gave him a bag of gold, requesting his prayers for her deceased relations. Blessed William at once said aloud : " Eternal rest give to them, O Lord ; and let perpetual light shine upon them. May they rest in peace," and stopped short—much to the disappointment of his visitor, who plainly intimated that she expected more prayers for the money. The holy priest replied by bidding her write down his prayer and weigh it in a balance with her bag of gold. She did so, and lo ! it was the money which kicked the beam, while down came the scale with the prayer. Blessed William had a great reputation for delivering those possessed by devils, but he was himself frequently attacked by evil spirits, who sometimes appeared to him in visible form and tried to do him bodily harm. He died on May 18, 1369, and his cult was confirmed by Leo XIII in 1893.

The short life by Nicholas Bertrand which is printed in the *Acta Sanctorum*, May, vol. iv, was written a century and a half after the death of Bd. William. There is also a brief historical summary in the decree approving the cult ; and a compendious account of the Beato by N. Mattioli, in Italian, was published in Rome in 1894.

ST FELIX OF CANTALICE, Conf.
A.D. 1587

St Felix was born in humble circumstances at Cantalice near Città Ducale in Apulia. His parents were very devout peasants and he himself early evinced such extraordinary piety that his little companions, when they saw him approach, would cry out : " Here comes Felix, here comes the Saint ! " As a mere child he acted as a cowherd and often, after driving his cattle to some quiet pasturage, he would spend several hours praying at the foot of a tree in the bark of which he had cut a cross. At the age of twelve he was hired out, first as a shepherd and afterwards as a ploughman, to a well-to-do landowner of Città Ducale, named Mark Tully Pichi or Picarelli. In his childish years, before the faculties of his mind were sufficiently developed for anything more ambitious, his prayers consisted of the Our Father, the Hail Mary, the Glory be to the Father, etc. and the Creed—the only prayers he knew, but when still quite young he taught himself to meditate during his work and he soon attained to a high degree of heavenly contemplation. In God, in himself, and in all creatures round him, he found a perpetual fund of pious thoughts and affections. In his later life a religious once asked him how he contrived to keep himself constantly in the presence of God amid the bustle of daily cares and the multiplicity of earthly distractions. "All earthly creatures can lift us up to God," he replied, "if we know how to look at them with an eye that is single." But most of all he loved to dwell upon the sufferings of Our Lord : he was never weary of contemplating that great mystery. Always cheerful, always humble, and always meek, he never resented an insult or an injury. If anyone reviled him he would only say : "I pray God that you may become a saint." An account he heard read of the Fathers in the Desert attracted him to the life of a hermit, but he decided that it might prove to be a dangerous one for him. He was still in doubt as to his future vocation when the question was decided for him through an accident. He was ploughing one day with two fresh young bullocks when his master unexpectedly entered the field. Either his sudden appearance or possibly the black garb he was wearing scared the animals and they bolted, knocking down Felix as he tried to hold them in. He was trampled upon ; the plough passed over his body, but in spite of this he arose unhurt. In gratitude for this miraculous deliverance he promptly betook himself to the Capuchin monastery of Città Ducale, where he asked to be received as a lay-brother. The Father Guardian, after warning him of the austerity of the life, led him before a crucifix, saying : "See what Jesus Christ has suffered for us ! " Felix burst into tears and impressed the superior with the conviction that a soul which felt so deeply must be drawn by God. He accordingly sent him to Rome with a letter to the Provincial.

During the noviciate, which he passed at Anticoli, he appeared already filled with the perfect spirit of his order—especially with a love of poverty, humiliations, and crosses. Often he would beg the novice-master to double his penances and mortifications and to treat him with greater severity than the rest who, he declared, were more docile and naturally more inclined to virtue. Although he thought everyone in the house better than himself, his fellow religious

like the children of Cantalice spoke of him amongst themselves as
" The Saint." In 1545, when he was about thirty, he made his
solemn vows. Four years later he was sent to Rome where for
forty years, practically until his death, he filled the post of questor—
in which capacity it was his daily duty to go round begging food and
alms for the sustenance of the community. The post was a trying
one, but Felix delighted in it because it entailed humiliations,
fatigue, and discomforts. His spirit of recollection was never
interrupted. On his rounds he never spoke unless obliged to do so,
and then in the fewest possible words. To the friar told off to
accompany him he would say : " Brother, let us go forth, rosary in
hand, with our eyes on the ground and our thoughts in heaven."
With the sanction of his superiors, who placed entire confidence in
his discretion, he assisted the poor liberally out of the alms he
collected. When free to do so, he loved to visit the sick, tending
them with his own hands, and consoling the dying. St Philip Neri
held him in great regard and delighted in conversing with him.
The two holy men, as a greeting, would wish each other sufferings
for Christ's sake. When St Charles Borromeo sent to St Philip the
rules he had drawn up for his Oblates with a request that he would
revise them, St Philip excused himself but referred the book to the
poor Capuchin lay-brother. In vain did St Felix protest that he
was illiterate : the rules were read to him and he was commanded
under obedience to give his opinion about them. He advised the
omission of certain regulations which struck him as being too
difficult. These emendations were accepted by St Charles who
expressed great admiration for the judgement that had prompted
them.

St Felix always preserved his purity of mind and body. He
chastised himself with almost incredible severity and invariably
went barefoot, without sandals. He wore a shirt of iron links and
plates studded with iron spikes. When he could do so without too
much singularity, he fasted on bread and water, privately picking
out of the basket for his own dinner the crusts left by other religious.
He tried to conceal from notice the remarkable spiritual favours
he received, but often, when he was serving Mass, he was so
transported in ecstasy that he could not make the responses. For
everything that he saw, for all that befell him, he gave thanks to
God, and the words " Deo gratias " were so constantly on his lips
that the Roman street urchins called him Brother Deogratias.
When he was old and was suffering from a painful internal complaint,
the Cardinal Protector, who loved him greatly, told his superiors
that he ought to be relieved of his wearisome office. But Felix asked

to be allowed to continue his rounds, on the ground that the soul grows sluggish if the body is pampered. He died at the age of seventy-two, after being wonderfully consoled on his death-bed by a vision of our Lady attended by many angels. There is record of a great number of miracles worked after his death.

The Bollandists, in the *Acta Sanctorum*, May, vol. iv, have published a considerable selection of materials presented in the beatification process, a process which was begun only a short time after Brother Felix's death, when witnesses were still available who had lived with him and had been the spectators of his virtues. There is no lack of other biographies, but they are mostly based on the same materials, *e.g.*, those by John Baptist of Perugia, Maximus a Valenza, Angelo Rossi, etc. In English Lady Amabel Kerr published in 1900 a very acceptable sketch entitled *A Son of St Francis*. See also Léon, *Auréole Séraphique* (Eng. trans.), vol. ii, pp. 198–213.

MAY 19

ST PETER CELESTINE, Pope

A.D. 1296

IN all papal history no figure is more pathetic than that of Peter Morone, the aged hermit who, after a pontificate of five short months, voluntarily abdicated, and died virtually a prisoner in the hands of his successor. His unprecedented act of resignation has been variously judged : it has been lauded by some critics as a proof of humility, while it has been severely condemned by others—notably by Dante, who has placed the venerable pontiff in his Inferno on the Circle of the Cowards for having basely made "the great refusal." The Church, however, has set the seal of her approval upon him by raising him to her altars as a canonised saint.

St Peter, who was the eleventh of twelve children, was born of peasant parents about the year 1210 at Isernia, in the Abruzzi. Because he showed unusual piety, his mother, though she was early left a widow, sent him to school—against the advice of her relations. Even as a boy, Peter was favoured with visions, and when he was twenty he retired from the world to live as a hermit on a solitary mountain where he made himself an underground cell so circumscribed that he could scarcely stand upright or lie down in it. In this place, which was infested with toads and reptiles, he remained for three years, practising great austerities and assailed by violent temptations. In spite of his desire to remain hidden, he had occasional visitors, some of whom persuaded him to seek holy orders. He accordingly went to Rome and was ordained priest, but in 1246 he returned to the Abruzzi. On the way back he received the Benedictine habit from the Abbot of Faizola, by whom he was permitted to resume the solitary life. For five years he dwelt on Mount Morone near Sulmona and experienced great favours from heaven at the price of severe interior trials. He was also tormented by scruples which made him afraid for a time to say Mass, but he was reassured in a vision and told to regard such scruples as temptations of the devil. In 1251 the wood was cut on Monte Morone, and the saint, finding his privacy too much invaded, took refuge with two companions in the fastnesses of Monte Majella.

His disciples, however, tracked him thither. After two further ineffectual attempts to live in solitude he resigned himself to the inevitable, and returning to Monte Morone, he became the head of a community of hermits who lived at first in scattered cells, but afterwards in a monastery. His own mode of life continued to be most austere. His flesh he treated with almost incredible severity until he was warned in a vision not to destroy that body which God required him to support. The greater part of the night he devoted to prayer and penance whilst throughout the day he busied himself in hard manual work or in copying books. When he slept, he lay on the ground with a log or a stone for his pillow. He never ate flesh : he fasted every day except Sunday. He kept four Lents in the year, during three of which he lived on bread and water, as he also did on Friday. The bread he used was so hard that it had to be chopped with an axe. He always wore a shirt of horse-hair full of knots and an iron chain round his waist. Five days in the week he gave direction or spiritual advice, but on Wednesdays, Fridays, and during Lent he kept inviolable silence. He gave his disciples a strict rule based on that of St Benedict and in 1274 he obtained from Pope Gregory X the approbation of his Order, the members of which were afterwards known as Celestines. St Peter lived to see thirty-six communities constituted, containing six hundred monks and nuns.

After the death of Nicholas IV, the chair of St Peter remained vacant for two years and three months owing to the rivalry between the two great parties neither of which would give way to the other. To the cardinals assembled at Perugia came a message from the hermit of Monte Morone threatening them with the wrath of God if they continued to delay. His name was mentioned with reverence and, as though moved by a common impulse, the conclave chose the hermit himself to become Christ's Vicar upon earth. The five envoys who climbed the steeps of Morone to bear the official notification to the pope-elect found the old man red-eyed with weeping and appalled at the tidings of his election which had already reached him. He even attempted flight, but was intercepted and was eventually prevailed upon to accept the council's decision as being the will of God. At the convent of Santo Spirito, in the valley below, he was invested with the pontifical robes in preparation for his consecration which was to take place at Aquila. Boundless enthusiasm prevailed amongst the populace at the choice of a Pope so holy and so unworldly, while to many pious souls it seemed an inauguration of the new era foretold by Joachim del Fiore—the reign of the Holy Ghost—when the religious orders would rule the

235

world in peace and love. Two hundred thousand persons are said to have been assembled in Aquila to acclaim the Pontiff as he rode to the cathedral on an ass, the bridle of which was held on the one side by the King of Hungary and on the other by Charles of Anjou, King of Naples. Scarcely, however, were the ceremonies of consecration and coronation completed than it became evident that Celestine V, as he was now called, was quite unequal to the task of ruling the Church. In his utter simplicity he became unwittingly a tool in the hands of King Charles, who used him for the furtherance of his schemes and induced him to live in Naples. He gave great offence to the Italian cardinals by refusing to go to Rome and by creating thirteen new cardinals—nearly all in the Franco-Neapolitan interest. Knowing little Latin and no canon law, his want of worldly experience led him into mistakes of all kinds, whilst the affairs of the Curia fell into hopeless confusion. He shrank from taking part in public ceremonies and strove as far as possible to lead a retired life with two companions in a cell he had constructed of planks in the royal palace. As Advent approached he proposed withdrawing into complete solitude and silence, leaving three cardinals to govern in his place, but was warned that by so doing he was practically creating three rival Popes. Conscious of failure, discouraged, and utterly weary of office, the aged Pontiff began to consider how he might lay down a burden he felt unable to bear. It was an unprecedented thing for a Pope to abdicate, but Cardinal Gaëtano and other learned men whom he consulted decided that it was permissible as not being contrary to canon law and even advisable in certain circumstances. Although the King of Naples and others strongly opposed the proposal, nevertheless on December 13, 1294, at a consistory of cardinals held in Naples in the monarch's presence, St Celestine read a solemn declaration of abdication in which he pleaded his age, his ignorance, his incapacity, and his rough manners and speech. He then laid aside his pontifical robes and, having resumed a religious habit, he cast himself at the feet of the assembly, begging pardon for his many errors and exhorting the cardinals to repair them as well as they could by choosing a worthy successor of St Peter. The assembly, deeply moved, accepted his resignation, and the old man joyfully returned to his hermitage on Monte Morone.

He was not, however, destined to remain there in peace. Within a very short time Cardinal Gaëtano, who as Boniface VIII had been chosen Pope in his place, found himself opposed by a bitterly hostile party and requested the King of Naples to send his too popular predecessor back to Rome lest he should be used to create a schism. St Celestine, duly warned, decided to run away, and took ship with a view to crossing the Adriatic. He was, however, driven back by contrary winds, captured and conveyed to Boniface by whose orders he was imprisoned under a guard of soldiers in the castle of Fumone near Anagni. There he suffered many indignities which never drew from him one word of complaint. On the contrary, he sent word to Boniface by two cardinals who visited him that he was content with his condition and desired no other. He used to say with wonderful tranquillity : " I wished for nothing in the world but a cell : and a cell they have given me." He sang the divine praises almost without interruption with two of his monks who were assigned to him as companions. On Whit Sunday, 1296, he was taken ill of a fever from which he died within six days. During the ten months of his captivity he had never modified any of his austerities. He was buried with great pomp in the Church of Ferentino, but his relics were afterwards translated to Aquila, where they are preserved in the Church of Santa Maria del Colle.

So excellent an account of St Celestine's whole history has been given by Mgr Mann in vol. xvii of his *Lives of the Popes in the Middle Ages*, pp. 247–341, that other references seem hardly necessary. Mgr Mann points out that apart from a rather slender collection of papal documents—the official *Registrum* is lost—Cardinal James Gaetani de' Stephaneschi, in his *Opus Metricum*, and the biographical materials printed by the modern Bollandists in their *Analecta Bollandiana*, vols. ix, x, xvi and xviii, must be regarded as our principal authorities. See also F. X. Seppelt, *Monumenta Celestiniana* (1921) ; B. Cantera, *S. Pier Celestino* (1892) ; G. Celidonio, *Vita di S. Pietro del Morrone* (1896) ; and J. Hollnsteiner, " Die Autobiographie Celestins V " in the *Römische Quartalschrift*, vol. xxxi (1923), pp. 29–40.

SS. PUDENTIANA AND PUDENS, Marts.

(?) FIRST OR SECOND CENTURY

In the Roman Martyrology for May 19 we read : " At Rome (the commemoration) of St Pudentiana, Virgin, who after innumerable contests, after caring reverently for the burial of many of the martyrs, and distributing all her goods to the poor, at length passed from earth to heaven. In the same city of St Pudens, a senator, father of the aforesaid Virgin, who was by the Apostles adorned for Christ in baptism, and guarded his vesture immaculate unto a crown of life." Opinions are divided as to whether this Pudens is to be identified with the Pudens mentioned in 2 Tim. iv, 21. But there can be no reasonable doubt that at an early date there was a Christian so named in Rome who gave a plot of ground with which was subsequently connected a church and " title." It was first known as the *ecclesia Pudentiana* or *titulus Pudentis* ; but by a later confusion people came to speak of the *ecclesia Sanctæ Pudentianæ*, and this supposed patroness was honoured as a martyr and a daughter of Pudens. Owing to a slurred pronunciation the name was also often written Potentiana. After the close of the eighth century a story was fabricated purporting to be the " Acts " of SS. Pudentiana and Praxedis, in which the two maidens were described as sisters (Pudentiana being only sixteen years old) and the daughter of Pudens. They were probably associated in the story because Praxedis and Pudentiana stand together first in the list of the virgins whose bodies were transferred from the catacombs to the church of Praxedis by Pope Paschal I (817–824).

The " Acts " of St Pudentiana are printed by the Bollandists in their fourth volume for May. A commission appointed by Pope Benedict XIV to revise the Breviary declared them to be fabulous and unworthy of credit. Many points connected with Pudens, Pudentiana and Praxedis still remain matters of controversy, but all the material issues are summed up by Père Delehaye in his commentary on the *Hieronymianum*, p. 263, where references are also given to other authorities. Add also Marucchi in the *Nuovo Bulletino di arch. crist.*, vol. xiv (1908), pp. 5–125.

SS. CALOCERUS AND PARTHENIUS, MARTS.

A.D. 304

The two brothers Calocerus and Parthenius, whom the Church honours together on this day, are said to have been eunuchs occupying the post of *praepositus cubiculi* and *primicerius* in the household of Tryphonia, the wife of the Emperor Decius. They were professing Christians and, on the outbreak of persecution, they suffered martyrdom rather than offer sacrifice to the gods. According to their reputed acts, which are quite untrustworthy, they were Armenians who had come from the East with a consul called Æmilianus. Their patron died, leaving them in charge of his daughter Calista or Anatolia as well as of his property, part of which was to be distributed to the poor. They were summoned before Decius on the double charge of being Christians and of dissipating the heritage of Anatolia. After making a bold defence and confession of faith they were condemned to be burnt alive. They emerged unscathed from the flames and were then beaten on the head with lighted stakes until they died. Their bodies were buried by Anatolia in the cemetery of Callistus.

Two texts of the supposed " Acts " are known. One is printed in the *Acta Sanctorum*, May, vol. iv, the other in the *Analecta Bollandiana*, vol. xvi (1897), pp. 240–241. De Rossi attaches some importance to this latter recension, and argues from it in favour of the date 250 ; but Père Delehaye has returned a very sufficient answer in the *Analecta Bollandiana*, vol. xlvi (1928), pp. 50–55, and see further his commentary on the *Hieronymianum*, pp. 261–262.

ST DUNSTAN, ARCHBISHOP OF CANTERBURY

A.D. 988

St Dunstan, the most famous of all the Anglo-Saxon saints, was born (*c.* A.D. 910) near Glastonbury of a noble family closely allied to the ruling race. He received his early education from some Irish scholars, priests who formed part of the community at Glastonbury, and then, while still a lad, he was sent to the court of King Athelstan. There he incurred the ill-will of his fellow-pages, some of whom were his relatives : they accused him of practising incantations—he was a very studious youth—and obtained his expulsion. As he was leaving, they further vented their spite by throwing him into a pond of mire which was probably a cesspool. He had already received the tonsure, and his uncle, St Elphege the Bald, Bishop of Winchester, to whom he now betook himself, urged him to embrace the religious life. Dunstan demurred for a time, but after his recovery from a skin trouble which he took to be leprosy, he hesitated no longer, receiving the habit and subsequently holy orders at the hands of his saintly kinsman. Returning to Glastonbury, he built himself a small cell, five feet by two and a half feet, with an oratory adjoining the old church dedicated to the Mother of God. There he divided his time between prayer, study, and manual labour which took the form of making bells and sacred vessels for the church and of copying or illuminating books. He also played the harp, for he was very musical. Indeed we probably possess the actual music of one or more of St Dunstan's compositions, as the late Abbot Cuthbert Butler contended in the article he wrote in 1886 in the *Downside Review*. The chant known as the *Rex splendens* is especially famous.

Athelstan's successor, Edmund, recalled St Dunstan to court and in 943 appointed him abbot of Glastonbury. Historians differ as to his age at this time : he was certainly young, but the date 925 given by the Anglo-Saxon Chronicle as that of his birth can scarcely

be correct.   At once the new abbot set about reconstructing the
monastic buildings and restoring the Church of St Peter.   By
introducing monks amongst the seculars already in residence, he
was able without too much friction to enforce regular discipline.
Moreover, he made of the abbey a great school of learning.   The
murder of King Edmund after a reign of six and a half years was
followed by the accession of his brother Edred.   The new monarch
summoned Dunstan to court, gave him the custody of the royal
treasures, and practically made him his chancellor and chief adviser.
The policy which the saint then initiated and which continued to
be his throughout his career was vigorous and far-seeing: he stood
out for reform—especially in morals—for the spread of regular
observance to counteract the laxity of the secular clergy and for
the unification of the country by conciliating the Danish element.
He became the acknowledged leader of a party which found its
chief support in East Anglia and in the north, but he made bitter
enemies amongst those whose vices he opposed and amongst the
mass of West Saxon nobles who were reactionary in their views.
Edred died in 955 and was succeeded by his nephew Edwy, a boy of
sixteen, who, on the very day of his coronation, left the royal banquet
to seek the society of a beautiful girl called Elgiva of whom he was
enamoured and was sternly rebuked by St Dunstan for his unseemly
conduct.   This reproof the young prince bitterly resented.   With
the support of the opposition party St Dunstan was disgraced, his
property confiscated, and he was driven into exile.   He found a refuge
in Flanders under the patronage of the Count, who was a grandson
of the great English King Alfred.   In the Netherlands St Dunstan
came into contact for the first time with the Cluniac reform, then
in the fulness of its pristine vigour, and it gave him a vision of
Benedictine perfection which was to be an inspiration to him in all
his after labours.   His banishment, however, did not last long.
A rebellion broke out in England, and the north and east, throwing
off Edwy's yoke, chose for their ruler his brother Edgar.   The new
monarch immediately recalled St Dunstan, upon whom he bestowed
first the see of Worcester and afterwards that of London.   Upon
Edwy's death the kingdom was reunited under Edgar, whose reign
was a peaceful and a prosperous one for England.   In 961 St Dunstan
became Archbishop of Canterbury and upon going to Rome to receive
the pallium was appointed by Pope John XII a legate of the Holy See.
Armed with this authority the saint set himself energetically to re-
establish ecclesiastical discipline, being powerfully protected by
King Edgar and ably assisted by his two former disciples, St
Ethelwold, Bishop of Winchester, and St Oswald, Bishop of

Worcester and Archbishop of York. These three prelates restored most of the great monasteries which had been destroyed during the Danish incursions and founded new ones. They were no less zealous in reforming the clergy, many of whom were leading worldly or scandalous lives, openly disregarding the canonical law binding them to celibacy. Where the seculars proved recalcitrant—notably in the cathedral chapter of Winchester—they were ejected, their places being supplied by monks. Laymen in high places were also brought under discipline, for no motives of human respect ever daunted the saintly archbishop. Even King Edgar himself was subjected to a lengthy and humiliating penance for having assaulted a maiden who had been educated in the nunnery of Wilton and who, though not a religious, had for a time assumed the veil to elude his advances. Throughout the sixteen years' reign of Edgar the Peaceful, St Dunstan remained his chief adviser and he continued to direct the state during the short reign of the next king, Edward the martyr. The death of the young prince was a grievous blow to his ecclesiastical prime minister, who when he crowned Edward's half-brother Ethelred in 979, foretold the calamities which were to mark his reign. The archbishop's political career was now over. He took no further part in state matters, but retired to Canterbury. He had always been a great patron of education, and in his old age, he loved to teach the scholars attached to his cathedral and to tell them stories. One of them, afterwards a priest, but only known to us by the initial of his name as " B," became his first biographer. The saint's memory did not readily fade, and long years after his death the boys used to invoke the aid of their " sweet Father Dunstan " to obtain a mitigation of the savage corporal punishment then in vogue. On the feast of the Ascension, 988, the Archbishop, though ill, said Mass and preached thrice to his people, to whom he announced his impending death. In the afternoon he went again to the cathedral and chose a place for his burial. Two days later, after receiving the holy viaticum, he peacefully expired, and was buried in the spot he had selected. St Dunstan has always been honoured as the patron of goldsmiths, jewellers, and locksmiths. His dexterity as a metal-worker seized upon the popular imagination and, in the eleventh century, gave rise to the popular legend that he once, with a pair of blacksmith's pincers, seized the nose of the devil who was trying to tempt him under the form of a beautiful girl.

The outstanding sources for the life of St Dunstan have been pains-takingly edited by Bishop Stubbs in a volume of the Rolls Series, *Memorials of St Dunstan* (1874). There is good reason, however, to believe that Stubbs was mistaken in assigning Dunstan's birth to 924. See on this E. Bishop and L. Toke in *The Bosworth Psalter* (1908), pp. 126–143. Consult further Dom D. Pontifex, " The First Life of Dunstan," in *The Downside Review*, vol. 51 (1933), pp. 20–40 and 309–325, and Dean Armitage Robinson, *The Times of St Dunstan* (1923). Besides such obvious sources as the *Acta Sanctorum*, Lingard's *History of England*, Stanton's *Menology*, etc., much useful information may be gathered from the series of articles on monastic observances, published at intervals by Dom T. Symons in the *Downside Review*, from 1921 to 1933.

ST IVO HÉLORY, Conf.

A.D. 1303

The patron of lawyers, St Ivo Hélory, was born near Tréguier in Brittany at Kermartin where his father was lord of the manor. At the age of fourteen he was sent to Paris, and before the end of a ten years' stay in its famous schools, he had gained great distinction in philosophy, theology, and canon law. He then passed on to Orleans to study civil law under the celebrated jurist, Peter de la Chapelle, afterwards Bishop of Toulouse and a Cardinal. In his student days he began to practise austerities which he continued and increased throughout his life. He wore a hair shirt, abstained from meat and wine, fasted during Advent and Lent (as well as at other times) on bread and water, and took his rest—which was always short—lying on a straw mat with a book or a stone by way of a pillow. Upon his return to Brittany after the completion of his education, he was appointed by the Archdeacon of Rennes diocesan " Official," or, in other words, judge of the cases that came before the ecclesiastical court. In this capacity he protected orphans, defended the poor and administered justice with an impartiality and kindliness which gained him the goodwill even of the losing side.

Before very long, however, his own diocesan claimed him, and he returned to his native district in the capacity of Official to Alan de Bruc, the Bishop of Tréguier. Here his championship of the downtrodden won for him the name of " the poor man's advocate." Not content with dealing out justice to the helpless in his own court, he would personally plead for them in other courts, often paying their expenses, and visiting them when they were in prison. Never would he accept the presents or bribes which had become so customary as to be regarded as a lawyer's perquisite. He always strove, if possible, to reconcile people who were at enmity and to induce them to settle their quarrels out of court. In this manner he prevented many of those who came to him from embarking on costly and unnecessary lawsuits. St Ivo had received minor orders when he was made Official at Rennes—that post being always held by a clerk. In 1284, he was ordained priest and was given the living of Trédrez. Three years later he resigned his legal office and devoted the last fifteen years of his life to his parishioners—first at Trédrez, and afterwards in the larger parish of Loyannec. He built a hospital in which he tended the sick with his own hands. He would often give the clothes off his back to beggars, and once, when he discovered that a tramp had passed the night on his doorstep, he made the man occupy his bed the following night, whilst he himself slept on the doorstep. He was as solicitous about the spiritual welfare of the people as about their temporal needs, losing no opportunity of instructing them. In great demand as a preacher, he would deliver sermons in other churches besides his own, giving his addresses sometimes in Latin, sometimes in French, and sometimes in Breton. All differences were referred to him, and his arbitration was nearly always accepted. He used to distribute his corn, or the value of it, to the poor directly after the harvest. When it was suggested that he should keep it for a time so as to obtain a better price for it, he replied : " I cannot count upon being alive then to have the disposal of it." From the beginning of Lent, 1303, his health failed visibly, but he would not abate his accustomed austerities. On Ascension Eve he preached and said Mass, although he was so weak that he had to be supported. He then lay down on his bed, which was a hurdle of twigs, and received the last sacraments. He died on May 19, 1303, in the fiftieth year of his age.

We are particularly well informed regarding the life of St Ivo Hélory. In the *Acta Sanctorum*, May, vol. iv, the Bollandists have reprinted a great part of the documents collected twenty-eight years after his death for the process of canonisation. These have been edited again with supplementary matter by A. de La Borderie, *Monuments Originaux de l'Histoire de S. Yves* (1887). Some further biographical material will be found in the *Analecta Bollandiana*, vol. ii and vol. viii. For details see *Bibliotheca Hagiographica Latina*, nn. 4625–4637. There are a number of small popular Lives, notably *Saint Yves* by Ch. de la Roncière (1901) in the series " Les Saints."

BD. AUGUSTIN NOVELLO, Conf.

A.D. 1309

Augustin Novello was the name adopted in religion by Matthew of Termini, otherwise called Taormina, in Sicily. After a brilliant career at Bologna where he studied and taught law, he became prime minister or chancellor to King Manfred. Wounded and abandoned for dead at the battle of Benevento, in which his royal master perished, Matthew vowed that if he recovered, he would devote himself to God's service. In accomplishment of this promise he entered the Order of the Hermits of St Augustine as a simple lay-brother, concealing his identity. When the community found itself involved in a very complicated lawsuit, Blessed Augustin offered to set forth their case, and produced a statement so clear, terse, and convincing, that the advocate of the opposition is said to have exclaimed : " This must be the work of an angel, or of the devil, or of Matthew de Termini—but he perished at Benevento." Confronted at his own request with the author of the statement, the lawyer recognised him at once and congratulated the superior upon possessing among his subjects so great a legal luminary. Augustin Novello accompanied Blessed Clement Osimo to Rome, where they drew up together the new constitutions of the Order. Pope Nicholas IV appointed him Penitentiary to the Papal court, and Boniface VIII sent him as legate to Siena. In 1298 Blessed Augustin was elected General, but he resigned the office two years later to retire into the hermitage of St Leonard which he had built near Siena. He died there on May 19, 1309.

A short Life which purports to have been written by a contemporary is in the *Acta Sanctorum*, May, vol. iv. See also the *Analecta Augustiniana*, vol. iv (1908), pp. 326 *seq.*, and vol. vi (1910, pp. 120–133). There are a number also of short popular Lives, *e.g.* that of P. Sanfilippo (1835).

BD. PETER WRIGHT, MART.

A.D. 1651

The parents of Blessed Peter Wright were pious Catholics who lived at Slipton in Northamptonshire. Obliged by poverty to enter service when very young, Peter, in Protestant surroundings, temporarily lost his faith, but on reaching manhood he recovered it, and went over to Liége, where he was reconciled to the Church by the English Jesuit Fathers in that city. He entered the Society of Jesus, and was sent on a mission to the English soldiers in Flanders—a congenial task which he accomplished with conspicuous success. So greatly did he endear himself to their colonel, Sir Henry Gage, that the gallant officer made the priest his constant companion in the Netherlands and in England. After Sir Henry had died, fighting for the King in 1644, Blessed Peter lived mainly with the Marquis of Winchester, upon the roof of whose house he was arrested by priest-catchers, on Candlemas Day, 1650. At his trial before the Lord Chief Justice, he was condemned mainly on the testimony of an apostate, Sir Henry Gage's younger brother. He received the sentence of death with the utmost serenity, and confided to a priest of the Society sent to him by the Provincial that he had never in his life experienced so much joy. At Tyburn, where he was to be executed with thirteen criminals, he addressed the crowd in a few well-chosen, dignified, yet touching words. After being strung up he was allowed to hang until he was dead, and his friends were suffered to carry away his head and other parts of his body when the usual horrible butchery had been consummated. Father Wright's deportment on the scaffold profoundly impressed many of the spectators and led to several conversions.

See Challoner, *Memoirs of Missionary Priests* (ed. Pollen), pp. 499–504 ; and Foley, *Records of the English Province S.J.*, vol. ii, pp. 506–566.

MAY 20

ST BERNARDINO OF SIENA, Conf.

A.D. 1444

THE Apostle of the Holy Name, St Bernardino, was born in the Tuscan town of Massa Marittima, in which his father, a member of the noble Sienese family of the Albizeschi, occupied the post of governor. The little boy lost both his parents before he was seven and was entrusted to the care of a maternal aunt called Diana and of her daughter Tobia—both excellent women, who gave him a pious training and loved him as though he had been their own child. Upon reaching the age of eleven or twelve, he was placed by his uncles at school in Siena where, under the best masters, he passed with great credit through the course of studies deemed requisite for a boy of his rank. He grew up a good-looking lad, so merry and entertaining that in the opinion of his companions it was impossible to be dull in his company, and so pure-minded that a coarse or blasphemous remark would always bring a blush to his cheek and generally a remonstrance to his lips. Once when a man of position sought to lead him into vice, Bernardino struck him in the face with his fists, and on a second and similar occasion he incited his comrades to join him in pelting the tempter with mud and stones. Except when thus moved by righteous indignation, Bernardino was singularly sweet-tempered. Indeed, throughout his life he was noted for his unfailing affability, patience, and courtesy. At the age of seventeen he enrolled himself in the Confraternity of Our Lady, the members of which pledged themselves to certain devotional practices as well as to the relief of the sick; and he at once embarked upon a course of severe bodily mortification. In 1400 Siena was visited by the plague in a virulent form. It had already broken out in other Italian cities and it seems to have been disseminated in many instances by the numerous pilgrims who were on their way to and from the Holy City for the jubilee. So serious was its toll in Siena that from twelve to twenty persons died daily in the famous Hospital of Santa Maria della Scala, which found itself bereft of almost all those who tended the sick. In this extremity Bernardino offered to take entire charge of the establishment with the help of some ten or twelve other young men whom he had fired with the determination to sacrifice their lives if necessary to aid the sufferers. Their services were accepted, and for four months the noble band worked tirelessly, day and night, under the direction of Bernardino, who, besides nursing the patients and preparing them for death, saw to everything and brought order as well as cleanliness into the hospital. Though several of his companions died, Bernardino escaped the contagion and returned home after the epidemic was over. He was, however, so exhausted by his labours that he fell an easy prey to a fever which laid him low for several months.

Upon his recovery he found that his immediate duty lay close at hand. An aunt named Bartolomea, to whom he was much attached, had become blind as well as bedridden, and to her he devoted himself as he had done to the plague-stricken in the hospital. When, fourteen months later, God called the invalid to Himself, it was in the arms of her nephew that she breathed her last. Free now from all earthly ties, Bernardino retired to a house near the Tufi gate of the city, where he built an oratory and all alone set himself by prayer and fasting to learn God's will as to his future. By this means he was led to enter the Franciscan Order, the habit of which he received shortly afterwards in the Convent of San Francesco in Siena. The house, however, proved too accessible to the novice's many friends and relations, and, with the consent of his superiors, he retired to the Convent of Colombaio outside the city—one of the few establishments in which the rule of St Francis was strictly observed. Here in 1403 he was professed and here he was ordained priest—exactly a year later, on the Feast of the Nativity of Our Lady which was his birthday and the anniversary of his baptism and of his clothing. From that time his fervour seemed to increase daily. He took a real delight in humiliations and, strict though the rule of the house already was, he was ingenious in contriving fresh austerities. When boys mocked and stoned him for his threadbare habit he would say to his companion : " Never mind : they are only helping us to attain to everlasting glory."

History has little to tell us about the saint during the next twelve years : he preached occasionally, but his life was mainly spent in retirement. His chief outward activity seems to have been the founding of a small convent called Capriolo on the site of an old hermitage, belonging to Santa Maria della Scala, which was readily ceded to him in gratitude for his services to the hospital during the plague. He helped with his own hands to build it, he became its first guardian and he often returned to it in after days. Gradually he was being prepared by God for the twofold mission of an Apostle and of a Reformer. When at last his hour had come, the way was made clear in a singular manner. A novice in the Convent at Fiesole in which the saint was staying, startled the community on three consecutive nights after Matins by exclaiming: " Brother Bernardino ! Hide no longer the gift that is in you. Go to Lombardy for all are awaiting you there ! " Reprimanded and questioned as to why he had thus spoken, he replied : " Because I could not help it ! " To Bernardino and to his superiors this seemed to be a call from on high and he at once obeyed. He opened his apostolic career at Milan to which he went as a complete stranger towards the end of 1417, but soon his eloquence and zeal began to attract enormous congregations. At the close of a course of Lenten sermons, before he was allowed to leave the city to preach elsewhere in Lombardy, he was obliged to promise that he would return the following year. At first he was hampered in his delivery by hoarseness and inability to make himself heard, but afterwards, as the result, he firmly believed, of fervent prayer to our Lady, his voice became singularly clear and penetrating. It is impossible to follow him on his missionary journeys, for in them he covered nearly the whole of Italy with the exception of the Kingdom of Naples. He travelled always on foot, preached sometimes for three or four consecutive hours and often delivered several sermons on the same day. In large cities he frequently had to speak from an open-air pulpit because no church could contain the multitudes who crowded to hear him. Everywhere he preached penance, denounced the prevalent vices and kindled popular fervour by spreading devotion to the Holy Name. At the end of every sermon he would hold up for veneration a tablet upon which he had written the letters I.H.S., surrounded by rays, and after telling the people to implore God's mercy and to live in peace he would give them a blessing with the Holy Name. In cities torn by faction he would heal deadly feuds and would persuade men to substitute the sacred monogram for the Guelph or Ghibelline emblems that too often surmounted their front doors. In Bologna, which was overmuch addicted to games of hazard, he preached with such effect that the citizens gave up gambling and brought their cards and dice to be burnt in a public bonfire. A card-manufacturer who complained that he was deprived of his only means of livelihood was told by St Bernardino to manufacture tablets inscribed with the I.H.S., and so great was the demand for them that they brought in more money than the playing-cards had ever done. All over Italy men spoke of the wonderful fruit of St Bernardino's missions— the numerous conversions, the restoration of ill-gotten goods, the reparation of injuries and the reform of morals. Nevertheless there were some who took exception to his teaching and accused him of encouraging superstitious practices. They went so far as to denounce him as a heretic to Pope Martin V, who summoned him to Rome and for a time commanded him to keep silence. However, an examination of his doctrine and conduct led to a complete vindication and he received permission to preach wherever he liked. The same Pope, in 1427, urged him to accept the bishopric of Siena, but he refused it, as he afterwards declined the sees of Ferrara and of Urbino. His excuse was that if he were confined to one diocese he could no longer minister to so many souls.

In 1430, nevertheless, he was obliged to give up missionary work to become Vicar General of the Strict Observance. This movement within the Franciscan Order had originated about the middle of the fourteenth century in the little convent of Brogliano between Camerino and Assisi and had only maintained a struggling existence until the coming of St Bernardino, who became its organiser and its second founder. When he received the habit there were only three hundred friars of the Observance in all Italy ; when he died there were four thousand. Wherever he went on his missionary tours, fervent young men were drawn to the Order with which he was identified, and pious persons desirous of founding convents offered to bestow them upon the Observants. It was therefore right and fitting that he should be officially empowered to consolidate and regulate the Reform. He accomplished this task with so much wisdom and tact that many convents passed voluntarily and without friction from the Conventual to the Observantine rule. The original Observants had shunned scholarship as they had shunned riches, but St Bernardino was aware of the danger of ignorance especially in face of the ever-increasing demand for Observant friars to act as confessors. He therefore insisted upon instruction in theology and canon law as part of the regular curriculum. He was himself a learned man, as may be judged from a series of Latin sermons which he wrote at Capriola and which are still extant, and also by the fact that, at the Council of Florence summoned by Pope Eugenius IV to heal the schism between the East and the West, St Bernardino was able to address the Greek delegates in their own tongue.

Important as was the work with which he was now entrusted, the saint longed to return to his apostolic labours which he regarded as his only vocation, and in 1442 he obtained permission from the Pope to resign his office as Vicar General. He then resumed his missionary journeys which led him through the Romagna, Ferrara, and Lombardy. He was by this time in failing health, and so emaciated that he looked like a skeleton, but the only concession he would allow himself was the use of a donkey to convey him from one place to another. At Massa Maritima in 1444 he preached on fifty consecutive days a course of Lenten sermons which he wound up by exhorting the inhabitants to preserve harmony among themselves, and by bidding a pathetic farewell to his native town. Though obviously dying, he still continued his apostolic work and set out for the Kingdom of Naples, preaching as he went. He succeeded in reaching the town of Aquila, but there his strength gave out and he died on the eve of the Ascension in the monastery of the Conventuals. He had almost reached the age of sixty-four years, forty-two of which he had spent as a religious. His tomb at Aquila was honoured by many miracles and he was canonised within six years of his death, the eulogy being pronounced by the Pope in person.

The number of early Latin biographies of St Bernardino is considerable, and it must suffice to note that a detailed enumeration is supplied in the *Bibliotheca Hagiographica Latina*, nn. 1188–1201. Some are given in full and extracts made from others in the *Acta Sanctorum*, May, vol. v. Excellent modern studies of the life and apostolate of the saint are numerous. The first edition of that by P. Thureau-Dangin, de l'Académie française, was published in 1896. Others which deserve special notice were written by Dr. K. Hefele, in German (1912); by A. G. Ferrers Howell, in English (1913); by Father V. Facchinetti (1933) and by Piero Bargellini (1933), both in Italian, but the number of such works is very great. A considerable amount of fresh material has been brought to light and printed in modern times, for most of which see the *Archivum Franciscanum Historicum*, more especially vols. vi, viii, xi, xii, xv, etc. For a fuller bibliography consult B. Stasiewski, *Der hl. Bernardin von Siena* (1931), and V. Facchinetti, *Bolletino Bibliografico* (1930). A very pleasant English sketch in small compass is that of M. Ward (Mrs. Sheed), *St Bernardino, the People's Preacher*, 1914.

ST THALELÆUS, MART.

(?) A.D. 284

On the ground that St Thalelæus was a physician who gave his services gratis, the Greeks called him "the Merciful," and reckon him amongst their so-called "Moneyless" or disinterested saints. In the Roman Martyrology he is entered as having suffered at Edessa in Syria, but this is a mistake : the actual scene of his martyrdom was Ægæ in Cilicia. Said to have been a native of the Lebanon and the son of a Roman general, he practised at Anazarbus. When persecution broke out against the Christians during the reign of the Emperor Numerian, he escaped to an olive grove where he was captured. After being conveyed to the coast town of Ægæ, he was strung up on a rope passed through his feet behind the ankles, and was then cast into the sea. He managed to swim to shore and was beheaded. This, at least, is the story told in his quite unreliable Greek " Acts." With him are associated a number of other martyrs, including Alexander and Asterius, who were either officials charged with his execution but converted by his fortitude, or else sympathising bystanders. In the Russian Church St Thalelæus is invoked at the blessing of water.

Two Greek texts have been printed in the *Acta Sanctorum*, May, vol. v, and there is also an Armenian rendering, which F. C. Conybeare has translated into English in his *Apology and Acts of Apollonius, etc.* (1894). See also Delehaye, *Origines du Culte des Martyres*, p. 195, who shows that there is no reason to question the fact of the martyrdom of St Thaleleus and that there was a considerable cultus.

ST BASILLA, or BASILISSA, Virg. and Mart.

A.D. 304

According to the Roman Martyrology, St Basilla was a maiden related to the imperial family who suffered in Rome about the middle of the third century. Affianced in her childhood to a distinguished patrician named Pompeius, she refused, after her conversion to Christianity, to carry out the contract because she had consecrated herself to Our Lord at the time of her baptism. Pompeius denounced her to the Emperor Gallienus who left her free to choose between marriage and death by the sword. She preferred the latter fate and was beheaded on the Salarian Way. These details, and in particular the mention of Gallienus in the third century are probably wholly erroneous. In 1654 in the Catacomb of St Cyriacus a tomb was discovered which bore the inscription " Basilla," together with a palm branch and a dove—the symbols of a virgin martyr. The bones found within were translated with great pomp to the Hôtel Dieu at Bayeux in Normandy as being those of our third-century saint, but this identification is now generally discredited, and the Bayeux relics are regarded as being those of an unknown martyr.

Though we have no detailed " Acts " of Basilla, but only a passing reference in the quite untrustworthy Passion of St Eugenia, there can be no question that Basilla was an authentic martyr. Her name is entered with a date (= 304) in the Roman *Depositio Martyrum*. Inscriptions invoking her have been found in the catacombs, and there is mention of her in the *Hieronymianum* on this day. See Delehaye, *Origines du Culte des Martyres*, p. 310. The only difficulty is that the *Depositio Martyrum* assigns her martyrdom to September 22.

ST BAUDELIUS, MART.

(?) A.D. 380

It is certain that a very large number of churches in France and Spain have been dedicated to St Baudelius, whose tomb was formerly one of the most venerated shrines in Provence, but little is actually known of his history except that he perished for the faith at Nîmes. Even the date of his martyrdom is uncertain : some authorities give it as 187, others as 297, and others place it as late as the close of the fourth century. If we may put any trust in his fabulous " Acts," he was a married man who came with his wife from a foreign land to evangelise Southern Gaul. He arrived at Nîmes one day when a feast was being celebrated in honour of Jupiter and was moved to harangue the people on the truths of Christianity and the errors of paganism. At the instigation of the priests he was arrested, and his head was struck off with an axe. St Gregory of Tours, who wrote in the sixth century, mentions the numerous miracles wrought at the tomb of St Baudelius, adding that his cultus had spread all over the Christian world. He is the principal patron of Nîmes.

See the *Acta Sanctorum*, May, vol. v ; and there are also other Latin texts enumerated in the *Bibliotheca Hagiographica Latina*, nn. 1043–1047. St Baudelius is commemorated on this day in the *Hieronymianum* and Père Delehaye's commentary thereon furnishes references to the evidence for early cultus.

ST AUSTREGISILUS (OUTRIL), Bp.

A.D. 624

At the court of King Guntramnus at Chalon-sur-Sâone, the youth Austregisilus (St Outril), who was the son of an impoverished nobleman of Bourges, bore a high reputation. He did not, however, escape the tongue of calumny, and was sentenced to face his accuser in the ordeal by battle in order to clear himself of a serious charge. The death of his opponent by a fall from his horse just before the fight was regarded by all as a special intervention of Providence. It confirmed Austregisilus in an intention which he had previously formed of retiring from the world, and, when the King urged him to marry, he replied by expressing a wish to consecrate himself to God in the religious life, for which he obtained a reluctantly given permission. St Aetherius, the political adviser of King Guntramnus, had been in the confidence of Austregisilus when they were living together at the court and as soon as Aetherius had become Archbishop of Lyons the younger man followed him thither. Austregisilus was ordained priest by his friend who also nominated him abbot of Saint-Nizier at Lyons. As a superior he gained a great reputation for wisdom and miracles. In 612 he was elected Bishop of Bourges and pontificated in this his native city until his death, twelve years later. Amongst his disciples was St Amandus, who, as a young man, came to Bourges and lived in a cell near the cathedral under the direction of the holy bishop.

The Life printed in the *Acta Sanctorum*, May, vol. v, has also been critically edited in the *M. G. H.*, *Script. rer. meroving.*, vol. iv, pp. 188–208. B. Krusch considers that the writer's claim to be a contemporary is fictitious, and that the text was really compiled a couple of centuries later. See also Duchesne, *Fastes Épiscopaux*, vol. i, p. 29.

ST ETHELBERT, KING AND MART.

A.D. 793

When he was still very young, St Ethelbert succeeded his father Ethelred as King of the East Angles, over whom he reigned for forty-four years. It was a saying of his that the higher a man's station in life, the greater is his call to humility and benevolence, and that precept he carried out in his own conduct. To secure the tranquillity of his country by providing it with an heir, he was at last persuaded to marry. He accordingly paid a visit to Offa, King of the Mercians, who was then at Sutton Wallis, that he might obtain the hand of his daughter Alfreda. At the Mercian court he was received with outward courtesy, but after several days he was treacherously murdered at the instigation of Offa's wife, Cynethryth, who desired to add his kingdom to their own. Though he was buried at Mardon, his relics were afterwards translated to a " fair church " at Fernley—now known as Hereford. Cynethryth died miserably within three months, Alfreda retired to live a solitary life at Croyland, and Offa subsequently made a penitential pilgrimage to

Rome, where he founded a school for the English. St Ethelbert is patron of Hereford Cathedral.

It must be confessed that John Brompton, whose account is printed in the *Acta Sanctorum*, May, vol. v, is not a very satisfactory authority, but the Bollandists apparently had also before them a transcript of a manuscript account by Giraldus Cambrensis, which perished in the Cottonian fire. The story has to be pieced together from scraps of information furnished by the A-S. Chronicle, Florence of Worcester, William of Malmesbury, etc. See the *Dictionary of National Biography*, vol. xviii, pp. 17–18 ; and Stanton's *Menology*. From Mr. Edmund Bishop's notes on the English calendar, incorporated in this last, it is clear that St Ethelbert had a considerable cultus as a martyr. He was also represented in the paintings at the English College in Rome. Consult further the account furnished in that undeservedly neglected work, W. B. MacCabe's *A Catholic History of England*, vol. i, pp. 683–697, and the Appendix to A. T. Bannister, *The Cathedral Church of Hereford*, pp. 109–114.

BD. COLOMBA OF RIETI, Virg.

A.D. 1501

In the chronicles of Perugia, we find many references to Blessed Colomba, a humble Dominican, who, by virtue of her sanctity and spiritual gifts, became, whilst yet living, so completely the city's patroness that her mediation was officially sought by the ruling magistrates in all times of danger and perplexity. She was a native, not of Perugia, but of Rieti, where her father and mother earned a modest livelihood as weavers and tailors in a small way. Although her angelic looks as a tiny baby led her parents to choose for her the name of Angiolella, she was always called Colomba, in allusion to a dove which made its appearance during the baptismal ceremony and alighted on the infant's head. It was indeed a prophetic emblem foreshadowing the peace-making rôle the child was destined to play. As she grew in years so she grew in beauty of soul and body. From the Dominican nuns who taught her to read she acquired a great veneration for St Dominic and St Catherine of Siena. During her childhood and throughout her life they often appeared in visions to encourage or to direct her. At the age of ten, she secretly dedicated herself to God and, when her parents urged that she should be betrothed to a wealthy young man, she cut off her hair, declaring that her whole heart belonged to Jesus Christ. She now gave herself up to austerities, hidden as far as possible from the eyes of men, and she strove to tread in the footsteps of St Catherine. She went barefoot, lived only on bread and water, scourged herself with thistles, took the discipline thrice during the night and kept five Lents in the year besides fasting completely on Fridays and Saturdays. On one occasion after a cataleptic trance in which she had lain as though dead for five days, she described in detail the holy places of Palestine which she had been visiting in spirit. But it was at the age of nineteen, when she had been invested with the Dominican Tertiary habit which she had long desired, that she emerged from her retirement and entered upon what may almost be described as her public life.

A resident of Rieti lay under sentence of death for murder, and Colomba's prayers were asked on his behalf. She visited him in prison, brought him to repentance and, after he had made a good confession, assured him that his execution would not take place. Her prophecy was fulfilled when, at the eleventh hour, a reprieve arrived for the condemned man. Her reputation was further enhanced by miracles and by her almost complete abstention from food. At Viterbo where she cured a demoniac, and also at Narni, the inhabitants sought to detain her by force, but she eluded them. She was not, however, to remain long at Rieti. It was revealed to her that her mission lay elsewhere, and accordingly early one morning she slipped out of the house in secular clothes—bound she knew not whither. Upon her arrival at Foligno she was arrested on suspicion that she was a fugitive for whom the authorities were searching and thus her relations were communicated with. Joined there by her father, her brother, and an elderly matron, she was then able to pursue her mysterious journey which led her finally to the gates of Perugia—perhaps the most turbulent city in Italy. She was received in a humble dwelling already occupied by several tertiaries, and immediately she seems to have been made the object of a popular demonstration. Her fame, no doubt, had preceded her. Not only the poor, but many of the rich, including the ladies of the Baglioni family then in power, welcomed her with open arms. On the other hand, certain excellent persons—notably the Franciscan and Dominican friars—were openly suspicious of a young woman who was said to subsist on a few berries and who was constantly falling into ecstacies. Amongst them was Father Sebastian Angeli, afterwards her confessor and biographer. In his book he confesses his early doubts and the incredulity with which he received the information that she had resuscitated a child. " Wait for ten years," he said to young Cæsar Borgia, who suggested ringing the city bells, " and then if her conduct has not belied her reputation we can reckon her a saint." The citizens generally, however, had no such doubts, and they offered to provide her with a convent. On January 1, 1490, Colomba, with a few companions, took the triple vows of a Dominican religious of the Third Order. A few years later, on the outbreak of plague, her position was so well established that the magistrates applied to her for advice and adopted her suggestion of instituting penitential processions. Many of the sick were healed by her touch, some in her convent where they were tended by her nuns, some outside. She had offered herself to God as a victim; and when, in answer to her prayers, the plague abated, she contracted it in a virulent form. Her recovery she attributed to St Catherine in whose honour the magistrates decreed an annual procession which was continued for a hundred years. In the bitter quarrels that rent the city Colomba invariably acted as an angel of peace, and once she warned the rulers of a projected attack from outside which they were consequently able to frustrate.

Pope Alexander VI, when he came to Perugia, asked specially to see her, and was so greatly impressed by her that at a later date he sent his treasurer to consult her on certain secret projects—only to receive reproaches and warnings the details of which were never made public. But if the Pontiff himself was favourably disposed towards her, it was otherwise with his daughter, Lucrezia Borgia, whom Colomba had refused to meet and who, it is said, became her bitter enemy. Apparently as the result of her hostile influence, Blessed Colomba was subjected to a period of persecution, when, by a decree issued from Rome, she was accused of magic and deprived of her confessor. She uttered no complaint and bore all in patience until the attack passed. Towards the end of her life she suffered much bodily pain, but her interest in Perugia continued to the end. To the city fathers who came to visit her in her last illness she gave an exhortation to observe Christian charity and to do justice to the poor. She died at the age of thirty-four, early in the morning on the Feast of the Ascension, 1501. The magistrates contributed to provide for her a public funeral which was attended by the whole city.

In the *Acta Sanctorum*, May, vol. v, the Bollandists have published a Latin biography of Bd. Colomba which was written by her confessor, Father Sebastian degli Angeli, a Dominican friar of Perugia. Very little other material seems to have been available from Dominican sources, and Father Leander Alberti, who produced an Italian Life in 1521, did little more than translate the Latin text of Father Sebastian. It must be confessed that there are many points in his rather surprising narrative which one would have liked to see presented from another angle. Bd. Colomba has never been canonised, but her cult was formally confirmed by Pope Urban VIII. In view of this confirmation or of the continuation of the cause, a summary statement with a brief catalogue of miracles was presented to the Congregation of Rites, and this also may be found in the same volume of the Bollandists. The Dominican, Father D. Viretti, using these sources, compiled in 1777 a *Vita della B. Colomba da Rieti* which was translated into English for the Oratorian Series and edited by Father Faber in 1847. The best modern biography of this interesting Beata seems to be that of Ettore Ricci, *Storia della B. Colomba da Rieti*, Perugia, 1901 ; but see also M. C. de Ganay, *Les Bienheureuses Dominicaines* (1913), pp. 305–354. A short sketch in English will be found in Procter, *Dominican Saints*, pp. 133–136.

MAY 21

ST GODRIC, Hermit

A.D. 1170

ST GODRIC was born of very poor parents at Walpole in
Norfolk, and in his youth earned a living by peddling small
wares in the neighbouring villages. As he improved his
stock he was able to go further afield to the great fairs and cities.
Then the spirit of adventure seized him, and he took to a seafaring
life which he pursued for sixteen years. He made voyages to
Scotland, Flanders, and Scandinavia, during the course of which
he became so expert in navigation that he was often called upon to
steer the ship in times of danger. He probably traded in the ports
he visited, for he was able to purchase a half-share in one merchant
vessel and a quarter-share in another. The life was a rough one
with many temptations, but Godric's thoughts gradually turned to
higher things and a visit which he paid to Holy Island or Lindisfarne
seems to have been the turning-point in his career. He was deeply
impressed by his intercourse with the monks—especially by the
account they gave him of the life of St Cuthbert, whom he ever
afterwards regarded with special veneration. In the fervour of
what was practically his conversion he undertook a penitential
pilgrimage to Jerusalem, which had lately been captured by the
Crusaders. On the homeward journey he visited Compostella.
After his return to England he became house-steward to a wealthy
Norfolk landowner, but the retainers plundered the poorer neighbours unmercifully and Godric soon gave up the post, partly because
he could not induce the master to check this pillaging, partly because
he himself had—knowingly or unknowingly—partaken of the
booty. He then set out on two more pilgrimages, the one to
the shrine of St Gilles in Provence and the other to Rome in the
company of his mother who, we are told, made the whole journey
barefoot. We hear of him next in Cumberland, worshipping in
the churches and acquiring from a kinsman at Carlisle a psalter
which he learnt by heart and which became his most treasured
possession.

But the call to a life of solitude would not suffer him to remain long near the haunts of men.　Having made his way eastward into the wilds of Durham, he fell in at Wolsingham with a recluse called Aelric or Godwin, who had formerly spent a considerable time in the monastery of Durham and who was well qualified to direct a novice.　Godric was permitted to join this aged hermit, in whose company he spent two happy and fruitful years, praising God day and night.　Then Aelric died and Godric made a second pilgrimage to Jerusalem.　It was the last of his foreign journeys, for St Cuthbert in a vision had promised him a hermitage in England.　After a sojourn at Eskdale and another in Durham, where he acted for a time as bell-ringer, he discovered the place of his dream in the midst of Bishop Flambard's hunting-park on the river Wear, three miles from Durham.　There, at Finchale, in a forest which teemed with big and small game, he spent the remaining years of his life, practising mortifications which would have killed any but a very robust man.　He wore an iron cuirass and a rough hair shirt, scourged himself unmercifully, subsisted mainly on berries and roots when he was not fasting from all food, and spent long winter nights immersed in icy water.　Shy creatures such as stags, hares, and birds were not afraid of him, nor did he fear wolves or snakes.　All wild animals were his friends, disporting themselves in his company and fleeing to him from danger.　With his own hands he constructed first a wattle oratory and then a church which he dedicated to St John the Baptist.　As far as possible he lived in silence and seclusion, but he was under the direction of the Prior of Durham who, besides supplying him with a priest to say Mass in his chapel, would often send strangers to be edified by his conversation.　Among his visitors was a monk called Reginald, who obtained from him, though with difficulty, the story of his early years and wrote a biography which is still extant.　St Godric was endowed with extraordinary powers—notably with the gifts of prophecy and a knowledge of distant events.　He foretold the death of Bishop William of Durham, and the exile, return, and martyrdom of St Thomas à Becket, whom he had never seen in the flesh.　He often beheld scenes that were being enacted far away, occasionally breaking off a conversation to pray for vessels in imminent danger of shipwreck.　He also knew beforehand the date of his own death which occurred on May 21, 1170, after he had spent some sixty years in his hermitage.　At a later period there was built at Finchale a stately monastery, the ruins of which survive to this day.

We have two distinct accounts of St Godric, one written by Reginald of Durham who had visited the hermit and had induced him to talk freely of his early life.　This, which is preserved to us in different recensions, was printed by the Surtees Society in 1845. The second, by Galfrid, is also the work of one who had himself seen him, and who had before him the memoir of Prior German who had been St Godric's confessor. This is printed in the *Acta Sanctorum*, May, vol. v. See also the *Dictionary of National Biography*, vol. xxii, pp. 47–49 ; Stanton's *Menology*, etc.

ST HOSPITIUS, HERMIT

A.D. 581

On a narrow tongue of land jutting out from the peninsula of St Jean between Villefranche and Beaulieu stands Cap Saint-Hospice. Here, in an old ruined tower during the latter part of the sixth century, lived the holy hermit Hospitius or Hospice. He bound himself with a heavy iron chain, subsisted on a small pittance of bread and dates, subjected his body to terrible mortifications, and was endowed with the gifts of miracles and prophecy. Owing to the timely warning he gave of the invasion of the Lombards, many of his neighbours were able to save themselves and their property by flight. When the monks of the nearest monastery demurred at the prospect of saving themselves and leaving him to his fate, he assured them that the barbarians would not kill him. The event proved him right. According to St Gregory of Tours, the invaders, at the sight of his chains, took him for a criminal and would have dispatched him. But when one of them raised his sword to strike his arm fell powerless to his side, and it remained as though paralysed until the saint restored it.

We know little of this holy ascetic beyond what is recorded by St Gregory of Tours. See the *Acta Sanctorum*, May, vol. v.

ST THEOBALD (THIÉBAUD), ARCHBP. OF VIENNE

A.D. 1001

Fifty-eighth in the succession of Archbishops of Vienne, and the fourth of their number to be raised to the altars of the Church, St Theobald, who was of a noble family allied to royalty, rebuilt with great magnificence the cathedral of St Maurice. Nothing in detail is recorded of his history, but the people of Vienne had so great a veneration for the holy prelate that they dedicated to his memory four chapels which were afterwards added to his basilica. Of these the largest served as a shrine for his relics which were preserved there until the Revolution. His cultus was approved in 1903.

A short notice of St Theobald is given in the *Acta Sanctorum*, May, vol. v. The decree confirming the cultus may be read in the *Acta Sanctæ Sedis*, vol. xxxvi (1904), pp. 423–426, but it supplies no biographical details. Consult, however, the *Mémoires etc. Soc. Savois.*, vol. xv (1901), pp. 34–43.

BD. BENVENUTUS OF RECANATI, Conf.

A.D. 1289

Few incidents marked the life of Blessed Benvenutus Mareni. He was born at Recanati, a hill-town in the Marches of Ancona at a short distance from Loreto, and entered as a lay-brother amongst the Franciscan Conventuals of his native city. He was remarkable for his piety and for his humility which made him always desirous of the lowliest offices. Often during Mass and especially when he had received Holy Communion he would fall into an ecstasy, his body at such times appearing to be completely insensible. From one of these trances he awoke to realise that it was long past the hour for him to begin to prepare the brethren's meal. Hastily he made his way to the kitchen, where he was greeted by an angelic deputy who had been engaged in doing his work. All who partook of the repast that day agreed that they had never tasted better fare. Bd. Benvenutus had many other supernatural experiences and was once permitted to hold the Infant Saviour in his arms. The saintly friar died on May 5, 1289. Pope Pius VII confirmed his cultus.

In the account which Père Léon, *Auréole Séraphique* (Eng. trans.), vol. ii, pp. 175–176, gives of this Beato he remarks that the annalists of the Order have left few details of his life. This observation seems to be thoroughly borne out by an inspection of such chroniclers as Mazzara or Mark of Lisbon.

BD. ANDREW BOBOLA, Mart.

A.D. 1657

Blessed Andrew Bobola, whom Catholics regard as the Apostle of Lithuania, was nicknamed by schismatics " Duszochwat," or " the Robber of Souls," because of his extraordinary success in reconciling so-called " Orthodox " Christians to the true Church. He came of an aristocratic Polish family and was born in the palatinate of Sandomir. Devout and serious from childhood, he entered in

1611 the Jesuit noviciate at Vilna in Lithuania.   From the end of the
thirteenth century, Poland had occupied a unique position as the
only Slavonic power to remain faithful to the Catholic faith whilst
standing outside the Holy Roman Empire.   Lithuania, on the other
hand, which had become united with Poland in 1391 through the
marriage of Queen Hedwig with Duke Jagiello,* had been largely
won over to the Greek schism—mainly as the result of immigration
and of constant invasion from Russian tribes.   After he had been
raised to the priesthood, Blessed Andrew was appointed preacher
in the Church of St Casimir at Vilna, where his apostolic zeal made
a great impression upon the people.   At a later date he was chosen
superior of the Jesuit house at Bobrinsk and, during his term of
office, distinguished himself by his devotion to the sick and dying
when a terrible epidemic was raging in Lithuania.   As soon as he
was relieved of his charge, he resumed the missionary career which
he had pursued untiringly for more than twenty years, travelling up
and down the country and bringing whole villages back to communion with the Church, besides converting numerous lax Catholics.
His marvellous success brought upon him hatred and opposition.
One form of petty persecution he found particularly trying.   For
several years, whenever he entered a village with a sufficiently large
anti-Catholic population, he was met by an organised band of children
who, in accordance with instructions they had received from their
elders, followed him about, hurling abusive epithets at him and trying
to shout him down.   He never lost patience with them, nor was he
ever daunted or discouraged by threats or opposition.   Poland at
this time had become the scene of a sanguinary conflict in which
the revolted Cossacks took a prominent part.   The Jesuit missionaries
were driven from their churches and colleges by these relentless foes
of Catholic teaching.   They took refuge in a district of swamps,
lakes, and marshland formed by branches of the Pripet and Berezina
and known as Podlesia, or the Woods.   Thither Prince Radziwil,
a good Catholic, invited the Jesuits, to whom he offered one of
his residences at Pinsk.   Blessed Andrew accepted the invitation
although he fully anticipated the fate that was in store for him.
His advent was bitterly resented and a plot was formed against his
life.   One day, just after he had finished saying Mass, he was set
upon by a party of Cossacks who stripped him, tied him to a tree
and beat him.   They then took him to Janow, where they subjected
him to appalling tortures, tearing out an eye, singeing him with
torches and partially flaying him alive.   Two hours later a passer-by
dispatched him with his sword.   The Catholics recovered his body

* See the February volume, pp. 387–388.

and took it to Pinsk, from whence it was subsequently translated to Polozk.

Apart from Polish archives the most reliable source of information concerning Bd. Andrew Bobola is the collection of documents printed for the Congregation of Rites in the Beatification process. These have been used in the compilation of various devotional sketches, notably by the Bollandist Victor de Buck (1853), Père Olivaint (1854), etc., but the most satisfactory Life of Bd. Andrew at present available is that of Padre L. Rocci, S.J., *Vita del B. Andrea Bobola, martire Polacco* (Rome, 1924). The extraordinary history of the conveyance to Rome in 1922 of the mutilated but incorrupt body of the Beato, which had been carried off by the Bolsheviks to Moscow, is told by Father L. J. Gallagher in *The Month*, for February, 1924.

BD. THEOPHILUS A CORTE, CONF.

A.D. 1740

The little town of Corte in Corsica was the birthplace of Blessed Theophilus, or, to give him his baptismal and family names, Blasius de' Signori. He was the only child of aristocratic and devout parents who fostered, up to a certain point, the boy's early piety. They encouraged him to invite his little schoolfellows on Sundays to his home, where he would pray with them and repeat to them the morning's sermon. But when, at the age of fifteen, he ran away to enter a Capuchin monastery, he was not permitted to remain there. Nevertheless, as he continued to show a marked vocation for the religious life, his father and mother allowed him two years later to take the Franciscan habit in his native town. After studying philosophy and theology at Corte, in Rome and at Naples he was ordained in 1700 at Naples. In the Retreat-house of Civitella, to which he was appointed Lector in Theology, he formed an intimate friendship with Blessed Thomas of Cori. In 1705, while still at Civitella, he was chosen for mission preaching and, overcoming a natural shrinking from publicity, he went forth as an evangelist among the people. At once it became evident that he had great oratorical gifts which enabled him to touch the hearts not only of careless Christians, but also of hardened sinners. The influence exerted by his eloquent words was enhanced by the holiness of his life and by miracles. At Civitella, of which he became Guardian, he won the love and veneration of the whole community. In 1730 his superiors sent him back to Corsica in order that he might form one or more houses there on the lines of Civitella. He found himself confronted by many difficulties, but he succeeded in establishing a

Retreat at Luani, where the rule of Civitella was followed in all its poverty and austerity. Four years later he was recalled to Italy to do similar work in Tuscany, and at Fucecchio, some twenty English miles from Florence, he made his second foundation. That same year he was summoned to Rome to give evidence for the beatification of Blessed Thomas of Cori. So great was the impression he then made upon the Bishop of Nicotera, who was in charge of the case, that the prelate afterwards exclaimed : " I have been questioning one saint about another saint." Blessed Theophilus died at Fucecchio on May 20, 1740. As his body lay awaiting burial in the church, immense crowds gathered round to venerate it. They kissed his hands and feet and tore so many pieces from his clothing that it became necessary to dress the sacred corpse in a new habit. Blessed Theophilus was beatified in 1896.

The brief of beatification which includes a biographical summary may be read in the *Analecta Ecclesiastica*, vol. iv (1896), pp. 5–7. There is an excellent account in French by the Abbé Abeau, *Vie du B. Théophile de Corte* (1896)—it runs to more than 400 pages—and an almost equally lengthy Italian Life, in which the archives of the Franciscans of the Observance have been utilised, by Father Dominichelli, *Vita del B. Teofilo da Corte* (1896).

BD. CRISPIN OF VITERBO, Conf.

A.D. 1750

The Romans have a great devotion to Blessed Crispin of Viterbo, whose relics rest under a side altar in the Church of the Immaculate Conception in the Holy City. He was the son of pious parents, and at an early date learnt from his mother the deep veneration to Our Blessed Lady which characterised him throughout his life. After he had received a little schooling at the Jesuit College, Peter—as he was named in his baptism—served his apprenticeship with an uncle from whom he learnt the trade of a shoemaker. The Franciscan Order attracted him greatly and, when he was about twenty-five, he asked and obtained admission to the Capuchin Convent at Viterbo, choosing the name of Crispin because of his trade. In the novice house at Paranzana to which he was sent, the Guardian hesitated to receive him because he looked so delicate and was diminutive in stature, but the Provincial, who had previously admitted him, overruled all objections. As it turned out, Brother Crispin proved equal to the heaviest tasks and loved to call himself the Capuchin ass—deeming himself unfit to be regarded as anything more exalted than a beast of burden. At Viterbo he dug the garden and acted as cook, and at Tolfa, where he was infirmarian during an epidemic, he effected some wonderful cures. The inhabitants of Tolfa, consequently, wished to retain him in their midst, but were told that it was contrary to the rule for a brother to remain long in the same convent. A short residence in Rome was followed by a stay at Albano and another at Bracciano, where he again nursed the sick during an epidemic and seems to have healed many of them miraculously. At Orvieto where he was questor—charged with soliciting alms—he was so greatly beloved that the citizens were determined to keep him. When the time came for his departure the housewives with one consent decided to close their doors to his successor, and, as the convent depended on the charity of the faithful, the Guardian was compelled to re-appoint Brother Crispin rather than allow the brethren to starve. The holy friar's last years, however, were spent in Rome. He was then noted for his prophecies, his miracles, his multiplication of food, and for his wise sayings— some of which have been preserved. He died in his eighty-second year on May 19, 1750, and was beatified in 1806.

There is an anonymous *Vita del B. Crispino da Viterbo* printed at the time of the beatification in 1806, and there have been many others since— notably two in French, by Ildephonse de Bard (1889), and by Pie de Langogne (1901); and two in Italian by P. Pacilli (1908) and by Paolo di Campello (1923). See also Léon, *Auréole Séraphique* (Eng. trans.), vol. ii, pp. 280–285.

MAY 22

ST JULIA, Mart.

Sixth Century (?)

THE name of St Julia appears in many ancient Western martyrologies and she is described as a martyr of Corsica. In the opinion of the Bollandists she suffered in the sixth or seventh century at the hands of Saracen pirates. Her legend, as related in her so-called Acts, is confessedly based on a late tradition and has been freely embellished with imaginative detail. It runs as follows: Julia was a noble maiden of Carthage, who, when the city was taken by Genseric in 439, was sold as a slave to a pagan merchant of Syria called Eusebius. She lived an exemplary life and became so valuable a servant to her master that he took her with him on a journey he was making to Gaul as an importer of Eastern goods. Having reached the northern part of Corsica, now known as Cape Corso, their ship cast anchor. Eusebius went on shore to take part in a local pagan festival, whilst Julia remained behind, refusing to assist at the superstitious ceremonies which she openly denounced. Questioned by Felix, the governor of the island, regarding this woman who had dared to insult the gods, Eusebius admitted that she was a Christian and his slave, but declared that he could not bring himself to part with so faithful and efficient a servant. When the governor offered four of his best female slaves in exchange for her, Eusebius replied : " If you were to offer me all your possessions, they could not equal the value of her services ! " However, when Eusebius was drunk and asleep, the governor took it upon himself to induce her to sacrifice to the gods. He offered to obtain her liberation if she would comply, but she indignantly refused, protesting that all the liberty she desired was freedom to continue serving her Lord Jesus Christ. Her boldness enraged the governor, who gave orders that she should be beaten on the face and that her hair should be torn out by the roots. She finally died by crucifixion. Monks, we are told, from the island of Giraglia rescued her body and kept it until 763, when it was translated to Brescia by the Lombard King Desiderius. St Julia is patroness of Corsica and of Leghorn, which claims to possess some of her relics.

There are two texts of the " Passion " of this martyr, one of which is printed in full in the *Acta Sanctorum*, May, vol. v. The insertion of her name on this day in the *Hieronymianum* affords strong presumption of her historical existence, as Delehaye notes in his commentary. See also particularly Mgr Lanzoni both in his *Diocesi d'Italia*, pp. 685–686, and in the *Rivista Storico-Critica*, vol. vi (1910), pp. 446–453.

SS. CASTUS AND ÆMILIUS, MARTS.
A.D. 250

In a book which he wrote upon the " Lapsed," St Cyprian mentions with sympathy the case of two African Christians, Castus and Æmilius by name, who at the time of the great persecution of Decius gave way under the stress of severe torture but afterwards repented, and gained the crown of martyrdom by confessing their faith and boldly facing death by fire. Nothing further is known about their life or the circumstances of their passion. Their name occurs in several old martyrologies, and St Augustine, in a sermon preached on the occasion of their festival, says that they fell like St Peter through presuming too much on their own strength.

The names are entered on this day in the Calendar of Carthage, a document which can hardly be dated later than the middle of the fifth century. See also the *Acta Sanctorum*, May, vol. v, and Delehaye's commentary in the *Hieronymianum*.

ST QUITERIA, VIRG. AND MART.
FIFTH CENTURY (?)

Many churches in southern France and northern Spain have been dedicated to the Virgin Martyr St Quiteria, who still enjoys a wide cultus—especially at Aire in Gascony where her reputed relics were preserved until they were scattered by the Huguenots. On the other hand, though her name appears in the Roman Martyrology, no mention of her is made in any of the ancient calendars. She is popularly supposed to have been the daughter of a Galician prince and to have fled from home because her father wished to force her to marry and to abjure the Christian religion. She was tracked to Aire by emissaries from her father, by whose orders she was beheaded. Most of the details of the story, in the form in which it was most widely circulated, are fabulous, having been borrowed from the well-known legend of King Catillius and Queen Calsia, and nothing is certain about St Quiteria except her name and her cultus. Because she is invoked against the bites of mad dogs, she is always depicted with a dog on a lead. It seems that Portugal is equally devout to St Quiteria, but tells a different story of her martyrdom and claims to possess her relics.

The modern Bollandists seem inclined to put faith in the Aire tradition, being influenced mainly by the researches of the Abbé A. Degert, who in the *Revue de Gascogne*, vol. 48 (1907), pp. 463–469, has printed the most ancient texts of the life of this martyr. See also the *Revue de Gascogne*, vol. 46 (1905), pp. 333–337, and vol. 44 (1903), pp. 293–309, with the *Analecta Bollandiana*, vol. xxvii (1908), p. 457. The more commonly received account of St Quiteria may be gathered from A. Breuils, *Les Légendes de Sainte Quitterie*, Pau, 1892.

ST ROMANUS, Conf.

c. A.D. 550

When the youthful St Benedict had abandoned the world and was wandering about on the rocky height of Monte Subiaco, he came face to face with a holy monk called Romanus who belonged to a neighbouring monastery. They entered into conversation, and St Benedict opened his heart to the older man and told him he desired to live as a hermit. Romanus not only encouraged him, but showed him a cave very difficult of access which would make him a suitable cell. For three years the monk was the only connection the young recluse had with the outside world and kept his presence a secret. Every day he saved part of his portion of food which, at stated times, he let down by a rope over a cliff to St Benedict. According to the legend, St Romanus left Italy when it was being overrun by the Vandals and betook himself to the neighbourhood of Auxerre in France, where he founded the monastery of Fontrouge and where he died. Auxerre, Sens, and Vareille claim to possess some of his relics.

See also the March volume of this series, p. 353. St Romanus is honoured with a separate elogium on this day in the Roman Martyrology and there is consequently a notice of him in the *Acta Sanctorum*, May, vol. v, which reprints a long and mainly fictitious account of his life and miracles compiled by Gislebert or Gilbert in the middle of the eleventh century. Consult further C. Leclerc, *Vie de S. Romain, éducateur de S. Benoît* (1893) which, though quite uncritical in the matter of his life, supplies some useful information regarding his cultus in Gaul.

ST AIGULPHUS, OR AIOUL, BP. OF BOURGES
A.D. 836

After the death of his parents, when he was still a young man, St Aigulphus left his native city of Bourges to live as a holy solitary in a neighbouring forest.   There he led a most austere life and acquired so great a reputation for sanctity that when the see of Bourges fell vacant, about the year 811, the clergy and people unanimously chose him for their bishop.   Although he only accepted office with reluctance, yet he ruled the diocese wisely and successfully for twenty-four years.   He was one of the signatories at the Council of Toulouse in 829 and was one of the judges selected to examine the case of Ebbo, Archbishop of Rheims, and two other prelates who had been deposed for joining the sons of Louis the Pious in their rebellion against their father.   When he felt that his last hour was approaching, St Aigulphus retired to his old hermitage, where he died and was buried.   Over his tomb a church was afterwards built. On the occasion of an elevation or of a translation of his body, the word " Martyr " was added to the inscription on his tomb, but this was a mistake, due probably to confusion with St Aigulphus, Abbot of Lérins, who was a martyr.

Little is known of St Aigulphus beyond what can be gleaned from the poem which St Theodulphus, Bishop of Orleans, addressed to him.   It is printed with some other fragments of information in the *Acta Sanctorum*, May, vol. v.   See also *Dictionnaire d'Histoire et de Géog. ecclés.*, vol. i, cc. 1142–1143.

ST BOBO, OR BEUVON, CONF.
c. A.D. 985

St Bobo, Bovo, or Beuvon was a Provençal knight—a devout Christian and a gallant soldier—who helped his fellow-countrymen on several occasions to repel the attacks of marauding Saracens from Spain and Africa.   The pirates mostly arrived in ships but they had also established a permanent stronghold in the castle of Garde-Fresnet, situated on a peninsula in the Bay of Tropez.   St Bobo at the head of a band of soldiers attacked this fortress and, with the aid of a doorkeeper, gained entrance into the citadel.   All the garrison were captured, but St Bobo spared and pardoned those who were prepared to embrace the Christian faith.   When peace and tranquillity was fully restored, the good knight retired into solitude from which he emerged once a year to make a pilgrimage to Rome. On the last of his homeward journeys he was taken ill in the Lombard town of Voghera and died there. St Bobo is honoured throughout Lombardy and is invoked against cattle-disease, an appeal which is probably entirely due to the fact that his name is suggestive of an interest in things bovine.

There is a Latin life which is printed in the *Acta Sanctorum*, May, vol. v, and with it a long catalogue of miracles. We may assume that the repute for miracles was mainly responsible for the popular cultus.

ST PETER PARENZI, Mart.

A.D. 1199

During the closing years of the twelfth century the city of Orvieto was greatly influenced by the teaching of the Albigenses or, as they were called in Italy, Cathari, and also Patarini. So unsatisfactory was the whole attitude of the citizens towards the Holy See that Innocent III detained their bishop in Rome for nine months to clear up the charges of undue severity which had been made against him. In February 1199 a noble Roman, Peter Parenzi, was sent to Orvieto as Papal Governor, or Podesta, with special instructions to protect the Catholics and to put down heresy. His first act was to prohibit the public combats which took place in Lent and which invariably led to bloodshed. He then issued a warning to the heretics, assuring them of forgiveness if they would return to the bosom of the Church within a stated time, but menacing with punishment those who should prove obstinate. These threats he carried out with great severity, by fines, by imprisonments, by scourgings, and in some cases by causing the houses of heretics to be burnt down. Upon his arrival at Orvieto he had been met with palms and olive branches, but by the time he went to Rome at Easter to give a personal report to the Holy Father he had, as he knew, made many bitter enemies in Orvieto. Innocent III exhorted him to be faithful unto death, inasmuch as his enemies could only kill his body, and he promised him full absolution at the hour of death if he should fall by the hands of the heretics. Peter had no illusions as to his probable fate. Before leaving Rome he bade farewell to his mother and to his wife, and divided part of his property among his brothers. In the meantime a conspiracy had been started at Orvieto. Soon after his return, on May 21, his house was entered at night and he was dragged out and cruelly murdered. His body was buried in the Church of

St Andrea, but it was afterwards translated to the Cathedral of Orvieto where it still rests.

Canon John of Orvieto, a contemporary, has written an account of all that happened.   It is printed in the *Acta Sanctorum*, May, vol. v, but consult in particular Mgr Mann, *The Lives of the Popes*, vol. xi, pp. 104–107.

ST HUMILITAS, Recluse

A.D. 1310

The foundress of the Order of Vallombrosan nuns was born at Faenza in the Romagna in the year 1226. Her parents, who were people of high rank and of considerable wealth, called her after the town of Rosana with which they were in some way connected, but she has always been known by the name of Humilitas which she adopted when she entered religion. From early childhood she had given proof of an ardent devotion to Our Lady and to St John the Evangelist and she wished to enter a convent. Her father and mother, on the other hand, intended their only daughter to make a good marriage. Although they permitted her to decline an offer from one of Barbarossa's kinsmen who was serving with the imperial army that took Faenza, they practically compelled her when she was about fifteen to marry a local nobleman called Ugoletto—a young man as frivolous as his bride was earnest and devout. She had the misfortune to lose both her little sons shortly after their baptism and for nine years she strove, apparently in vain, to appeal to her husband's better nature. A dangerous illness, however, then brought him to death's door and upon his recovery he was induced by his doctors to consent for his own benefit to his wife's request that they should from thenceforth live as brother and sister. Soon afterwards they both retired from the world, he to become a serving-brother in the monastery of St Perpetua at one of the gates of Faenza and she to be a sister in the nunnery attached to it. At this period Humilitas was twenty-four years of age and very beautiful. She discovered before long that the rule afforded her insufficient opportunity for solitude and austerity and, on this account, she withdrew first to a house of Poor Clares and then to a cell which was constructed for her by a kinsman whom she had cured of a painful infirmity of the feet. It adjoined the church of St Apollinaris, and into this there was an opening—what archæologists call a " squint "—which enabled her to follow Mass and to receive Holy Communion. The church seems to have been served by religious from a priory dependent on the Vallombrosan Abbey of St Crispin, the abbot of which, following the ceremonial provided for such cases, solemnly enclosed her in her cell. Her life was now one of heroic mortification : she subsisted on a little bread and water with occasionally some bitter herbs : she wore a cilicium of bristles, and the short snatches of sleep she allowed herself were taken on her knees with her head leaning against a wall. She had never consented to see her husband after she had left the world, but he could not forget her and, in order that he might keep in touch with her, he left St Perpetua to become a monk at St Crispin, where he died a holy death three years later. After Humilitas had lived twelve years as a recluse, the Vallombrosan Master General and several other persons persuaded her to emerge from her retirement to organise a foundation for women. At a place called Malta outside the walls of Faenza, she established the first Vallombrosan nunnery, of which she became abbess and which was known as Sta Maria Novella alla Malta. Long years afterwards—actually in 1501—the convent was removed for safety into the city and occupied the site once covered by the monastery of St Perpetua. Before her death St Humilitas founded in Florence, under the dedication of St John the Evangelist, a second house of which she was also abbess and where she died at the age of eighty on May 22, 1310.

Tradition credits her with the authorship of several treatises— she is said to have dictated them in Latin, a language she had never studied. One of these deals with the angels and in it she speaks of living in constant communion with two heavenly beings, one of whom was her guardian angel and the other was a celestial spirit sent to her when she was thirty years of age, to guide and advise her in the difficult work with which she was entrusted.

A contemporary Life is printed in the *Acta Sanctorum*, May, vol. v, from a MS. notarially attested in 1332 to be an exact copy. There is a modern biography by M. Ercolani (1910), and many popular accounts of earlier date. The Latin tractates of St Humilitas were edited by Torello Sala at Florence in 1884. They are said to be very obscure and the Latin to be stiff and artificial.

BB. JOHN DE CETINA AND PETER DE DUEÑAS, Marts.

A.D. 1397

Blessed Peter de Dueñas is sometimes known as Peter Tolentinus —apparently because he was, in early boyhood, a page at the court of Toledo. His actual birthplace was Palencia, where his parents held an honourable position. When still very young, he received the Franciscan habit and was a novice of fifteen when there arrived in his convent a holy priest of the order, John de Cetina, who was inflamed with an ardent desire to evangelise the Spanish Moors and thereby possibly gain the crown of martyrdom. Peter was infected by his zeal; and their superiors, to whom they applied for permission, after serious consideration consented to send them to the Mohammedan city of Granada. Peter having been professed, the two friars set out for their destination, which they reached on January 8, 1396. At once they embarked on their mission, which from the first encountered bitter opposition. On May 19 they were arrested by order of King Bambalva, by whose orders they were tortured and then beheaded. Their bodies, after being dragged through the streets, were hacked in pieces, but part of the sacred relics were rescued by pious Christians.

The Bollandists mention these martyrs among the "*prætermissos*" of May 19, but a tolerably full account of them is given both by Mazzara in his *Leggendario Francescano* (ed. 1676), vol. i, pp. 729–733, and by Marco da Lisbona (Italian ed., 1591), Parte Terza, ff. 9–10.

ST RITA OF CASCIA, WIDOW

A.D. 1457

In the year 1381 there was born in a humble peasant home at Roccaporena in the Central Apennines a little girl who, as an exemplary daughter, matron, and religious, was destined to attain to great heights of holiness in this life, and afterwards to merit from countless grateful clients by her intercession in heaven the title of " the saint of the impossible and the advocate of desperate cases."

The child of her parents' old age, Rita—as she was named— showed from her earliest years extraordinary piety and love of prayer. She had set her heart upon dedicating herself to God in the Augustinian Convent at Cascia, but when her father and mother decreed that she should marry, she sorrowfully submitted, deeming that in obeying them she was fulfilling God's will. Her parents' choice was an unfortunate one. Her husband proved to be brutal, dissolute, and so violent that his temper was the terror of the neighbourhood. For eighteen years with unflinching patience and gentleness Rita bore with his insults and infidelities. As with a breaking heart she watched her two sons fall more and more under their father's evil influence, she shed many tears in secret and prayed for them without ceasing. Eventually there came a day when her husband's conscience was touched so that he begged her pardon for all the suffering he had caused her, but shortly afterwards he was carried home dead and covered with wounds. Whether he had been the aggressor or the victim of a vendetta she never knew. Poignancy was added to her grief by the discovery that her sons had vowed to avenge their father's death, and in an agony of sorrow she prayed that they might die rather than commit murder. Her prayer was answered. Before they had carried out their purpose they contracted an illness which proved fatal. Their mother nursed them tenderly and succeeded in bringing them to a better mind so that they died forgiving and forgiven.

Left alone in the world, Rita now began to practise great austerities : her longing for the religious life returned and she tried to enter the Convent at Cascia. She was informed, however, to her dismay that the constitutions forbade the reception of any but virgins. Three times she made application, begging to be admitted in any capacity, and three times the Prioress reluctantly refused her. Nevertheless, with the help of her three patrons, St John Baptist, St Augustine, and St Nicholas of Tolentino, her persistence triumphed : the rules were relaxed in her favour and she received the habit in the year 1413.

In the convent St Rita displayed the same submission to authority which she had shown as a daughter and wife. No fault could be found with her observance of the rule, and when her superior, to try her, bade her water a dead vine in the garden, she not only complied without a word, but continued day after day to tend the old stump. On the other hand, where latitude was allowed by the rule—as in the matter of extra austerities—she was pitiless to herself. She kept long night watchings, she wore a rough hairshirt, she confined herself to a single meal of bread and water, and she scourged herself thrice daily—the first time for the dead, the second time for benefactors, and the third time for all sinners. Her charity to her neighbour expressed itself especially in her care for her fellow religious during illness and for the conversion of negligent Christians, many of whom were brought to repentance by her prayers and persuasion. But all that she said or did was prompted primarily by her fervent love of God which was the ruling passion of her life. From childhood she had had a special devotion to the sufferings of Our Lord, the contemplation of which would sometimes send her into an ecstasy, and when in 1441 she heard an eloquent sermon on the Crown of Thorns from St James of Montebrandone (della Marca), a strange physical reaction seems to have followed. While

she knelt, absorbed in prayer, she became acutely conscious of a pain
—as of a thorn which had detached itself from the crucifix and had
embedded itself in her forehead. It developed into an open wound
which suppurated and became so offensive that she had to be
secluded from the rest and confined to her cell. We read that the
wound was healed for a season—in answer to her prayers—to
enable her to accompany her sisters on a pilgrimage to Rome during
the year of the Jubilee, but it was renewed after her return and
remained with her until her death, obliging her to live practically
as a recluse.

During her later years she was afflicted also by a wasting disease
which she bore with perfect resignation. She would never relax
any of her austerities or sleep on anything softer than rough straw.
She died on May 22, 1457, and her body has remained incorrupt
until modern times. The roses which are St Rita's emblem and
which are blessed in Augustinian churches on her festival refer to
an old tradition. It is said that when the saint was nearing her
death she asked a visitor from Roccaporena to go to her old garden
and bring her a rose. It was early in the season and the friend
had little expectation of being able to gratify what she took to be a
sick woman's fancy. To her great surprise, on entering the garden,
she saw on a bush a rose in full bloom. Having given it to St Rita
she asked if she could do anything more for her. " Yes," was the
reply. " Bring me two figs from the garden." The visitor hastened
back and discovered two ripe figs on a leafless fig tree.

St Rita's great devotion to the Passion has caused her to be chosen
patroness of a confraternity in Rome which exists to venerate the
Sacred Crown of Thorns. She is also joint-patroness of a kindred
association—the Sodality of St Rita and St Clare of Montefalco.

However attractive may be the story of St Rita as it is popularly presented,
the evidence upon which it rests cannot be described as altogether satisfactory. The Saint died in 1457, but the first biography of which anything
is known, written by John George de Amicis, only saw the light in 1600 and
we can learn little or nothing of the sources from which it was compiled.
A considerable number of Lives have appeared in recent years, but in spite
of the diligence of their various authors they add hardly anything in the way
of historical fact to the slender sketch which may be read in the *Acta
Sanctorum* (May, vol. v), and which is derived mainly from the seventeenth
century Life by Cavallucci. There are also many chronological problems,
which, *pace* Father Vannutelli, still remain unsettled. In English we have
The Life of St Rita of Cascia, by R. Connolly (London, 1903), and *Our Own
Saint Rita*, by M. J. Corcoran (New York, 1919). Of the numerous Italian
biographies those by P. Marabottini (1923) and by L. Vannutelli (1925)
seem most in favour.

BD. JOHN FOREST, Mart.

A.D. 1538

At the age of seventeen Blessed John Forest entered the Franciscan Convent of the Strict Observance at Greenwich, and nine years later he was sent to Oxford to study theology. His studies completed, he seems to have returned to his friary with a great reputation for learning and wisdom. Not only was he invited to preach at St Paul's Cross, but he was also chosen to be Queen Catherine's confessor when the court was in residence at Greenwich. He was also probably at one time Provincial. The close relations into which he was brought with the King and Queen and the uncompromising attitude taken up by the Observants with regard to Henry VIII's schemes for divorcing Catherine, rendered his position a delicate one. At a chapter in 1525 he told his brethren that the King was so incensed against them that he had contemplated suppressing them, but that he—Blessed John—had succeeded in dissuading him. The relief, however, was only temporary. In 1534, after the Pope's decision had been made known, Henry ordered that all Observantine convents in England should be dissolved and that the friars should pass to other communities. Captivity was the punishment for such as proved refractory and we know from a legal report that Blessed John was imprisoned in London in the year 1534. How long he remained there is uncertain as we have no record of the next four years. According to the testimony of his enemies he admitted to having made an act of submission " with his mouth but not with his mind " which would appear to have gained him his liberty. On the other hand in the year 1538 we find him living in the House of the Conventual Grey Friars at Newgate under the supervision of a superior who was a nominee of the crown, in a state of semi-captivity but able to minister to those who resorted to him. Because he was thought to have denounced the oath of supremacy to Lord Mordaunt and other penitents, he was arrested and brought to trial. During the trial he was inveigled or browbeaten into giving his assent to some articles propounded to him, but when they were submitted to him afterwards for him to read and sign and he realised that one of them would have amounted to apostasy, he repudiated them altogether. He was thereupon condemned to the stake. He was dragged on a hurdle to Smithfield and almost to the last he was offered a pardon if he would conform, but he remained unshaken. Asked if he had anything to say, he protested that if an angel should come down from heaven and should show him anything other than that which he had believed all his life, and that if he should be cut joint after joint and member after member—burnt, hanged, or whatever pains soever might be done to his body—he would never turn from his " old sect (i.e. profession) of this Bishop of Rome." Owing to the wind the flames took a long time in reaching a vital part, but the martyr bore his sufferings with unflinching fortitude. With him was burnt a wooden statue of a saint known as " Derfel Gatheren," and much venerated in Wales, concerning which it had once been predicted that it would set a *forest* on fire.

The best documented account of this martyr is that by J. H. Pollen, contained in *Lives of the English Martyrs*, edited by Dom Bede Camm, vol. i (1904), pp. 274–326. See also Father Thaddeus, *Life of Blessed John Forest*, and J. M. Stone, *Faithful unto Death* (1892), pp. 46–70.

BD. JOHN BAPTIST MACHADO, Mart.

A.D. 1617

When Blessed John Baptist Machado, as a little boy of seven, heard his elders talking about Japan, he made up his mind that some day he would go there as a missionary, and that determination never left him. He was of Portuguese origin, having been born in the island of Terceira, one of the Azores. At the age of seventeen he was admitted to the Society of Jesus at Coimbra and in 1609 his wish was fulfilled, for he was sent on the Japanese Mission. After having laboured for eight years at Nagasaki, he was called to the Goto Islands, but was arrested immediately after landing. He was taken back to Japan where he was confined in the prison of Omara, or Vomura, a town to the north of Nagasaki. The conditions were dreadful, but Blessed John Baptist had as a fellow-prisoner a Franciscan priest, Blessed Peter of the Ascension, and the two were able to offer holy Mass daily from the Feast of Pentecost until the Monday after Trinity Sunday—the day appointed for their execution.

" God grant that I may suffer something for the love of Him," wrote Blessed John Baptist. " I heartily thank Him for all the favours He had shown me and which I have never deserved. I can truthfully assure you that I would not exchange my present state for any worldly or spiritual dignity. I have never been so happy, so content, and so free from care or unrest as I now am." He reckoned as the three happiest days of his life the day he entered the Society of Jesus, the day he was cast into prison and the day he learnt

. that he was condemned to death. The two priests heard each other's confession, recited the Litany of the Saints and then walked, crucifix in hand and followed by a huge crowd, to the place of execution between Omura and Nagasaki. After Blessed Peter had addressed the crowd, the martyrs embraced each other and with perfect resignation laid their heads upon the executioner's block. With them perished a Japanese youth called Leo who had been server to Blessed John Baptist.

See Boero, *Les Martyrs du Japon* (1868), pp. 8–14, Broeckaert, *Vie du B. Charles Spinola*, pp. 133 and 225–6 ; as well as the fuller histories of Christianity in Japan by Bartoli, Charlevoix, Pagès and others.

MAY 23

ST JOHN BAPTIST ROSSI, Conf.

A.D. 1764

THIS holy priest was born in 1698 at the village of Voltaggio in the diocese of Genoa, and was one of the four children of an excellent and highly respected couple. As a little boy he was remarkable not only for his piety, but also for his gift of inspiring his playfellows with something of his own religious fervour. When he was ten, a nobleman and his wife who were spending the summer at Voltaggio asked and obtained permission from his parents to take him back with them to Genoa to be trained in their house. He remained with them three years, winning golden opinions from all—notably from two Capuchin friars who came to his patron's home. They carried such a favourable report of the boy to his uncle who was then Provincial of the Capuchins that a cousin, Lorenzo Rosso, a canon of Sta Maria in Cosmedin, invited him to come to Rome. The offer was accepted and John Baptist entered the Roman College at the age of thirteen. Popular with his teachers and with his fellow pupils, he had completed the classical course with distinction when the reading of an ascetical book led him to embark on excessive mortifications. The strain on his strength, at a time when he was working hard, led to a complete breakdown which obliged him to leave the Roman College. He recovered sufficiently to complete his training for the priesthood at the Dominican College of the Minerva, but he never was again really robust. Indeed, his subsequent labours were performed under the handicap of almost constant suffering. On March 8, 1721, at the age of twenty-three he was ordained, and his first Mass was said in the Roman College at the altar of St Aloysius Gonzaga, to whom he always had a special devotion. Even in his student days he had been in the habit of visiting the hospitals, often in the company of his fellow pupils, over whom he exercised the same influence that he had wielded over the children of Voltaggio. Now, as a priest, he could do far more for the poor patients. Very particularly did he love the hospice of St Galla, a night refuge for paupers which had been founded by Pope Celestine III. For forty years he

laboured amongst the inmates consoling and instructing them—
often himself supporting the feeble and the crippled to help them
to the chapel. The hospital of the Trinità dei Pellegrini was also a
field of his labours. But there were other poor people for whom,
as he discovered, no provision had hitherto been made : these
called for his special sympathy and efforts. First and foremost
there were the cattle-drivers and teamsters who came up regularly
from the country to sell their beasts at the cattle-market then held
in the Roman Forum. In the early morning and late evening he
would go amongst them, winning their confidence, instructing them
and preparing them for the sacraments. Another class to whom his
pity was extended comprised the homeless women and girls who
wandered about begging or who haunted the streets by night. He
had absolutely no money except the little that came as Mass stipends,
but with the help of 500 scudi from a charitable person and of 400
scudi from the Pope, he hired a house behind the Hospice of
Sta Galla and made of it a refuge which he placed under the
protection of St Aloysius Gonzaga.

For the first few years after his ordination his diffidence made
him shrink from undertaking the work of a confessor. It was not
until he had gone to convalesce after an illness to the house of
Bishop Tenderini of Civita Castellana that he was persuaded by
his friend to make a beginning in his diocese. At once he and his
penitents realised that he had found his true vocation and he
followed it up upon his return to Rome. " I used often to wonder
what was the shortest road to heaven," he remarked to another
friend. " It lies in guiding others thither through the confessional.
. . . What a power for good that can be ! "

In the year 1731, Canon Rossi obtained for his kinsman the post
of assistant priest at Sta Maria in Cosmedin. The church, partly
owing to its position, had been poorly attended, but it soon began
to fill with penitents of all classes who flocked to St John Baptist's
confessional. So much of his time came to be spent there that, at a
later date, two successive Popes, Clement XII and Benedict XIV,
dispensed him from the obligation to say the choir offices when he
was on duty in the tribunal of penance.

Upon the death of Canon Lorenzo Rossi in 1736, his canonry was
conferred upon his cousin, who accepted it but gave up its emoluments
to provide the church with an organ and the stipend of an organist.
Even the house which he inherited from Canon Lorenzo he presented
to the chapter whilst he himself went to live in a miserable attic.
His personal wants were very few : his fare was frugal in the extreme,
and his attire, although always scrupulously neat, was of the plainest

material.　One very congenial task was undertaken at the request of Pope Benedict XIV who inaugurated courses of instruction for prison officials and other state servants and selected the young priest to deliver them.　Amongst his penitents was the public hangman.　Once he was called in to settle a serious quarrel between that official and a younger subordinate.　" To-day I have brought a great state affair to a happy conclusion," he afterwards humorously remarked.

As a preacher the saint was in great demand for missions and also for giving spiritual addresses in religious houses of both men and women.　The Brothers of St John of God, in whose hospitals he often ministered, held him in such high esteem that they chose him to be their own confessor-in-ordinary.　Failing health obliged him in 1763 to take up his residence in the Trinità dei Pellegrini, and in the December of that year he had a stroke and received the last sacraments.　He rallied sufficiently to resume saying Mass, but he suffered greatly and on May 23, 1764 he succumbed to another apoplectic seizure.　He was sixty-six years of age.　He left so little money that the hospital of the Trinità had to undertake to pay for his burial.　As it turned out, however, he was accorded a magnificent funeral : two hundred and sixty priests, many religious, and innumerable lay persons took part in the procession : Archbishop Lercari of Adrianople pontificated at the Requiem in the Church of the Trinità whilst the Papal Choir provided the music.　During his life the saint had been endowed with supernatural gifts, and numerous miracles followed his death.　The process of his beatification, begun in 1781, was completed by the bull of canonisation in 1881.

For those who wish to get in touch with the ultimate evidence for the saint's holy life, the documents printed for the process of beatification and canonisation afford the best available sources ; but there are also a number of excellent modern Lives, notably that by the Dominican Père Cormier in French (1901), and that written in Italian by E. Mougeot (1881), which was translated into English by Lady Herbert and issued with a preface by Cardinal Vaughan (1906).　A contemporary biography was published by one of de Rossi's friends, J. M. Toietti, as early as 1768, and another was issued in the same year by Father Tavani, S.J.

ST DESIDERIUS, OR DIDIER, Bp. OF VIENNE, MART.

A.D. 608

At the time when Queen Brunhildis was exercising her baleful influence over the courts of her grandsons Theodebert King of

Austrasia and Theodoric King of Burgundy, the diocese of Vienne was administered by a holy and learned bishop named Desiderius. He was one of the French prelates to whom St Gregory the Great specially commended St Augustine and his companion missionaries on their way to evangelise England. The zeal of St Desiderius in enforcing clerical discipline, in repressing simony, and in denouncing the profligacy of the court made him many enemies, the chief of whom was Brunhildis herself. Attempts were made to discredit him with the Pope by accusing him of paganism on the ground of his scholarly liking for reading the great Latin classics, but St Gregory, after receiving his apologia, completely exonerated him. Brunhildis then persuaded a servile council at Châlons to banish the good bishop on charges trumped up by false witnesses. Recalled after four years, St Desiderius found himself hampered in the exercise of his duties by the governor of Vienne and other old opponents, but he did not scruple boldly to rebuke King Theodoric (who had expressed a wish to see him), for his shameless immorality. On the way home from the court he was set upon by three hired assassins and was murdered at the place where now stands the town of St Didier-sur-Chalaronne.

The " Passion " which was edited in the *Analecta Bollandiana*, vol. ix (1890), pp. 250–262, seems to be a trustworthy document and to be the work of a contemporary. Another account attributed to Sisebut, the Visigothic King, is also probably authentic, but tells us little. Both are included by B. Krusch in his third volume of the *Scriptores Merovingici*. See also Duchesne, *Fastes Episcopaux*, vol. i, pp. 207–208.

ST GUIBERT, or WIBERT, Abbot

A.D. 962

Gembloux or Gemblours in Brabant, which is now a centre for agriculture and for the manufacture of cutlery, covers the site once occupied by a celebrated Benedictine monastery. It was founded by St Guibert who, about the year 936, gave his estate of Gemblours with all its dependencies for that purpose. He came of one of the most illustrious families of Lorraine and had served with distinction in warlike campaigns, when he was moved to abandon the world and to make trial of the solitary life on one of his estates. It was whilst he was living as a hermit that he conceived the idea of establishing a religious house where men, drawn from worldly affairs, would honour God unceasingly by singing His praises.

St Guibert's grandmother Gisla helped to endow the new foundation over which he placed a holy man called Eusebius to be the first abbot. He himself, as soon as the new monastery was well launched, retired to the Abbey of Gorze, where he received the habit. This step he took from humility, to avoid the respect with which he was regarded at Gemblours and the complacency he might feel in his own foundation. At Gorze he hoped to live in obscurity as a simple monk. He soon discovered, however, that he could not thus easily sever his connection with Gemblours. The land he had given to the new abbey appears to have been an imperial fief, and busybodies represented to the Emperor Otto I that the saint was not entitled thus to dispose of it. The monarch, who was curious to see St Guibert, summoned him to appear before him to plead his cause. The holy man defended his action and his rights so successfully that Otto confirmed the establishment of the abbey by charter and subsequently granted to it great privileges, including the right to hold public markets and to coin money. Nevertheless, in spite of the Emperor's letters, the monks of Gemblours were not left in peaceful possession of the domain. The Count of Namur, St Guibert's brother-in-law, claimed it on behalf of his wife and seized the revenues of the abbey. He was excommunicated from Rome, but St Guibert was obliged for a time to return to Gemblours to assert his own claims and to check the excesses of the Count's soldiery. At the same time he did missionary work, and succeeded in converting and baptising a certain number of pagans—the descendants of Hungarian and Slav settlers who had remained in the country after the great invasion of 954. St Guibert's last years, which he spent at Gorze, were troubled by a long and painful illness. When he was dying the monks of Gemblours came to assist at his death-bed and to claim his relics. He died on May 23, 962, in his seventieth year, and his tomb was afterwards celebrated for the miracles wrought there.

There is a Life written in some detail by the chronicler Sigebert of Gembloux, who lived a century later. It is printed in the *Acta Sanctorum*, May, vol. v, and elsewhere. A good deal of attention has been paid by various writers to the foundation of Gembloux. See especially Dom U. Berlière, *Monasticon Belge*, vol. i, pp. 15–26, and also the *Revue Bénédictine*, vol. iv (1887), pp. 303–307.

ST YVO, Bishop of Chartres

A.D. 1115

To the Order of Canons Regular of St Augustine the Church in the eleventh century was indebted for one of the most venerated of her ecclesiastical rulers. Yvo, Bishop of Chartres, was born of noble parents in the territory of Beauvais and studied theology under the celebrated Lanfranc in the Abbey of Bec. After occupying a canonry at Nesle or Nelle in Picardy, he took the habit at the monastery of St Quentin, a house of Regular Canons which had been founded in 1078 by Guy, Bishop of Beauvais. St Yvo bestowed part of his patrimony upon the community and was appointed to lecture on theology, canon law, and the holy scriptures. Afterwards he ruled as provost or superior for fourteen years, during the course of which he raised the house to a high pitch of discipline and learning, so that he was constantly being called upon by bishops and princes to send his canons to other places either to reform ancient chapters or else to found new ones. At that period the rule of the order was extremely severe. The canons never ate either flesh or fish, and they observed almost perpetual silence unless the duties of charity required them to speak. Prayer and penitential exercises constituted their principal employment, although they also applied themselves to the instruction of the people and to the study of sacred science.

When, in the year 1091, Geoffrey, Bishop of Chartres, was deposed for simony and other misdemeanours, the clergy and people demanded Yvo for their bishop. He was very unwilling to emerge from his retirement, but Urban II confirmed his election and King Philip gave him the investiture by placing a crozier in his hand. Yvo immediately set out for Rome, where he was consecrated by the Pope, who subsequently checked the endeavours of Richerius, Archbishop of Sens and Metropolitan of Chartres, to reinstate Geoffrey. Scarcely was St Yvo firmly established in his see than he found himself faced with the necessity of opposing the will of his sovereign. King Philip had become so greatly enamoured of Bertrada, the third wife of Fulk, Count of Anjou, that he had determined to marry her and to divorce his queen Bertha in spite of the fact that she had borne him two children. With a view to finding means of legalising his proposed action, he called a conference to which he invited Yvo and other prelates. The saintly Bishop of Chartres did his utmost to dissuade the King from proceeding further, but when he found his remonstrances unavailing he declared openly that he would prefer to be cast into the sea with a mill-stone round his neck rather than countenance such a scandal. Philip in revenge had him put in prison, seized his revenues and sent officers to plunder his lands. Strong representations, however, were made by the Pope, by influential personages, and by the citizens of Chartres, and he was released. Philip indeed could scarcely fail to realise that the saintly bishop was amongst his most loyal subjects, for St Yvo, while actually in custody, nipped in the bud a conspiracy of nobles against their sovereign. He also held up for a considerable time the Papal letters condemning the prince's proposed adulterous marriage lest their publication should furnish the malcontents with a pretext for taking up arms against Philip. For the same reason he delayed publishing the excommunication which the Holy Father launched against the King. At a later date he exerted himself to reconcile Philip to the Holy See and took part in the Council of Baugency which decided upon the absolution of the King in 1104. Though he was devoted to the Holy See, St Yvo maintained a sufficiently independent attitude to enable him to act as mediator in the dispute over investitures and to protest openly against the greed of certain Roman legates and the simony of members of the papal court.

St Yvo died on December 23, 1115, after having governed his see for twenty-three years. He was a voluminous writer and many of his works have survived. His most famous literary undertaking was a collection of decrees drawn from papal and conciliar letters and canons accepted by the fathers. This is preserved to us in two, if not three, independent compilations. We have also 24 sermons and 288 letters which shed an interesting light on contemporary history and ecclesiastical discipline.

Although no formal early biography of St Yvo of Chartres is preserved to us, we have a great deal of information supplied by his letters and by references in contemporary chronicles and correspondence. See the *Acta Sanctorum*, May, vol. v. Yvo has been much studied recently, especially from the point of view of his work as a canonist. A most valuable contribution to this aspect of the subject may be found in the treatise of P. Fournier and G. Le Bras, *Histoire des Collections canoniques en Occident depuis les Fausses Décrétales, etc.*, vol. ii (1932), pp. 55–114. St Yvo's views as to the superiority of the cenobitical life to that of hermits and solitaries are discussed by Dom G. Morin in the *Revue Bénédictine* for 1928, vol. xl, pp. 99–115.

BD. GERARD OF VILLAMAGNA, HERMIT

A.D. 1245

The origins of the Franciscan Third Order for lay-folk are involved in great obscurity, and it is curious to notice how little evidence is forthcoming to support the claim that certain holy people in the early part of the thirteenth century were admitted as Tertiaries by St Francis himself. Something has already been said (see April volume, p. 321) of the case of Blessed Luchesius, and here again when we ask for proof that Gerard of Villamagna was received into the Third Order by the Saint of Assisi, we are told that all early documents have perished. Gerard was a solitary who occupied a hermitage near his native village of Villamagna in Tuscany. He led a very austere life, absorbed for the most part in contemplation, but also giving direction at times to many struggling souls who came to consult him. We are told that he had been left an orphan at the age of twelve, had been brought up as a kind of page boy in the household of some wealthy Florentine, had attended his master as a body-servant when he joined the third crusade, had been captured by the Saracens and afterwards ransomed, that he had again returned to the Holy Land with another crusader, and had himself eventually been admitted as a Knight of the Holy Sepulchre. Wearied of the world, it is stated that he came back to Italy to lead the life of a hermit, that he received the cord of the Third Order from St Francis himself, and that he died some twenty years later famous for his miracles and prophecies. His cult was confirmed in 1833.

The Bollandists could find no better materials to print in the *Acta Sanctorum* (May, vol. iii) than an account compiled after the year 1550 by the parish priest of Villamagna. See also Wadding, *Annales*, vol. v, p. 19.

BD. BARTHOLOMEW PUCCI-FRANCESCHI, CONF.

A.D. 1330

Amongst the numerous persons of all ranks who were led by the example of the early Franciscans to abandon all things in order to embrace holy poverty was a prominent citizen of Montepulciano named Bartholomew Pucci-Franceschi. He was a married man and had lived an exemplary Christian life with his family for many years when the call came to him to serve God in complete renunciation of the world. With the consent of his wife, who herself took the vow of chastity, he entered the Franciscan Order. Soon he surpassed all his brethren in piety, and was induced, though against his wish, to receive holy orders. He had frequent visions of Our Lady and of angels, and performed many miracles—particularly in the multiplication of food. To avoid human respect he tried to become a "fool for Christ's sake," behaving at times in such a manner as to be ridiculed and pelted by children in the streets. He lived to be very old, and died at Montepulciano on May 6, 1330.

See Ausserer, *Seraphisches Martyrologium* (1889); Léon, *Auréole Séraphique* (Eng. trans.), vol. ii, pp. 375–376.

MAY 24

ST VINCENT OF LÉRINS, Conf.

c. A.D. 445

ST VINCENT OF LÉRINS is described by St Eucherius in his *Instructiones* and in his letter *De Laude Eremi* as a man "pre-eminent in eloquence and learning." He is supposed to have been the brother of St Lupus (St Loup) of Troyes, and he would seem to have been a soldier before he took the habit at the Abbey of Lérins in the island off the coast of Cannes now called Saint Honorat, after the founder of the great monastery. St Vincent was living there as a monk and a priest when, in the year 434— nearly three years after the close of the Council of Ephesus—he composed the book upon which his fame rests, his so-called *Commonitorium* against Heresies. In this book he speaks of himself as a stranger and pilgrim who had fled from the military service of this world with all its empty vanities and passing pleasures in order to enter the service of Christ as one of His lowliest servants in the seclusion of the cloister. He explains that, in the course of his reading, he had gathered from the Fathers certain principles or rules for distinguishing Catholic truth from heresy, and that he had jotted them down primarily for his own use—to aid his poor memory. These notes he expanded into a treatise in two parts, the second of which dealt with the recent Council of Ephesus. This latter portion, however, was lost or stolen, and St Vincent contented himself with adding to the first part a general summary or recapitulation of the whole. In this book of forty-two short chapters, which St Robert Bellarmine described as being "small in bulk but very great in value," we find enunciated for the first time the axiom that for a dogma to be regarded as Catholic truth, it must have been held always, everywhere, and by all the faithful—" quod ubique, quod semper, quod ab omnibus creditum est." Doubtful points must be settled by this test of universality, antiquity, and consent, *i.e.* the agreement of all or nearly all bishops and doctors. The Holy Scriptures cannot be regarded as the sole test of truth, because they are subject to different interpretations and are quoted as much in the interests of heterodoxy as of orthodoxy. The letter of the Law must be interpreted according to the tradition of the Church, which alone has the right to expound it. If a new doctrine is advanced, it must be confronted with the universal teaching of the Church and, where the universality test appears to be defective by reason of widespread apostasy at any period, appeal must be made to the teaching of the primitive Church. If the error is one which had its counterpart in primitive times, then the final court of appeal would be the faith of the majority. Progress indeed there must be, but it must be like the growth of the acorn, or the development of the infant into a man : it must preserve identity and all essential characteristics. The chief work of the Councils has been to elucidate, define, and emphasise that which had already been widely taught, believed, and practised. Any private opinion, even that of a saint and martyr, should be set aside. Behind all the testimony of the fathers, the doctors, and the councils stands the authority of the Holy See.

An immense body of literature has been provoked by this treatise and it has been very variously judged. It appeared at a time when the controversy over grace and free-will was raging, especially in the South of France, and many authorities regard the book as a thinly veiled attack upon the extreme Augustinian doctrine of predestination. In support of this view they point to the fact that at the time when the *Commonitorium* was written, the Abbot of Lérins and many of the monks were Semi-Pelagians ; that in many passages St Vincent uses Semi-Pelagian terms ; and that a celebrated vindication of Augustinianism by Prosper of Aquitaine purported to be a refutation of a book of objections composed by a certain Vincent, whom they identify with St Vincent of Lérins. On the other hand it is beyond question that Vincent was a very common name and also that, if Semi-Pelagian ideas appear in the *Commonitorium*, it has other passages which are so similar to clauses of the Athanasian Creed, that St Vincent has sometimes been credited with the authorship of that most orthodox confession of faith. In any case the Semi-Pelagian controversy had not then been authoritatively settled, and if St Vincent erred in that direction he erred in company with many other holy men. The exact date of his death is not certain, but it seems to have been about the year 445.

We know very little in detail regarding the life of St Vincent of Lérins. The brief account in the *Acta Sanctorum* (May, vol. v), is mainly derived from the *De Viris Illustribus* of Gennadius of Marseilles. See also the

Dictionary of Christian Biography, vol. iv, pp. 1154–1158, the *Dictionnaire Apologétique*, vol. iv, cc. 1747–1754, and the *Historisches Jahrbuch*, vol. xxix 1908), pp. 583 *seq.* There is an excellent translation of the *Commonitorium* in French (1906) by de Labriolle and H. Brunetière.

ST AFRA OF BRESCIA, MART.

A.D. 133 (?)

The name of a local martyr called St Afra is held in great honour at Brescia, where her reputed relics lie in a church which is dedicated to her. Her true history is unknown, but tradition connects her with the legend of St Faustinus and St Jovita (see February 15). She is supposed to have been the wife of the Praetor Julian who was destroyed at Brescia by the wild animals to whom he had condemned the two martyrs. Afra was converted as a result of the tragic fate of her husband, and withdrew into the wilderness, where she lived for some time. She then went to Rome and was baptised by Pope St Linus. This statement involves a grave anachronism, for Pope Linus had died nearly half a century earlier. Upon Afra's return to Brescia she was arrested and beheaded.

No better evidence is forthcoming than the lessons of a medieval Brescian breviary. See the *Acta Sanctorum*, May, vol. v. St Afra is commemorated in the Roman Martyrology, where it is stated that she suffered under Hadrian (117–137), but there is no mention of this St Afra in early liturgical books or calendars.

SS. DONATIAN AND ROGATIAN, MARTS.

(?) A.D. 289 OR 304

During the reign of the Emperor Maximianus there was living at Nantes in Brittany a young man called Donatian who belonged to a prominent Romano-Gallic family and who was a zealous Christian. After the outbreak of persecution his elder brother Rogatian was moved by his example and piety to desire baptism, but the sacrament was deferred because the bishop was in hiding. The emperor had issued an edict directing that all who refused to sacrifice to Jupiter and Apollo should be put to death. Upon the arrival of the prefect at Nantes, Donatian was brought before him on the charge of professing Christianity and of withdrawing others—notably his brother—from the worship of the gods. He made a bold confession and was cast into prison, where he was soon joined by Rogatian who, in the face of cajolery and threats, had remained constant to his newly-found faith. He only grieved that he had not been baptised, but he prayed that the kiss of peace which he had received from his brother might supply the necessary grace. He was destined to receive the baptism of blood. They spent the night together in fervent prayer and were brought up again the following day before the prefect to whom they expressed their willingness to suffer for the name of Christ whatever torments might be in store for them. By his order they were tortured on the rack, their heads were pierced with lances, and they were finally decapitated. The two martyrs are greatly venerated at Nantes where they are popularly known as " Les Enfants Nantois." A few of their reputed relics are preserved in a church dedicated in their honour.

The comparatively sober " Passion " of these martyrs has been included in the *Acta Sincera* of Ruinart. This may be read also in the *Acta Sanctorum*, May, vol. v, and another redaction has been printed in the *Analecta Bollandiana*, vol. viii (1889), pp. 163–164. Though it is impossible to regard the text as the report of a contemporary, still it cannot be treated as a mere pious romance. Mgr Duchesne, who touches upon the matter in his *Fastes Épiscopaux* (vol. ii, pp. 359–361), remarks that in the whole of western Gaul these are the only martyrs whose death can confidently be assigned to the Roman persecutions. See further La Borderie, *Histoire de Bretagne*, vol. i, pp. 187–194. Delanoue, *Saint Donatien et Saint Rogatien de Nantes* (1904), G. Mollat in *Annales de Bretagne*, vol. xxii (1907), pp. 205–213. Dom H. Leclercq has also discussed the question at some length in the *Dictionnaire d'Archéologie et de Liturgie*, vol. xii (1935), *cc.* 628–634, giving abundant bibliographical references.

BD. GERIUS, GÉRY, OR GIRIO, CONF.

A.D. 1298 (?)

Nothing can be positively asserted about Blessed Gerius except that he is the principal patron of the little town of Monte Santo near Loreto and that he has a cultus which is said to go back to the end of the thirteenth century and was approved by Pope Benedict XIV in 1742. According to his breviary legend, which is quite unreliable, he came of one of the most ancient families of Languedoc —that of the lords of Castelnaud of the house of Sabran. Born at Lunel between Nîmes and Montpellier, he was invested at the age of five with the habit of the Third Order of St Francis. On reaching manhood, he and his brother went to live as hermits at Pont du Gard where, on the occasion of an inundation which cut him off from the mainland, Blessed Gerius was fed for several days by an eel. Afterwards the two brothers undertook pilgrimages to Rome and Jerusalem, encountering strange adventures. Once, when they were lost in a thicket, a bear indicated to them the right road. Gerius never reached Jerusalem, for he was taken ill on the way to Ancona, and died at Colombaro near Monte Santo. Many miracles took place at his tomb which became a favourite place of pilgrimage. The saint is invoked against headaches and fits. It is or was usual to clothe epileptics who were brought to his shrine for healing in the light green habit of the special confraternity founded in 1735.

Here is another of those alleged Franciscan Tertiaries, whose history, from the point of view of evidence, is so unsatisfactory. Père Léon (*Auréole Séraphique*, Eng. trans., vol. ii, p. 285) asserts of Géry that " when barely five years old he earnestly begged to have the habit of the Third Order of St Francis given to him," and he adds that " the Friars Minor did not hesitate to enrol him in the Franciscan family." For all this there is not a fragment of evidence. The decree approving the cultus simply states that Géry had been venerated at Monte Santo from time immemorial. Père Léon gives a reference to a Life of Bd. Gerard in the *Acta Sanctorum*, which refers to an entirely different person and makes not the slightest mention of Géry.

BD. PHILIP OF PIACENZA, Conf.

A.D. 1306

Very little seems to be known about Blessed Philip. He belonged to the nobility of Piacenza, his family, that of the Suzani, occupying a prominent position in the city. At a date which is not specified he joined the hermits of St Augustine, and is described in the martyrology of his order as having been "distinguished for his contempt of worldly vanities, for his deep humility, and for his spirit of prayer." It is stated that Pope Clement XIII in 1756 confirmed his immemorial cultus. In 1808 his relics were translated to Piacenza Cathedral, where they were enshrined anew in 1884.

The Bollandists in the *Acta Sanctorum*, May, vol. v, supply a brief notice of Bd. Philip, but confess themselves at a loss to find any materials for his history. Augustinian writers themselves are divided upon the question whether he was born at Mantua or Piacenza. If his cultus was ever confirmed, it certainly was not confirmed by Pope Clement XIII in 1756, for Pope Clement XIII was only elected in 1758.

BD. JOHN OF PRADO, Mart.

A.D. 1631

Amongst the heroes of the Friars Minor of the Observance, great honour is paid to Blessed John of Prado, who won the crown of martyrdom at Morocco in the seventeenth century even as the Franciscan pioneers of Morocco and Ceuta had won it in the thirteenth. He was born of a noble Spanish family at Morgobejo in the Kingdom of Leon, and, after being educated at Salamanca University, received the habit as a Discalced Friar of the Strict Observance in the Province of St Gabriel in the year 1584. From the day of his ordination to the priesthood he desired to go as a missionary to the pagans, but his aspirations could not be realised for some time. His superiors set him to preach in his own country and he also filled the offices of Novice-master and Guardian in several convents. Though one of the holiest and humblest of men, he became the victim of cruel calumny, and his Provincial removed him from his post of Superior. He accepted the disgrace with resignation. " God wills that I should suffer," he said. " May His will be done. The only thing that grieves me is the discredit it may bring upon our order and the scandal it may cause to the weak." His innocence was, however, afterwards completely vindicated and in 1610 he was made Provincial of the newly formed province of San Diego. Three years later a widespread epidemic of plague carried off all the Franciscans who were labouring in the Moroccan mission. Blessed John's term of office had just expired and he begged to be sent to the relief of the Christians. Pope Urban VIII accordingly named him missionary apostolic with special powers. Accompanied by Father Matthias and Brother Genesius, he arrived in the city of Morocco and immediately embarked upon the work of ministering to the Christian slaves. Though ordered by the Emperor to leave Barbary, they continued their labours, administering the sacraments to the faithful, and reconciling those who had apostatised. They were consequently arrested, cast into prison, fettered and set to grind saltpetre. After a while they were brought into the monarch's presence, but when they still boldly made profession of Christianity, they were scourged and were ordered back to their dungeon. On the occasion of a second public examination a little later, insidious attempts were made to break down their constancy by assuring them that compliance with the Emperor's desires would be well rewarded. " I have served my crucified Master for more than fifty years," was John's reply,

" how could I be so mad as to forsake Him when He is about to give me my crown ? Your Mahomet has nothing but hell to bestow on those who follow him." The Emperor was so incensed that he struck him with his sword, and thereupon, after being tortured and shot through with arrows, the martyrs were stoned to death. Their remains were subsequently conveyed to Spain and enshrined in Seville cathedral.

See Francisco de San Juan de el Puerto, *Mision historial de Marruecos*, Seville, 1708 ; P. P. Ausserer, *Seraphisches Martyrologium*, 1880 ; Léon, *Auréole Séraphique* (Eng. trans.), vol. ii, pp. 292–296 ; and F. Fernandez y Romeral, *Los Franciscanos en Marruecos* (1921).

ST GREGORY VII, POPE

A.D. 1085

THE Bollandist compilers of the *Acta Sanctorum* remark by
way of a preface to the life of Gregory VII that he suffered
much from persecutions during his lifetime and from
calumnies after his death. It is, however, satisfactory to note that,
whereas it was once the fashion to depict the great Pope as an
ecclesiastical tyrant, modern historians are agreed in recognising
his whole policy to have been inspired, not by ambition, but by an
unquenchable thirst for justice—the establishment of righteousness
upon the earth.

St Gregory was born in the hamlet of Rovaco, near Saona in
south Tuscany, and received at his baptism the name of Hildebrand.
Nothing is known of his parentage, but he was sent when very
young to Rome, to the care of an uncle who was superior of the
monastery of Sta Maria on the Aventine. From there he attended
the Lateran school where one of his masters, John Gratian, formed
so high an opinion of him that, upon being raised to the Papacy
as Gregory VI, he chose his former pupil as one of his palace officials
or " capellani." The affection was reciprocated and when, after
the Council of Sutri, the Pope had to lay down his office and
accompany the Emperor Henry III back to Germany, Hildebrand
went with him and remained with him till his death. He then
retired into a monastery which—if we accept the tradition—was
actually the great Abbey of Cluny, then ruled over by St Odilo as
abbot and by St Hugh as sub-prior. Gladly would Hildebrand
have spent the rest of his life in the cloister, but Bruno, Bishop of
Toul, who was chosen to fill the chair of St Peter, persuaded him to
re-enter the world and to return with him to Rome. There, as
economus to Pope St Leo IX, he restored financial stability to the
treasury and order to the city, besides co-operating with all that
pontiff's attempted reforms. He was appointed sub-deacon of the
Roman Church, steward of St Paul's outside the Walls and, in 1053,
legate to France. Under St Leo's four successors he continued to
act as chief counsellor and indeed was regarded by many as the

power behind the throne. In 1055 he was sent again as legate to France, where he deposed six bishops for simony; and where, at a synod in Tours, he received the retractation of Berengarius. He visited the court of the Empress Agnes on behalf of Stephen IX who, when on his deathbed, directed that his legate's return should be awaited and his advice followed in the election of the new Pope. By his counsel Nicholas II and, after his death in 1061, Alexander II, were invested with the supreme Pontificate. In the capacity of Archdeacon, to which he had been raised by the former Pope, Hildebrand governed Rome remarkably well, with the help of the militia which he raised to great efficiency. His name was on all men's lips. Therefore when, at the funeral obsequies of Alexander II, a cry was raised, "Hildebrand bishop!" the cry was taken up by clergy and people. Very much against his will, he was declared to be elected and was carried off to the church of St Peter ad Vincula to be enthroned. He had indeed reason to be appalled at the magnitude of the task which lay before him. It was one thing to denounce the abuses which were corrupting the Church, as his friend St Peter Damian was doing, or even to wield the sword of justice in the service of other Popes as he himself had done. It was quite another thing to feel directly responsible to God as Christ's Vicar on earth for the suppression of those abuses. No man was better qualified for the task. "On you, who have reached the summit of dignity, are fixed the eyes of all men," wrote William of Metz. "They know the glorious combats you have sustained in a lower station, and one and all now long to hear great things of you." In the presence of the Empress Agnes, the Countess Beatrice and the Chancellor Gregory of Vercelli, he was consecrated on June 30, 1073, having chosen the name of Gregory in honour of his former patron, Gregory VI.

To aid him in the reforms he was about to undertake he could expect little help from those in authority. Of the great rulers, the best was William the Conqueror, ruthless and cruel though he showed himself at times. Germany was governed by Henry IV, a young man of twenty-three, dissolute, greedy of gold, tyrannical and without one redeeming quality; whilst of Philip I, King of France, it has been well said: "His reign was the longest and most discreditable which the annals of France have known." The lesser princes, as St Gregory himself expressed it, were "worse than Jews or pagans." The leaders of the Church were as corrupt as the rulers of the state, to whom indeed they had become subservient, bishoprics and abbeys being sold by kings and nobles to the highest bidder or bestowed on unworthy favourites. Simony was general, while the law of clerical celibacy had become so far relaxed that in many districts priests openly lived as married men, squandered the tithes and offerings of the faithful on their families and even, in some cases, bequeathed their livings to their children. The rest of Gregory's life was to be spent in heroic efforts to free and purify the Church by putting down simony and clerical incontinency, and by abolishing the whole system of investitures, *i.e.* the bestowal of preferments by laymen and their symbolical conveyance by presentation of the crozier and the ring.

It was necessary first for the new Pope to consolidate his position. With that object in view he visited Southern Italy, where he concluded treaties with Landolfo of Benevento, Richard of Capua, and Gisolfo of Salerno, all of whom took the oath of fealty to him as their suzerain. To Spain, which he regarded as also a fief of the Holy See, he sent a legate who was empowered to enforce the reforms he had at heart and to substitute the Roman Mass for the Mozarabic rite then prevalent. Regarding himself as the father of all Christians, he sent the Archbishop of Venice to the court of the Greek schismatic Emperor, Michael VIII, who had congratulated him on his election. In his sympathy for the Eastern Christians he even sought to promote a Crusade against the Turks, but his appeal fell on deaf ears and he soon found his whole attention required for matters nearer home.

Shortly after his accession, he deposed Godfrey, Bishop of Milan, who had obtained his office by bribery, and, in his very first Roman synod, he enacted stringent decrees against simoniacal and married priests. Not only were they disqualified from exercising ecclesiastical jurisdiction or holding any benefice, but the faithful were warned not to avail themselves of their ministrations. These decrees roused great hostility, especially in France and Germany. The Bishops of Passau and Chur, and the Archbishop of Rheims nearly lost their lives in endeavouring to promulgate them, and a council assembled in Paris declared them intolerable, irrational, and calculated to make the validity of a sacrament dependent on the character of the celebrant. St Gregory, however, was not one to be daunted by opposition or deflected from pursuing the right course. A second synod held in Rome the following year went still further, and abrogated, in one single decree, the whole system of lay investiture. It pronounced the excommunication of "any person, even if he were emperor or king, who should confer an investiture in connection with any ecclesiastical office." To publish and enforce his decrees he made use of legates, for he could not trust the bishops. These representatives, sent to every country and equipped with full powers, claimed obedience by virtue of the spiritual overlordship the Pope was entitled to exercise over Christian lands, many of which had also, at some time or other, placed their temporalities under the protection of the Holy See. Gregory's legates, who were nearly all monks whom he had known and tested, served him courageously and well in these times of exceptional difficulty.

In Italy discontent at the new measures led to a conspiracy against St Gregory, promoted in the first instance by Wibert, Archbishop of Ravenna, and carried into effect by Cencius, the unscrupulous and dishonest son of a former prefect of Rome. While the Holy Father was celebrating the Christmas Midnight Mass, he was attacked by armed men who wounded him and carried him off to a stronghold belonging to Cencius. The people of Rome, however, rose in a body, rescued him and would have stoned Cencius had not St Gregory himself pleaded for him and forgiven him. In France, after a severe struggle, the reforms were carried out, thanks largely to the efforts of the legate, Hugh de Die, and after the deposition of so many bishops that the hierarchy was practically a new one. In England, William the Conqueror absolutely refused to give up investiture, but managed to escape excommunication—partly because he zealously enforced the Pope's other decrees and partly, no doubt, because, in spite of his vices, he was sincerely attached to the Holy See. It was far otherwise with the Emperor Henry IV, who was to prove St Gregory's life-long enemy. At first indeed the relations between them were amicable. Soon after the Pope's accession and when Henry's position was jeopardised by the insurrection of his Saxon subjects, he wrote a filial and submissive letter in which he deplored his past misconduct and promised amendment, but, as soon as he felt himself secure, he showed himself in his true colours, and reverted to his evil practices. Constantly requiring money to pay for his excesses, he found the easiest way of raising it was by the spoliation of the Church or the sale of benefices. After he had defeated the Saxons he deposed and imprisoned their bishops, replacing them by creatures of his own. So outrageous was his conduct, both public and private, that the Pope threatened to excommunicate him unless he made atonement. Henry retorted by holding at Worms a council of his supporters and of those opposed to the reforms. At his bidding they declared the pontiff guilty of heinous crimes and pronounced his election illegal and void. But the Emperor had gone too far. Once St Gregory had launched the excommunication, many of the German princes, uneasy at the prospect of finding themselves also under the Church's ban and tired of their monarch's misrule, met at Tribur, near Darmstadt, from whence they issued an ultimatum.   They declared the crown forfeit unless within a year Henry became reconciled with the Holy See and appeared before a council to which the Pope was also invited, to be held at Augsburg in the following February.   Thoroughly alarmed, the Emperor resolved to forestall the tribunal.   With his wife, his infant son, and one attendant he crossed the Alps in mid-winter to intercept and make his peace with St Gregory, who had already started for Augsburg.   For three whole days he had to wait in the garb of a penitent outside the gates of the Castle of Canossa where the Pope was staying.   At the close of that time he was admitted, made his submission, and received conditional absolution.

But the humiliation he had endured led to no amendment after his return to Germany, nor were the conditions ever fulfilled.   In 1077 Rupert of Suabia was chosen Emperor by a section of the nobles and civil war ensued.   Though for a time St Gregory tried to remain neutral, he found himself compelled to renew the excommunication and declared in favour of Rupert who, however, was slain in battle. Henry on his part promoted the election of Wibert, Archbishop of Ravenna, as anti-pope and, as soon as death had freed him of his rival, marched an army into Italy.   For two years he unsuccessfully besieged Rome, but the third year he succeeded in taking it.   St Gregory retired into the then almost impregnable Castle of St Angelo, where he remained until he was rescued and released by an army under Robert Guiscard, the Norman Duke of Calabria.   The excesses of Guiscard's followers, however, roused the Romans to fury, and St Gregory, because he had summoned the Normans to his aid, shared their unpopularity.   He withdrew first to Monte Cassino and then to Salerno, where he died the following year.   His last recorded words, spoken on his death-bed, are an epitome of his life.   " I have loved justice and hated iniquity . . . therefore I die in exile."

The Bollandists in the *Acta Sanctorum*, May, vol. vi, print with other material three documents which to some extent help us to appreciate Hildebrand as a man and a saint.   The first is a formal biography by Paul Bernried, completed only in 1128, but founded on the recollections of those who knew Gregory VII and upon a study of his Registers.   The second is a memoir of which Pandulfus is the probable author ; the third an adaptation by Cardinal Boso, the Englishman, of Bonizo's *Liber ad Amicum*, which last work was written in Gregory's lifetime.   But the great Pope belongs to all history, and official documents such as the Regesta, at least what is left of them, do in this case very much help to elucidate his character.   From Mgr Mann's *Lives of the Popes*, vol. vii (1910), pp. 1–217, a full and satisfactory account of the pontificate, especially in its external aspects, may be obtained.   There is also a good bibliography, in which Mgr Mann judiciously goes out of his way to commend J. W. Bowden's *Life and Pontificate of Gregory VII*, though it was published as far back as 1840.   The literature of the subject is very vast and has grown immensely since Mann wrote in 1910. An admirable sketch, based on more profound but scattered studies published elsewhere, is the *S. Grégoire VII* of A. Fliche (in the series " Les Saints," 1920), and M. Fliche has since published a more exhaustive work, *La Réforme grégorienne* (1925), on which *cf.* the *Analecta Bollandiana*, vol. 44 (1926), pp. 425–433. See also W. Wühr, *Studien zu Gregors VII Kirchenreform* (1930), and on the problem of Gregory's *Regesta* consult the studies of W. M. Peitz and of E. Caspar.

ST URBAN I, POPE AND MART.

A.D. 230

The notice in the Roman Martyrology reads : " At Rome on the Via Nomentana, the birthday of Blessed Urban, Pope and Martyr, by whose exhortation and teaching many persons, including Tiburtius and Valerian, received the faith of Christ, and underwent martyrdom therefor ; he himself also suffered much for God's Church in the persecution of Alexander Severus and at length was crowned with martyrdom, being beheaded." It is to be feared that even this short notice is mainly apocryphal. The reference to Tiburtius and Valerian is derived from the very unsatisfactory " Acts " of St Cecilia, from which also the account of Urban in the *Liber Pontificalis* has borrowed. It is quite certain in any case that Pope Urban was not buried in the Via Nomentana, but in the cemetery of St Callistus, on the Via Appia, where a portion of his sepulchral slab, bearing his name, has been found in modern times. Not far from the cemetery of Callistus on the same main road was the cemetery of Prætextatus, and there another Urban, a martyr, had been buried. Confusion arose between the two, and an old building close beside the Prætextatus catacomb was converted into a small church, afterwards known as St Urbano alla Caffarella.

The confusion of the two Urbans and the muddle hence resulting in the notices of the *Hieronymianum* are points full of interest, but too complicated to be discussed here. See Delehaye's commentary on the document last named, pp. 262 and 273 ; Duchesne, *Liber Pontificalis*, pp. xlvii, xciii and 143 ; De Rossi, *Roma Sotterranea*, vol. ii, pp. xxii–xxv, 53, 151. Besides the " Passio " of Pope Urban in the *Acta Sanctorum*, May, vol. vi, several other texts have been printed in the Bollandist catalogues of Latin MSS. ; see B. H. L., nn. 8372–8392.

ST DIONYSIUS, Bp. of Milan
c. A.D. 359

Amongst the few faithful bishops who upheld the cause of St Athanasius when the whole world seemed to have turned against him, a place of honour must be accorded to St Dionysius, who succeeded Bishop Protasius in 351 as metropolitan of Milan. An ardent champion of the Catholic faith, he found himself summoned in 335 to attend, in his own episcopal city but at the imperial palace, a synod which the Arian Emperor Constantius had convoked to pronounce the condemnation of Athanasius. Although nearly all the prelates present were overawed into signing the decree, St Dionysius, St Eusebius of Vercelli, and Lucifer Bishop of Cagliari absolutely refused to do so. They were accordingly banished, and St Dionysius retired into Cappadocia, where he died about the year 360—probably shortly before the Emperor Julian sanctioned the return of the exiles to their churches. A point of great interest is the fact that the remains of the Saint were sent back to Milan all the way from Cappadocia by St Basil. The letter in which Basil describes to St Ambrose the care taken to authenticate the relics is still preserved and is printed in Migne, *P. G.*, vol. 33, pp. 712–713.

In the *Acta Sanctorum*, May, vol. vi, a life of St. Dionysius is given. It is of little historical value, as the document, or possibly some earlier text upon which it is based, was probably, as Father Savio has shown, compiled by the unscrupulous chronicler Landulfus at the end of the eleventh century. Father Savio's comments will be found in his book, *Gli Antichi Vescovi d'Italia, La Lombardia*, pp. 114 *seq.* and 753 *seq.* See also Lanzoni, *Le Diocesi d'Italia*, vol. ii (1927), p. 1014, and especially Père Delehaye's commentary on the *Hieronymianum*, pp. 81 and 271, with Hefele-Leclercq's *Conciles*, vol. i, pp. 873–877.

ST ZENOBIUS, Bp.
c. A.D. 390 (?)

Fact and fiction are intermingled in the traditional history of St Zenobius, the principal patron of Florence, and there are no contemporary records from which to reconstruct a reliable biography. A member of the Geronimo family of Florence, he is said to have been baptised at the age of twenty-one by Bishop Theodore, who afterwards ordained him and made him his archdeacon. The virtues and learning of Zenobius won him the friendship of St Ambrose of Milan, by whose advice he was called to Rome by Pope

Damasus. After carrying out successfully a mission from the Holy See to Constantinople, he returned to Italy. Upon the death of St Theodore he was chosen Bishop of Florence, and edified all men by his eloquence, his miracles, and the holy life he led with his deacon St Eugenius and his sub-deacon St Crescentius. Five dead persons, we are told, were resuscitated by him, including a child who was run over by a cart as he played before the Cathedral. St Zenobius died at the age of eighty and was buried at first in San Lorenzo and then in the Cathedral. Scenes from the life of St Zenobius form the subject of many pictures by old masters in the Florentine galleries.

The text of several short Lives is printed in *Acta Sanctorum*, May, vol. vi, but no one of them can be dated earlier than the eleventh century. The existence of Bishop Theodore is doubtful, it was St Ambrose who was called upon to dedicate the cathedral. See especially Davidsohn, *Forschungen zur älteren Geschichte von Florenz*, vol. i, and with regard to the reputed relics of the Saint, Cocchi, *Ricognizioni, etc., delle Reliquie di S. Zenobio*.

ST LEO (LYÉ), ABBOT

c. A.D. 550

At Mantenay, a village in the diocese of Troyes, St Leo's whole life was passed : there he was born and there he entered a monastery which had been built not very many years earlier by St Romanus, afterwards Bishop of Rheims. First as a simple monk, afterwards as abbot in succession to St Romanus, St Leo led an edifying but uneventful existence. One night when he lay, as was his custom, on the baptistery floor, St Hilary, St Martin of Tours, and St Anastasius of Orléans appeared to announce his death which, they told him, was to take place in three days—after he should have buried the priest Maurelius. At the expiration of the three days, the celestial visitors returned, but St Leo asked for a three days' respite to enable him to obtain a mortuary habit which a pious woman had promised him. The delay was granted and a messenger was despatched from the abbey to ask for the garment. The good lady acknowledged that she had not yet made it, as the father abbot seemed hale and hearty, but said he should have it in three days. The promise was kept : the habit was duly sent : and St Leo at the appointed time passed to his eternal reward.

A short account of St Leo is given both in Mabillon and the *Acta Sanctorum*, May, vol. vi, but the materials merit little confidence. His name, however, has been included in certain later recensions of the *Hieronymianum*.

ST ALDHELM, Bp. of Sherborne
A.D. 709

The first Englishman to attain distinction as a scholar in his native land and across the seas was St Aldhelm or Ealdhelm. Sufficient is preserved of his Latin writings in prose and in verse to give an idea of his obscure and turgid style. A near relation to Ine, King of the West Saxons, he was born about the year 639, and received his early education at Malmesbury under an Irish teacher named Maildubh. It is not clear where he spent his first years of manhood, but when he was between thirty and forty we find him at Canterbury, which had become a great centre of religious and secular learning under Archbishop Theodore and the Abbot of St Augustine's, a learned monk called Adrian, who had formerly been at Monte Cassino, but who had come to England in the Archbishop's train. It was to Abbot Adrian that St Aldhelm attributed the literary proficiency he afterwards developed. While he was at Canterbury or perhaps earlier he received the tonsure and took the habit. Upon the death or retirement of Maildubh, St Aldhelm returned to Malmesbury to take charge of the school and about the year 683 he was appointed Abbot. In his dual capacity he did much to foster religion and education in Wessex, especially after the accession of King Ine, whose counsellor he became. For the edification and instruction of the poor, whose spiritual needs he had at heart, he composed verses in the vernacular, and songs—for he was a skilled musician. King Alfred dearly loved St Aldhelm's English hymns, and the holy man's ballads were popular down to a much later date, but unfortunately they are not now extant. His life as an abbot is described as having been most austere. Amongst other pious practices he used daily to recite the whole psalter while standing up to the shoulders in cold water—even in mid-winter. With the assistance, doubtless, of King Ine, he founded subsidiary monasteries at Frome and Bradford-on-Avon, besides building several churches. A little chapel at Bradford-on-Avon dedicated by him to St Lawrence is standing to this day. At the request of a synod summoned by King Ine, he addressed a letter to Geraint, King of Cornwall and Devon, which proved the means of reconciling to the Roman use a number of ecclesiastics who had till then adhered to the Keltic tradition in such matters as the date of keeping Easter and the shape of the clerical tonsure. St Aldhelm is said to have made a journey to Rome and to have obtained from Pope Sergius special privileges for his abbey, but of this visit we have no satisfactory evidence. When, after the death of Hedda in 705, Wessex was divided into two dioceses, the more westerly was bestowed upon Aldhelm, who fixed his episcopal seat at Sherborne. Four years later he died, while on a visitation to Dilton, near Westbury. His body was conveyed back to Malmesbury with great solemnity, crosses being erected at the places where the holy relics had rested on the way. The best known of St Aldhelm's writings is a treatise on virginity dedicated to the nuns of Barking. There are also a number of Latin poems and a book on prosody containing as illustrations certain metrical riddles.

The accounts of St Aldhelm furnished by Faricius of Abingdon and by William of Malmesbury (both printed in the *Acta Sanctorum*, May, vol. vi) are not very trustworthy, as coming from twelfth century writers. Bede refers to him in respectful terms, but does not tell us very much. The best edition of Aldhelm's works is that edited by Ehwald in *M. G. H. Auctores Antiquissimi*, vol. xv. See also the *Cambridge History of English Literature*, vol. i, pp. 72–79 ; Stanton's *Menology*, which shows that his name was entered in many English calendars ; G. F. Brown, *St Aldhelm* ; and Howorth, *The Golden Days of the Early English Church*, vol. ii, pp. 451–500. These two last works, though supplying useful archæological illustrations, are disfigured by a strong anti-Roman bias.

ST GENNADIUS, Bp. of Astorga

A.D. 936

St Gennadius, whom the Spaniards invoke against fever, was trained as a monk from an early age by Abbot Arandisellus. He was afterwards the Abbot and restorer of San Pedro de Montes, which St Fructuosus had founded at Vierzo in the Cantabrian Mountains. About the year 895, or possibly later, he was chosen Bishop of Astorga and during his episcopate he built and restored several religious houses. Five years before his death he resigned his office to resume the life of a monk or hermit in a mountain desert. He died about the year 936 and was buried in his monastery of St Peter at Peñalba. He is described as a man of the deepest piety whose only preoccupation was the honour of God and the salvation of souls.

There is an account pieced together by Mabillon from various materials. See the *Acta Sanctorum*, O.S.B., vol. v, pp. 33–38. Consult also Yepez, *Coronica General de la Orden de San Benito*, vol. iv, folios 266 *seq.* ; Florez, *España Sagrada*, vol. xvi, pp. 129–147 ; V. de la Fuente, *Historia ecclesiastica de España*, vol. iii, pp. 239 *seq.* The very interesting renunciation, or testament, of St Gennadius is printed in Mabillon and elsewhere.

BD. CLARITUS, Conf.

A.D. 1348

There stood in old Florence, for two centuries and more, a convent of Augustinian nuns which was popularly known as " Il Chiarito." It was founded in 1342 by Blessed Claritus or Chiarito, the last male scion of the Voglia family and was dedicated by him to Our Lady the Queen of Heaven. His wife Nicolasia having taken the veil in the new foundation, he himself entered it as servant to the nuns. In that humble capacity he remained until he was carried off by an epidemic of the plague which decimated the city in 1348. His body was held in great veneration in the convent church and was credited with the property of emitting a peculiar odour whenever one of the nuns was about to die.

There is the usual dearth of reliable evidence which seems characteristic of saints of the Augustinian Order. The Bollandists could find no better materials than a Life written nearly three centuries after the event by A. M. V. Racconisi. It is printed in a Latin translation in the *Acta Sanctorum*, May, vol. vi. See, however, the *Bolletino Storico Agostiniano*, vol. i (1924), pp. 15–20.

ST MADELEINE SOPHIE BARAT, Virg.

A.D. 1865

The foundress of the Society of the Sacred Heart, St Madeleine Sophie Barat was born on December 12, 1779, in the Burgundian town of Joigny, where her father was a cooper and the owner of a small vineyard. At her baptism, which took place the following day, a brother eleven years her senior stood godfather. Louis was intended for the priesthood, and when, after completing his course at the Grand Séminaire of Sens, he returned as a deacon to take up a post as master in the College of his native city, he found his godchild a sprightly intelligent little girl of ten. Almost immediately the conviction forced itself upon him that she was destined by God to accomplish some great work for which it was his duty to fit her. This he proceeded to do by imparting to her an education similar to that which his boy pupils received, coupled with a discipline calculated to teach her to repress her emotions and control her will. All day long, without companionship and almost without relaxation, she had to study in her little garret to acquire a grounding in Latin, Greek, history, physics, and mathematics under the direction of a stern young taskmaster whose policy it was frequently to blame and punish, but never to praise. It was fortunate for her that she developed a great love of learning, seeing that the only reward she ever received was instruction in a fresh subject. Human emotion of any kind was severely repressed; so much so, that once, when she offered a little present to her brother, it was thrown into the fire. The system, harsh as it was, worked well and Madeleine Sophie was making remarkable progress when she was suddenly deprived of her teacher.

In the year 1793 which saw the execution of Louis XVI and the inauguration of the Reign of Terror, Louis Barat, who had openly withdrawn his adherence to the Civil Constitution of the Clergy as soon as it had been condemned by the Pope, fled from Joigny to escape prosecution, but it was only to be arrested in Paris and to remain for two years a prisoner in constant expectation of death. Sophie in the meantime had grown up a charming and vivacious girl, the idol of her parents and the centre of an admiring circle of friends. To Louis, when he revisited Joigny as a priest after his liberation, there seemed a real danger that she might lose that sense of vocation to the religious life which she had formerly evinced, and he never rested until he had transplanted her to Paris, where he was living and where he could resume his course of training. To the repressive discipline of her childhood were now added bodily penances and constant self-examinations, whilst the classics were replaced by the study of the Bible, the Fathers, and theological treatises. She submitted with cheerful resignation, little anticipating the great future which in God's providence lay before her.

As soon as the first fury of the French Revolution had spent itself, thoughtful men were confronted with the problem of providing education for the younger generation, seeing that all Christian schools had been swept away. Amongst those who took a deep interest in this question were a group of young priests who had formed an association pledged to work for the restoration of the Society of Jesus suppressed by Clement XIV thirty years earlier. Their superior, Father Varin, had for some time been desirous of forming an institute of consecrated women for the training of girls, and when he heard from the Abbé Barat of his sister's abilities and training, he sent for her and questioned her. After a very short acquaintance he satisfied himself that the simple Burgundian maiden possessed all the qualifications he required. In reply to her timid admission that she hoped to become a Carmelite lay-sister, he said bluntly : " No, that is not your vocation. The gifts God has given you and your education point elsewhere." He then expounded to her his ideal of a great educational work for girls, a work deriving its inspiration from devotion to the Sacred Heart of Jesus. Humbly and diffidently she responded to the call. " I knew nothing : I foresaw nothing : I accepted all that was given me," she said long afterwards, referring to that time.

On November 21, 1800, the Feast of the Presentation of Our Lady in the Temple, Madeleine Sophie and three other postulants began their religious life, and the following year she was sent to Amiens to teach in a school which had been taken over and which was the first convent of the new Order. Soon a second school—a free one for poor children—was opened. More postulants came to the little community, but their first superior left them after two years, having proved herself devoid of ability to govern and lacking a true religious vocation. To her dismay Madeleine Sophie was appointed superior by Fr. Varin although she was only twenty-three and the youngest of all. She was to retain that office for sixty-three years.

The success of their educational ventures in Amiens led to requests for other foundations, and in 1804 Mother Barat travelled to Grenoble to take over the derelict old convent of Ste Marie-d'en-Haut as well as to receive into her institute the remnant of a community of Visitation nuns which it had sheltered. Foremost amongst these was Philippine Duchesne, who was destined later on to introduce the Society of the Sacred Heart into America. The next settlement was at Poitiers, where an ancient Cistercian house, the Abbey of the Feuillants, had been offered as a gift. St Madeleine Sophie made it the noviciate, and it became her headquarters for two years, which were perhaps the happiest of her life. There she trained her novices and from there she made occasional journeys across France and into Flanders to open fresh houses at Belley, Niort, Ghent, and Cugnières. Everything seemed to be going well when the saint was faced with one of those fierce trials which seem almost invariably to beset the founder of a new religious order. During her absence from Amiens a number of important changes had been made without consulting her by the local superior, Madame Baudemont, in conjunction with M. de Saint-Estève, an ambitious young priest who had succeeded Fr. Varin as chaplain. For eight years these two carried on a persistent campaign, striving, it seemed, to supersede the Superior General, to undermine her influence, and to mould the society according to their own ideas. Patience and prayer were the weapons with which Mother Barat met their attacks, and they mistook her strength for weakness. M. de Saint-Estève went so far as to draw up for the Order constitutions of his own which would have changed its nature and transformed its very name. However, just when his success seemed assured, he over-reached himself, and the Constitutions as passed by the General Congregation of 1815 were not his, but a code which had been framed by Mother Barat and by Fr. Varin—now a Jesuit. The collapse of the opposition was followed by a period of great expansion, and in 1818 Mother Duchesne was sent with four companions to North America. Two years later Mother Barat summoned all the available local superiors to Paris—now the headquarters of the Order—to draw up a general plan of study for the schools. Certain definite principles were laid down, but with characteristic clear-sightedness she insisted from the first that there should be facilities for development and adaptation. Indeed, when she arranged that the General Council should meet every six years, one of her reasons was the opportunity that would be afforded to its members of revising the curriculum in order to keep abreast of the educational needs and systems of the day. Under her inspiration, the Paris boarding schools attained a reputation which brought applications from all sides for similar establishments.

It is difficult for us in these days of easy communication to realise the arduous nature of St Madeleine Sophie's labours in the foundation of no less than one hundred and five houses. To establish and maintain them she many times traversed the length and breadth of France, thrice she visited Rome, once she went to Switzerland to make a home for the novitiate driven out of France in 1830 by the July Revolution, in 1844 she came to England and twelve years later she travelled to Austria. "I am always on the road," she once remarked, and her journeys often entailed great discomforts and even hardships on one who had never been robust.

In her great love for children she tried, wherever it was possible, to provide for the opening of a day-school for poor girls as well as a boarding-school for the daughters of well-to-do parents. With those foundations which she could not personally visit she kept in touch by correspondence, which necessitated the writing of innumer-able letters. Even when she was living at the Mother-house she was ceaselessly employed either in administrative work or in giving interviews to the many persons who sought her advice. Words which she addressed to one of her daughters were singularly applic-able to herself. "Too much work is a danger for an imperfect soul . . . but for one who loves Our Lord . . . it is an abundant harvest."

In the December of 1826, in response to a memorandum drawn up by St Madeleine Sophie and presented by her to Pope Leo XII, the Society of the Sacred Heart received the formal approbation of the Holy See. This must have seemed to all to set the seal of stability on the new Order, but thirteen years later a crisis arose which might easily have led to disruption or to something worse. At the General Congregation of 1839 certain fundamental alterations in the Constitutions were proposed and carried in spite of Mother Barat's disapproval. It was characteristic of her tact and fairness that, instead of exercising her veto, she consented to allow them to be tried for three years. Time proved her to have been right : the new regulations did not work well : Pope Gregory XVI refused to sanction them, and they were reversed by the next General Congregation. Once more prayer and patience had prevailed and those who had promoted the changes were the first to acknowledge their mistake.

Within narrow limits it is not possible to deal with the activities of the Saint's later years : they form part of the history of her Order. She lived to see her daughters firmly established in France, Italy, Belgium, Spain, Austria, Germany, Holland, England, Ireland, Canada, the United States, and South America. In 1864, when eighty-five years of age, she begged the General Congregation to allow her to lay down her office, but all she could obtain was permission to choose a Vicar General to assist her. The following year on May 21 she was stricken with paralysis and four days later, on the Feast of the Ascension, her soul flew to God.

As in the case of most modern saints, the fullest and most authentic materials for the Life, regarded from its spiritual side, are the testimonies printed in the process of beatification. But St Madeleine Sophie has also been privileged in her biographers. The admirable *Histoire de la Ven. Mère Madeleine Sophie Barat*, written by Mgr Baunard, was excellently translated into English by Lady Georgiana Fullerton. Another satisfactory present-ment in two volumes was that of one of her own religious, Mère Cahier (1884). A short sketch is provided in the series " Les Saints " ; it is written by Geoffroy de Grandmaison (1909). Finally, for English readers, the first place in order of merit must be accorded to the work of Mother Maud Monahan, *Saint Madeleine Sophie* (1925).

MAY 26

ST PHILIP NERI, Conf.

A.D. 1595

ST PHILIP NERI was born in Florence in the year 1515 and was one of the four children of a notary called Francesco Neri. Their mother died while they were very young, but her place was well supplied by an excellent stepmother. From infancy Philip was remarkable for his docility and sweet disposition, which caused him to be spoken of as " Pippo buono "—" good little Phil." Indeed, the only time he ever merited and received a reprimand from his elders was when he once pushed away his elder sister because she persisted in interrupting him and his little sister while they were reciting some of the psalms. His first religious teachers were the Dominicans of San Marco, whose instructions and example made a deep and permanent impression. He grew up a pious, attractive, cheerful lad—very popular with all who came in contact with him. When he was eighteen he was sent to San Germano, to a childless kinsman who was supposed to have a flourishing business and who was likely to make him his heir. Philip, however, did not stay there long. Soon after his arrival he passed through a mystical experience which in after years he spoke of as " conversion," and from thenceforth worldly affairs had no more attraction for him. The atmosphere in which he was living became uncongenial, and he set out for Rome, without money and without plans, trusting entirely to the guidance of Divine Providence. In Rome he found shelter under the roof of Galeotto Caccia, a Florentine Customs official who provided him with an attic and the bare necessaries of life. It was little enough that Philip needed. His entire fare consisted of bread, water, and a few olives or vegetables which he usually took once a day : and his room was practically bare except for a bed, a chair, some books, and a line on which he hung his clothes. In return for his hospitality Philip gave lessons to his host's two small sons who, if we may accept the testimony of their mother and their aunt, became veritable little angels of goodness under his direction.

Except for the hours he devoted to his young charges, St Philip seems to have spent the first two years of his residence in Rome almost like a recluse—giving up whole days and nights to prayer in his garret. It proved to be a period of inward preparation, at the close of which he emerged from his retreat, with his spiritual life strengthened and his determination to live for God confirmed, while he proceeded to take up courses of philosophy and theology at the Sapienza and at St Agostino. For three years he worked with diligence and with such success that he was regarded as a promising scholar. Then, quite suddenly—perhaps in response to some intuition or intimation—he threw up his studies, sold most of his books and embarked upon an apostolate amongst the people. Religion at that time was at a low ebb in the papal city, which was very slowly recovering from the effects of the Sack of Rome in 1527. There were several contributory causes. Grave abuses had crept into the Church : they had long been generally recognised, but nothing was being done to remove them. Elections to the Sacred College had been controlled by the Medici, with the result that the Cardinals, with few exceptions, were princes of the state rather than of the Church. The enthusiasm for classical authors, fostered by the Renaissance, had gradually substituted pagan for Christian ideals, thereby lowering the moral standard and weakening the faith. Indifference, if not corruption, was rife amongst the clergy, many of whom seldom said Mass, let their churches fall into disrepair and neglected their flocks. It was small wonder that the people were lapsing into semi-paganism. To re-evangelise Rome was to be St Philip's life-work, and he accomplished it with such success as to earn from posterity the title of " the Apostle of Rome."

He began in a small way. He would stand about the street-corners and market-place, entering into conversation with all sorts of people—especially with the young Florentines employed in the banks and shops of the Sant' Angelo quarter. He had an attractive personality with a notable sense of humour, and he readily won a hearing. Then he would put in a word in season or speak to his audience about the love of God and the state of their souls. In this manner he gradually prevailed upon many to give up evil practices and to reform their lives. His customary greeting : " Well, brothers, when shall we begin to do good ? " found them willing enough to respond provided he would show them the way. So he took them with him to wait upon the sick in the hospitals and to visit the Seven Churches—a favourite devotion of his own. His days were given up to men, but towards evening he would retire into solitude, sometimes spending the night in a church porch, sometimes in the catacombs of St Sebastian beside the Appian Way. Here, in the "grotte" as they were then called, he was fervently praying for the gifts of the Holy Spirit on the eve of Pentecost 1544, when there appeared to him, as it were, a globe of fire which entered his mouth and which he afterwards felt dilating his breast. Immediately he was filled with such paroxysms of divine love that he rolled upon the ground exclaiming : "Enough, enough, Lord, I can bear no more !" When he had risen and was more composed, on putting his hand to his heart he discovered a swelling as big as a man's fist, but neither then nor subsequently did it give him pain. From that day, under the stress of spiritual emotion, he was apt to be seized with violent palpitations which caused his whole body to tremble and sometimes the chair or the bed on which he rested to be violently shaken. The fervour which consumed him often obliged him to bare his breast to relieve the heat within and he would ask God to mitigate His consolations lest he should die with love. After his death it was discovered that two of the saint's ribs were broken and had formed an arch which added to the normal space for the beating of his heart.

In the year 1548, with the help of his confessor, Fr. Persiano Rossa, who lived at San Girolamo della Carità, St Philip founded a confraternity of poor laymen who met for spiritual exercises in the Church of San Salvatore in Campo. With their aid he popularised in Rome the devotion of the Forty Hours and undertook the care of needy pilgrims. This work was greatly blessed and developed into the celebrated hospital of Sta Trinità dei Pellegrini which, in the year of the Jubilee 1575, assisted no less than 145,000 pilgrims and afterwards undertook the charge of poor convalescents. Thus by the time he was thirty-four, St Philip Neri had accomplished much, but his confessor was convinced that he could do still more as a priest. Though the saint's humility made him shrink from the idea of taking holy orders, he eventually deferred to his director's wishes. He was ordained on May 23, 1551, and went to live with Fr. Rossa and other priests at San Girolamo della Carità. His apostolate was now exercised mainly through the confessional as the best means of saving souls. From before daybreak until nearly midday and often again in the afternoon he sat in the tribunal of penance, to which flocked a host of penitents of all ages and ranks. He had a wonderful power of reading the thoughts of those who resorted to him and effected an enormous number of conversions. For the benefit of those penitents who desired to lead a holy life, he would hold informal spiritual conferences and discussions, followed by visits to churches or attendance at vespers and compline. Often they would read aloud the lives of martyrs and missionaries. The account of the heroic career and death of St Francis Xavier so inspired St Philip himself that he was tempted to volunteer for the foreign mission field. However, a holy Cistercian whom he consulted assured him that Rome was to be his Indies, and the saint accepted the decision as a definite message from on high.

A large room was built over the nave of San Girolamo to accommodate the increasing numbers of those who attended the conferences in the direction of which St Philip was aided by several other priests. The people called them Oratorians because they rang a little bell to summon the faithful to prayers in their "Oratory," but the real foundation of the Congregation so named was laid a few years later, when St Philip presented five of his young disciples for ordination and sent them to serve the church of San Giovanni, the charge of which had been entrusted to him by his fellow-Florentines in Rome. For these young priests, amongst whom was Cæsar Baronius the future historian, he drew up some simple rules of life. They shared a common table and spiritual exercises under his obedience, but he forbade them to bind themselves to this state by vows or to renounce their property if they had any. Others joined them and their organisation and work developed rapidly— the more so, perhaps, because it met with opposition and even persecution in certain quarters. However, in 1575 the new Congregation received the formal approbation of Pope Gregory XIII, who afterwards gave to it the ancient church of Sta Maria in Vallicella. The edifice, besides being in a ruinous condition, was far too small, and St Philip decided to demolish it and to rebuild it on a large scale. He had no money, but contributions came in from rich and poor. The holy Father and St Charles Borromeo were generous in their donations, as were also many of the most prominent men in Rome. Cardinals and princes were amongst his disciples, though he not infrequently disconcerted them by the strange things he did and said—sometimes spontaneously, for he was the most unconventional of saints, but often deliberately in order to conceal his spiritual emotion or to lower himself in the esteem of onlookers. Humility was the virtue which, of all others, he strove to practise himself and to instil into his penitents. He could not succeed, however, in blinding others to his own sanctity or in wholly concealing from them the extraordinary gifts and graces with which he was endowed.

Always a delicate man, he was once cured of a severe attack of stone by Our Lady, who appeared to him in a vision. He had been lying in a state of exhaustion when he suddenly rose up with out-stretched arms exclaiming : " Oh, my beautiful Madonna ! Oh, my holy Madonna ! " A doctor who was present took him by the arm, but St Philip entreated him to let him be. " Would you not have me embrace my holy Mother who has come to visit me ? " he asked. Then, realising the presence of two physicians at his side, he hid his head in the bedclothes like a bashful child. Many sick persons were restored by him to health and it is said that he once, for a short time, recalled a dead boy to life. On several occasions he prophesied future events—all of which came to pass. He lived in such constant touch with the supernatural that sometimes it was with the greatest difficulty that he could pursue his worldly avocations. He would fall into an ecstasy when saying his office, when offering Holy Mass, or even while he was dressing. Men looking upon his face declared that it glowed with celestial radiance.

By April 1577, work on the Chiesa Nuova, as it was called, had advanced sufficiently for the Congregation of the Oratory to be transferred to the Vallicella, but their Superior went on living at San Girolamo as before. He had become attached to the room he had occupied for thirty-three years, and it was not until 1584 that he took up residence at the Chiesa Nuova, in compliance with the Pope's expressed wishes. Even then he continued to live and have his meals apart from the community, although his spiritual sons had free access to him. So far, indeed, was he from leading the life of a solitary that his room was constantly crowded by visitors of all descriptions. The Roman people, in his later years, held him in extraordinary veneration : the whole College of Cardinals resorted to him for counsel and spiritual refreshment : and so great was his reputation that foreigners coming to Rome were eager to obtain an introduction to him. It was thus, in his own room, that he continued his apostolate when increasing age and infirmities precluded him from going about freely. Rich and poor mounted the steep steps that led to his apartment at the top of the house, with its loggia looking out above and beyond the roofs—the holy man always loved open spaces—and to each person he gave advice suited to his special needs.

Towards the close of his life St Philip had several dangerous attacks of illness from which he rallied wonderfully after receiving the last sacraments. Two years before the end he succeeded in laying down his office of Superior in favour of his disciple Baronius. He also obtained permission from the Pope to celebrate Mass daily in a little oratory adjoining his room. So enraptured did he become when offering the Holy Sacrifice that it became the practice for those who attended his Mass to retire at the *Agnus Dei*. Even the server would leave the chapel after extinguishing the candles, lighting a little lamp and placing outside the door a notice to give warning that the Father was saying Mass. Two hours later he would return, relight the candles and the Mass would be continued. On the Feast of Corpus Christi, May 25, 1595, the saint appeared to be in a radiantly happy mood, bordering on exultation, and his physician told him he had not looked so well for ten years. St Philip alone realised that his hour had come. All day long he heard confessions and saw visitors as usual, but before retiring he said : " Last of all, we must die." About midnight he was seized with an attack of hæmorrhage so severe that the fathers were called. He was obviously dying, and Baronius, who read the commendatory prayers, besought him to say a parting word, or at least to bless his sons. Though St Philip was past speaking, he raised his hand, and, in bestowing his benediction, passed to his eternal reward. He was eighty years of age and his work was done. His body rests in the Chiesa Nuova which the Oratorians serve to this day. St Philip Neri was beatified six years after his death and was canonised by Pope Gregory XV in 1622.

The Abbé Louis Ponnelle and the Abbé Louis Bowet, in the best documented and most painstaking Life of St Philip which has yet been published (*St Philip Neri and the Roman Society of his Times*, translated by Father R. F. Kerr, 1932), devote a preliminary chapter to an exhaustive review of the " Sources." It is therefore only necessary here to indicate a few of those earlier publications by which Catholics, and more particularly Catholics of English speech, have become familiarised with the lovable personality of the " Apostle of Rome." The earliest biography is that of the Oratorian, Father Gallonio, which was written in Latin and published in 1600. It is reproduced in the *Acta Sanctorum*, May, vol. vi, together with another by Father Bernabei, probably chosen because it amounts to little more than a summary of the process. The Life by Bacci appeared in Italian in 1622, and it was supplemented by G. Ricci, O.P., in 1678. This standard work was translated into English and, as part of the Oratorian Series, edited by Father Faber, went to press in 1847. Another edition, revised by Father Antrobus, was issued in 1902. The Life by Cardinal Capecelatro, written in Italian, has also been twice printed in English, viz. in 1882 and 1926. Finally may be mentioned an excellent little sketch, in much more compendious form, published by Father V. J. Matthews in 1934.

ST QUADRATUS, Bp. of Athens

c. A.D. 129

The first of the great line of Christian apologists was St Quadratus or Codratus who, as some suppose, became Bishop of Athens after the death of St Publius. Eusebius and other ecclesiastical writers speak of a certain Quadratus (who may or may not be identical with the apologist) with special respect, as a prophet and as a holy man who had been the disciple of the apostles. When the Emperor Hadrian came to Athens to be present at the Eleusinian Games, St Quadratus addressed to him a written treatise in defence of the Christians, which had the effect of checking the persecution, or at least of preventing the promulgation of any fresh decrees against them. The apology was known to Eusebius and possibly to St Jerome, but it has now, unfortunately, been lost. In it he quotes Our Lord's miracles as an evidence of the truth of His teaching and mentions the fact that he himself had actually known persons who had been healed or raised to life by Our Lord. The date of his death is uncertain : it probably occurred about the year 129 or a little later.

The passages from Eusebius and St Jerome upon which we depend for all our knowledge of St Quadratus are quoted in the *Acta Sanctorum*, May, vol. vi. Quadratus was not an uncommon name, and it is very doubtful whether the apologist, the Bishop of Athens, and the prophet in Asia Minor were one and the same person. See Bardenhewer, *Geschichte der altkirch-lichen Literatur*, vol. i, pp. 168–169 ; Harnack in *Texte und Untersuchungen*, vol. i, part 1, pp. 100 *seq.* ; also Harnack, *Chronologie der altchristlichen Literatur*, vol. i, pp. 269–271.

ST ELEUTHERIUS, Pope

A.D. 189

As in the case of all the other early Roman pontiffs, we have very little reliable information concerning Pope Eleutherius. It is stated that he was a Greek by origin and also that he was a deacon of the Roman church in the time of Pope Anicetus, which implies that he must have been resident in Rome for at least ten years before his election. Under Commodus the persecution had relaxed, but trouble was brewing in another form owing to the heretical attitude of the Montanists, whose views were spreading westwards. The Christians of Lyons were disturbed by these new doctrines. They wrote on the subject to their brethren in Phrygia, and St Irenæus, afterwards bishop, came from Lyons to Rome, bringing with him another communication addressed to Pope Eleutherius. We gather from Eusebius that the letter, while recognising the gravity of the evil, deprecated violent action and urged that every effort should be made to preserve peace and unity. It is possible that a decree attributed to Eleutherius and ruling that no form of nourishment commonly partaken of by mankind should be deemed unlawful for Christians, preserves the vestige of a condemnation of some Montanist or Gnostic extravagance. On the other hand there are indications in Tertullian (*Adv. Praxeam*) that a conciliatory letter was sent by the Pope to the Montanists, but afterwards recalled.

Eleutherius is now chiefly remembered from his supposed correspondence with a British King Lucius who wrote to ask his warranty to be admitted into the Christian fold (*ut per ejus mandatum Christianus efficeretur*). This statement, made in the *Liber Pontificalis*, is repeated by Bede, who traces to the same incident the first preaching of Christianity in Britain.

See the *Liber Pontificalis* (Duchesne, vol. i, pp. cii–civ, 58 and 136) ; Stanton's *Menology*, pp. 580–581 ; J. P. Kirsch, in the *Catholic Encyclopedia*, vol. v, pp. 378–379. The question of King Lucius will be more appropriately discussed under his name on December 3.

ST PRISCUS AND COMPANIONS, MARTS.

c. A.D. 272

The persecution initiated under the Emperor Aurelian was carried on with peculiar ferocity in Roman Gaul—notably in the town of Besançon. Mindful of the precept " When they persecute you in one city, flee to another," two prominent citizens, Priscus and Cottus, retired with a number of other Christians to Auxerre, which was surrounded by forests. They were, however, hunted down and slain by the sword. The bodies of the saints were discovered in the first half of the fifth century by St Germanus, who built two churches in their honour and who propagated a cultus of these martyrs of Auxerre which became very general. Besançon and Auxerre still celebrate the feast of St Priscus as a double.

Although the legend of these martyrs printed in the *Acta Sanctorum*, May, vol. vi, is comparatively free from extravagance, it cannot be regarded as trustworthy. On the other hand, the insertion of the name of Priscus in the *Hieronymianum* points to the existence of a genuine and early cultus.

ST LAMBERT, BP. OF VENCE

A.D. 1154

St Lambert was born at Bauduen, in the diocese of Fréjus, and became a monk in the Abbey of Lérins, where he had lived from his childhood. Though kindly to all and popular with his brethren, he was so great a lover of solitude and study that he never left his cell except when obedience required him to do so. Much against his will he was made Bishop of Vence in 1114. For forty years he ruled his diocese, instructing the people and healing many sick persons by prayer and the laying on of hands. He was famous for his learning and for his miracles. Beloved of all, he died in the year 1154, and was buried in his own cathedral church.

The life printed in the *Acta Sanctorum*, May, vol. vi, seems to have been written within ten years of St Lambert's death, but its dullness is only relieved by the narration of some very dubious miracles. A copy of his epitaph has been published in the *Revue des Sociétés savantes*, vol. iv (1876), p. 196.

BD. EVA, OR HEVA, OF LIÉGE, RECLUSE

c. A.D. 1266

When Blessed Juliana was Prioress of Cornillon, one of her closest friends was a holy recluse, Eva or Heva of Liége, whom she inspired with her own enthusiastic purpose to obtain the institution of a feast in honour of the Blessed Sacrament. It was in Eva's cell near the church of St Martin that Juliana found refuge when she was driven for the first time from Cornillon, and it was Eva who took up her mission after she died. The accession of Pope Urban IV raised her hopes, for he had formerly shown himself sympathetic when, as James Pantaléon, the papal legate, he had been approached on the subject by Blessed Juliana. Eva's hopes were fulfilled. Not only did he institute the Festival of Corpus Christi, but he sent to her the bull of authorisation as well as the special office for the day which St Thomas Aquinas had compiled at his desire. Pope Leo XIII confirmed the cultus of Blessed Eva in 1902.

The brief authorising the cultus may be read in the *Analecta Ecclesiastica*, vol. x (1902), pp. 245. See also Demarteau, *La première auteur wallonne, Eve de Saint Martin* (1898); *Analecta Bollandiana*, vol. xvi (1897), pp. 531–532; and cf. the bibliography given under Bd. Juliana, April 5, p. 67.

BD. MARIANNA DE FLORES Y PAREDES, VIRG.

A.D. 1645

The present capital of Ecuador was a Peruvian town in 1618— the year which saw the birth of its famous citizen, Blessed Marianna de Flores y Paredes, the Lily of Quito. Her parents, who came of noble Spanish stock, died when she was very young, leaving her to the care of an elder sister and brother-in-law, who loved her as they did their own little daughters. She was remarkable for her piety almost from infancy and, when a mere child, liked to engage her nieces, still younger than herself, in saying the rosary or in making the stations of the cross, and she would manufacture disciplines for her own use from thorn bushes or prickly leaves. So precocious did she appear that her sister obtained permission for her to make her first communion at the then unusually early age of seven. When she was twelve she decided to start off with a few companions to convert the Japanese, and after that scheme had been discovered and frustrated she inspired them with the idea of living as hermits on a mountain near Quito. Somewhat perturbed at the adventurous turn her piety was taking, her relations proposed placing her in a convent to try her vocation. But, although on two occasions all preparations were made, her departure was prevented at the last moment by what appeared to be some special interposition of Providence. Marianna accordingly remained at home, and, under the direction of her Jesuit confessor, entered upon the life of a solitary in her brother-in-law's house, which she never again left except to go to church. Gradually she embarked upon a succession of austerities which can only be regarded as horrifying when practised by a frail young girl delicately reared. In the ante-chamber of her apartment she kept a coffin, in which she spent each Friday night : at other times it contained the semblance of a corpse in a Franciscan habit and with shrouded face—a constant reminder of death. Heavy chains bound her arms and legs, and besides a wire girdle, she wore a hair shirt over her breast and a spiked iron cincture wound about her body. Every Friday she put on two crowns, the one of thorns and the other of spiked iron. She would then mount up to a cross affixed to her wall and would hang two hours or more suspended by her hair and by her wrists which were passed through nooses attached to the extremities of the cross-beam. She never slept more than three hours, the rest of her time being employed in religious exercises, according to a detailed time-table which was found after her death. Little by little she reduced her diet until she came to subsist on the Holy Communion and a small portion of bread taken once a day. Towards the end of her life she deprived herself of drink in order the better to realise Our Lord's thirst on the cross. To add to her sufferings she would raise a glass of water to her parched lips in very hot weather and would then withdraw it untasted. She was also the recipient of many spiritual favours and was endowed with the gifts of prophecy and miracles.

In 1645 Quito was visited by earthquakes and by a deadly epidemic which swept away many of the inhabitants. On the fourth Sunday in Lent Blessed Marianna, after listening to an eloquent sermon preached by her confessor in the Jesuit church, was moved by the Holy Spirit to offer herself publicly as a victim for the sins of the people. We read that the earthquakes ceased immediately but that as soon as the epidemic began to abate, Marianna was seized with a complication of maladies which soon brought her to the grave. She died on May 26, 1645, at the age of twenty-six. The whole city mourned for one whom they regarded as their saviour. A beautiful white lily is said to have sprung up in the garden in a place which had served as the receptacle for the blood drawn from her veins during the numerous bleedings to which she had been subjected in her last illness.

There is a Life in Italian and in French by Father Boero, S.J. (1854), and in Spanish others by J. Moràn de Bertròn (1854) and A. Bruchez (1908).

BD. PETER MARTYR SANZ, Bp., AND COMPANIONS, MARTS.

A.D. 1747 AND 1748

It is one of the glories of the Catholic Church that so many of her sons in the prime of life have always been eager to surrender all that the world prizes in order to court persecution and death on the foreign mission field. Amongst the number must be reckoned the five Dominican priests who were martyred in the Chinese province of Fu-kien in the years 1747 and 1748. Their names were Peter Martyr Sanz, Francis Serrano, James Royo, John Alcober, and Francis Diaz : all five were Spaniards : and all five from early youth were inflamed with the desire to spread the gospel of Christ amongst the heathen. In response to their petitions and with the sanction of their superiors they were set aside for missionary work in the far East. Their future leader, Peter Sanz, a native of Asco in Catalonia, was sent in 1713 to the Philippine Islands, but was transferred the following year to the Chinese province of Fu-kien, where he laboured successfully until 1730 when he was named Bishop of Mauricastro and Vicar Apostolic of Fu-kien with the general supervision of the whole mission. The previous year, persecution had broken out against the Christians and it had required great circumspection on the part of the bishop to escape capture. The storm had died down, although there remained penal enactments which could be enforced at any time. Nevertheless Blessed Peter and his priests continued to work untiringly until practically the whole town of Fogan had been converted to Christianity. In 1749 persecution broke out again on a much greater scale. An avaricious man, who had applied to the bishop for money and had been refused, drew up a formal indictment of the European missionaries who, as he complained, were infringing the laws with impunity and were winning thousands in the city to the Catholic faith. The case came before the Viceroy, a bitter enemy to Christianity, and stern measures were adopted. The houses of the Catholics were entered and searched, the sacred vessels were confiscated, and Bishop Peter, Father Royo, and Father Alcober were imprisoned. After some time they were transferred, loaded with chains and emaciated by hunger, to the city of Foochow, where their patience under barbarous ill-treatment won the admiration even of their enemies. For a year they languished in prison under appalling conditions, and then, by the Viceroy's orders, Blessed Peter was beheaded. His last words to his companions were : " Be of good courage : must we not rejoice that we are to die for the law of our God ? "

The other four captives—Father Serrano and Father Diaz had by now joined their brethren in prison—gave themselves to almost unceasing prayer. They had not very long to wait. The arrival of a document appointing Father Francis Serrano Coadjutor to Bishop Sanz, the news of whose death had not yet reached Rome, sealed their fate. At the command of the Viceroy, Father Serrano— bishop-elect of Tipasa—Father Royo, Father Alcober, and Father Diaz were cruelly executed in prison.

See M. J. Savignol, O.P., *Les Martyrs Dominicains de la Chine au XVIIIe siècle* (1894) ; André Marie, *Missions Dominicaines dans l'Extrême Orient* (1865); *Monumenta O. P. historica*, vol. xiv, pp. 128 *seq.*; Wehofer, *Die Apostel Chinas* (1894).

MAY 27

ST BEDE, Conf. and Doctor of the Church

A.D. 735

ALMOST all that is known about the life of St Bede is derived from a short account he has given of himself and from a touching description of his last hours written by one of his disciples, a monk called Cuthbert. In the closing chapter of his famous work—the *Ecclesiastical History of the English People*, the Venerable Bede says : " Thus much concerning the ecclesiastical history of Britain and especially of the race of the English, I, Bæda, a servant of Christ and priest of the monastery of the Blessed Apostles St Peter and St Paul, which is at Wearmouth and at Jarrow, have with the Lord's help composed as far as I could gather it either from ancient documents or from the traditions of the elders or from my own knowledge. I was born in the territory of the said monastery and at the age of seven I was, by the care of my relations, given to the most reverend Abbot Benedict (St Benedict Biscop) and afterwards to Ceolfrid to be educated. From that time I have spent my whole life in that monastery, devoting all my efforts to the study of the Scriptures, and amid the observance of monastic discipline and the daily charge of singing in the Church it has ever been my delight to learn or teach or write. In my nineteenth year I was admitted to the diaconate and in my thirtieth to the priesthood—both by the hands of the most reverend Bishop John (St John of Beverley) and at the bidding of Abbot Ceolfrid. From the time of my ordination up till my present fifty-ninth year I have endeavoured for my own use and that of the brethren, to make brief notes upon the Holy Scriptures either out of the works of the venerable fathers or in conformity with their meaning and interpretation." He goes on to give a list of his writings and concludes with the words : " And I pray Thee, loving Jesus, that as Thou hast graciously given me to drink in with delight the words of Thy knowledge, so Thou wouldst mercifully grant me to attain one day to Thee, the fountain of all wisdom and to appear for ever before Thy face."

322

That Bede sometimes visited friends in other monasteries has been inferred from the fact that in 733 he stayed for a few days in York with Archbishop Egbert and only refused another invitation from the same quarter the following year on the score of ill health. Except for such brief interludes, his life seems to have been spent in a round of prayer and praise, of writing and of study. His last illness seems to have been of an asthmatic nature. A fortnight before Easter 735 he began to be much troubled by shortness of breath, and all seem to have realised that the end was near. Nevertheless his pupils continued to study by his bedside and to read aloud—though their reading was often interrupted by tears. He for his part unceasingly gave thanks to God. During the " Great Forty Days " from Easter to the Ascension, in addition to singing the office and instructing his pupils, he was engaged on two literary works—a translation of St John's Gospel into his native Anglo-Saxon, and a collection of notes from St Isidore, for he said : " I will not have my scholars read what is false or labour unprofitably on this after my death." On Rogation Tuesday he began to be much worse, but he passed the day peacefully and dictated in school, saying occasionally : " Go on quickly : I do not know how long I shall hold out and whether my Maker will soon remove me." After a wakeful night spent in thanksgiving he began to dictate the last chapter of St John. At three in the afternoon he sent for all the priests of the monastery, distributed to them some pepper, some incense and a little linen which he had in a box and asked for prayers and masses. They wept much when he announced that they would see his face on earth no more, but they rejoiced when he said that he was about to return to his Creator. In the evening the boy who was acting as his amanuensis said : " There is still one sentence, dear master, which is not written down," and when that last passage had been supplied and he was told that it was finished, the dying saint exclaimed : " You have well said . . . all is finished. Take my head in your hands that I may have the comfort of sitting opposite the holy place where I used to pray and that, so sitting, I may call upon my Father." And on the pavement of his cell, singing " Glory be to the Father and to the Son and to the Holy Ghost," he breathed his last. All who were present declared that they had never seen anyone die with such devotion and peace of soul. Several fantastic stories have been invented to account for the title of " Venerable " by which Bede is known, but it was actually a term of respect not infrequently bestowed in days of old upon distinguished members of strict religious orders. We find it applied to Bede by the Council of Aix-la-Chapelle in 836, and the title

seems to have struck the public imagination as peculiarly suitable.
It has clung to him through the succeeding centuries and, though
in 1899 he was authoritatively recognised as Saint and Doctor of
the Church, it remains his special designation to this day.

A Benedictine scholar of our own days, the late Cardinal Gasquet,
has left us a sympathetic appreciation of Bede's literary work.
The following extract from it may suitably find a place here. "When
we compare," he writes, "the work done under the inspiration
of Bede at Wearmouth and Jarrow with the other literary efforts of
the seventh and eighth centuries, one characteristic at once strikes
us. The work of that northern school is what may be called
' thorough and scholarly '. . . . It will bear the test of examination :
it carries with it evidence of wide reading and full knowledge
utilised with judgement and critical tact, and for this it became
a model to subsequent generations. Whether we take the History
of Bede for chronology and the careful determination of dates ; or
his treatise of metre which is really philological ; or his Scripture
commentaries, and compare them with the efforts of a century or
two before, or even with those of a century or two later, we can at
once detect the difference. . . . Or look at his History. . . . Reflect
how this great record of our own country was composed. Remember
that its author was a man who lived his whole life within the narrow
circuit of a few miles ; remember also the difficulty of obtaining
information in those days. Still, to acquire knowledge, and accurate
knowledge, he went to work precisely as the historian would at the
present day, never resting till he had got at the best sources of
information attainable at the cost of whatever time or patience or
labour it might involve. It is only now, in this age of minute
criticism, that we can realise the full excellence of Bede's historical
methods.

The chief study of St Bede and his fellow-monks of Wearmouth
and Jarrow was, however, the Bible. It was from this monastery
that has come to us the most correct manuscript of the Vulgate—a
scientific achievement of the highest quality. . . . Remember too
what the work was upon which St Bede was engaged upon his
deathbed—it was a translation of the Gospels into English. . . .
Here, too, in devotion to the Scripture and in a desire to break the
word to the poor and unlearned we may all of us take a useful lesson
from the life of St Bede."

Concerning the life and spirit of St Bede there is nothing to add to what
has been said above. With regard to his writings it may be noted that
much has been done of late years to make clear what can be authentically
attributed to his authorship and what is spurious. Dom G. Morin, for

instance, has identified the genuine collection of St Bede's Homilies, and they are not quite those which have previously been printed under his name (see the *Revue Bénédictine*, vol. ix, 1892, pp. 315–326). So again, Dom Quentin, in his book *Les Martyrologes historiques* (1908), has for the first time enabled us to understand what Bede's martyrologium really was. Similarly in 1896 Prof. C. Plummer edited what may be regarded as a definitive edition of the historical works. The scriptural commentaries, however, still await a competent editor. Many books have been written about St Bede and his times, especially by Anglicans. Dr. William Bright's *Chapters of Early English Church History* (first edn. 1878) may in some respects be open to objection from a Catholic point of view, but no one has written more eloquently or sympathetically of Bede's own character. Of G. F. Brown's *Bede* and Sir Henry Howorth's *Golden Days*, the same comment needs to be repeated which was made above under Aldhelm. In the *Acta Sanctorum*, May, vol. vi, we have little but what purports to be a Life by Turgot, really an extract from Simeon of Durham, and an account of the translation of Bede's remains to Durham cathedral. See T. D. Hardy, *Descriptive Catalogue* (Rolls Series), vol. i, pp. 450–455.

ST RESTITUTA OF SORA, Virg. and Mart.

A.D. 271 (?)

St Restituta was a Roman maiden of patrician rank who is said to have suffered martyrdom about the year 271 in the town of Sora, of which she is the principal patroness and which claims to possess her relics. Her so-called " acts " are altogether fabulous. According to this legend, she was told by Our Lord to go to Sora and an angel transported her there. She lodged in the house of a widow whose son she cured of leprosy. Thereupon the young man, his mother and thirty-nine other persons were converted to Christianity. The Proconsul Agathius, when he was informed of her activities, cast her into prison. As she refused to sacrifice to the gods she was scourged with scorpions and sent back to her dungeon, where she was left without food or drink for seven days, seven heavy chains having been bound round her. Upon the appearance of an angel in the prison the chains melted like wax, her wounds were healed, and she felt neither hunger nor thirst. This miracle converted several of her guards, who suffered martyrdom for the Christian faith. St Restituta herself, the priest Cyrillus, whom she had converted, and two other Christians were decapitated, their bodies being cast into the River Liri from whence they were afterwards recovered.

In the *Acta Sanctorum*, May, vol. vi, these fabulous Acts are printed in full, together with the report of a number of miracles said to have been worked by her intercession, and also the description of the recovery of her remains in the seventeenth century after they had long been lost sight of. The miracles, real or supposed, worked at her shrine, seem to have resulted in a considerable local cultus. Although we know little about either, this Roman saint would seem to be entirely different from the African Restituta commemorated on May 17. See above p. 219.

ST JULIUS AND COMPANIONS, OF DUROSTORUM, MARTS.
A.D. 302 (?)

St Julius was a veteran soldier and was arraigned by his officers for the Christian faith before Maximus, governor of Lower Moesia, at Durostorum, now Silistra in Rumania. Pasicrates and Valentio, men belonging to the same legion, had received the crown of martyrdom a short time before. The judge used threats and promises but Julius declared that he desired nothing more than to die for Christ in order to live eternally with Him. Thereupon he was sentenced to be beheaded, and was led forth to the place of execution. As he went, Hesychius, a Christian soldier who was also a prisoner and suffered martyrdom a few days after him, said : " Go with courage and remember me who am about to follow you. Commend me to the servants of God, Pasicrates and Valentio who, for confessing the holy name of Jesus, are gone before us." Julius, embracing Hesychius, replied : " Dear brother, make haste to come to us : those whom you salute have already heard you." Julius bound his eyes with a handkerchief and, as he presented his neck to the executioners, said : " Lord Jesus, for whose name I suffer death, vouchsafe to receive my soul in the number of Thy saints." His martyrdom took place on May 27, two days after the execution of St Pasicrates, at Durostorum on the Lower Danube, probably about the year 302.

In the Roman Martyrology Pasicrates and Valentio are commemorated separately on May 25 ; but the story is all one piece, and the historical value of these Acts, as Père Delehaye points out (*Analecta Bollandiana*, vol. xxxi, 1912, pp. 268–269), has never been called in question. The portion relating to Pasicrates and his companion has only been preserved to us in the summary of the Greek Synaxaries, but the section which deals primarily with St Julius is extant and has been printed in Ruinart, *Acta Sincera*, and in the *Acta Sanctorum*, May, vol. vi. See P. Franchi de' Cavalieri in the *Nuovo Bulletino di arch. crist.*, vol. x (1904), pp. 22–26, and especially Delehaye's *Hieronymianum*, p. 272, where it is pointed out that Pasicrates is probably to be recognised in a mention of " Polycarp " in the early Syriac *breviarium* ; " Policratus," which appears in the Epternach text, suggesting how the confusion has arisen. The word " coronatorum " in the same notice has been transformed into the name of a town, Gortuna in Crete.

ST EUTROPIUS, Bp. of Orange
c. A.D. 476

Although Eutropius, a native of Marseilles, seems to have led a careless life at the beginning of his career in that city, still he sobered down after marriage, and when his wife died, he was induced by Bishop Eustachius, despite his own sense of unworthiness, to enter the ranks of the clergy. His conversion, aided, we are told, by heavenly favours, was very thorough. He gave himself up to prayer and fasting, and when Justus, the Bishop of Orange, departed this life, Eutropius was chosen as his successor. The see of Orange unfortunately had just been ravaged by the Visigoths, and the material and moral desolation of the people was such that Eutropius, losing heart at the sight of the burden imposed upon him, meditated taking refuge in flight. But a holy man whom he consulted showed him where his duty lay, and from that time forth the new bishop set an admirable example. The terms in which he is addressed by Sidonius Apollinaris in a letter still preserved plainly indicate the repute for piety and learning in which he was held. He is named as bishop in a letter written by Pope Hilary in 463, and he signed in 475 a protest drafted by Faustus of Riez against the views on predestination adopted by the priest Lucidus.

A fragmentary biography by Verus, his successor in the see of Orange, is printed in the *Acta Sanctorum*, May, vol. vi. A sepulchral inscription described him as *innocentissimus*, meaning, probably, that his conduct as a bishop was faultless, and his name is commemorated in the *Hieronymianum*. See also Duchesne, *Fastes Épiscopaux*, vol. i, pp. 265–266.

ST JOHN I, Pope and Mart.
A.D. 526

A Tuscan by birth, John I joined the Roman clergy while still young and was an archdeacon when, after the death of Hormisdas in 523, he was chosen Pope. Italy had been for some thirty years ruled by Theodoric the Goth who, though an Arian by birth and by conviction, treated his Catholic subjects with toleration and even with favour during the greater part of his reign. About this time, however, his policy changed—partly as the result of what he regarded as treasonable correspondence between leading members of the Roman Senate and Constantinople, partly in consequence of a severe edict against heretics enacted in 523 by the Emperor, Justin I, the first strictly Catholic occupant of the Byzantine throne for fifty years. Appealed to by his co-religionists in the East, Theodoric at first threatened war but eventually decided to send an embassy to negotiate with the Emperor. Much against his own wishes, John was made head of this mission, which comprised five bishops and four senators. His arrival in Constantinople was greeted with extraordinary enthusiasm ; all the inhabitants went out to meet him, headed by Justin, who knelt to receive his blessing, and on Easter Day he pontificated in the Cathedral. Accounts vary as to the exact nature of the message he bore and the manner in which he carried out his mission, but he appears to have induced the Emperor to moderate his measures against the Arians lest reprisals should be made at the cost of the Catholics in Italy. At the same time his presence sealed the healing of the schism which had rent the Church in the East and in the West since the publication of Zeno's *Henoticon* in 482. But Theodoric's suspicions had been growing. During the absence of the embassy he had ordered the execution of the philosopher Boethius and his father-in-law Symmachus on a charge of high treason and he seems to have regarded the friendly relations between the Pope and the Emperor as part of a great conspiracy against him. No sooner had the mission reached Ravenna, Theodoric's capital, than the Pope was cast into prison, where he died not many days later from the treatment he received.

The text and notes of Duchesne's edition of the *Liber Pontificalis*, vol. i, pp. 275–278, tell us almost all that is known of Pope John I ; cf., however, what is said in the *Acta Sanctorum*, May, vol. vi, and in Hartmann, *Geschichte Italiens im Mittelalter*, vol. i, pp. 220–224. G. Schnürer in the *Festschrift*, published in honour of Prof. F. Porsch (pp. 211–217), has contributed a paper on Pope John's coronation of the Emperor Justin I. Pope John's title to be regarded as a martyr has been contested by G. Pfeilschifter, *Theodorich der Grosse*, etc. (1896), pp. 184–203), and defended by Fr. Grisar, *Geschichte Roms und der Päpste*, vol. i, pp. 481–483. See also F. X. Seppelt, *Der Aufstieg des Papsttums* (1931), pp. 274–276.

BD. FREDERICK, BP. OF LIÉGE

A.D. 1121

After the death of Obert, the fifty-fifth bishop of Liége, there was some delay in choosing a successor. Then the Archdeacon Alexander, Treasurer of the Cathedral, backed by the Count of Louvain and other powerful nobles, purchased the nomination from the excommunicated Emperor Henry V, who not only granted him the temporalities, but also, in defiance of the canons so lately revived, gave him spiritual investiture by bestowal of the cross and the ring and sent him back to Liége.   Frederick, the Provost of the Cathedral, with the chapter and most of the clergy, refused to accept him, having been warned by the Archbishop of Cologne that his appointment was simoniacal and uncanonical.   A proper election was held at Cologne and the choice fell upon Frederick, who went to Rheims to be consecrated by Pope Calixtus II, and returned barefoot to his diocese.   The partisans of Alexander, however, took up arms, and a pitched battle was fought at Huy on the Meuse between the rival parties.   Frederick's supporters, amongst whom was his brother the Count of Namur, were victorious and Alexander submitted.   Bd. Frederick only ruled for two years.   He died on May 27, 1121—poisoned, it was commonly reported, by a servant at the instigation of the Count of Louvain.   The relics of Bd. Frederick are said to have been discovered in 1919 during the restoration of Rheims Cathedral.

A Life by Nizo, a monk of St Laurence's Abbey at Liége, has been edited in Pertz, *Monumenta Germaniæ, Scriptores*, vol. xii, pp. 502–506 ; and there is also a metrical Life printed in the *Analecta Bollandiana*, vol. ii (1883), pp. 264–269.   See especially P. Magnette, *S. Frédéric, évêque de Liége*, 1895.

MAY 28

ST AUGUSTINE, Bishop, Apostle of England

A.D. 605

WHEN Pope Gregory the Great decided that the time had come for carrying out his long-cherished plan of attempting the evangelisation of Anglo-Saxon England, then sunk in idolatry, he chose as missionaries some thirty or more monks from the monastery of St Andrew which he had founded in his paternal home on the Cœlian Hill. As their leader he gave them their own Prior, Augustine. Nothing is known of the early history of the Apostle of the English, but St Gregory must have esteemed him highly to have made him responsible for a scheme so dear to his heart. The party set out from Rome in the year 596, bearing letters addressed to the bishops of the various French cities they were to visit on their way to England, but no sooner had they arrived in Provence than they were assailed with warnings about the ferocity of the Anglo-Saxons and the dangers of the Channel. Greatly discouraged, they persuaded Augustine to return to Rome and obtain leave to abandon the enterprise. St Gregory, however, had received definite assurance that the English were well disposed towards the Christian faith and was more eager than ever to bring about their conversion. He therefore sent Augustine back to his brethren with words of encouragement which gave them heart to proceed on their way. After adding to their number several French-men qualified to act as interpreters, they crossed the Channel and landed in the Isle of Thanet in the territory of Ethelbert, King of Kent. He was a pagan, but his wife Bertha, the daughter of Charibert, King of Paris, was a devout Christian. How the missionaries sent messengers to Ethelbert, how he received them sitting under an oak and listened to their words, how he made over to them a dwelling-place in Canterbury with the use of the old church of St Martin, and how he gave them leave to propagate the faith among his subjects, has been already described in the February volume of this series under the article St Ethelbert (p. 334). The King was baptised at Pentecost 597, and almost immediately after-wards St Augustine paid a visit to France, where he was consecrated

330

Bishop of the English by St Vergilius, metropolitan of Arles, who was also papal legate in Gaul. At Christmas of that same year, ten thousand of Ethelbert's subjects were baptised in the Swale near the mouth of the Medway—as St Gregory joyfully related in a letter to Eulogius, the patriarch of Alexandria. Soon after his return to England, St Augustine sent two of his monks, Lawrence and Peter, to Rome to give a full report of the success of his mission, to ask for more helpers and obtain advice on various points. They came back bringing the pallium for Augustine and accompanied by a fresh band of missionaries, amongst whom were St Mellitus, St Justus, and also St Paulinus, afterwards Archbishop of York. With these " ministers of the word," says Bede, " the holy pope sent all things needed in general for the divine worship and the service of the church, viz. sacred vessels, altar cloths, ornaments for churches, and vestments for priests and clerks and also many books." In a notable letter he outlined for Augustine the course he should take to develop a hierarchy for the whole country, which was to be divided into a northern and a southern province with twelve suffragan bishops for each one. That scheme could not immediately be carried out, but St Gregory, writing to Mellitus, gave very practical instructions on other points. Pagan temples were not to be destroyed, but were to be purified and consecrated for Christian worship. Local customs were as far as possible to be retained, days of dedication and feasts of martyrs being substituted for heathen festivals since, as St Gregory wrote to St Mellitus, " he who would climb to a lofty height must go by steps—not leaps." In Canterbury itself St Augustine reconsecrated and rebuilt an ancient church which, with an old wooden palace bestowed upon him by St Ethelbert, formed the nucleus for his metropolitan basilica and for the adjacent monastery of Christchurch. These buildings, which were destroyed by fire in 1067, stood on the site of the present cathedral begun by Lanfranc in 1070. Round another converted temple outside the walls of Canterbury he made a second religious foundation which he dedicated to St Peter and St Paul and placed under the rule of his disciple Peter. After his death this Abbey became known as St Augustine's.

The evangelisation of the Kingdom of Kent was proceeding apace, but St Gregory had expressly stated : " All the bishops of Britain we commend to your Fraternity." These, at the time he wrote, consisted of the prelates of the ancient British church which had been driven by the Saxon conquerors of England into the fastnesses of Wales and Cornwall. Cut off from much communication with the outside world, the British Church, though sound in doctrine, clung to certain usages at variance with those of the Roman tradition. In virtue of his jurisdiction, St Augustine invited the leading ecclesiastics to meet him at a place just outside the confines of Wessex, still known in Bede's day as Augustine's Oak. There, during the course of a long conference, he urged them to comply with the practice of the rest of Western Christendom at least in the matter of the date of Easter, and more especially to co-operate with him in evangelising the Anglo-Saxons. Fidelity to their local traditions, however, and bitterness against their conquerors made them unwilling to accede to his demands, even though he wrought a miracle of healing in their presence to demonstrate the supernatural nature of his authority. Nevertheless, they consented to a second conference which was attended by seven British bishops and the Abbot of Bangor in Flintshire. It proved a sad failure. Because St Augustine failed to rise when they arrived, they decided that he was lacking in humility and would neither listen to him nor acknowledge him as their metropolitan.

The saint's last years were spent in spreading and consolidating the faith throughout Ethelbert's realm, which comprised the greater part of England south of Northumbria. Some progress was also made in Essex, then under Ethelbert's suzerainty. Episcopal sees were established in London and at Rochester, St Mellitus being set over the one and St Justus over the other. Seven years after his arrival in England and two months after the death of his patron St Gregory, St Augustine passed to his eternal reward.

The text and notes of Prof. C. Plummer's edition of Bede's *Historia Ecclesiastica* supply almost all that can be regarded as trustworthy material for the life of St Augustine. Such later biographers and chroniclers as Goscelin (in the *Acta Sanctorum*, May, vol. vi), William of Malmesbury, Thomas of Elmham, John Brompton, etc., add nothing of value. The Welsh sources are equally late and unreliable. A curious perversity, which can with difficulty be reconciled with any " continuity " theory, has led most Anglican writers of recent times to claim kinship with the British Church and to judge harshly St Augustine's relations with the British bishops. For this reason such works as Canon Mason's *Mission of St. Augustine*, or Sir H. Howorth's *Augustine the Missionary* are open to objection. There is an excellent account of *St. Augustine of Canterbury and his Companions* (Eng. trans., 1897), by Père A. Brou. The longest contribution to Newman's *Lives of the English Saints*, that devoted to St Augustine by Canon F. Oakeley, is thorough and sympathetic, but was written, of course, in his Anglican days.

ST SENATOR, Bp. of Milan
A.D. 475

When the Church in the East was threatened with schism or lapse into heresy as the result of the vindication of the Monophysite Eutyches and the condemnation of St Flavian by the so-called "Robber Synod," St Leo the Great decided to send legates to Constantinople to urge upon the Emperor Theodosius II the calling of a General Council at which the true doctrine of Our Lord's two natures should be definitely and decisively enunciated. For this mission men of learning, tact, and integrity were required, and the Pope chose St Abundius, Bishop of Como (see April, p. 22), and a distinguished priest called Senator, as being suitable representatives. By the time these envoys reached Constantinople, Theodosius was dead, but their mission resulted in the summoning of the Council of Chalcedon under the Emperor Marcian. The year after his return to Italy, St Senator attended a synod at Milan in the same capacity of papal legate. Upon the death of St Benignus he succeeded to the bishopric of Milan, over which he ruled for three years, dying probably in 475. He was buried in the Church of St Euphemia—a saint for whom he had conceived a special devotion during his stay in Constantinople, and in whose honour he constructed this church.

The fragmentary materials for the history of St Senator have been brought together in the *Acta Sanctorum*, May, vol. vi. The laudatory reference to him in the verses of Ennodius on the Bishops of Milan will be found in the *M. G. H. Auct. Antiquissimi*, vol. vii, p. 166. But see especially Father Savio, *Gli antichi Vescovi d' Italia, Milano*, vol. i, pp. 197–199.

ST JUSTUS, Bp. of Urgel
c. A.D. 550

The Spanish bishopric of Urgel seems to have been founded in the first quarter of the sixth century, and its earliest recorded ruler is St Justus, whose three brothers were Justinianus, Bishop of Valencia, Nebridius, Bishop of Egara, and Elpidius of Huesca, also a bishop. St Justus took part in the Councils of Toledo and Lerida in the years 527 and 546 respectively. He was the author of a short mystical exposition of the Canticle of Canticles which he dedicated to his metropolitan, Archbishop Sergius of Tarragona.

The tone of this treatise and of its dedication leaves a very favourable impression of the writer's intelligence and piety.

Almost all the little we know of St Justus is due to a paragraph in the *De Viris Illustribus* of St Isidore of Seville, quoted in the brief notice of the *Acta Sanctorum*, May, vol. vi. See also Florez, *España Sagrada*, vol. xlii, pp. 75 and 187 ; but especially Dom. H. Quentin in the *Revue Bénédictine*, vol. xxiii (1906), pp. 257–260 and 487–488.

ST GERMANUS, Bp. of Paris
A.D. 576

St Germanus, one of the chief glories of France in the sixth century, was born near Autun about the year 496. After a careful training under a pious clerical cousin called Scapilion, he was ordained priest by St Agrippinus, Bishop of the diocese, and was subsequently chosen Abbot and administrator of St Symphorianus in one of the suburbs of Autun. Happening to be in Paris when that see became vacant on the death of Bishop Eusebius, he was nominated by King Childebert I to fill the episcopal chair. His promotion made no change in the austerity of his life : he retained his simplicity of dress and diet, but his house was always crowded by a throng of beggars whom he entertained at his own table. Through his eloquence and example he brought many sinners and careless Christians to repentance, including the King himself who, from being entirely absorbed in worldly interests, became a generous benefactor to the poor and the founder of many religious establishments. By the holy bishop's zeal the remains of idolatry were extirpated in many parts of France. Childebert, possibly at his instigation, though this seems to have taken place in 554, before Germanus was bishop, issued an edict commanding the destruction of all idols throughout his dominions and prohibiting the excesses which in certain places disgraced the celebration of Christian festivals. St Germanus had the principal share in drawing up the canons passed by the Third Council of Paris in 557 ; he also took part in the Second Council of Tours in 566 and in another Parisian council in 573. When Childebert fell ill at his palace of Celles, near Melun, the saint visited him, and we are told that on hearing that he had been given up by the physicians, he spent the whole night in prayer for his recovery. In the morning he cured the royal patient by the imposition of his hands. The King is said to have related this miracle himself in letters patent in which he declared that, out of gratitude to God, he bestowed upon the church of Paris and Bishop Germanus the land of Celles where he had received this favour. Unfortunately, however, the authenticity of this charter is more than doubtful. Among Childebert's foundations was a church built to contain the stole of St Vincent which the people of Saragossa had given him in return for his raising the siege of their city. The edifice which, with the adjoining monastery, was dedicated to the Holy Cross and to St Vincent was consecrated by St Germanus, who added to it the chapel of St Symphorianus, which eventually contained his tomb. After his death the church was renamed St Germain-des-Prés and became for several generations the burial-place of the royal family. Throughout his episcopate St Germanus strove to check the licentiousness of the nobles. He did not scruple to reprove and even to excommunicate King Charibert for his shameless immorality. During the fratricidal wars in which the nephews of Childebert became involved, he made every effort to induce them to suspend their hostilities—even writing to Queen Brunhildis in the hope of enlisting her influence with her husband to that end. All his remonstrances and appeals, however, were ineffectual, and it was not until a year after his death that peace was restored. The saint died on May 28, 576, at the age of eighty, mourned by all the people, but by none more than by King Chilperic, who himself composed his epitaph in which he extolled the holy bishop's virtues, his miracles, and his zeal for the salvation of souls.

The principal source for the history of St Germanus is the Life by Venantius Fortunatus, a contemporary. From a biographical point of view it leaves much to be desired and it is mainly a record of rather dubious miracles. It has been printed many times (*e.g.* in the *Acta Sanctorum*, May, vol. vi), but the most critical text is that of B. Krusch in *M. G. H. Script. meroving.*, vol. vii (1920), pp. 337–428, with a valuable preface, notes and supplementary matter. There are satisfactory articles on St Germanus in the *Kirchenlexikon* and in the *Dictionary of Christian Biography*. One point of special interest in connection with St Germanus is the fact that the two letters on liturgical observances which were formerly attributed to him and which were believed to furnish a detailed and trustworthy description of the so-called " Gallican " liturgy in the middle of the sixth century, have of late been shown to be a century or more later in date. See the convincing article of Dom A. Wilmart in the *Dictionnaire d'Archéologie, etc.*, vol. vi, *cc.* 1049 to 1102. There follows in the same volume a very full discussion by Dom H. Leclercq of the history of Saint-Germain-des-Prés.

ST WILLIAM OF GELLONE, Conf.

A.D. 812

Under Pepin the Short, Charlemagne's father, the wife of Theoderic, Count of Toulouse, gave birth to a son to whom they gave the name of William. They were a pious couple and were careful that their boy should have a religious upbringing as well as a thorough training in all military exercises. Upon attaining manhood William went to court, where he soon became a prime favourite with Charlemagne, who by this time had succeeded to his father's throne. He filled various offices to the monarch's satisfaction and then was sent by him against the Saracens who were threatening to invade France. At the same time he was created Duke of Aquitaine—the kingdom which Charlemagne had created for his son Louis. St William vanquished the Saracens in several encounters, and not only regained for the Christians in those parts liberty and freedom, but also raised the prestige of the Catholic cause amongst the Moslems by his bravery, justice, and piety. Amongst those of his own faith also he came to be regarded as the ideal Christian knight, and he figures as the principal character in an ancient French heroic romance entitled " William of Orange." He could not, however, rest satisfied with serving his king and his fellow-Catholics : he desired to place himself at the disposal of the King of kings. With this object in view he sought for a suitable site on which to build a monastery, and discovered it at Gellone, in the diocese of Lodève, at about an hour's distance from the celebrated Abbey of Aniane. There he erected his monastery, which he peopled with monks from the neighbouring religious houses—especially from Aniane. He also built in the vicinity a convent for women, in which his sisters Albana and Bertana took the veil. For some time he continued to live in the world, attending the royal court, where he was regarded with great favour, but the call to abandon all came to him as it had done to his sisters. With some difficulty he obtained the requisite permission from Charlemagne, who offered him rich presents and parted from him in tears. But St William would accept nothing except a piece of the True Cross which had been sent from Jerusalem. He made his way to Brioude in the Auvergne and hung up his weapons in the Church of St Julian after he had laid a costly offering on the altar. From thence he went to the Abbey of Gellone, where he presented the fragment of the True Cross with other valuable gifts and asked to be admitted as a lay brother. Amid general rejoicing he received the habit from St Benedict of

Aniane, who became from that time his director and spiritual guide. Perfect as had been St William's conduct as a layman, it was equally perfect as a monk. He died on May 28, 812, and was buried in his own monastery, which was afterwards renamed St William of the Desert.

The Life printed in the *Acta Sanctorum*, May, vol. vi, cannot be the work of a contemporary, as it purports to be, but it is relatively sober. See " L. Clarus " (W. Volk), *Herzog Wilhelm von Aquitanien* (1865) ; Dom G. Morin in the *Revue Charlemagne*, vol. ii (1913), pp. 116–126 ; A. Becker, *Die alt-französische Wilhelm-sage* (1896) ; Bédier, *Les Légendes épiques ; le cycle de Guillaume d'Orange* (1908).

ST BERNARD OF MENTHON, Conf.

A.D. 1081 (?)

The founder of the two celebrated hospices of the Great and Little St Bernard which have saved the lives of so many Alpine travellers has a claim to the grateful recognition of posterity and it is strange that until comparatively recent years no attempt was made to deal critically with the matter contained in the obviously highly coloured biographies of St Bernard of Menthon. He was born near Annecy in Savoy, the only son of Richard, Count of Menthon, and of Bernoline de Duyngt, of the family of the Counts of Geneva. Bernard's education, which was begun at home when he was seven, was completed at Paris. Upon his return his parents arranged a desirable marriage for him although he had set his heart upon becoming a priest. He is said to have fled from home on the eve of his wedding-day and to have found a refuge and the training he needed with Peter of the Val d'Isère, Archdeacon of Aosta. After his ordination he devoted himself especially to apostolic work, and was appointed by the Bishop of Aosta his " Official " and afterwards Vicar General, entrusted with the administration of the diocese. For forty-two years he travelled up and down the country, visiting the most remote Alpine valleys where the remnants of pagan superstition still lingered, and extending his missionary labours even beyond his own jurisdiction into the neighbouring dioceses of Novara, Tarantaise, and Geneva. In the territory under his immediate control he founded schools, restored clerical discipline, and insisted that the churches should be well kept. His piety went out to all those in need, but especially to the travellers—often French or German pilgrims on their way to Rome—who attempted the crossing of the Alps by the two mountain passes which led into the territory of Aosta. Some lost their way and were frozen to death, some wandered into snowdrifts, whilst others who could face the severity of the climate were plundered or held to ransom by brigands. With the help of the bishop and other generous donors, St Bernard built hospices on the summit of the two passes which were renamed after him the Great and the Little St Bernard. Actually, his was not the first venture of the kind in those regions. Some sort of hospice under clerical auspices is known to have existed in the ninth century on the Mons Jovis, as it was then called, but the enterprise had lapsed long before the days of St Bernard. The rest-houses which he constructed were absolutely new foundations. Provision was made in them for the reception of all travellers indiscriminately, and the hospices were placed under the care of Augustinian canons regular, for whom a monastery was built close at hand. The same Order has continued to direct them to the present day. The boon thus conferred on travellers soon made St Bernard's name famous, and princes of the Church and of the state were eager to visit the hospices and contributed to their endowment. The legend narrates that amongst those who made their way thither were the Count of Menthon and his wife, still sorrowing over the loss of their son, and that St Bernard to whom they opened their heart filled them with joy by disclosing to them his identity. At some time St Bernard went to Rome, where he is said to have received from the then Pope the formal approbation of the hospices together with the privilege of receiving novices to perpetuate his congregation. The saint lived to the age of eighty-five and died most probably on May 28, 1081, in the monastery of St Lawrence at Novara.

In the *Acta Sanctorum*, June, vol. iii, a Life is printed which purports to have been written by a contemporary, Richard, Archdeacon of Aosta, as well as some other texts. All these documents are certainly of much later date, and no confidence at all can be placed in the legends which they recount. It seems, in fact, to have been clearly demonstrated that St Bernard of Menthon died, not in 1008, but in 1081. See the article of A. Lütolf in the *Theologische Quartalschrift*, vol. 61 (1879), pp. 179–207. This conclusion is supported by a text printed in the *Bibliotheca de la Società Storica Subalpina*, vol. xvii (1903), pp. 291–312, which is probably the oldest known account of the saint, and which records a meeting of Bernard with the Emperor Henry IV at Pavia in 1081. See also Mgr Duc in *Miscellanea di Storia Italiana*, vol. xxxi (1894), pp. 341–388. Other dates have also been suggested, as, for example, by Gonthier, *Œuvres historiques*, vol. iii, who holds that the saint died in 1086. The legend of St Bernard in its older form, after having been presented in the Middle Ages as a mystery play, has been revived by Henri Ghéon in his very beautiful drama *La merveilleuse Histoire du jeune Bernard de Menthon* (English trans. by Barry Jackson). In 1923 His Holiness Pope Pius XI, in a Latin letter of quite singular eloquence, proclaimed St Bernard Patron of all Alpinists and mountain climbers. The text is in the *Acta Apostolicæ Sedis*, vol. xv (1923), pp. 437–442.

BD. MARGARET POLE, Mart.

A.D. 1541

Niece to two English kings, Edward IV and Richard III, Margaret Plantagenet was the child of their brother the Duke of Clarence by Isabel, daughter of Warwick the Kingmaker. Henry VII, whose wife was her first cousin, gave her in marriage to Sir Reginald Pole, a Buckinghamshire gentleman who did him good service in the Scottish campaign and elsewhere. At the time of Henry VIII's accession, Margaret was a widow with five children, and the young monarch, who described her as the saintliest woman in England, gave her back her brother's estates which had been forfeited by attainder in the previous reign, creating her also Countess of Salisbury in her own right. Upon the birth of Princess Mary she was appointed governess to the royal infant, but her disapproval of Henry's marriage to Anne Boleyn led to her retirement from court with the consequent loss of her post and of the King's favour. A treatise which her fourth son Reginald—afterwards Cardinal Pole—wrote against the royal claim to ecclesiastical supremacy, and which he sent to the King, still further incensed Henry, who told the French ambassador that he meant to get rid of the whole family. After Sir Henry Neville's rising in the north, emissaries were sent to examine Blessed Margaret in the hope of incriminating her as privy to the conspiracy, but though they questioned her from the forenoon till the evening they could obtain from her no damaging admission. They had to own that the tall, dignified woman had the brains as well as the stature of a man. She was nevertheless taken into custody and was imprisoned, first in Lord Southampton's house at Cowdray and afterwards in the Tower, where she suffered greatly during the winter from lack of firing and from insufficient clothing. She was never brought to trial : it was thought that no jury would convict her ; but a servile Parliament passed an Act of Attainder against her. On May 28, 1541, she was led out into the square to be beheaded. It is said by Lord Herbert that she refused to kneel down and lay her head on the block, saying she was no traitor, and that the executioner, who was a novice, struck at her several times unsteadily with the axe before he felled her. This, however, is contradicted by the French ambassador's account, in which we are told that the regular executioner being absent, his understudy, as she knelt, hacked at her neck very clumsily. The most weighty authorities reject Lord Herbert's story as improbable. She was seventy years of age when she suffered. An interesting portrait of Blessed Margaret Pole is in the National Portrait Gallery.

A full and well documented account of Blessed Margaret is given by Father E. S. Keogh in the *Lives of the English Martyrs*, edited by Dom Bede Camm, vol. i, pp. 502–540. The *Letters and Papers, Foreign and Domestic*, of Henry VIII are our principal source of information, and Blessed Margaret's fate is, of course, treated in some detail by Lingard, Gairdner, and other historians of the reign.

BD. MARIA BARTOLOMEA DE BAGNESIIS, VIRG.

A.D. 1577

The history of Blessed Maria Bartolomea de Bagnesiis is practically the record of a life of suffering heroically borne. Though she came of a noble and wealthy Florentine family, her health was so greatly undermined in infancy by the starvation to which she was subjected by a foster-mother in whose care she had been left, that she was never able in after life to eat a normal meal. A pious child, she had decided even then to devote herself to the religious life as two of her elder sisters had already done, but the death of her mother, when she was seventeen, placed her in charge of her father's household. It does not seem to have occurred to her that she would be expected to marry, and when her father told her that he had actually chosen a bridegroom for her the shock was so great that she had a complete breakdown which not only precluded all possibility of marriage, but also made of her a bedridden invalid. Various grave complications supervened—all of which she bore with unfailing resignation, just as she submitted to the often revolting and most painful remedies prescribed for her by the charlatans her father called in. From her bed of sickness she exercised a wonderful spiritual influence over the numerous persons who visited her. Enemies were reconciled, the sorrowful consoled, sinners converted and the sick healed by one who forgot her own sufferings in her sympathy for others. When she was thirty-two she was clothed as a Dominican Tertiary, and for a short time regained strength enough to rise and go to church, but the improvement was only temporary and she had to take to her bed once more. Her sufferings were intense, aggravated no doubt by the austerities she never ceased to practise. We are told that on eight occasions she received extreme unction. She had the great privilege granted her of having Mass said in her room and of receiving Holy Communion frequently. At times she was rapt in ecstasy, but humility made her loth to speak of her spiritual experiences on these occasions even to her directors. She died after being an invalid for forty-five years and was buried by her own wish in the Carmelite Church dedicated to St Mary of the Angels.

A full account translated from the Italian Life written by her domestic chaplain will be found in the *Acta Sanctorum*, May, vol. vi, Appendix.

BB. THOMAS FORD, JOHN SHERT, AND ROBERT JOHNSON, MARTS.

A.D. 1582

On May 28, 1582, three English priests, Thomas Ford, John Shert, and Robert Johnson, were hanged, drawn, and quartered at Tyburn—actually for exercising their sacerdotal functions and for denying that Elizabeth was head of the Church, but professedly for participation in a fictitious conspiracy against the Queen, known as the plot of Rome and Rheims.

Thomas Ford was a Devonshire man who had taken his M.A. degree at Oxford and had become a Fellow of Trinity. Religious scruples having compelled him to leave the University, he went to the English College at Douai where he was raised to the priesthood —being one of the first batch of its students to be presented for holy orders. About the year 1576 he was sent upon the English Mission and laboured successfully in winning souls until, in 1581, he was arrested with Blessed Edmund Campion at the house of Mr. Yates at Lyford in Berkshire. He was committed to the Tower and was condemned to death on the evidence of informers, who had never seen him or his fellow martyrs before their imprisonment. In the cart, as he was being taken to execution, he declared : " I am a Catholic and do die in that religion." With regard to the Queen, he stated on the scaffold that he acknowledged her for his sovereign and queen and had never in his life offended her. His last words were : " Jesu, Jesu, Jesu, esto mihi Jesus."

John Shert was also an Oxford man, but a student of Brazenose and a native of Cheshire. For some time after he had left the University he was a schoolmaster in London. Like Blessed Thomas Ford, however, he became dissatisfied with the established religion and crossed over to Douai to study for the priesthood : having received ordination in Rome, he returned to the College, which had been transferred to Rheims. In 1579 he was sent to England, where he worked for two years. He was arrested on July 14, 1581, and was imprisoned in the Tower. Though no real evidence could be adduced against him, he was condemned to be hanged. On the scaffold at Tyburn he was made to watch the execution and disembowelling of Blessed Thomas Ford. Far from being dismayed, he cried out : " O blessed soul : happy art thou : pray for me ! " He could have saved himself at the last moment by asking pardon and by affirming that Elizabeth was the head of the Church in England, but he stoutly declared : " She is not, nor cannot be, nor any other but only the supreme pastor," *i.e.* the Pope.

Robert Johnson, sometimes confused with Lawrence Richardson (see p. 367), came from Worcester. After being a manservant in a private family, he went to Douai, studied, became a priest, and was sent on the English Mission in 1576. Some four years later he was committed to the Tower, where he was cruelly racked three times. In November 1581 he was sentenced to death on the same charge of conspiracy as his two brother martyrs and suffered in the same place on the same day. As the rope was placed about his neck he prayed aloud in Latin. Bidden rather to pray in English, he replied : " I pray that prayer which Christ taught in a tongue I well understand." " Pray as Christ taught," exclaimed one of the ministers present. To which the martyr spiritedly retorted : " What ! do you think Christ taught in English ? " He was still reciting Latin prayers when the cart was drawn away from under him.

See Challoner, *Memoirs of Missionary Priests* (ed. Pollen), pp. 44–51, and *Lives of the English Martyrs* (ed. B. Camm), vol. ii, pp. 443–490.

MAY 29

ST MARY MAGDALEN DE' PAZZI, Virg.

A.D. 1607

THE family of the Pazzi was one of the most illustrious in
Florence and was closely allied to the Medici, the ruling
house : it gave to the state a long line of eminent politicians,
governors, and soldiers ; and to religion one great woman who in
fame has eclipsed them all. The father of St Mary Magdalen de'
Pazzi, Camillo Geri by name, had married Maria Buondelmonte,
the descendant of a family as distinguished as his own. The saint
was born in Florence in the year 1566, and in honour of St Catherine
of Siena received her name in baptism. Almost from infancy she
began to display an intense attraction for piety and good works.
At the age of seven she would stint herself of food to give it to the
poor, and when she was old enough to go to school and was provided
with a little basket containing her dinner, she would distribute
the contents to the prisoners who, through their gratings, were
allowed to beg of passers-by. Constantly she would steal away
from her playmates to spend her time in prayer or would instruct
poor children in what she knew of the catechism. On one occasion,
when she had begun to teach the child of one of her father's tenants
on their country estate and was told that it was time to return to
Florence, she wept so bitterly that she was allowed to take her little
pupil with her to complete her instruction. By the time she was
eight or nine, she would pass whole hours in prayer. Childish
amusements were without attractions for her : her only pleasure
lay in speaking to God or of God. Often in the night she would
leave her bed to lie on straw or on the bare floor. As the result of
much pondering on the sufferings of Jesus Christ, she made a crown
of thorns and rushes which she bound round her head at night.
Once on St Andrew's day in the course of her meditation her heart
was so much affected by the intensity of her desire to suffer with
and for Our Lord that she fainted away and her mother thought
that she was dying. In her intense devotion to the blessed Eucharist
she liked to be near those who had received Holy Communion, as

though by love she could detect in them the odour of Christ's presence. She made her first communion with wonderful fervour when she was ten, and two years later by a secret vow consecrated her virginity to God. Her father having been appointed governor of Cortona, she was placed at the age of fourteen as a boarder in the convent of St John in Florence. There she could give full scope to her devotion and spent four hours every morning in meditation on her knees. She also learnt to love the atmosphere of a religious house, although out of humility she rarely sought the company of the nuns, whom she venerated as the chosen spouses of Our Lord.

Fifteen months later her father took her home with a view to arranging a marriage for her. Several desirable suitors were proposed, but her heart was so strongly set upon embracing the religious life that her parents after some opposition reluctantly gave way to her desire. She chose the Carmelite Order in preference to any other because its members made their communion almost every day. On the eve of the Assumption, 1582, she entered the Convent of St Mary of the Angels upon the understanding that she should continue to wear her secular clothes until she had had full experience of the rule. She had only been there fifteen days when her parents fetched her home—hoping, no doubt, that she would reconsider her decision. Her resolution, however, was unbroken, and three months later she re-entered the convent with their full approbation and blessing.

On January 30, 1583 she received the habit. When the priest placed the crucifix in her hands with the words : " God forbid that I should glory save in the Cross of Our Lord Jesus Christ," her face was suffused with an almost unearthly radiance and her heart was filled with an ardent desire to suffer during the rest of her life for her Saviour. That desire was never to leave her. After a most fervent novitiate she was allowed to take her vows unusually early, because she was dangerously ill and her superiors wished her to have the privilege of dying as a professed nun. The ceremony took place on May 17, 1584. As her sufferings were obviously very severe, one of the sisters asked her how she could bear so much pain without a murmur, and without any alleviation. The saint pointed to the crucifix and said : " See what the infinite love of God has suffered for my salvation. That same love sees my weakness and gives me courage. Those who call to mind the sufferings of Christ and who offer up their own to God through His passion find their pains sweet and pleasant." In religion she changed her name Catherine for that of Mary Magdalen, out of devotion to that great saint. When she was conveyed back to the infirmary after her profession, she sank into an ecstasy which lasted over an hour; and for forty days she enjoyed great heavenly consolations in addition to frequent raptures—as though her divine Spouse desired by these favours to celebrate with her His mystical nuptials. It has often been noticed by the great writers on the spiritual life that God is wont thus to visit elect souls with special consolations after their first act of complete self-surrender. He does it in order to brace them for the trials which never fail to ensue. Our Lord, who is infinitely jealous of the hearts of His servants, will not brook in them any rival to Himself. Therefore, in order to crucify in them all self-seeking, to teach them to know themselves, and to prepare them to be vessels of His pure love, He refines them in the crucible of internal tribulation. Usually the higher the degree of sanctity to which they are to rise, the fiercer are the cleansing fires. This we find exemplified in the state of desolation into which our saint fell after her first transports of spiritual joy. But she did not desire spiritual consolations. Her ardent aspiration was to suffer for her Saviour's sake, and this thirst for the cross seemed insatiable —springing as it did from her unbounded love of her heavenly Spouse. Fearing that she might have offended God by over-eagerness to be professed, she asked and obtained permission to live as a novice two years after she had made her vows. At the expiration of that time she was appointed second directress of the extern girls, and three years later, she was set to instruct young nuns. She was now being tried by the most severe interior trials. Although she fasted always on bread and water except on Sundays and holidays when she took Lenten fare, she was assaulted with the most violent temptations to gluttony and impurity. Loathsome ideas and scenes from which her pure soul shrank in horror forced themselves upon her imagination whilst hellish monsters seemed to try to entice her or threaten her. To resist them she chastised her body with disciplines, hair shirts, girdles studded with iron points, and similar contrivances, while she never ceased to implore the help of her heavenly Spouse and of Our Blessed Lady. She seemed to be plunged into a state of darkness in which she saw nothing but what was horrible in herself and in all around her. Thoughts of blasphemy and infidelity obsessed her so continuously that she would sometimes say to the sisters: " Pray for me that I may not blaspheme God instead of praising Him." The very nuns themselves began to despise her, thinking her former graces which they had admired to have been only illusions.

To her interior trials were added exterior ones. She suffered much from ill health and also from physical violence at the hands of unseen powers. Nevertheless she never repined or prayed for release from her trials. All she asked was for grace to bear them. Her chief support and comfort was in meditation on Christ's passion, which made her aspire to resemble her Lord more and more in His sufferings. For five whole years she remained in this state of desolation and spiritual dryness, and then God restored to her soul His holy peace together with the comfort of His divine presence. In 1590, on Whitsunday at Matins when the *Te Deum* was intoned, she fell into a rapture. On emerging from it, she pressed the hands of the prioress and the novice-mistress, exclaiming : " Rejoice with me, for my winter is now at an end ! Help me to thank and glorify my good Creator." From this time onwards God was pleased to manifest His graces in her. She read the thoughts of others and predicted future events. To Alexander dei Medici who visited her she foretold that he would one day be Pope. Repeating the prophecy on a subsequent occasion she added that his reign would be a short one : it actually lasted twenty-six days. During her lifetime she appeared to several persons in distant places and she also cured a number of sick people. As time went on, her ecstasies became more and more frequent. Sometimes in that state she would appear rigid and lifeless, sometimes she would carry on her customary duties while remaining entranced. Occasionally from her words and gestures it was evident that she was in some way participating in the Passion of Our Lord or conversing with her divine Spouse and the denizens of heaven. So edifying were the words that fell from her lips that a record was kept of them by her sisters who collected them after her death into a book. Her union with God seemed unbroken : the very mention of His name was enough to transport her soul in raptures of love. She would call upon all created things to glorify their Creator and longed for all mankind to love Him as she did. Falling on her knees she would pray with tears for the conversion of the heathen, of unbelievers, of heretics, and of sinners. She would cry out : " O Love, love is not loved, not known by His own creatures. O my Jesus ! If I had a voice sufficiently loud and strong to be heard in every part of the world, how I would cry out to make this Love known, loved, and honoured by all men as the one incomprehensible good ! " When she was summoned away by her duties or obliged to go to rest while thus engaged in prayer she would often say : " How can I rest when I consider how God is offended on earth ? " Then the spirit of holy discipline asserting itself, she would quickly add : " O Love, I will obey, and thus fulfil Thy holy will ! "

In 1598 St Mary Magdalen was chosen novice mistress for three years—according to the custom of the house—and in 1601 she was reappointed. Afterwards she was made sub-prioress, an office she continued to discharge until her death. The esteem of the community, the veneration of the outside world, and the spiritual favours heaped upon her never affected her profound humility. She regarded herself as the basest of creatures and a disgrace to her Order. She would have preferred to be despised, reproached, and charged with the most menial duties rather than occupy a post of dignity.

In 1602 she contracted a severe chill accompanied by a cough : this was followed by the bursting of a blood vessel and frequent hæmorrhages. However, she recovered sufficiently to be again elected sub-prioress. In 1604 she had a serious relapse, after which she became bedridden. She was now subject to violent headaches and sweats, her teeth dropped out and she lost all power in her limbs although she suffered agonies if touched. Besides being in constant pain she experienced much spiritual dryness. Nevertheless, the greater her suffering the greater grew her desire for it. " O Lord," she prayed, " let me suffer or let me die—or rather—let me live on that I may suffer more ! " She even rejoiced if her prayers were not granted because it meant that God's will was being done, not hers. When she knew that her last hour was approaching, she gave a parting injunction to the nuns assembled round her. " Reverend mother and dear sisters," she said, " I am about to leave you ; and the last thing I ask of you—and I ask it in the name of Our Lord Jesus Christ—is that you love Him alone, that you trust implicitly in Him and that you incite one another continually to suffer for the love of Him." After extreme unction had been administered, she lingered on twelve days, receiving Holy Communion daily. On May 25, 1607 she went to her eternal reward at the age of forty-one years, twenty-four of which she had spent as a religious. Her body, which was untouched by corruption, still lies in a sumptuous shrine in the church attached to her convent in Florence.

In the *Acta Sanctorum*, May, vol. vi, the Bollandists print a Latin translation of the two earliest Lives of St Mary Magdalen de' Pazzi. The first appeared in 1611 and was written by Vincent Puccini, the saint's confessor in her last years. The narrative portion is comparatively brief, but it is accompanied by a supplement of some 700 pages consisting of extracts from her visions and letters. Father Cepari, S.J., who had also acted as her confessor, had likewise a biography in preparation, but he withheld it out of consideration for Puccini. It appeared, however, in 1669 with additions borrowed from the process of canonisation. These two works, combined with her letters and five manuscript volumes of notes of her revelations and dialogues in ecstasy, taken down by her fellow nuns, constitute our sources. A new selection of her utterances, called *Estasi e Lettere scelte*, was edited in 1924 by Maurice Vaussard, who has further contributed a short Life in French to the series " Les Saints," *Ste Marie Madeleine de Pazzi* (1925). The Life by Cepari was translated into English for the Oratorian Series and was printed in 1849.

ST CYRIL, MART.

A.D. 251 (?)

Of this boy martyr we are told that without the knowledge of his pagan father he had become a Christian. The father, discovering that the child refused to pay any mark of respect to the idols, turned him out of doors. This happened at Cæsarea in Cappadocia, and the governor of the city hearing of the matter gave orders that Cyril should be brought before him. Cajoleries and threats proved equally ineffectual to shake the boy's resolution. Then the governor ordered him off as if to execution, but he gave directions that after the youth had seen the blazing pyre into which he might be thrown, he was to be brought back to the court. On his return Cyril only complained that the sentence had not been carried out, and the governor, infuriated, had him put to death by the sword.

The so-called *Passio*, which exists only in Latin, looks more like a fragment of a panegyric than a historical document. It is printed in the *Acta Sanctorum*, May, vol. vii, and in Ruinart. The real interest of the case lies in the fact that Cyril's name, with a mention of Cæsarea in Cappadocia, was included already in the Syriac *breviarium* of the early fifth century under May 28, and that the same entry also appears on May 29 in the *Hieronymianum*, revised in Gaul a century or two later.

ST MAXIMINUS, BP. OF TREVES

c. A.D. 349

St Maximinus, who was a native of Poitiers and closely related to St Maxentius, left his home in early youth for Treves, attracted by the reputation for sanctity of its bishop, St Agritius. There he completed his education and there he was raised to the episcopate to become the successor of St Agritius. When St Athanasius went to Treves as an exile in 336, St Maximinus received him with honour, deeming it a privilege to be able to entertain so illustrious a saint. St Athanasius stayed with him two years ; and his writings emphasise the courage, vigilance, and noble qualities of his host who was, moreover, already famous for his miracles. St Paul, patriarch of Constantinople, when banished by Constantius, likewise found a retreat at Treves and a powerful protector in its bishop. St Maximinus convened the synod of Cologne which condemned Euphratas as a heretic, depriving him of his see. He warned the Emperor Constans, whose favourite residence was at Treves, against the errors of the Arians and he himself opposed them on every possible occasion. Either in person or by correspondence he took part in the Council of Sardica in 347 and his name was coupled with that of St Athanasius in the excommunication which the Arians afterwards launched against their opponents at Philippopolis. In Treves St Maximinus built a great church as a cathedral. He is said to have died in Poitou when on a visit to his relations. He was buried near Poitiers, but his body was afterwards translated to Treves. The date of his death is uncertain : but we are told that it cannot have been later than 349, because his successor Paulinus is known to have been in possession of the see of Treves that same year. Although St Maximinus seems to have written much, none of his works have survived.

A Life of Maximinus is printed in the *Acta Sanctorum*, May, vol. vii, but the biography written by Servatus Lupus in the ninth century is probably preferable. It has been edited by B. Krusch in *M. G. H. Rer. meroving. Scrip.*, vol. iii, pp. 71–82. The question of the Council of Cologne in 346 has been much debated. Mgr Duchesne denied the existence of any such Council ; see *Revue d'Histoire ecclésiastique*, vol. iii (1902), pp. 16–29 ; but consult Dom H. Quentin in *Revue Bénédictine*, vol. xxiii (1906), pp. 477–486, and Hefele-Leclercq, *Histoire des Conciles*, vol. i, pp. 830–836. On Maximinus, *cf.* Duchesne, *Fastes Épiscopaux*, vol. iii, p. 35.

SS. SISINNIUS, MARTYRIUS, AND ALEXANDER, MARTS.

A.D. 397

Amongst the many strangers who came to sojourn in Milan during the reign of Theodosius the Great were three pious natives of Cappadocia—Sisinnius and the two brothers Martyrius and Alexander. St Ambrose esteemed them so highly that he commended them to St Vigilius, Bishop of Trent, who was in great need of missionaries. Sisinnius having been ordained a deacon and Martyrius a lector, the three Cappadocians were commissioned to preach the gospel in the Tyrolese Alps where Christianity had made but little way. They laboured especially in the valley of Anaunia (Val di Non). There, in spite of opposition and ill-treatment, they gained a great number of souls and Sisinnius built a church in the village of Methon or Medol, where he assembled his converts to complete their instruction. The pagans, enraged at the success of the missionaries, resolved to force the newly baptised Christians to take part in one of their festivals. Sisinnius and his companions, however, did their best to keep their converts away. The pagans thereupon attacked the missionaries in their own church, beating them so severely with their clubs that Sisinnius died within a few hours. Martyrius managed to creep away into a garden, but his enemies found him the following day, and dragged him by the legs over sharp stones till he expired under this brutal treatment. Alexander also fell into their hands. They tried by threats to make him renounce his faith as they were burning the bodies of his companions in the fire. Finding their efforts unavailing, they cast him alive into the same fire, where he soon expired.

The ashes of the saints were collected by the faithful and were taken to Trent. Afterwards St Vigilius erected a church on the spot where they suffered.

Though the details supplied in the supposed " Acts " of Sisinnius, in the Bollandists, May, vol. vii, are of little account, the fact of the martyrdom is most certain. We possess the letters written by Vigilius himself to the Bishop of Milan and to St John Chrysostom. St Augustine also speaks of them and St Maximus of Turin. See further the references given in Père Delehaye's commentary on the *Hieronymianum*, p. 281.

ST THEODOSIA, Virg. and Mart.

A.D. 745

The history of St Theodosia was written in the fourteenth century by Constantine Acropolites, who seems to have drawn upon early written records and on oral tradition. He inhabited a house at Constantinople near the martyr's tomb and was one of her great votaries. According to him she came of a noble family and lost her parents when she was still very young. She afterwards took the veil in the monastery of the Anastasia in Constantinople. She lived in the days of the Iconoclastic Emperors Leo the Isaurian and his son, Constantine Copronymus, who strove to abolish the public veneration of sacred images. When the order had gone forth for the destruction of a greatly revered statue of Our Lord, Theodosia at the head of a band of women shook the ladder which supported the official who was about to hew down the figure. The man fell and was killed. The women then stoned the palace of the pseudo-patriarch Anastasius, obliging him to flee. Summary punishment was meted out to the women but especially to Theodosia as their ringleader. She was tortured in prison, her throat was torn and she died of the ill-treatment she had received. Her relics were long venerated in the church which was called Dexiocrates, and her name is still commemorated in the liturgy of the Orthodox Church.

A sufficient account is provided in the *Acta Sanctorum*, May, vol. vii. Probably the most reliable text is that of the *Constantinople Synaxary* (ed. Delehaye), *cc.* 828–829, under July 18. See also Martinov, *Annus Ecclesiasticus Græco-Slavicus*, p. 142. A translation of the " Passion " will be found in Dom Leclercq, *Les Martyrs*, vol. iv.

SS. WILLIAM, STEPHEN, RAYMUND, AND COMPANIONS, MARTS.

A.D. 1242

The twelve martyrs who are commemorated together on this day were all directly or indirectly connected with the branch of the Inquisition which had been set up by the Synod of Toulouse in 1228 to combat the errors and propaganda of the Albigensians and other heretics in Languedoc. Six years after the synod, Pope Gregory IX specially commissioned the Order of Preachers to expound the faith in Toulouse and the neighbouring districts, to hunt down heretics and to deliver them over to the secular arm. In the execution of this task the Dominicans encountered great hostility and drew upon themselves the bitter hatred of the Albigensians. They were driven out of Toulouse, Narbonne, and other places by the mob at the instigation of the heretics. As they went, the friars, undaunted by the treatment they were receiving, chanted aloud the Salve Regina and the Apostles' Creed. At Avignonet, to the south-west of Toulouse, they conducted a preaching mission with the assistance of other priests, and were offered hospitality in the local castle which belonged to Count Raymund VII of Toulouse but which was then in charge of his bailiff. All unsuspecting they accepted the invitation. On the Vigil of the Ascension, as they were retiring for the night, they were set upon and treacherously butchered by a band of soldiers who had been secretly introduced into the building. Unarmed as they were, they could put up no defence. They uttered no cry, but with their dying breath they praised God in the words of the Te Deum. The little company of martyrs included three Dominicans—William Arnaud or

Arnoldus of Montpellier, Bernard of Rochefort, and Garcias of Auray ; two Franciscans—Stephen of Narbonne and Raymund of Carbonier ; and two Benedictines—the Prior of Avignonet and a monk from Clusa. The remaining five were Raymund Reginald of Costigan, canon of Toulouse and archdeacon of Lézat or Villelongue, his secretary Bernard, two apparitors, Fontanerius and Ademar, and finally the layman Peter of Arnauld, notary to the Inquisition. Shepherds watching in the vicinity of the castle of Avignonet testified to having seen the souls of the martyrs ascend to heaven in glory. Other phenomena and many cures led to a cultus which was confirmed more than eight hundred years later by Pope Pius IX in 1866.

A summary compiled from the Chronicle of Toulouse and other sources will be found in the *Acta Sanctorum*, May, vol. vii. See also the *Monumenta O. P. Historica*, vol. i, pp. 231 *seq.*, Mortier, *Histoire des Maîtres généraux O. P.*, vol. i, pp. 357 *seq.*, Léon, *Auréole Séraphique* (Eng. trans.), vol. ii, pp. 356–374, Procter, *Lives of Dominican Saints*, pp. 152–155.

BD. PETER PETRONI, Conf.

A.D. 1361

In the Carthusian Order Peter Petroni of Siena is held in great veneration. Born of a distinguished family in that city, he seems to have manifested from his earliest childhood an extraordinary attraction for the things of God. He loved to go apart and pray, and spent even as a boy a great part of the night in pious exercises. He sought out little ragamuffins in the streets to teach them and relieve their needs, spoiling his rich clothes, so his parents complained, by living in such company. When the Carthusian monastery of Maggiano was built near by through the munificence of one of his relatives, he was eager to enter there, and in spite of opposition he accomplished his purpose at the age of 17. His superiors wished him later to be ordained priest, but he in his humility so shrank from the responsibilities entailed that after all his remonstrances had proved fruitless, he chopped off the index finger of his left hand to render himself for ever disqualified for ordination. His life was marked by what might seem an almost fanatical determination to have nothing to do with his own family, but on the other hand he is said to have been favoured by God with marvellous graces and with preternatural knowledge. Shortly before his death he commissioned a devoted *protégé* of his, Gioacchino Ciani, to warn the famous humanist,

Boccaccio, that unless he gave up his wanton literary work and mended his life, God would very soon summon him to judgement. The message was delivered, Boccaccio demurred, but when Ciani proceeded to remind him of secrets in his past, which were known to no human being, but which he had learnt from Blessed Peter's disclosures, the scholar was converted. Sixty years after Blessed Peter's death his body was disinterred, and it was found that no trace of corruption had touched either flesh or clothing.

There is an Italian Life of Bd. Peter, written at least in part by his disciple, St John Colombini, which has been translated into Latin in the *Acta Sanctorum*, May, vol. vii. See also the *Annales Ordinis Carthusiani*, by Dom Le Couteaulx, vols. v, vi and vii. The conversion of Boccaccio is confirmed by his correspondence with Petrarch.

BD. RICHARD THIRKILD, Mart.

A.D. 1583

Blessed Richard Thirkild was already an old man when he was ordained a priest in 1579, after having studied at Douai and at Rheims. Previous to that date he had been a student, probably a " scholar," at Queen's College, Oxford. He was born at Ginsley, in the diocese of Durham, and for eight years he had prayed daily to be allowed to suffer death for the faith. He was sent upon the English Mission, where he exercised his ministry chiefly at York and in the neighbouring districts. A night visit which he paid to a Catholic prisoner aroused suspicion, and nine days after the execution of Blessed William Hart he was arrested on the charge of being a priest. Unhesitatingly he at once acknowledged his priesthood, explaining the purpose for which he had come to England. He was accordingly imprisoned in the Kidcote prison at York. Two months later he was tried by a jury which pronounced him guilty of treason, mainly on the score of his admission that he had absolved and had reconciled to the Church of Rome some of the Queen's subjects. Remitted to the condemned cell, he spent the whole night instructing some of the criminals by whom he was surrounded and preparing them for death. The following day he came up again before the court and was condemned to be hanged, to be cut down alive, to be dismembered, disembowelled and quartered. Upon hearing his sentence he fell upon his knees and gave thanks to God, saying : " This is the day which the Lord hath made : let us be glad and rejoice therein." The sentence was duly carried out, but no details are available because extraordinary pains were taken by the authorities to prevent the public in general from being present—so universal was the admiration and sympathy felt for the holy and venerable-looking old priest.

An account is printed in Challoner, *Lives of Missionary Priests* (ed. Pollen), pp. 79–83, but more fully in *Lives of the English Martyrs* (ed. Bede Camm), vol. ii, pp. 635–653.

MAY 30

ST JEANNE D'ARC, Virg.

A.D. 1431

ST JEANNE LA PUCELLE, or Joan of Arc as she has always been called in England, was born on the Feast of the Epiphany, 1412, at Domrémy, a little village of Champagne on the left bank of the Meuse. Her father, Jacques D'Arc, was a peasant farmer of some local standing, a worthy man, frugal and rather morose; but his wife was a gentle affectionate mother to their five children. From her the two girls of the family received a good training in household duties. "In sewing and spinning I fear no woman," Jeanne afterwards declared : reading and writing, however, she never learnt. Impressive and often touching testimony to her piety and exemplary conduct appears in the sworn depositions of her former neighbours presented in the process for her rehabilitation. Priests and former playmates amongst others recalled her love of prayer and church, her frequent use of the sacraments, her care of the sick and her sympathy with poor wayfarers to whom she often gave up her own bed. "She was so good," it was stated, "that all the village loved her." A happy childhood hers seems to have been, though clouded by the disasters of her country as well as by the dangers of attack to which a frontier town like Domrémy bordering on Lorraine was specially exposed. On one occasion at least before she began her great undertaking Jeanne had been obliged to flee with her parents to the town of Neufchatel, at eight miles distance, to escape a raid of Burgundian freebooters who sacked Domrémy, setting fire to the church. She had been but a very young child when Henry V of England invaded France, overran Normandy and claimed the crown of the insane king, Charles VI. France, in the throes of civil war between the contending parties of the Dukes of Burgundy and Orleans, had been in no condition from the first to put up an adequate resistance, and after the Duke of Burgundy had been treacherously murdered by the Dauphin's servants the Burgundians threw in their lot with the English, who supported their claims. The death of the rival kings in 1422 brought no relief to France. The Duke of Bedford, as regent for the infant King of England, prosecuted the war with vigour, one fortified town after another falling into the hands of the allies, while Charles VII, or the Dauphin as he was still called, seems to have regarded the position as hopeless and spent his time in frivolous pastimes with his court. St Jeanne was in her fourteenth year when she experienced the earliest of those supernatural manifestations which were to lead her through the path of patriotism to the death of a martyr. At first it was a single voice addressing her apparently from near by, and accompanied by a blaze of light : afterwards, as the voices increased in number, she was able to see her interlocutors whom she identified as St Michael, St Catherine, St Margaret, etc. Only very gradually did they unfold her mission : it was a mission which might well appal her : she, a simple peasant girl, was to save France ! She never spoke about these voices in Domrémy ; she was too much afraid of her stern father. By May 1428 they had become insistent and explicit. She must present herself at once to Robert Baudricourt, who commanded the King's forces in the neighbouring town of Vaucouleurs. Jeanne succeeded in persuading an uncle who lived near Vaucouleurs to take her to the general, but Baudricourt only laughed at her and dismissed her, saying that her father ought to give her a good whipping.

At this time the military position was well-nigh desperate, for Orleans, the last remaining stronghold, had been invested by the English and was in danger of falling. After Jeanne's return to Domrémy her voices gave her no rest. When she protested that she was a poor girl who could neither ride nor fight, they replied : " It is God who commands it." Unable to resist such a call she secretly left home and went back to Vaucouleurs. Baudricourt's scepticism as to her mission was somewhat shaken when official confirmation reached him of a serious defeat of the French which Jeanne had previously announced to him. He now not only consented to send her to the King but gave her an escort of three men-at-arms. At her own request she travelled in male attire to protect her from outrage. Although the little party reached Chinon, where the King was residing, on March 6, 1429, it was not till two days later that Jeanne was admitted to the royal presence. Charles had purposely disguised himself, but she identified him at once and, by a secret sign communicated to her by her voices and imparted by her to him alone, she obliged him to believe in the supernatural nature of her mission. She then asked him for soldiers whom she might lead to the relief of Orleans. This request was opposed by La Trémouille, the King's favourite, and by a large section of the court who chose to regard the girl as a crazy visionary or a scheming impostor. To settle the matter it was decided to send her to be examined by a learned body of theologians at Poitiers. After a searching interrogatory extending over three weeks this council decided that they found nothing to disapprove of and advised the King to make prudent use of her services. Accordingly after her return to Chinon arrangements were pushed forward to equip her to lead an expeditionary force. A special standard was made for her bearing the words Jesus, Maria, together with a representation of the Eternal Father to whom two kneeling angels were presenting a fleur-de-lis. On April 27 the army left Blois with Jeanne at their head clad in white armour, and in spite of some contretemps Jeanne herself entered Orleans on April 29. Her presence in the beleaguered city wrought marvels. By May 8, the English forts which surrounded Orleans had been captured and the siege raised after she herself had been wounded in the breast by an arrow. All these events with their approximate dates she had prophesied before starting the campaign. She would fain have followed up these successes, for her voices had told her that she would not last for long, but La Trémouille and the Archbishop of Rheims were in favour of negotiating with the enemy. They persisted in regarding the relief of Orleans merely as a piece of good luck. However, the Maid was allowed to undertake a short campaign on the Loire with the Duc d'Alençon, one of her best friends. It was completely successful and ended with a great victory at Patay in which the English forces under Sir John Fastolf suffered a crushing defeat. Jeanne now pressed for the immediate coronation of the Dauphin. The road to Rheims had practically been cleared and the last obstacle was removed by the unexpected surrender of Troyes. But the French leaders dallied, and only very reluctantly did they consent to follow her to Rheims where on July 17, 1429, Charles VII was solemnly crowned, Jeanne standing at his side with her standard. That event, which completed the mission originally entrusted to her by her " voices," marked also the close of her military successes. A boldly planned attack on Paris failed, mainly for lack of Charles's promised support and presence. During the action Jeanne was wounded in the thigh by an arrow and had to be almost dragged into safety by the Duc d'Alençon. Then followed a truce which entailed on the Maid a winter of inaction spent for the most part in the entourage of a worldly court where she was regarded with thinly veiled suspicion. Upon the resumption of hostilities she hurried to the relief of Compiègne which was holding out against the Burgundians. She entered the city at sunrise on May 23, 1430, and that same day led an unsuccessful sortie. Through panic or some miscalculation on the part of the governor the drawbridge over which her company was retiring was raised too soon, leaving Jeanne and some of her men outside at the mercy of the enemy. She was dragged from her horse with howls of execration and led to the quarters of John of Luxembourg, one of whose soldiers had been her captor. From that time until the late autumn she remained the prisoner of the Duke of Burgundy. Never during that period or afterwards was the slightest effort made on her behalf by King Charles or any of his subjects. With the basest ingratitude they were content to leave her to her fate. But the English leaders desired to have her if the French did not : and on November 21 she was sold to them for a sum equivalent to about £23,000 in modern money. Once in their hands her execution was a foregone conclusion. Though they could not condemn her to death for defeating them in open warfare, they could have her sentenced as a sorceress and a heretic. In an age when fear of witchcraft was general the charge would not seem preposterous, and already the English and Burgundian soldiers attributed their reverses to her spells.

In the Castle of Rouen to which she was transferred two days before Christmas she was confined at first—we are told, but this is doubtful —in an iron cage, for she had twice tried to escape. Afterwards she lay in a cell where, though chained to a plank bed, she was watched day and night by soldiers. On the 21st day of February, 1431, she appeared for the first time before a tribunal presided over by Peter Cauchon, Bishop of Beauvais, an unscrupulous man who hoped through English influence to become Archbishop of Rouen. The judges were composed of dignitaries and doctors carefully selected by Cauchon, as well as of the ordinary officials of an ecclesiastical court. During the course of six public and nine private sessions the prisoner was examined and cross-examined as to her visions and " voices," her assumption of male attire, her faith and her willingness to submit to the Church. Alone and undefended she bore herself fearlessly, her shrewd answers and accurate memory astonishing and frequently embarrassing her questioners. Only very occasionally was she betrayed into making damaging replies through her ignorance of theological terms and lack of education. Nevertheless, at the conclusion of the sittings a grossly unfair summing-up of her statements was drawn up and submitted first to the judges, who on the strength of it declared her revelations to have been diabolical, and then to the University of Paris, which denounced her in violent terms.

In a final deliberation the tribunal decided that she must be handed over to the secular arm as a heretic if she refused to retract. This she declined to do though threatened with torture. Only when she was brought into the cemetery of St Ouen before a huge crowd to be finally admonished and sentenced was she intimidated into making some sort of retractation. The actual terms of this retractation are uncertain and have been the occasion of much controversy. She was led back to prison but her respite was a short one. Either as the result of a trick played upon her by those who thirsted for her blood or else deliberately of her own free-will she resumed the male attire which she had consented to discard, and when Cauchon with some of his satellites visited her in her cell to question her concerning what they chose to regard as a relapse, they found that she had recovered from her weakness. Once again she declared that God had truly sent her and that her voices came from God. " Be of good cheer ! ", Cauchon is reported as having exclaimed exultingly to the Earl of Warwick as he left the Castle, " we shall get her again." On Tuesday, May 29, 1431, the judges after hearing Cauchon's report condemned her as a relapsed heretic to be delivered over to the secular arm, and the following morning at eight o'clock Jeanne was led out into the market-place of Rouen to be burned at the stake. Her demeanour on that occasion was such as to move even strong men to tears. When the faggots had been lighted, a Dominican friar at her request held up a cross before her eyes and as the flames leaped up she was heard to call upon the name of Jesus before surrendering her soul to God.

She was not yet twenty years old. After her death her ashes were contemptuously cast into the Seine, but there must have been many amongst the spectators to echo the remorseful exclamation of John Tressart, one of King Henry's secretaries : " We are lost : we have burned a saint ! "

No adequate bibliography of St Jeanne d'Arc is possible within these narrow limits. The list made in 1906 by Canon U. Chevalier contains some 1500 entries, and this was before she was even beatified. Innumerable books and articles have been written since then. The most important sources were first published in Quicherat's *Procès de Condamnation et Réhabilitation*, 5 vols. (1841–1849) ; these are in Latin, but may be read in translations, *e.g.* by P. Champion in French and T. D. Murray in English. There is also a vast collection of materials, mostly translated, in the five volumes of Père Ayroles, *La Vraie Jeanne d'Arc* (1890–1901), but it is unfortunate that the polemical note is here so much emphasised. The same exception may also be taken to the otherwise excellent books of Canon Dunand, *Histoire complète de Jeanne d'Arc*, 4 vols. (1912) ; and *Études Critiques*, 4 vols. (1909). Consult further Denifle's *Chartularium Universitatis Parisiensis*, with its supplement; and Ch. Lemire, *Le Procès de Jeanne d'Arc*. In English no author has written more convincingly on the subject than the non-Catholic, Andrew Lang, *The Maid of France*, and especially in his criticism of Anatole France's misleading volume. Among minor English biographies may be mentioned those of Hilaire Belloc (1930) ; C. M. Antony, and C. F. Oddie (1931).

ST FELIX I, POPE

A.D. 274

According to the Roman Martyrology and the *Liber Pontificalis*, Felix I (a Roman by birth) ended his life as a martyr. This is almost certainly a mistake due to confusion with a certain Felix, a martyr who was buried on the Via Aurelia. The same confusion has led to the undoubtedly incorrect statement in the *Liber Pontificalis* (second edition) that Pope Felix " built a church on the Via Aurelia where he was also buried." Very little is known of this pontificate, though Felix seems to have sent some reply to the report of the Synod of Antioch—announcing the deposition of Paul of Samosata—which had been brought to Rome in the time of his predecessor, Pope Dionysius. On the other hand the quotation from what purported to be Felix's letter which was read at the Council of Ephesus is declared by such modern scholars as Duchesne, Bardenhewer, Harnack, and others to have been an Apollinarian forgery. The statement that Pope Felix " decreed that Masses should be celebrated on the tombs of the martyrs " may possibly refer to some practice initiated by him of placing an obstruction to block the hollow space (*arcosolia*) left above the tombs in the catacombs, exception only being made for tombs which were known to be those of martyrs. Thus the decree would mean that Masses should be celebrated (only) on the tombs of martyrs. The true date of his death was December 30 (III *kal. jan.*), but a misreading of *jun.* for *jan.* has led to its being assigned to May 30. The *Depositio Episcoporum* which reveals this error also informs us that Felix was buried in the cemetery of Callistus.

See J. P. Kirsch in the *Catholic Encyclopedia*, vol. vi, pp. 29–30 ; Duchesne in *Liber Pontificalis*, vol. i, p. 158 ; Delehaye's Commentary on the *Hieronymianum*, pp. 14–16 ; Bardenhewer, *Geschichte der altkirchlichen Literatur*, vol. ii, pp. 645–647.

ST ISAAC OF CONSTANTINOPLE, ABBOT

c. A.D. 410

When the Arian Emperor Valens was persecuting his Catholic subjects, a pious hermit named Isaac was inspired to leave his solitude in order to remonstrate with the monarch. Coming to Constantinople he warned the Emperor several times that unless he ceased his oppression and restored to the Catholics the churches which he had given to the Arians, a great disaster awaited him and a miserable end. Valens treated these warnings with scorn and on one occasion when the hermit seized the bridle of his horse as he was riding out of the city, he gave orders that the prophet should be thrown into a neighbouring swamp. Isaac escaped—miraculously as it seemed—but on repeating his prophecy he was put in prison. His words were fulfilled shortly afterwards, for the Emperor was defeated and killed at the battle of Adrianople, the greatest catastrophe that had befallen the Imperial forces since Cannæ. St Isaac was released by the successor of Valens, Theodosius, who always held him in great veneration. The holy man attempted to resume the solitary life, but soon found himself surrounded by disciples who refused to leave him. For them he founded a great monastery which is said to have been the oldest in Constantinople. From St Dalmatus, one of St Isaac's disciples and his successor, it was afterwards called the Dalmatian monastery. St Isaac took part in the first Council of Constantinople—usually described as the Second Ecumenical Council of the Church. He died at an advanced age and was buried in the Church of St Stephen.

A Greek Life of St Isaac is printed in the seventh volume for May of the *Acta Sanctorum*, from the last paragraph of which it has been inferred that the saint died in 383. This, however, is a mistake, as J. Pargoire has shown in *Échos d'Orient*, vol. ii (1899), pp. 138–145 ; the one reliable life of St Dalmatus proves that Isaac must have lived at least until 406. See the *Analecta Bollandiana*, vol. xviii (1899), pp. 430–431.

ST EXUPERANTIUS, Bp.

A.D. 418

The successor of St Ursus as metropolitan of Ravenna was St Exuperantius or Superantius—a holy man who did much to promote the temporal as well as the spiritual welfare of his flock. He lived during the reign of the Emperor Honorius, and when Stilicho invested Ravenna with his army, St Exuperantius prevailed upon him to restrain his soldiers from desecrating and looting the cathedral. The saintly bishop built the town of Argenta—so-called because it paid a tribute in silver to the Church of Ravenna. After a peaceful and uneventful episcopate of twenty years St Exuperantius died in 418 and was buried in the Church of St Agnes. His relics now rest in the cathedral of Ravenna.

There is a short account in the *Acta Sanctorum*, May, vol. vii, but the ultimate authority seems to be the not very trustworthy *Liber Pontificalis seu Vitæ Pontificum Ravennatum* of Andreas Agnellus. This may conveniently be consulted in Migne, P. L., vol. 106, *cc.* 525–528, but a better text is provided by Holder-Egger in *M. G. H. Scriptores Rerum Langobardicarum*, pp. 265 *seq.*

ST MADELGISILUS (MAUGUILLE), HERMIT

c. A.D. 655

St Madelgisilus, or Mauguille, is said to have been an Irishman and the inseparable companion of St Fursey, with whom he went to England and afterwards to Gaul. After the death of St Fursey, Madelgisilus joined the monks of Saint-Riquier at Centula, where he edified all by his sanctity. Dismayed at finding himself regarded with veneration by his brethren he obtained leave from the abbot to retire into the solitude of Monstrelet, on the river Authie. Here he lived an austere life of contemplation alone until he was visited by a holy English recluse named Vauban who, finding him very ill, nursed him back to health. A great friendship sprang up between them and they continued to practise the eremitic life together or side by side until Vauban's death. St Madelgisilus did not long survive his friend. He was buried in the hermitage chapel, but his relics were afterwards removed to a church of his name built near Saint-Riquier.

A Life by Hariulphus, who, though he wrote as late as the beginning of the twelfth century, was a painstaking compiler, is printed in the *Acta Sanctorum*, May, vol. vii. See also Corblet, *Hagiographie du diocèse d'Amiens*, vol. iii, pp. 226, *seq.*, and *cf.* Gougaud, *Gaelic Pioneers of Christianity*, pp. 19 and 134.

ST FERDINAND III, KING OF CASTILE AND LEON

A.D. 1252

The father of St Ferdinand III was Alphonsus, King of Leon, and his mother was Berengaria, who was the elder daughter of Alphonsus IX, King of Castile and the maternal aunt of St Louis of France. After she had borne him two sons and two daughters, Berengaria was obliged by Pope Innocent III to separate from her consort and to return to her father because her marriage had been contracted within the prohibited degrees, and dispensations to legalise such unions were not conceded at that time. Nevertheless, as it had been solemnised in good faith, the children were declared legitimate. The death of her brother Henry in 1217 left Berengaria heiress to the throne of Castile, but she resigned her rights in favour of her eighteen-year-old son Ferdinand, whom she caused to be proclaimed king at Palencia, Valladolid, and Burgos. In quelling the disturbances and in allaying the opposition with which he had at first to contend, the young monarch displayed a degree of prudence and clemency remarkable in one so young. He was greatly assisted by the wise counsels of his mother, whom he consulted and obeyed to the day of her death. By her advice he chose as his wife in 1219 Beatrice, daughter of the Emperor Philip of Suabia—a most accomplished and virtuous princess. Their union, which was never clouded by the least discordance, was blessed by a numerous family of seven sons and three daughters. St Ferdinand was severe in the administration of justice, but readily pardoned all personal injuries, and no sooner were rebellions crushed than he granted general amnesties. His wisdom manifested itself particularly in the choice he made of governors, magistrates, and generals. Rodriguez, Archbishop of Toledo and chancellor of Castile, was during thirty years at the head of all his councils and so perfectly in agreement with Ferdinand and Berengaria as to seem to have but one soul with them. To exercise some check upon inferior tribunals he established a court, afterwards called the royal council of Castile, to which appeal could be made from other courts. A code of laws which he caused to be compiled continued to be in use till modern times. Nothing ever troubled the saint so much as when his own father, the King of Leon, laid claim to his dominions and invaded them. Ferdinand attempted to give him all reasonable satisfaction and lent him his own forces to fight against the Moors. For his own part he was resolved never to wage war against any but the enemies of the Christian faith. For that reason he restored several places the claims to which seemed doubtful and refused to be drawn into quarrels with the kings of Portugal and Aragon or with Eleanor of England in Gascony. He founded several bishoprics and contributed munificently to the building or repairing of cathedrals, churches, and monasteries. No necessity could ever make him impose any heavy tax on his subjects. When it was suggested that he should raise a subsidy in this way for his wars against the Moors he rejected the proposal indignantly, saying that God would provide him other means, and that he feared the curse of one poor old woman more than the whole army of the Moors.

From the year 1225 when he opened his first campaign against the infidels until his death, he continued almost uninterruptedly to wage war against Islam. In 1230 he took some twenty strongholds in Andalusia and in the kingdoms of Cordova and Jaën. His vassal, Aben Mohammed, having been murdered by his subjects for serving under a Christian sovereign, he took occasion to conquer the whole Kingdom of Baëza. Totally devoid of personal ambition he was far less concerned to add to his territories than to rescue Christians and Christian property from the hands of the unbelievers. With perfect truth could he protest: "Thou, O Lord, who searchest the heart of man, Thou knowest that I desire Thy glory—not mine—and the increase of Thy faith and holy religion—not of any temporal kingdom." He set his soldiers an example of devotion by fasting rigorously, praying much, spending whole nights in pious exercises—especially before an engagement—and giving to God the glory of his victories. A large picture of Our Lady was carried before him into battle, whilst a small one was attached to his saddle-bow. With the spoils of war he richly endowed the cathedral of Toledo, of which he laid the first stone.

St Ferdinand was about to besiege Jaën when his father died, leaving his kingdom to the two daughters of his second marriage. The clergy and people of Leon, however, declared for Ferdinand. It took him two or three years to settle the affairs of his new kingdom, which from that time became united with Castile, but in 1234 he resumed his wars against the Moors by the siege and capture of Ubeda. In the meantime the infante Alphonsus with fifteen hundred men defeated at Xeres the formidable army of Abenhut, King of Seville, divided into seven corps, each of which was more numerous than the whole Christian army. This victory, which only cost Alphonsus the lives of nine soldiers and one knight, was regarded on all sides as a miracle. St James, mounted on a white horse, is said to have been seen leading the Christian army. About the beginning of 1236 Queen Beatrice died, deeply regretted by her husband and by her subjects, but grief for her loss did not suspend warlike operations for long. While James, King of Aragon, wrested from the Moors the kingdoms of Minorca and Valencia, Ferdinand completed the conquest of the two Moorish kingdoms of Baëza and Cordova. The city of Cordova had been in the hands of the Mussulmans five hundred and twenty years and had long been the capital of their empire. St Ferdinand, after a long siege, entered it on SS. Peter and Paul's day, 1236. The chief mosque was converted into a church and the great bells which had been brought from Compostella by the labour of Christian slaves were returned to their proper home, transported by Moors. In the campaigns which followed Cordova, St Ferdinand made himself master of twenty-four other towns, of which Ecija was the first and Moron the last.

The Kings of Murcia and Granada having voluntarily made themselves his vassals, he then proceeded to lay siege to Seville, the largest, strongest, and most densely populated city in Spain. When, after a valiant defence which lasted sixteen months, the garrison capitulated on November 23, 1249, the Moors were allowed a month in which to dispose of their property; 300,000 removed to Xeres and 100,000 passed over to Africa. Axataf, governor-general of the Moors in Seville, as he looked from the top of a hill at the city for the last time, declared with tears that only one specially favoured by God could have taken so strong a city with so few men. In thanksgiving for his great victory St Ferdinand rebuilt the cathedral of Seville with such magnificence that it seemed inferior to no church in Christendom, save possibly that of Toledo. During the last three years of his life St Ferdinand made his headquarters at Seville that he might settle the tribunals and regulate the affairs of this important conquest. He also added to his dominions the towns of Xeres, Medina-Sidonia, Alcalá, Cadiz, Arcos, and other strongholds. He was preparing an expedition against the Moors in Africa when he was attacked by his last illness. Realising that his death was approaching, he prepared himself by a devout confession, and after receiving the last sacraments, died on May 30, 1252, in the fifty-third year of his age and the thirty-fifth of his reign in Castile. As his second wife he had married Jane of Ponthieu, who bore him two sons and one daughter—Eleanor, the future wife of Edward I of England. The body of St Ferdinand was buried in the cathedral of Seville, where it is still venerated.

The Bollandists in the *Acta Sanctorum*, May, vol. vii, have translated into Latin those portions of the chronicle of Roderick Ximenes, Archbishop of Toledo (a contemporary), which refer to St Ferdinand. With this we have also the summary account of Luke, Bishop of Tuy, who was likewise a contemporary, and other miscellaneous documents. Further, there is preserved a narrative by the Franciscan, Giles of Zamora, (*c.* A.D. 1300). This will be found in the *Boletin de la real Academia de la Historia*, vol. v (1884), pp. 308–321. St Ferdinand, of course, plays a conspicuous part in all Spanish histories which cover this period. Among modern biographies may be mentioned those by J. Laurentie in French (1910), F. Maccono in Italian (1924), and a popular Life in Spanish by J. R. Coloma (1928).

BD. ANDREW FRANCHI, Bp. of Pistoia

A.D. 1401

Blessed Andrew was a member of the noble family of the Franchi Boccagni of Pistoia—his native city—and early entered the

Dominican order. A great preacher, he was also endowed with administrative powers which led to his being made prior of three convents in Italy. In 1378 he was appointed Bishop of Pistoia. For twenty-three years he ruled his diocese wisely and well, promoting peace and spending his revenues over the restoration of churches and the relief of the poor. In assisting the needy he always felt as though he were being privileged to give to Our Lord in person. He had a great devotion to the Child Jesus, to Our Blessed Lady, and to the Magi. As a bishop he led a life of extreme simplicity, striving as far as possible to observe the rule to which he had been bound as a simple friar. A year before his death he resigned his office and retired to his old convent in Pistoia, where he prepared himself for the end. He died on May 26, 1401. In 1921 Pope Benedict XV sanctioned his cultus for the whole Dominican Order and for the diocese of Pistoia.

In the decree confirming the cultus (see the *Acta Apostolicæ Sedis*, vol. xiv, 1922, pp. 16–19) there is a short biographical summary. A longer account will be found in the *Année Dominicaine*, vol. v (1891), pp. 689–693 ; and in 1922 Padre Taurisano published a brief Life in Italian.

BD. JAMES PHILIP BERTONI, Conf.

A.D. 1483

At the age of nine, Blessed James Philip Bertoni was placed in the Servite Priory of Faenza in fulfilment of a vow which his father had made during a dangerous illness. Even as a little boy James Philip practised austerities to the best of his ability and in later years as a professed Servite he proved himself a most holy religious. So great was his horror of sin that he made his confession every day. In appearance he was tall, thin, and very pallid. After his ordination he became procurator of the Priory of Faenza and held other responsible offices. He died on May 25, 1483, at the age of thirty-nine. Miracles wrought at his tomb in the church of St John at Faenza led to a popular cultus which was formally approved by Pope Clement XIII in 1766. Soon after his death, in recognition of his sanctity, his father was declared a burgher of Faenza and was granted exemption from all imposts and taxes. Prince Galeotti II of Faenza had the mortal remains of Blessed James interred in his own burial chapel, at the same time granting to the holy man's family full proprietary rights over the tomb.

A short Latin life written by Nicholas Borghesi was printed in the *Acta Sanctorum*, May, vol. vi, as also in the *Monumenta Ordinis Servorum B.V.M.*, vol. iv (1901), pp. 63-67. There is also a modern sketch by L. Trebbi (1867).

BB. WILLIAM FILBY, LUKE KIRBY, LAWRENCE RICHARDSON and THOMAS COTTAM, Marts.

A.D. 1582

On May 30, 1582, two days after the martyrdom of Blessed John Shert and Blessed Robert Johnson, four other Catholic priests were executed at Tyburn. Their names were William Filby, Luke Kirby, Lawrence Richardson *alias* Johnson, and Thomas Cottam. All four had been educated at English universities before going abroad to be trained for the Catholic ministry and all four had been tried the previous November with Blessed Edmund Campion and condemned—nominally for being concerned with a bogus plot called the conspiracy of Rheims and Rome, but practically for the offence of coming as Catholic priests to minister to the Queen's subjects. The six months between their condemnation and their execution they spent as prisoners in the Tower.

William Filby, a native of Oxford, had been a student at Lincoln College. Religious scruples led him to leave the University and he soon afterwards entered the English Seminary at Rheims. Ordained priest in 1581, he was sent to England where he was promptly arrested in company with Blessed Edmund Campion at the house of Mr. Yates of Lydford. From July 1581 he was imprisoned in the Tower and after his trial—for six whole months—he was loaded with iron manacles. Together with his three companions he was taken at seven in the morning of May 30, 1582, to Tyburn, where he was the first to suffer. He met his fate with great composure, commending his soul to God. He was only twenty-seven years of age.

Luke Kirby was a North-country man from Durham or York-shire and a Master of Arts. He joined the Douai College in 1576 and was ordained the following year. After a short stay in England he went to the English College in Rome to pursue further studies. Returning to England he was soon arrested and imprisoned. While in the Tower he was cruelly tortured.

Lawrence Richardson, who was born in Lancashire and whose true name was Johnson, quitted Brazenose College, Oxford, to embrace the Catholic faith. After studying at Douai and being raised to the priesthood he laboured with great zeal and success in his native county of Lancashire. He was apprehended in the early part of 1581. Offered mercy on the scaffold if he would confess his treason and renounce the Pope, he answered : " I thank her Majesty for her mercy ; but I must not confess an untruth or renounce my faith."

Thomas Cottam was also a native of Lancashire and a graduate of Brazenose College, Oxford. For a time he worked as a schoolmaster in London but, on becoming a Catholic, he went abroad, first to the Douai College and then to Rome, where he entered the Society of Jesus. Persistent ill-health prevented his completing his noviceship, but he was ordained a priest at Rheims and, at his own earnest entreaty, was sent on the English Mission. The British authorities had been furnished with an exact description of him by a notorious informer called Sledd who had feigned to be his friend. By this means he was identified upon landing at Dover. One of his fellow-travellers, a Douai professor named Dr. Ely, escaped detection and was actually instructed to deliver Father Cottam up to Lord Cobham. He acquiesced, not intending to carry out the order. After their arrival in London he succeeded, though not without difficulty, in persuading his companion to proceed on his way. As soon, however, as the authorities began to press Dr. Ely, Father Cottam voluntarily gave himself up. He was imprisoned first in the Marshalsea and afterwards in the Tower where he and Father Kirby were subjected to the instrument of torture known as the Scavenger's Daughter. He was the last of the four to be executed, and was compelled to watch the dismemberment of his fellow-martyrs.

Full details of the history, capture and imprisonment of all four martyrs will be found in *The Lives of the English Martyrs* (ed. Bede Camm), vol. ii, pp. 491–563. The account in Challoner, *Memoirs of Missionary Priests* (ed. Pollen), pp. 51–66, is less complete.

BB. WILLIAM SCOTT AND RICHARD NEWPORT, MM.

A.D. 1612

Blessed William Scott was studying law at Trinity Hall, Cambridge, when he was converted by reading Catholic literature. He went abroad, and took the Benedictine habit in the Abbey of St Facundus, assuming in religion the name of Maurus. After his ordination he was sent on the English Mission. As he entered London he saw Blessed John Roberts, the priest who had received him into the Church, being hurried to execution, and three days later he was himself arrested and cast into prison where he remained a year. He was then deported, but soon made his way back to England. According to a contemporary he was imprisoned and exiled more than once and on each occasion he returned. After his final arrest, as he was being conveyed by boat from Gravesend to London he threw into the river a bag containing his breviary, his faculties, and some medals and crosses. The bag was caught in a fisherman's net and figured at the trial. In prison he had as his companion a secular priest called Richard Newport, a Northampton-shire man by birth, who after having been trained at Douai and in Rome, had laboured very successfully in the English Mission. He also had been several times imprisoned and twice banished. The two prisoners were brought up at the Old Bailey before the Lord Mayor, the Bishop of London, the Lord Chief Justice, and other magistrates. They made a bold defence, but their condemnation was a foregone conclusion and they were sentenced to death as traitors. They suffered at Tyburn with great fortitude on May 30, 1612.

See Challoner, *Memoirs of Missionary Priests* (ed. Pollen), pp. 323–329, and Dom Bede Camm, *Nine Martyr Monks* (1931), pp. 180–237.

MAY 31

ST ANGELA MERICI, Virg.

A.D. 1540

THE foundress of the Ursulines—the first teaching order of
women to be established in the Church—was born on March
21, 1470 or 1474, at the little town of Desenzano, on the
south-western shore of Lake Garda in Lombardy. She received a
good early training from her parents, a pious couple not overburdened
with this world's goods. They both died when Angela was ten
years old, leaving their two daughters and a son to the care of a
well-to-do uncle living at Salo. Already Angela and her elder
sister had shown signs of quite unusual piety, and in the house of
kindly and sympathetic relations they were allowed to follow this
inclination unchecked except when they ran away to try to live
the hermit life in a cave. On that occasion they found themselves
promptly pursued and obliged to return to the more humdrum
routine of a well-ordered home. The death of her elder sister came
as a great shock to Angela when she was thirteen. To her natural
grief at being separated from one who was almost a second self
was added apprehension as to her actual condition ; for the young
girl, although she had lived an almost angelic life, had passed away
before she could receive the last sacraments. Angela's first vision
—she was to have many in after years—seems to have been granted
to her at this time, in order to set her mind completely at rest as to
her sister's salvation. In overflowing gratitude she consecrated
herself more completely to God and soon afterwards was admitted
as a Franciscan Tertiary. Her life became one of extreme austerity.
Striving to emulate St Francis, she wished to possess nothing of
her own—not even a bed—and lived almost entirely on bread,
water, and a few vegetables.

After the death of her uncle when she was about twenty-two,
Angela returned to Desenzano. There, as she went about amongst
her neighbours, she was appalled by the ignorance which prevailed
amongst the poorer children whose parents could not or would not
teach them the simplest elements of religion. Gradually it was
borne in upon her that she was called to do something to remedy

this state of things and she talked the matter over with her friends. They were mostly fellow-tertiaries or young women of her own class with little money and less influence, but they were eager to help her if she would show them the way.   Though very small of stature, Angela had all the necessary qualifications for leadership, including charm of manner and good looks.   At her suggestion they set to work to gather together the little girls of the neighbourhood to whom they gave regular and systematic instruction.   The work so humbly begun prospered and developed.   St Angela was invited to go to Brescia to begin a similar school in that city.   She consented, and was cordially welcomed into the household of a noble couple whom she had consoled when they were in distress.   Through her hosts she was brought into touch with the leading families of Brescia and became the centre of a circle of devout women and men whom she inspired with her great ideals.   From time to time we find her making pilgrimages to various shrines.   Thus she visited the tomb of Blessed Osanna at Mantua and eagerly seized an opportunity which presented itself of going to the Holy Land with a young relative, sailing under the protection of Antonio de Romanis—an elderly merchant of Brescia.   They had travelled as far as Crete on the outward journey when St Angela was suddenly overtaken with complete blindness.   Her companions proposed abandoning their purpose, but the holy woman would not hear of their doing so.   With them she visited the Holy Places in Palestine, with as much devotion as if she could have beheld them with her bodily eyes.   On the return journey, as she was praying before a crucifix, her sight was restored in the very place where she had lost it a few weeks previously.   In the Holy Year—1525—she went to Rome to obtain the Jubilee Indulgence and, through the kind offices of a papal chamberlain whom she had met on pilgrimage, she had the privilege of at least one private audience.   Clement VII received her most graciously and suggested that she should stay in Rome to take charge of a congregation of nursing sisters, but a sense of her true vocation as well as a shrinking from publicity led her to decline the offer.   She accordingly returned to Brescia from whence however she was soon obliged to withdraw.   For war had broken out again in Italy, and when Charles V was on the point of making himself master of Brescia, it became essential that as many non-combatants as possible should leave the city.   St Angela with some of her friends retired to Cremona, where they remained until peace was finally concluded by the Treaty of Cambrai.   Her return to Brescia was greeted with joy by the citizens who, besides appreciating her charity, venerated her as a prophetess and a saint.   We read that as she was assisting at Mass shortly afterwards she fell into a prolonged ecstasy and was seen by a great number of persons to be upraised from the ground.

Years earlier, as a young woman at Desenzano, St Angela had seen in a vision a vast concourse of maidens ascending to heaven on a ladder of light and a voice had said : " Take heart, Angela : before you die you will found at Brescia a company of virgins similar to those you have just seen." And now the time was at hand for the fulfilment of that prophecy.

About the year 1533 she seems to have begun to train a select few of her companions in a kind of informal novitiate. Twelve of them came to live with her in a house she took near the Church of St Afra, but the greater number continued to live with parents or other relations. Two years later, on November 25, 1535, twenty-eight young women consecrated themselves with her to the service of God. She placed them under the protection of St Ursula, the patroness of medieval universities who was popularly venerated as a leader of women. Hence the name of Ursulines which her daughters have always borne. This date—November 1535—is reckoned as that of the foundation of the Ursuline Order. It was, however, during the lifetime of its foundress more in the nature of an association. No habit was worn, although a black dress was recommended ; no vows were taken and the sisters were not enclosed nor did they lead a community life. They met together for classes and spiritual exercises, carried out such duties as were allotted to them, and lived a holy life in the midst of their families. The idea of a teaching order of women was so novel that time was required in which to let it develop. Yet, although many changes and modifications have taken place, the Ursulines from the period of their foundation until the present day have never lost sight of the object for which they were instituted—the religious education of girls, especially of the poorer classes. At the first election St Angela was unanimously chosen superior, and she continued to fill that office for the last five years of her life. She was taken ill early in January 1540 and died on the twenty-seventh of the same month. Her body, which long remained incorrupt, was buried in the Church of St Afra, where she had asked to be laid. In 1544 Pope Paul III issued a bull confirming the Company of St Ursula and declaring it to be a recognised congregation.

The sources for the history of St Angela are very fully set out in English in the painstaking work of Sister M. Monica, *Angela Merici and her teaching idea* (1927). The saint's Rule, her " Testament," and her Counsels were taken down in writing by her secretary, the priest Cozzano. The first sketch of her life was compiled by the notary, G. B. Nazari, in 1560 and is printed as an appendix to the volume of Giuditta Bertolotti, *Storia di S. Angela Merici* (Brescia, 1923). The earliest printed biography seems to have been that of Ottavio Gondi, S.J. (1600), but it is full of legendary material. That of Carlo Doneda, compiled with a view to the process of canonisation, appeared in 1768, and owing to its relatively critical treatment, is more reliable. There are a number of others, but it is only necessary to mention the work of the Abbé Postel (1878), in two volumes, that of W. E. Hubert in German, and that entitled *Sainte Angèle Merici et l'Ordre des Ursulines, par une Religieuse du même Ordre*, 1922, two volumes. There is also an earlier Life in English by Bernard O'Reilly, *St Angela Merici and the Ursulines* (1880). Sister M. Monica's book is no doubt the least unsatisfactory, but it must be confessed that the appendix on St Ursula, which appeals to J. H. Kessel's monograph published in 1863 as a reliable authority on the problem of the 11,000 virgins, is not a little disconcerting. A reference to the article " Ursula " in the *Catholic Encyclopedia* would have been more to the point.

ST PETRONILLA, Virg. and Mart. (?)

A.D. 251 (?)

The Roman Martyrology for this day has the following entry : " At Rome, of St Petronilla, Virgin, daughter of the Blessed Apostle Peter, who refused to wed Flaccus, a nobleman, and accepting three days' delay for deliberation, spent them in fasting and prayer, and on the third day after receiving the Sacrament of Christ, gave up the ghost." It is quite certain that Petronilla was not the daughter of St Peter. The idea that St Peter had a daughter seems to have been derived from certain apocryphal publications of Gnostic origin, and her identification with the St Petronilla venerated in Rome was imported into the pious legends concerning her which were current in the sixth century or earlier. On the other hand, in the cemetery of Domitilla a fresco has been discovered, dating from the middle of the fourth century, which quite unmistakably represents Petronilla as a martyr. Despite De Rossi's adverse view, the opinion that Petronilla was beyond doubt a martyr has prevailed. The legend which survives in the notice just quoted from the Roman Martyrology, according to which the saint died in her bed, has no better authority than the quite worthless " Acts " of Nereus and Achilleus; see above on May 12, page 139.

Père Delehaye, in his publication *Sanctus* (1927), pp. 118–120, puts the question in its true light, and see further the references in his commentary on the *Hieronymianum*, pp. 285–286. There is also an excellent, if disproportionately long, article on St Petronilla by Mgr J. P. Kirsch in the *Catholic Encyclopedia*, vol. xi, pp. 781–782.

SS. CANTIUS, CANTIANUS, AND CANTIANELLA, MARTS.

A.D. 304 (?)

According to their "Acts" preserved in several recensions, the two brothers Cantius and Cantianus with their sister Cantianella were members of the illustrious Roman family of the Anicii and were closely related to the Emperor Carinus. Left orphans, they were brought up in their own palace in Rome by a pious Christian tutor and guardian called Protus, by whom they were instructed in the faith. When the persecution of Diocletian began to fill Rome with terror, they liberated their slaves, sold their possessions the proceeds of which they distributed to the poor, and retired to Aquileia where they had estates. Even there, however, the cruel edict was being rigorously enforced. No sooner were the authorities informed of the arrival of the young nobles than they cited them to appear and to sacrifice to the gods. At the same time a messenger was despatched to Diocletian for instructions, and the Emperor, who wished to be rid of them as much for political as for religious motives, sent word that they were to be beheaded unless they consented to sacrifice to the gods. The martyrs had left Aquileia in a chariot drawn by mules, but were held up by an accident four miles from the town of Aquæ Gradatæ. Here they were overtaken by their pursuers and when called upon to obey the Emperor's behest, they replied that nothing should make them unfaithful to the only true God. They were accordingly beheaded, together with their tutor Protus, in the year 304.

As to the accuracy of these details we have no certainty. The story, with variations, is preserved in many texts, one is printed in the *Acta Sanctorum*, May, vol. vii, and the others are catalogued in the *Bibliotheca Hagiographica Latina*, nn. 1543-1549. A sermon in honour of these martyrs attributed to St Ambrose is not genuine, but it may possibly be the composition of St Maximus of Turin. On the other hand there is much evidence which establishes the early cult of St Cantius and his companions at Aquileia. The casket of Grado on which their names are engraved (it is figured in Leclercq, *Dict. d'Archéologie, etc.*, vol. vi, *cc.* 1449-1453) may be as old as the early seventh century. But before this we have mention of them in the verses of Venantius Fortunatus, and in the earliest text of the *Hieronymianum*. See Delehaye's commentary on this last, p. 284, and his *Origines du Culte des Martyrs*, pp. 375-376.

BD. MECHTILDIS, ABBESS OF DIESSEN
A.D. 1160

Blessed Mechtildis was only five years old when she was placed by her parents, Count Berthold of Andechs and his wife Sophia, in the double monastery they had founded on their own estate at Diessen, on the Ammersee in Bavaria. Trained by the nuns, Mechtildis grew up a devout and exemplary maiden, much given to prayer and austerities. Her one weakness in youth was a somewhat quick temper which occasionally betrayed her into hasty speech, but over this she obtained complete control. Indeed, in later life she was remarkable for her silence, and it was said of her by the Cistercian monk Engelhard that on the rare occasions when she opened her lips to speak her words were as those of an angel. After she had received the habit, she made still further advance along the path of perfection. It was her great joy to perform the most distasteful offices and to make herself the servant of her sisters in religion. Upon the death of the superior, she was elected abbess—in which capacity she raised the tone of the whole community to a high pitch of virtue. This she effected far more by her example than by the strictness of her rule. So highly was she esteemed by the Bishop of Augsburg that he requested her to undertake the charge of the convent of Edelstetten which stood in great need of reform. Mechtildis shrank from the task : she was only twenty-eight, and felt incapable of coping with the difficulties of the situation. Nevertheless, in compliance with an injunction from Pope Anastasius IV, who reminded her that obedience is better than sacrifice, she allowed herself to be installed Abbess of Edelstetten by the bishop. At first she was well received, for her youth and noble rank commended her to her new daughters. But when she proceeded to enforce the rule, to insist upon enclosure and generally to tighten the reins of discipline she was met with violent opposition. It finally became necessary for the bishop to order the expulsion of the chief malcontents. The rest of the nuns were soon won over by the holy life of their superior, enhanced as it was by the extraordinary gifts and graces which, from this period onwards, became manifest to all. She healed the sick, restored speech to the dumb, and the sight of an eye to one of the nuns. Very often she was rapt in ecstasies which lasted for a long period. Her fame spread far and wide, and the Emperor Frederick I was proud to claim her as a kinswoman. Shortly before her death she had a premonition that her end was near. She thereupon laid down her office and

375

returned to Diessen, where she died on May 31, 1160. Her elder sister Euphemia, who became Abbess of Altomünster, was, like herself, locally venerated as a saint, but her cultus was never confirmed.

Her Life, written in some detail by Engelhard, Abbot of the Cistercian monastery of Langheim (*c.* A.D. 1200), is printed in the *Acta Sanctorum*, May, vol. vii. See also Rader, *Bavaria Sancta*, vol. i, pp. 241–244. This St Mechtildis is, of course, to be carefully distinguished from St Mechtildis of Hackeborn, the younger sister of St Gertrude of Helfta. Even Canon Chevalier, in the references he enumerates in his *Bio-bibliographie*, has occasionally confused them.

BD. JAMES SALOMONIUS, CONF.

A.D. 1314

Blessed James Salomonius or, as he is sometimes designated, James the Venetian, was born of a noble family at Venice in 1231. His father having died when he was very young, he was brought up partly by his mother who, however, retired after a few years into a Cistercian Convent, partly by a very pious grandmother. James was devout almost from infancy, and at the age of seventeen he distributed all his property to the poor and joined the Dominicans. Desiring in all things to emulate the holy founder of the Order, he preserved throughout his life his baptismal innocence. Very much against his will he was chosen to fill the office of Prior at Forlì, Faenza, San Severino, and Ravenna, but he was finally allowed to settle down at Forlì, where he led a life of great austerity, devoting himself especially to prayer, to reading, and to charity towards the sick poor, for whom he had a great affection. In addition to the Holy Scriptures he regularly studied the martyrology which, as he was wont to aver, provided him with constant food for meditation. The holy friar had many ecstasies, was endowed with the gift of prophecy, and miraculously healed a number of paralytics and other sick persons. Although he suffered for four years from a gnawing cancer, he never complained, appearing always to be cheerful and calm. The cancer is said to have been healed shortly before his death, which took place on May 31, 1314, when he was eighty-two years of age. He was buried in the Priory church and many miracles were wrought at his intercession. The year after he died a brotherhood was formed to promote his veneration. His cultus was sanctioned for Forlì by Pope Clement VII in 1526, for Venice by Pope Paul V, and for the whole Dominican Order by Gregory XV.

The Bollandists, in the *Acta Sanctorum*, May, vol. vii, print from MS. sources a copious Life by an anonymous contemporary. See also Procter, *Lives of Dominican Saints*, pp. 155–159.

APPENDIX

St Walstan, Conf.

A.D. 1016

NOT much can be stated with any certainty regarding St Walstan. There is no notice of him in the *Dictionary of National Biography*, and Sir T. D. Hardy in his *Materials relating to the History of Great Britain and Ireland* refers only to the account given in Capgrave, *Nova Legenda Angliæ*. But it is possible that Alban Butler had before him a copy of some manuscript materials which have now perished, perhaps in the fire which so seriously damaged the Cottonian collection. He wrote at any rate of St Walstan as follows, under May 30, appealing, besides Capgrave and Blomfield's *History of Norfolk*, to " an old manuscript Life " :

" St Walstan was formerly much honoured at Cossey and Bawburgh, commonly called Baber, two villages four miles from Norwich. He was born at Baber, and of a rich and honourable family. The name of his father was Benedict, that of his mother Blida. By their example and good instructions he, from his infancy, conceived an ardent desire to devote himself to God, with the greatest perfection possible. In this view, at twelve years of age he renounced his patrimony, left his father's house, and entered as a poor servant at Taverham, a village adjoining to Cossey. He was so charitable that he gave his own victuals to the poor, and sometimes even his shoes, going himself barefoot. He applied himself to the meanest and most painful country labour in a perfect spirit of penance and humility ; fasted much, and sanctified his soul and all his actions by assiduous, fervent prayer, and the constant union of his heart with God. He made a vow of celibacy, but never embraced a monastic state.

APPENDIX

God honoured his humility before men by many miracles. He died in the midst of a meadow where he was at work, on the 30th of May in 1016. His body was interred at Baber: it was carried thither through Cossey or Costessye, where a well still bears his name, as does another which was more famous at Baber, a little below the church. These places were much resorted to by pilgrims, especially to implore the intercession of this saint for the cure of fevers, palsies, lameness, and blindness. His body was enshrined in the north chapel of that church, which chapel was on that account pulled down in the reign of Henry VIII though the church is still standing. All the mowers and husbandmen in these parts constantly visited it once a year, and innumerable other pilgrims resorted to it, not only from all parts of England, but also from beyond the seas. The church is sacred to the memory of the Blessed Virgin, and of St Walstan."

The late Father Joseph Stevenson, S.J., in certain manuscript notes he has left concerning the English Saints, adds these details: "St Walstan, after giving away his shoes, loaded thorns in a cart without suffering any injury. His master offered to adopt him, but he refused, accepting, however, the gift of a cow, which produced two calves at one birth. When his approaching death was notified to him in a vision, he ordered his body to be placed on a cart drawn by two oxen who should be suffered to go on until they stopped of their own accord. They proceeded towards Costesheya (Cossey), and, though they passed through some water, the wheel-tracks then made are said to remain to the present day. The oxen came to a stop at Bawburgh, and there his body is buried."

In the *British Martyrology*, compiled by Bishop Challoner with the title, "A Memorial of Ancient British Piety" (1761), there is a brief mention of St Walstan under May 30. On the other hand, the name is apparently not to be found in any surviving pre-Reformation calendar, nor does it figure in the "Martiloge" of R. Whytford (1526), nor in that of Father Wilson (1608 and 1640). The Bollandists, writing in the seventeenth century, would seem never to have heard of St Walstan, for he is not mentioned even among the "Prætermissi" of May 30.

378

INDEX TO VOLUME V

[The figures in brackets give, as nearly as may be, the date of the Saint's death.]

A

Abellon, *see* Andrew Abellon.
Acacius, mart. (303 or 305), 97.
Achilleus, mart. (first century ?), 139.
Æmilius, mart. (250), 267.
Afra of Brescia, mart. (133 ?), 290.
Agathus, *see* Acacius.
Agricola, *see* Isidore Agricola.
Aigulphus, Bp. of Bourges (836), 269.
Aioul, *see* Aigulphus.
Albergati, *see* Nicholas Albergati.
Albert of Bergamo, conf. (1279), 132.
Albrici, or Albrizzi, *see* Magdalen.
Aldebrandus, bp. (early thirteenth century), 17.
Aldhelm, Bp. of Sherborne (709), 303.
Alexander, mart. (397), 349.
Alexander, Eventius and Theodulus, MM. (113 ?), 40.
Aloysius Rabata, conf. (1490), 134.
Alphius and Comps., MM. (251), 119.
Amator, bp. (418), 8.
Andeolus, mart. (208), 7.
Andrew Abellon, conf. (1450), 223.
Andrew Bobola, mart. (1657), 261.
Andrew Franchi, Bp. of Pistoia (1401), 365.
Andrew Hubert Fournet, conf. (1834), 168.
Anfrid, *see* Ansfridus.
Angela Merici, virg. (1540), 370.
Angelus, mart. (1220), 75.
Ansfridus, Bp. of Utrecht (1008 or 1010), 130.
Antoninus, Abp. of Florence (1459), 116.

Antony Middleton, mart. (1590), 84.
Apparition of St. Michael (492 ?), 92.
Asaph, bp. (*c.* 600), 14.
Athanasius, bp. and Doctor of the Church (373), 19.
Auguste Schöffler, mart. (1851–52), 18.
Augustin Novello, conf. (1309), 243.
Augustine, bp., Ap. of England (605), 330.
Austregisilus, bp. (624), 252.
Avertinus, deacon (1180 ?), 74.

B

Bagnesiis, *see* Maria Bartolomea de Bagnesíis.
Barat, *see* Madeleine Sophie.
Bartholomew Pucci - Franceschi, conf. (1130), 286.
Basilla, or Basilissa, virg. and mart. (304), 251.
Baudelius, mart. (380 ?), 252.
Baylon, *see* Paschal Baylon.
Beatrice of Este, virg. (1226), 123.
Beatus, hermit (112 ?), 110.
Bede, conf. and Doctor of the Church (735), 322.
Bellarmine, *see* Robert Bellarmine.
Benedict II, Pope (685), 101.
Benincasa, hermit (1436), 134.
Benvenutus of Recanati, conf. (1289), 261.
Bernard of Menthon, conf. (1081 ?), 337.
Bernardino of Siena, conf. (1444), 246.
Bertha, hermit (840 ?), 193.
Beuvon, *see* Bobo.
Bobo, conf. (985), 269.

379

S

Sacerdos, Bp. of Limoges (520 ?), 73.
Salle, see John Baptist de la Salle.
Salomonius, see James Salomonius.
Sanz, see Peter Martyr Sanz.
Saturninus and Comps., MM. (c. 304), 27.
Schöffler, see Auguste.
Scott, see William Scott.
Senator, Bp. of Milan (475), 333.
Serenicus, ab. (c. 669), 88.
Serenus, hermit (c. 669), 88.
Servais, see Servatus.
Servatus, Bp. of Tongres (384), 159.
Shert, see John Shert.
Sigismund, king (523), 12.
Simon Stock, conf. (1265), 211.
Sisinnius, Martyrius and Alexander, MM. (397), 349.
Solangia, virg. and mart. (880), 122.
Spellucci, see Ventura.
Stanislaus, Bp. (1079), 85.
Stephen, mart. (1242), 351.
Stock, see Simon.
Stone, see John Stone.

T

Thalelæus, mart. (284 ?), 250.
Thecusa, mart. (304 ?), 226.
Theobald, Abp. of Vierne (1001), 260.
Theodardus, Abp. of Narbonne (893), 16.
Theodemar, see Thethmar.
Theodosia, virg. and mart. (745), 350.
Theodotus, Thecusa and Comps., MM. (304 ?), 226.
Theodulus, mart. (? 113), 40.
Theophilus a Corte, conf. (1740), 263.
Thethmar, conf. (1152), 222.
Thiébaud, see Theobald.
Thirkild, see Richard Thirkild.
Thomas Cottam, mart. (1582), 367.
Thomas Ford, John Shert and Robert Johnson, MM. (1582), 341.

Timothy and Maura, MM. (c. 286), 41.
Torquatus and Comps., MM. (first century), 189.

U

Ubaldo, see Vivaldus.
Ubaldus, Bp. of Gubbio (1160), 209.
Ultan, ab. (c. 675), 28.
Urban I, Pope and mart. (230), 300.

V

Venantius, mart. (257 ?), 225.
Venerius, Bp. of Milan (409), 54.
Ventura Spellucci, Ab. (twelfth century), 44.
Victor and Corona, MM. (second century ?), 172.
Victor Maurus, mart. (303), 96.
Vincent of Lerins, conf. (c. 445), 288.
Vivaldus, hermit (1300), 133.

W

Waldebertus, Ab. of Luxeuil (c. 668), 29.
Walstan, conf. (1016), 377
Walter, ab. (1070), 131.
Wibert, see Guibert.
Wiborada, virg. and mart. (925), 30.
William Filby, mart. (1582), 367.
William of Gellone, conf. (812), 336.
William of Toulouse, hermit (1369), 229.
William Scott and Richard Newport, MM. (1612), 368.
William, Stephen, Raymund and Comps., MM. (1242), 351.
Wiro, conf. (seventh century), 100.
Wright, see Peter Wright.

Y

Yvo, Bp. of Chartres (1115), 284.

Z

Zenobius, bp. (c. 390 ?), 301.
Zoë, mart. (c. 135), 27.

Vol V only   .50¢